Belize Handbook

Alex & Gardênia Robinson

Belize was formed when Itzamná, the creator god of the Maya, took the best bits of Central America and put them all within easy reach of each other in the place where the Maya people began. "Why make people journey for hours to see wild rainforest filled with jaguars and hummingbirds, misty mountains and tumbling waterfalls, ruined cities and glittering caves?" he thought, whilst shaping the country. "Let me sprinkle them through the land and around the coral cayes, and let me add manatees and sea turtles, harpy eagles and spider monkeys".

But Itzamná was bad at PR; whilst lots of people heard about Costa Rica, Mexico and Guatemala, few heard about Belize. If they visited, they passed through, on their way from the Riviera Maya in Mexico to the temples of Tikal, or they took a vacation in San Pedro. The rest of Belize stayed almost empty. And it remains so to this day. Plenty of tourists visit Chichen Itzá, Cozumel and Playa del Carmen, just over the border in Mexico. But in Belize travellers have a Mayan city, a reef of rainbow fish, or even a whole island almost entirely to themselves. And they do so on a backpacker budget, or in chic comfort at one of many small, tastefully turned-out beach hotels or wilderness lodges.

There's never been a better time to visit. At the end of 2012 the Mayan Long Count calendar comes to a cyclical close. Some say this heralds the end of the world as we know it. They forget that it also marks the beginning of Itzamná's new, more perfect creation. In 2012 the world begins again in the place where it first began... in Belize.

THIS PAGE The giant pyramid of Caana in the ruined metropolis of Caracol is one of the largest in the Maya world.
PREVIOUS PAGE Aquamarine sea surrounds a coral caye in the Lighthouse Reef atoll.

iii

MEXICO

Corozal Town

Bahía de
Chetumal

Libertad

Little
Belize   Cocos

♦ **12**
Shipstern
Nature
Reserve

COROZAL

Ambergris Caye

Orange Walk
Town

San Pedro
1

Blue Creek   Shipyard

Maskall

Caye Caulker
2

ORANGE
WALK

La Milpa

Río Bravo

Santana

Altun Ha

Hick's Cayes

Lamanai

11
Gallon
Jug

Hill Bank

Bermudian
Landing

Burrell Boom

Ladyville

Drowned
Caye

Wamil

St Paul's

Big Falls

BELIZE

Burdon Canal

Belize
City

4
Turneffe
Atoll

To Lighthouse Reef & The Blue Hole

Spanish Creek
Wildlife Sanctuary

Guanacaste
National Park

Monkey Bay
Wildlife Sanctuary

Middle
Long
Caye

3

Belmopan

San
Ignacio

Santa
Elena

Mopan

Sibun
Forest
Reserve

Gales Point
Village

Barrier Reef

Xunantunich

San
Antonio

6
Actun
Tunichil
Muknal
(ATM Caves)

Five Blue
Lakes
National Park

Southern
Long Caye

Benque Viejo

To Tikal & Flores Island

5
Macal

CAYO

STANN
CREEK

Dangriga

7
Caracol

Cockscomb Basin
Wildlife Sanctuary

Victoria
Peak
(1120m)

8 ♦

Hopkins

Sittee
Village

9
South Water Caye
Marine Reserve

Mango
Creek

Maya Beach

Placencia
Peninsula

Gladden Spit

Placencia

TOLEDO

Paynes Creek
National Park

♦ Monkey River

Silk Cayes

Nim Li Punit

Lubaantun

10
San Antonio
Dump

Blue Creek

Gulf of
Honduras

Caribbean Sea

Pusilha

Toledo

Punta Gorda

Barranco

Bahía de
Amatique

N

20 km

20 miles

GUATEMALA

Cockscomb Basin Wildlife Sanctuary is home to all five of Belize's felines: jaguar, puma, ocelot, margay and jaguarundi.

Don't miss...

See colour map at end of book

Ambergris Caye is surrounded by shallow, warm turquoise seas.

Itineraries for Belize

Belize is only 180 miles long and 68 miles wide and it's easy to get anywhere within a day. This makes it tempting to base yourself in one place and take day trip excursions. Try and stay in at least two locations; the dawn chorus in the rainforest is as magical as the dawn light over the Caribbean sea, and a night safari is as captivating as a night dive over the sleeping reef.

ITINERARY ONE: 1 week – 10 days
Cayes, Cockscomb and Cayo

A week to 10 days is enough for you to sample a few of Belize's highlights: to catch a whiff of rainforest air, dip your toes into the Caribbean and get some rest and relaxation on the country's best beach. After flying into Belize City take the Western highway to Cayo District and

TRAVEL TIP

Book a full itinerary through Belize Travel Services or another operator to save on tours and transfers.

check in to a wilderness lodge nestled in the dense forest of the Macal River Valley. Spend two nights here birdwatching, kayaking on the river and taking a night safari in search

Weatherboard shacks on the cayes sell local snacks from beans and rice to fried patties or jacks.

Electric blue morpho butterflies flutter through the rainforests of Belize.

of wide-eyed nocturnal mammals. Visit the Mayan City of Xunantunich and climb its pyramids for sweeping views of forest stretching into Guatemala. Stop off at Belize Zoo – to see the animals you might have missed in the rainforest – on your way to the islands. Choose either San Pedro or Caye Caulker, depending on your budget, to dive and snorkel over the barrier reef and take a day trip to the inky deep Blue Hole in the Lighthouse Reef atoll. Then head to the beach in Hopkins, either to do very little or to search for jaguars in the Cockscomb Basin on a day trip or go birdwatching in Mayflower Bocawina National Park.

ITINERARY TWO: 2 weeks
Rainforest and reef

With two weeks, you could see Belize's most celebrated sights as well as getting well off the beaten track. Begin with a stay at a jungle lodge in Orange Walk District in the heart of the biggest stretch of tropical forest north of the Amazon. Choose Chan Chich, tucked in Mayan ruins in Gallon Jug forest reserve, for intimate luxury or La Milpa, for simpler accommodation in a similar setting. Then head south to Burrell Boom and the Black Orchid Resort, set in forest on the banks of the old Belize River. Spot Morelet's crocodiles and toucans from

The Blue Hole is a vast collapsed cavern in the heart of the Lighthouse Atoll.

vii

A river flows through the gaping mouth of the Actun Tunichil Muknal cave in Cayo District.

TRAVEL TIP
Bust your budget and splurge on a helicopter flight, dive excursion or stay in a luxury lodge.

your hotel balcony. Take a side trip to see the howler monkeys at the Community Baboon Sanctuary or the New River Lagoon and the towering temples of the Mayan city of Lamanai. Head to Cayo and the cool highlands of Mountain Pine Ridge for wildlife and 300-m-high falls, which plunge into a deep canyon. Then splurge on a helicopter flight to the Blue Hole, or spend less on a day trip to the spooky ATM caves, which are littered with Mayan artefacts covered in glittering flow stone. Finish up on the beach in Placencia, taking side trips to spot manatees and Morelet's crocodiles on the Monkey River or dive or snorkel with whale sharks off the southern cayes.

ITINERARY THREE: 3 – 4 weeks
Mayan Belize and Caribbean cayes
Begin in the Maya heartlands of the south with jungle immersion and Earl Grey tea

The Gallon Jug Reserve in northern Orange Walk District has some of the best birdwatching in Central America.

The iridescent emerald toucanet is the rarest and most beautiful of Belize's three toucan species.

at Hickatee Cottages. Spend a few days learning how to play marimba and make tortillas on a Mayan homestay programme in the hills of western Toledo. Then head to Cayo, stopping off at the Maya Centre (to buy copal incense and take a healing massage), Cockscomb Basin Wildlife Sanctuary (to see jaguar) and sights along the Hummingbird Highway. Stay in the wilderness in Mountain Pine Ridge or the Macal River Valley and take a day trip to the rainforest-clad Maya metropolises of Caracol or Guatemala's Tikal, just over the border. Visit

TRAVEL TIP
Homestays with the Maya can be as cheap as a night in a hostel dorm.

the howler monkeys at Bermudian Landing and the bird-filled lagoons of Crooked Tree Wildlife Sanctuary before learning to tag crocodiles and track jaguars at the Lamanai Outpost. Finish with total immersion in the Caribbean Sea on one of the cayes or atolls, diving, sea kayaking and soaking up the sun on a powdery fine beach.

A Mayan householder roasts coffee beans over a traditional wood-fired cooker in Stann Creek District.

Traffic is slow and life is easy on the laid-back island of Caye Caulker.

Southern stingrays congregate in huge numbers in Shark Ray Alley. Some are up to 2m across.

Contents

NORTHERN
BELIZE

SAN PEDRO &
THE NORTHERN
CAYES

BELIZE CITY
& DISTRICT

Tikal

CAYO &
THE MAYA
MOUNTAINS

SOUTHERN
BELIZE

Contents

Footprint features

Essentials

Planning your trip

Best time to visit Belize

The high season runs from mid-December to March. Until the end of May there are clear skies and warm temperatures (25-30°C). Inland, in the west, day temperatures can reach 35°C, but the nights are cooler and usually pleasant. Between November and January there are cold spells during which the temperature in Belize City may fall as low as 13°C. Humidity is normally high, making it sticky most of the time in the lowlands.

Belize experiences sharp variations in rainfall across the country. The southernmost district of Toledo is the wettest, with 4310 mm of rainfall a year. It is the only district in Belize with true tropical rainforest. Belize City gets around 1650 mm a year and northern Belize, 1270 mm. The driest months are April and May. In June and July there are usually heavy showers followed by blue skies. This is often followed by a mini-dry season of about six weeks in August and early September. Mid-September to November tend to be overcast and there are more insects during these months, especially sand flies on the coast and some of the cayes.

June to November is hurricane season, although this doesn't mean that you will necessarily experience a hurricane at this time. Since 1930, Belize has been hit by just 16 hurricanes, only eight of which were severe, and 17 tropical storms. Even if a hurricane hits it is likely to be localized and you'll have at least a day's warning; follow local advice. Most towns and large villages have hurricane shelters and 'Hurricane Preparedness' instructions are issued annually.

What to do in Belize

Archaeology

The protection of Belize's Mayan heritage and its development into tourism sites is high on the government's agenda. Further excavation and protection of sites, better access, the construction of facilities such as visitor centres and the availability of knowledgeable guides are all part of the plan. Belize has a number of impressive Mayan sites, most in beautiful settings. **Lamanai** (page 181) nestles in forest on the banks of the wild New River Lagoon; **Xunantunich** (page 105) occupies a ridge with sweeping views into neighbouring Guatemala, and **Caracol** (page 130), which was one of the largest Mayan cities in Mesoamerica, sits in the heart of the vast and little-tramped Chiquibul tropical forest reserve. **Tikal** (page 107), just over the border in Guatemala, can be visited on a day trip from Belize.

Birdwatching

Belize is one of the best destinations in the Americas for birdwatchers, with a broad range of habitats within easy reach of each other, excellent guiding and lodges, and some 600 species of birds in abundant numbers, more than half of which are only found in the Neotropics. There are some spectacular birds, such as harpy eagles, ocellated turkeys, orange-breasted falcons, jabiru storks and king vultures, as well as locally restricted, endangered or threatened species, including Yucatán vireos, black rails, black catbirds, brown pelicans, buff-breasted sandpipers and a very rare sub-species of

scarlet macaw. Top birding sites include **Crooked Tree Wildlife Sanctuary** (page 44), **Cockscomb Basin** (page 141), **Lamanai** (page 181), **Caracol** (page 130) and **Shipstern Nature Reserve** (page 190). See also Tour operators, page 23, and Birds, page 217.

Caving and cave tubing

Belize has some of the longest cave systems in the world, many of them littered with Mayan artefacts and sparkling with spectacular speleological formations. Facilities are good for novice cave-clamberers or specialist spelunkers, through agencies such as **Hun Chi'ik** (see page 119), who take visitors to **Actun Tunichil Muknal** (famous for its Maya remains) and **Crystal Cave**, or the Caves Branch Jungle Lodge (see page 127) near the entrance to the **Blue Hole National Park**. It is also possible to tube through the caves at locations like **Barton Creek**, see page 102.

Diving and snorkelling

With the third-longest barrier reef system in the world, Belize has more coral and fish species than any other location in the Caribbean. Couple this with an astonishing variety of dive and snorkel sites (from plunging walls, underwater caves and sinkholes to brightly coloured coral gardens, huge canyons and coral and sponge-encrusted wrecks), 3 atolls and excellent facilities and you have the best diving in the Atlantic Ocean. The top destinations include **Hol Chan Marine Reserve** and **Shark Ray Alley** (page 68), the **Blue Hole** (page 89) and **Turneffe Atoll** (page 87).

Fishing

Belize is a popular destination for anglers and fly fishing. There are abundant permits, tarpons and bonefish populating Belize's waters and they are easy to catch on the country's extensive flats. There's good game fishing for sailfish, marlin, wahoo, barracuda and tuna in deeper water. The rivers offer increasingly fewer opportunities for good fishing, and tilapia, escaped from regional fish farms, now compete with the catfish, tarpon and snook for the food supply.

Anglers require a licence to fish in Belize, whether you fish off a boat or from the shore. These must be obtained from the **Coastal Zone Management Authority and Institute** (CZMA) (www.coastalzonebelize.org), and cost BZ$20 a day or BZ$50 a week. There is an online form or the licences can be obtained through El Pescador (see page 73), Tres Pescados (see page 82) or any of the many designated angler-friendly tour operators mentioned in this guide.

Hiking

Belize is small but perfectly formed for the hiker. You could stroll for half an hour along deserted beaches under the palms; wander along forest paths to see floating butterflies and brilliantly coloured birds; hike for a few hours to a string of wispy waterfalls dropping into deep plunge pools, or spend days hiking the Mesoamerican Trails System or in the wild, unspoilt tropical forests of Cockscomb Basin, as you trek to the rugged heights of **Victoria Peak**, the country's second highest mountain, see page 142. See also 'Code Green for Hikers' in box, page 14.

A few of Belize's protected areas, including Cockscomb and Guanacaste National Park, have signposted trails. Some park visitor centres offer trail maps, either in paper form or on large displays in the visitor centres themselves. However, the country has no official self-guided trails; you will need a guide if you go hiking in Belize.

Kite and windsurfing

Belize is not a world-class destination, but flat waters within the reef, numerous lagoons and a steady prevailing breeze mean that places like **Ambergris Caye** (page 59) are a good and very easy place to learn or hone your novice skills.

Sailing

There's good sailing off the reef or between the numerous cayes set between the reef and the continental shore. The windiest months are Feb and Jun with 12–20 knots most days at the best location, **Ambergris Caye** (page 59).

Getting to Belize

Air

All international flights arrive and depart from the country's only international airport, **Phillip SW Goldson International Airport**, see below, in Belize City. Most other airports are just small airstrips. Try not to exceed the 23 kg weight limit when leaving Belize; airlines are far more stringent here than in almost any other country in the world and excess baggage charges are high. There is an airport departure tax of BZ$40 for all passengers.

From Europe and Australia and New Zealand

There are no flights connecting Belize with Europe. Europeans must transit through a US airport or fly via Cancún (Mexico), then catch the **ADO** bus south to Belize (see page 8). There are no direct flights from Australia or New Zealand. Again, visitors must travel via the US.

From North America

There are flights from NYC twice weekly with **United**, Miami twice daily with **American**, Atlanta six times a week with **Delta** and Houston two to four times a day with **United**. Return flights cost US$650-US$900, depending on the season. There are no direct flights from Canada.

From Central America

Tropic flies once daily to San Pedro Sula in Honduras and twice daily to Flores in Guatemala.

Airport information

Phillip SW Goldson Airport is small, with a short one-mile runway that is only fit for short-haul jets like Boeing 737s. However, it is currently undergoing a major expansion, due for completion in 2015, which will allow for wide-bodied jets to arrive from Europe. There are nominally two terminals. Terminal 1 serves **Continental**, **Grupo Taca**, **Atlantic Airlines**, **Maya Island Air** and **Tropic Air**. Terminal 2 serves **American**, **Delta** and **US Airways**. Both share the same rectangular building and walking between them takes fewer than five minutes. If transferring direct to the islands or elsewhere in Belize with a domestic carrier, be sure to stipulate that you would like a connection through the international airport. This will cost an extra BZ$40 or so, offset by avoiding an unnecessary transit through Belize City to the municipal airport or boat dock (and an associated BZ$50 taxi fare). Facilities in Phillip SW Goldson Airport include ATMs, a porter service (porters wear blue and white uniforms and charge around BZ$2 to carry bags), security (which operate a lost-and-found service, T225-2045 ext 107), a handful of shops (**Maya Endings** sell the best gifts, including CDs from **Stonetree** records; see page 210), bars and restaurants and car rental offices (including **Avis**, **Budget** and **Thrifty**). A Belize Tourist Board booth (open to coincide with all international flight arrivals) operates in the Arrivals Hall and has information on tours, accommodation and transport.

Road

There are two land border crossings between Belize and Mexico, one at Chetumal–Santa Elena (see box, page 193) and another at La Unión–Blue Creek (see box, page 183).

Bus
From Mexico ADO (www.ado.com.mx) buses connect Cancún, Mérida and destinations on the Riviera Maya with Belize City via Orange Walk (see page 40). There are also regular bus services between Chetumal, Corozal, Orange Walk and Belize City (see page 40). Buses are comfortable and air conditioned. They can be cold enough to merit bringing a jacket.

From Guatemala Linea Dorada (lineadorada.info) buses connect Guatemala City, Melchor and Flores with Belize City via the border at Benque Viejo (see box, page 40).

Car
The Northern Highway runs from Belize City to Chetumal in Mexico. The Western Highway runs from Belize City to the Guatemalan border via Belmopan, San Ignacio and Benque Viejo. Belize law requires that you carry ID documents and driving licences in Belize. EU or North American driving licences are accepted in Belize for visits under three months. For longer stays, an International Driving Permit is required. In the UK these can be obtained from the Automobile Association (www.theaa.com).

Sea

From Central America
San Pedro Jet Express and **San Pedro Belize Express** speedboats connect Chetumal in the south of Quintana Roo state with Ambergris Caye and Caye Caulker (see page 83). From late 2012 there will be a daily boat service between San Pedro and Xcalak in Mexico. From Guatemala boats connect Puerto Barrios in Guatemala with Punta Gorda (see box, page 176) in Toledo district in Belize's far south. From Honduras boats connect Puerto Cortés with Placencia (see page 154).

From the rest of the world
A number of cruise lines call in at Belize, with the most popular departing from Florida. Companies include **Carnival Cruise Lines** (www.carnival.com), **Royal Caribbean** (www.royal caribbean.co.uk), **Norwegian Cruise Line** (www2.ncl.com), **Oceania** (www.oceaniacruises. com) and **Holland America** (www.hollandamerica.com). See also the excellent website **Cruise Compete** (www.cruisecompete.com) for the latest cruise lines, ships and itineraries. As with most cruises, shore excursions tend to be very rapid and, as a result, rather unsatisfactory for the price (deals are often far cheaper from local tour operators than through the cruise ship itself).

Transport in Belize

Air

Tropic Air (www.tropicair.com) and **Maya Island** (www.mayaregional.com) operate an extensive network throughout the country. Destinations include Belize City, Caye Caulker, Corozal, Dangriga, Placencia, Punta Gorda and San Pedro (for Ambergris Caye). Both airlines also charter planes.

Road

Bicycle

Cycling is very popular in Belize with a calendar of events organized by the **Belize Cycle Association** (www.belizecycling.com), and you will often see groups of cyclists on the country's principal paved highways: the Northern, Western, Southern and Hummingbird Highways. You will need a mountain bike on dirt roads in areas like Mountain Pine Ridge. For cycle repairs and parts, you will need to visit Belize City; try **Bruce's Bike Shop** ① *1834 Chancellor St at Blue Marlin Blvd, T223-7979, brucebikeshop.com.*

Bus

Buses are the primary mode of transport for most Belizeans, and the country has an extensive bus network. There are five main bus companies in the country: **BBDC**, **James**, **Shaws**, **Gilharry** and **National**. Most do not have a website, but **Belize Bus** (belizebus. wordpress.com) and **Guide to Belize** (www.guidetobelize.info) have schedules of departures from the major cities. All are old US school buses; none have air conditioning.

Shuttles and airport shuttles Cayo-based **William's Belize Shuttle** (www.parrot-nest. com/belize_shuttle.html) offers a shuttle service pretty much anywhere in mainland Belize, though best rates are for travel between the major centres. **Belize Shuttles** (www. belizeshuttlesandtransfers.com) has a fast and reliable shuttle or private car service between Belize City, San Ignacio, Placencia and the international airport.

Car

Only four highways in Belize are paved: the Northern, Southern, Western and Hummingbird Highways. You will need a sturdy 4WD if you intend to get off the paved road.

Road traffic accidents are common, and driving is generally of a low standard. Drink driving is not unusual, and at night not all cars use their lights. Visitors should take great care when driving. In the southern districts of Stann Creek and Toledo, temporary bridges and unpaved roads in low-lying areas may flood during heavy rains. Drive carefully as road conditions are constantly changing and totally unpredictable, with speed bumps, cyclists and pedestrians appearing around every bend. When driving in the Mountain Pine Ridge area it is prudent to check carefully on road conditions at the entry gate; good maps are essential. Emory King's annually updated *Drivers' Guide to Belize* is helpful when driving to the more remote areas.

For more information on driving licence requirements, see page 8.

Car hire This is cheapest when booked from abroad. Cars can be hired in the international airport. For a list of companies see page 42. When choosing a company, check if it will release registration papers to enable cars to enter Guatemala or Mexico. Without obtaining them at the time of hire, it is impossible to take hire cars across international borders.

Car hire cost is high in Belize owing to the heavy wear and tear on the vehicles. You can expect to pay between BZ$140 for a Suzuki and BZ$250 for an Isuzu Trooper per day.

Belizean law does not require that toddlers use a child seat, and such devices are not available in the country. Those who are not comfortable getting in a taxi without a car seat or booster seat should bring one from home.

Hitchhiking
Hitchhiking is easy in Belize, though not recommended around Belize City or at night.

Taxi
Belizean taxis have green plates indicating their status as an official taxi. Be sure to negotiate the fare before you get into the taxi. Taxis in Belize never have meters. In Belize City taxis cost BZ$5 for rides within the city for up to two people and BZ$1 for each additional person. Taxis are a similar price in Cayo and Orange Walk districts, but are more expensive elsewhere in Belize, notably in Placencia where a trip from the city centre to the airstrip will cost BZ$10 and a drive to the northern peninsula village of Maya Beach as much as BZ$30 or BZ$40.

Sea

Three water taxi companies (see page 39) carry passengers to the most popular islands of Caye Caulker and Ambergris Caye, with regular daily services from the Marine Terminal by the swing bridge in Belize City. Further south, boat transport is available at Dangriga to nearby cayes and to Puerto Cortés, Honduras, via Placencia. From Punta Gorda, there is a service to Puerto Barrios in Guatemala. In the north there is a daily service between Corozal and San Pedro, Ambergris Caye, via Sarteneja.

Maps

Maps of Belize are limited, and topographical maps have not been readily available for several years. Maps produced internationally include an Adventure map by **National Geographic** and a 1:250,000 colour country map by **International Travel Maps (ITMB)**, www.itmb.com. **Borch GmbH** publishes a handy laminated 1:500,000 map, with a street map of Belize City and plans of the main archaeological sites.

Where to stay in Belize

Belize has a wide variety of accommodation, from upmarket beach resorts and luxurious lodges in private wildlife reserves to simple wooden huts on a caye or basic guesthouses. It is increasingly popular as a honeymoon destination, and there are romantic beach hotels on Ambergris Caye, Hopkins and on some of the smaller islands in the atolls and reef. There are many specialist hotels catering for wildlife enthusiasts, those into sports fishing or divers.

Belize Travel Services (www.belizetravelservices.com) have a good list of hotels and guesthouses, covering a range of price categories, and can organize tours and trips. Rates can be better than booking directly with a hotel.

Belize's high season extends from late November to April and reaches its absolute peak (when prices are highest and bookings essential for hotels) over Christmas and New Year and at Easter.

All hotels are subject to 9% government hotel tax (on room rate only); 10% service charge is also often added.

Wilderness lodges

There is a good selection of wilderness lodges to suit most budgets along the Macal River and Mopan River valleys in Cayo, in Mountain Pine Ridge and in the northern large private reserves of Gallon Jug and the Rio Bravo Conservation and Management Area. Lodges typically offer trips for wildlife watching and exploring the surrounding forest on foot or by kayak.

Budget accommodation

Travellers on a tight budget are well catered for in Belize. There is a good network of hostels and cheap guesthouses, both on the cayes (notably Caye Caulker) and in San Ignacio, Punta Gorda and Hopkins. You can stay in Maya communities in Toledo and Sarteneja cheaply (see below), whilst also helping to maintain the cultural identity of the region. There are other homestay options too. Monkey Bay (see page 55) can organize homestays in villages around the Sibun river. These can be combined with a wildlife or community-based volunteer programme.

Maya homestays

Experience life in a Maya village first hand through a Mayan homestay, with the **Toledo Ecotourism Association** or the **Sarteneja Homestay Programme** (see pages 169 and 192).

Camping

Campsites are gaining in popularity, and there are private camping facilities in most tourist areas, with a variety of amenities offered. Camping on the beaches, in forest reserves or in any other public place is prohibited. Butane gas in trailer/Coleman stove-size storage bottles is available in Belize, and white gas for camp stoves is available at **Brodie's** in Belize City, page 39, and in Belmopan.

Food and drink in Belize

Belize is not one of the world's great gourmet destinations. Menus suffer from a surfeit of rice and beans (usually served with chicken, fish or beef and plantain), and wholesome though the combinations are, the lack of variety becomes tedious after the first few meals. In Corozal, Orange Walk and San Ignacio there is often simple Mexican food available, including burritos, quesadillas and *huevos rancheros*. Restaurants such as **Nahil Mayab** (see page 187) in Orange Walk Town serve delicious traditional Yucatec Maya food. The best food in Belize is in the more heavily visited areas and the more exclusive resort hotels (most of whose dining rooms are open to non-guests). Highlights include **Chef Rob's** (see page 152) in Hopkins, **La Palmilla** (see page 78) in San Pedro and the **Mare** (see page 163) and **Maya Beach Hotel Bistro** (page 164) restaurants in Placencia.

Belize has almost 30 species of endangered or threatened reef fish (see www.earthsendangered.com for a complete list). They include many items on the menu like sea bass, red and Nassau grouper, mutton and cubera snapper. Avoid ordering these. Also avoid ordering lobster or conch out of season (between mid-February and mid-June and July and September, respectively) as stocks are worryingly low.

You'll find Marie Sharp's spicy sauces, jams, chutneys and spreads on tables and in shops all over the country. Sauces come with distinctive colourful labels advertising their potency. Jams and chutneys are made from tropical fruits grown on Marie's home farm.

Chocolate has been made in Belize for over 2000 years. The Maya drank it as a bittersweet and mildly hallucinogenic drink. Modern Belizean chocolatiers who include **Cotton Tree** (see page 174), **Cyrila's** (ecomayachocolate.com), **Kakaw** (www.belizechocolatecompany.com) and **Goss** (see page 156) make it to European and American tastes. Belize cacao and chocolate is held to be some of the best in the world. All national producers use organic Toledo cacao, as do **Green and Black's** (www.greenandblacks.com), who have been buying organic cocoa from the Toledo Cacao Growers' Association (TCGA) since 2003, in a joint investment programme with the British government.

There are just two kinds of beer in Belize: Lighthouse and Belikin beer. It is a federal offence to bring foreign beer into Belize. There are many brands of local rum and fire water, and even local wines. Sweet fruit liqueurs include *nanche*, made from crabou fruit, and cashew wine made from cashew fruit.

All imported food and drink is expensive. A 9% sales tax is added to meals and a 10% service charge may be added as well.

Festivals in Belize

Most businesses throughout the country close down from Good Friday to Easter Monday; banks close at 1300 on Maundy Thursday and buses run limited services from Holy Saturday to Easter Monday, though local flights and boats to the cayes are available. Christmas and Boxing Day are also limited in terms of services. Many shops will open for a few hours on holiday mornings, but may have limited choices for food.

Independence celebrations begin on St George's Caye Day, 10 September, with events occurring daily through to Independence Day, 21 September. The 'September Celebrations', as they are locally called, often start two or three days in advance and require a lot of energy.

The most colourful of Belizean festivals is Garífuna Settlement Day in November with celebrations concentrated around Dangriga, Hopkins, Seine Bight and Placencia. The tone of the festival varies greatly; there's a more public celebration of music and dance in Dangriga (with shows by many of the best Garífuna musicians like Aurelio Martinez) and a more spiritual and quieter ambience in Seine Bight.

Public holidays and major festivals

1 Jan New Year's Day.
Feb Weekend before or after Valentine's Day, Annual Sidewalk Arts Festival, Placencia.
9 Mar Baron Bliss Day.
Early Mar San José Succotz Fiesta.
Mar/Apr Easter (Fri-Mon).
Late Apr or May National Agricultural and Trade Show (Belmopan).
1 May Labour Day.
May (variable) Cashew Festival (Crooked Tree), Cayo Expo (San Ignacio), Coconut Festival (Caye Caulker).

24 May Commonwealth Day.
23-25 Jun Lobster Fest, Placencia.
Early to Mid-Jul Benque Viejo Fiesta.
Aug International Costa Maya Festival (San Pedro, Ambergris Caye).
10 Sep St George's Caye Day.
21 Sep Belize Independence Day.
11 Oct Pan-American Day.
19 Nov Garífuna Settlement Day, festival normally over the weekend.
25 Dec Christmas Day.
26 Dec Boxing Day.

Responsible travel

The tourism industry in Belize is very important for the country's economy and creates thousands of jobs. Many national parks, valuable archaeological sites and museums are funded by visitor entry fees, which, in turn, promote their protection. Additionally, some of the tour operators, private reserves and lodges fund conservation and community projects. By earning from tourism, the poorer people who rely on the land for their livelihoods are more likely to protect their environments for the benefit of tourism, and these projects are well worth supporting.

10 ways to be a responsible traveller

There are some aspects of travel that you have to accept are going to have an impact, but try to balance the negatives with positives by following these guidelines to responsible travel.

• **Cut your emissions** Plan an itinerary that minimizes carbon emissions whenever possible. This might involve, hiring a bike or booking a walking or canoeing tour rather than one that relies on vehicle transport. See opposite page for details of carbon offset programmes.

• **Check the small print** Choose travel operators that abide by a responsible travel policy (if they have one, it will usually be posted on their website). Visit www.responsibletravel.com.

• **Keep it local** If travelling independently, try to use public transport, stay in locally owned accommodation, eat in local restaurants, buy local produce and hire local guides.

• **Cut out waste** Take biodegradable soap and shampoo and leave excess packaging, particularly plastics, at home. The countries you are visiting may not have the waste collection or recycling facilities to deal with it.

• **Get in touch** Find out if there are any local schools, charities or voluntary conservation organizations that you could include in your itinerary. If appropriate, take along some useful gifts or supplies; www.stuffyourrucksack.com has a list of projects that could benefit from your support.

• **Learn the lingo** Respect local customs and dress codes and always ask permission before photographing people – including your wildlife tour guide. Once you get home, remember to honour any promises you've made to send photographs.

• **Avoid the crowds** Consider travelling out of season to relieve pressure on popular destinations, or visit a lesser-known alternative.

• **Take only photos** Resist the temptation to buy souvenirs made from animals or plants. Not only is it illegal to import or export many wildlife souvenirs, but their uncontrolled collection supports poaching and can have a devastating impact on local populations, upsetting the natural balance of entire ecosystems.

CITES, the Convention on International Trade in Endangered Species (www.cites.org) bans international trade in around 900 animal and plant species, and controls trade in a further 33,000 species. Several organizations, including WWF, TRAFFIC and the Smithsonian Institution have formed the Coalition Against Wildlife Trafficking (www.cawtglobal.org).

• **Use water wisely** Water is a precious commodity in many countries. Treating your own water avoids the need to buy bottled water which can contribute to the build-up of litter.

• **Don't interfere** Avoid disturbing wildlife, damaging habitats or interfering with natural behaviour by feeding wild animals, getting too close or being too noisy. Leave plants and shells where you find them.

Code green for hikers
• Take biodegradable soap, shampoo and toilet paper, long-lasting lithium batteries and plastic bags for packing out all rubbish.
• Use a water filter instead of buying bottled water, and save fuel at remote lodges by ordering the same food at the same time. Only take a hot shower if the water has been heated by solar power.
• If no toilet facilities are available, make sure you are at least 30 m from any water source.
• Keep to trails to avoid erosion and trampling vegetation. Don't take short cuts, especially at high altitude where plants may take years to recover.

Code green for divers and snorkellers
• Help conserve underwater environments by joining local clean-ups or collecting data for Project AWARE (www.projectaware.org).
• Choose resorts that properly treat sewage and wastewater and support marine protected areas.
• Choose operators that use mooring buoys or drift diving techniques, rather than anchors, which can damage fragile marine habitats such as coral reefs.

• Never touch coral. Practise buoyancy-control skills in a pool or sandy area before diving around coral reefs, and tuck away trailing equipment.
• Avoid handling, feeding or riding on marine life.
• Never purchase marine souvenirs.
• Don't order seafood caught using destructive or unsustainable practices such as dynamite fishing.

How should I offset my carbon emissions?
Carbon-offsetting schemes allow you to offset greenhouse gas emissions by donating to various projects, from tree planting to renewable energy schemes. Although some conservation groups are concerned that carbon offsetting is being used as a smoke-screen to delay the urgent action needed to cut emissions and develop alternative energy solutions, it remains an important way of counterbalancing your carbon footprint.

For every tonne of CO_2 you generate through a fossil fuel-burning activity, such as flying, you pay for an equivalent tonne to be removed elsewhere through a 'green' initiative. There are numerous online carbon footprint calculators (such as www.carbonfootprint.com). Alternatively, book with a travel operator that supports a carbon offset provider like TICOS (www.ticos.co.uk) or Reduce my Footprint (www.reducemyfootprint.travel).

It's not all about tree-planting schemes. Support now goes to a far wider range of climate-friendly technology projects, ranging from the provision of energy-efficient light bulbs and cookers in the developing world to large-scale renewable energy schemes such as wind farms.

Black coral

Beautiful tourmaline-black, shiny coral jewellery is available throughout Belize. It's as enticing as ivory, and buying it is about as environmentally friendly. Bringing it back home to the US (or to Europe) is a federal offence. A US Virgin Islands company was sentenced in late 2011 to pay a US$1.8 million criminal fine in a federal court in St Thomas, the largest ever non-seafood wildlife trafficking financial penalty and the fourth largest for any US case involving the illegal trade of wildlife.

The US Justice Department came down heavily to set a precedent. For black corals are too precious to wear. They grow incredibly slowly in the deep ocean, as little as 4 to 35 micrometres per year. Large black corals are among the oldest continuously living organisms on the planet, at more than 4000 years old.

Corals in general are under increased threat from ocean warming, acidification and destructive fishing practices. But the biggest threat to black, red and pink corals is from the jewellery trade.

For more information on black coral conservation, see www.seaweb.org.

Shopping in Belize

Art
The country has a nascent but developing contemporary arts scene, spearheaded by painters like Pen Cayetano, Piva and Eduardo Garcia. Many of these artists are represented by the **Image Factory** in Belize City (see page 38) and **Belizean Arts** in San Pedro (see page 80).

Food
Edible souvenirs include Marie Sharp's sauces (see page 139) and organic Toledo chocolate (see page 168), both available throughout the country.

Handicrafts
The preponderance of Guatemalan indigenous arts and crafts in Belizean tourist shops says much about the state of the local industry. There are precious few typically Belizean souvenirs. You'll find Mayan arts and crafts, including carved wooden objects, carved stone and slate glyphs, copal resin and copal candles in San Antonio village in Cayo (see page 101) and at the **Maya Centre** in Cockscomb (see page 142). **David's Woodcarving** in Hopkins (see page 153), the **National Handicraft Center** in Belize City (see page 39), and **Orange Gifts** in San Pedro (see pages 80) sell beautiful hand-crafted wooden bowls and other handicrafts.

Jewellery
If you're buying jewellery, avoid black coral. It is a criminal offence to bring this into the UK and a federal offence to bring it into the US (see box, above).

Music
CDs from the **Stonetree Records** catalogue, including albums by Andy Palacio, Aurelio Martinez, the Garifuna Women's Project and Paul Nabor (see page 209), are available in **Brodie's** stores and at the airport.

Essentials A-Z

Accidents and emergencies

For all emergencies, T911. For the tourist police, T227-6082.

Customs and duty free

Duty free items include 200 cigarettes or 50 cigars or 250 g of tobacco, 1 litre of wine or spirits, medicine and medical supplies suitable for personal use and animal feeding material. You can import and export up to BZ$100 per person in local currency and can import and export an unlimited amount of foreign cash providing it is declared upon arrival. You have to declare any currency in excess of BZ$10,000 or foreign currency equivalent.

Prohibited items
The import of plant and plant products, meat and meat products, milk and poultry products, beer and pornographic material is forbidden.

Disabled travellers

Belize is not an easy country for travellers with disabilities. Travel by public bus is nearly impossible; Belizean public buses are usually old US school buses, which sit very high off the ground and have narrow stair entrances. Water taxis have no ramps and most hotels do not have rooms on the ground floor or elevators.

An excellent online source of information is disabledtravelers.com, which has comprehensive lists of travel agents offering trips for people with disabilities, as well as regularly updated features on topics such as adventure travel and home exchanges. The **Handicapped Scuba Association** (www. hsascuba.com) are the leading source of information on disabled diving and organize

their own trips. Good general sources of information include www.tourismforall.org. uk, www.independentliving.org, www.makoa. org, www.access-able.com, www.radar.org.uk, www.acrod.org.au and www.dpa.org.nz.

Many of those with disabilities coming to visit Belize do so on a cruise. Many modern cruise ships are well equipped for those with disabilities, with fully accessible cabins for wheelchair-bound passengers, bathroom fixtures with grab rails, ADA kits for the hearing impaired and Braille elevator buttons for the visually impaired. Contact the **Disabled Cruise Club** (www. disabledcruiseclub.co.uk) or **Cruise Lines International Association** (www.cruising. org) for details of particular cruises.

Drugs

Drugs of any kind are illegal in Belize, even where they appear to be widely used, and police come down hard on tourists carrying even small amounts of cannabis. You will be touted weed and other drugs whilst in Belize. Be aware that you are liable for either 6 months in prison or a minimum BZ$6000 fine if you indulge.

Drug dealers in Belize, especially in urban areas, are often gang members involved in violent crime. Be especially careful in Belize City where touts can be aggressive and try to intimidate tourists.

Electricity

110/220 volts single phase, 60 Hz. Plugs are usually the US-style with 2 flat prongs, and occasionally European 2-pin plugs. Some hotels use 12-volt generators.

Wilderness lodges and hotels on the remoter cayes run on generators or partial solar power. A few do not have electricity 24 hrs a day. Check before charging up your cameras and computers, and bring a torch/flashlight.

Embassies and consulates

For all Belizean embassies and consulates worldwide and for all foreign embassies and consulates in Belize, see http://embassy.goabroad.com.

Gay and lesbian travellers

A prevalence of macho and homophobic attitudes, particularly among the uneducated, do not make Belize a gay- and lesbian-friendly travel destination in general. Homosexuality was only made legal in 1988, but there is no gay scene. For more information see gaytravelbelize.com.

Due to the high number of international visitors, however, San Pedro and Ambergris Caye are an exception to the rest of Belize. Ambergris is by far the most tolerant destination in the country and you are unlikely to receive any discrimination there.

There are just a handful of gay- or lesbian-owned hotels in Belize, including **Changes in Latitudes** on San Pedro (see page 71) and **Macaw Bank** in San Ignacio (see page 115). Gay- and lesbian-friendly bars and clubs include **Jaguar's Paw** and **1755 Lounge**, both in San Pedro. Gay- and lesbian-friendly hotels listed in this guide include **Caye Casa** in San Pedro (page 76), **Radisson Fort George** in Belize City (see page 35), **Chabil Mar** in Placencia (see page 159), and **Calico Jack's** in Cayo District (page 113).

Health

Before you go

See your doctor or travel clinic at least 6 weeks before your departure for general advice on travel risks, malaria precautions and vaccinations. Make sure you have travel insurance, get a dental check (especially if you are going to be away for more than a month), know your own blood group and,

if you suffer a long-term condition such as diabetes or epilepsy, make sure someone knows or that you have a **Medic Alert** bracelet/necklace with this information on it (www.medicalert.org.uk).

Vaccinations

Recommended vaccinations for Belize are diptheria, Hepatitis A, tetanus, yellow fever (if travelling from a country with risk of yellow fever transmission). But things change. Check with your doctor or travel clinic before leaving home.

A-Z of health risks
Bites and stings

To prevent mosquito bites wear clothes that cover the arms and legs, use effective insect repellent and a mosquito net treated with insecticide. Repellents containing 30-50% DEET (Di-ethyltoluamide) are recommended, or try a lighter repellent, such as Off. If you are a popular target for insect bites, use antihistamine tablets and apply a cream such as hydrocortisone. Alternatively, use our tried-and-tested recipe: 70% jojoba oil, 30% pure citronella essential oil, 10 drops of eucalyptus citriodora and 5-10 drops of clove and wintergreen essential oil.

Sandflies, especially seen on the cayes, are known as 'no see-ums' in Belize. These little blighters leave dozens of tiny red welts on limbs, which itch profusely and which often do not appear until 6-10 hrs after the bite. They are so small that they can fly through the holes in mosquito nets. Prevent them from doing so by impregnating the net with permethrin. The viscosity of the jojoba oil in our home-made repellent (see under mosquitoes above) traps the sand flies legs and makes it very difficult for them to settle on the skin. Grape-seed oil is a good alternative. Use plenty of both. Locals use Avon Skin So Soft (now available with an added chemical insect repellent) or Johnson's baby oil.

If you are unlucky (or careless) enough to be bitten by a venomous snake, spider, scorpion or sea creature, try to identify the culprit, without putting yourself in further danger (ie do not try to catch a live snake). Belize is home to black widow spiders, which rarely bite but are highly venomous, and brown recluse spiders, which look like a tiny British house spider and whose bite causes an ulcer. None of Belize's scorpions are deadly to healthy adults, though they can cause severe reactions in children and the elderly. They are found throughout Belize but you are only likely to encounter them in one of the forest lodges. The best way of avoiding bites or stings from spiders and scorpions is always to shake out shoes, towels and clothes left in the hotel overnight, before using them.

There are ticks in the Belizean forest – particularly in areas where there are peccary and/or deer. They can carry diseases but are usually just a painless annoyance; use tweezers to carefully remove them, or smother them overnight in Vaseline, and never twist.

There are a number of venomous snakes in Belize. Most are vipers, but there also coral snakes. Although the latter have a strongly neurotoxic venom which is deadly to most humans, they are not aggressive and, unless you step on or try to catch one, you are very unlikely to be bitten. Victims of bites from any snake should be taken to a hospital or a doctor without delay.

Belize has one dangerous insect, the bullet or 24-hr ant (*paraponera*). This large (18-25 mm long) solitary ant inflicts an agonising sting whose waves of burning, throbbing pain endure for 24 hrs. It is only found in the forest. Belize's brightly-coloured large centipedes can also inflict a painful, poisonous bite.

There are a number of dangerous water animals. Cone and auger shells are hunting molluscs with very attractive conically shaped colourful shells with large slit-like openings. They are sometimes washed-up on beaches. Both are poisonous, cones more so – with highly toxic venom that acts quickly to cause acute pain, swelling,

paralysis, blindness and possible death within hours. On the reef look out for fire corals, bright yellow-green or brown skeletal hydroids that look a little like seaweed; they inflict a painful sting. And, in the open water, beware of Portuguese man-of-war, a jellyfish with long (up to 35 ft) tendrils. Stings are painful and incapacitating, but rarely fatal. Poisonous fish include toad, scorpion and stone fish – pug-ugly camouflaged bottom-dwellers with big mouths and venomous spines. Stone fish look uncannily like small pieces of reef. Brightly banded lionfish with long wispy spines can inflict a painful wound. Kite-shaped stingrays have a sharp barb in their tail, leaving an extremely painful wound if stepped on. Some are venomous. You are unlikely to encounter any dangerous sharks in Belize.

Dengue fever

Dengue fever, also known as 'break-bone fever', is a viral disease spread by mosquitoes that tend to bite in urban areas during the day. The symptoms are fever and intense joint pain and some people also develop a rash. Symptoms last about a week but it can take a month to recover fully. Dengue can be difficult to distinguish from malaria, so it is important to get your blood tested as soon as possible. There are no effective vaccines or antiviral drugs. Rest, plenty of fluids and paracetamol (never aspirin, which can cause fatal complications in some strains) are the recommended treatment.

Diarrhoea

It is not uncommon to contract a short but unpleasant bout of diarrhoea while your body adjusts to changes in diet, climate and temperature. Bacterial diarrhoea is different and usually transmitted through contaminated food and drinking water. Be wary of salads, reheated foods or food that has been left out in the sun having been cooked earlier in the day. Avoid all unpasteurized dairy products. Adults can use medication such as loperamide to control the symptoms of diarrhoea, but only for up to 24 hrs. Keep well hydrated and eat bland foods only. Oral rehydration sachets are useful. If your diarrhoea persists for more than 5 days – or is accompanied by blood, fever and/or vomiting – seek medical attention immediately. Travellers to rural areas sometimes contract parasites which can cause medical complications if left untreated. Amoebas are the usual culprits and, if you suspect an infection, go straight to your nearest lab for stool tests. Note it can take 5 consecutive days of testing for a positive result.

Hepatitis
There are vaccines for hepatitis A and B (the latter is spread through blood and unprotected sexual intercourse, both of which can be avoided).

Malaria
The key advice is to guard against contracting malaria by taking the correct antimalarials and finishing the recommended course. Malaria can cause death within 24 hrs and can start as something resembling an attack of flu. You may feel tired, lethargic, headachy or feverish; or, more seriously, you may develop fits, followed by coma and then death. Have a low index of suspicion because it is very easy to write off vague symptoms, which may actually be malaria. If you have a temperature, visit a doctor as soon as you can and ask for a malaria test. On your return home, if you suffer any of these symptoms, have a test as soon as possible. Even if a previous test proved negative, this could save your life. Remember **ABCD: Awareness** (of whether the disease is present in the area you are travelling in), **Bite avoidance**, **Chemoprohylaxis, Diagnosis**.

Rabies
Rabies is quite rare in Belize and vampire bats are the main carriers. Rabies vaccination before travel can be considered for those intending to visit areas more than a day from hospital facilities. If bitten, always seek urgent medical attention – whether or not you have been previously vaccinated – after first cleaning the wound and treating with an iodine-base disinfectant or alcohol. Avoid handling wild or feral animals.

Sun
The sun is extremely fierce in Belize and over-exposure can quickly lead to sunburn and, in the longer term, skin cancers and premature skin aging. The best advice is simply to cover exposed skin, wear a hat and stay in the shade if possible, particularly between late morning and early afternoon. Apply a high-factor sunscreen (greater than SPF15) and be sure it screens against UVB. A further danger in tropical climates is heat exhaustion or, more seriously, heatstroke. These can be avoided with good hydration, which means drinking water past the point of simply quenching thirst. If you cannot avoid heavy exercise, it is also a good idea to increase salt intake. Note that cloud coverage does not mitigate the dangers posed by ultraviolet light; continue covering up and using sun block even if the weather is overcast.

Water
If you intend to get off the beaten track, bottled water may not be available and you should certainly purify whatever else is available. Dirty water must first be strained through a filter bag or coffee filter and then boiled or treated. When boiling, bring the water to a rolling boil for several minutes. Chemical sterilizers usually contain chlorine or iodine compounds. Their unpleasant taste can often be neutralized with additional products. In an emergency situation, add 3-5 drops of bleach to a litre of water and let it stand for 30-60 mins.

Useful websites
National Travel Health Network and Centre (NaTHNaC), www.nathnac.org.
World Health Organisation, www.who.int.

Insurance

Insurance is highly recommended for all travellers. It's best to buy this before you leave, as few companies will insure you once you are travelling. Shop around and check some online reviews before settling on a provider. The most important aspect of any policy is medical care and repatriation, but ideally you will want to be covered for personal items, too. Most policies have strict limits regarding the total value of lost or stolen items – as well as an excess – so if you are carrying digital cameras, laptops or other expensive equipment you may have to insure these separately. Adventure activities such as diving usually add cost to a policy. Before you leave, read all the small print and take digital photos of your valuables and their receipts, including serial numbers. Store all these images in a secure online facility (eg dropbox) along with electronic copies of your passport and insurance policy. If you need to make a claim, call your provider immediately to determine which documents (eg medical or police reports) they will require. Keep hard and digital copies of everything and always have the number of your insurance provider to hand in case of an emergency.

Internet and VoIP

It is easy to get internet access in Belize. Most hotels have Wi-Fi, usually free of charge, and there are internet cafés and LAN houses dotted about all of the larger towns and villages. In the unlikely event of you not having internet access in your hotel, ask for the nearest one. VoIP, including Skype, are outlawed in Belize and are blocked by the government. You will not be able to access them unless you use a programme like Hotspot Shield.

Language

English is the official language, but Spanish is widely used, especially in Orange Walk,

Corozal, Cayo and border areas; see also page 230. Kriol is spoken by some throughout the country. Mennonite settlers in the north speak Plautdietsch (Low German). Yucatec, Mopan and Quiché Mayan languages and Garífuna are spoken by those associated ethnic groups.

Media

Newspapers

There are no daily newspapers in Belize. News is available in the weeklies, which generally come out on Fri morning and on the newspaper websites which are more frequently updated. The *Belize Times* (www.belizetimes.bz) and the *Guardian* (www.guardian.bz) are supported by the PUP political party and the UDP, respectively. The *Reporter* (www.reporter.bz) and *Amandala* (www.amandala.com.bz) have less marked political affiliations. Local papers include the tourist-orientated *San Pedro Sun* on Ambergris Caye (www.sanpedrosun.com) and the *Placencia Breeze* (www.placenciabreeze.com) in Placencia. Small district newspapers are published sporadically.

Radio

Belize has a number of radio stations, including a Spanish-language station, **Estereo Amor** (103.7 FM, www.estereoamor.bz) and **Love FM** (95.1 FM, www.lovefm.com), the country's largest and most popular station. There are sadly no Garifuna stations. Internet radio is available on www.belizeweb.com.

TV

Belize has 3 national TV channels. **Channel 5** (edition.channel5belize.com) shows mostly re-runs of US and Caribbean programmes. **Channel 7** (www.7newsbelize.com) is more strongly news based, and **Plus TV** (www.plustvbelize.com) runs Christian programmes. All have online streaming. There are a handful of local TV channels (including **San Pedro Channel 7**and **Channel 3** in Orange Walk). Many hotels have US satellite TV.

Money

ATMs

Visa and MasterCard ATMs are available at branches of **Scotia Bank**, **Belize Bank**, **First Caribbean** and **Atlantic** banks. Most banks will charge up to 5% for a cash advance against a credit card over the counter.

Cost of living and travelling

Belize is cheap compared to Europe, the Caribbean or the US, about the same as Mexico and pricey when compared to the rest of Central America. Budget travellers should allow for BZ$50-80 per person per day if travelling in pairs, staying in hostels or low-end guesthouses, using public transport and opting for cheaper trips. Visits to Ambergris Caye or the outer atolls will push this up. Ambergris is half as expensive again as the rest of the country and, whilst there is budget accommodation on the outer atolls, transport costs are high. Prices for hotel rooms and meals in good restaurants are good value: around 30% cheaper than the equivalent in the US, and 50% cheaper than continental Europe, Japan, Australia or Brazil.

Areas like Mountain Pine Ridge and inland Toledo are difficult for budget travellers to reach as they involve private or expensive tour or transfer options. Be aware of hidden taxes in Belize.

Currency

The monetary unit is the **Belize dollar**. US dollars are accepted everywhere and the Belize dollar is currently tied to the greenback at BZ$2 for US$1.

Currency notes issued by the Central Bank are in denominations of 100, 50, 20, 10, 5 and 2 dollars, and coins of 2 dollars and 1 dollar; 50, 25, 10, 5 and 1 cent. The American expressions, quarter (25c), dime (10c) and nickel (5c) are widespread, although 25c is sometimes referred to as a shilling.

It is generally better to spend in US dollars when you have them, as you will lose out on the exchange rate when converting to Belize dollars if you change them at a money changer or bank.

A common cause for complaint or misunderstanding is uncertainty about which currency you are paying in. The price tends to be given in US dollars when the hundred Belizean dollar mark is breached; make sure it is clear from the start whether you are being charged in US or Belizean dollars.

Exchange

The government has recently restricted the exchange of foreign currency to government-licensed money-changers (*casas de cambio*), which operate only in major towns. You can still find some money changers at the borders, but the exchange rate is not as high as it has been, and there is a risk of both you and the money changer being arrested and fined.

Opening hours

Businesses Mon, Tue, Thu-Sat 0800-1200, 1300-1600; Wed 0800-1200; Fri also 1900-2100. Small shops open additionally most late afternoons and evenings, and some on Sun 0800-1000. **Government and commercial offices** Mon-Fri 0800-1200, 1300-1600.

Post

Airmail to Europe takes 8 days and costs BZ$0.60 for a letter, BZ$$0.50 for a postcard. A letter to USA costs BZ$0.45 and a postcard costs BZ$0.35. A letter to Australia costs BZ$1 and a postcard costs BZ$0.70, and takes 2-3 weeks. Parcels: BZ$8 per 0.5 kg to Europe, BZ$1 per 0.5 kg to USA. The service to Europe and USA has been praised, but surface mail is not reliable. Belize postage stamps are very attractive and much in demand, and a trip to the Philatelic Bureau in Belize City is worthwhile to pick up some great souvenirs.

Safety

Belize has a poor reputation for safety, due to high crime rates in Belize City (mostly driven by gang retaliations) and the country's increased involvement with international drug smuggling. Attacks on foreigners are, however, extremely rare and mostly occur when a tourist has unwittingly strayed into the wrong part of Belize City after dark.

But it is always best to be cautious in Belize and to follow a few rules. Do not walk around Belize City after dark, even in a group. Dress down in Belize City and avoid engaging with hustlers; politely ignore them and walk swiftly on. Do not walk around Dangriga or Orange Walk alone at night. Do not drive at night. Avoid wearing expensive jewellery, watches or cameras in urban Belize. If someone tries to rob you, do not resist; give them what they ask; robbers are often armed.

Taxes

VAT has been replaced by a 10% sales tax, which is charged on all services. There is an additional 9% tax on most hotel rooms. There are sometimes additional taxes imposed on top of these, such as service taxes of around 10% or even a surcharge for paying by credit card. These taxes are not usually included in the quoted price, to the indignation of all but US and Canadian travellers, even on hotel websites (particularly those owned by people from the US), US online travel agents and travel advisory pages. Belize also charges a 1% 'environmental tax' on all goods brought into the country.

Telephone

Country code: T+501; **Information**: T113; **International operator**: T115.
If you have many calls to make, a phone card works out much cheaper. There is a direct-dialling system between the major towns and to Mexico and the US. Local calls cost BZ$60 for 3 mins, BZ$$0.20 for each extra

min within a city, BZ$0.35-0.75 depending on zone. For Belize's telephone directory see www.belizetelemedia.net.

There is decent mobile phone coverage in Belize through **Belize Telecom**. Prices are high for international users and it works out much cheaper to buy a local SIM card. **Belize Telemedia** is the GSM provider in Belize and a BTL SIM with a local phone number and around BZ$10 of credit will cost about BZ$50. These can be purchased from one of the telecom shops immediately opposite the terminal building at the international airport or in supermarkets. If you are travelling on to Guatemala or Mexico, you will have to buy a new SIM card in those countries.

VoIPs do not work in Belize (see Internet above).

Time

Belize is GMT - 6 hrs.

Tipping

In restaurants, tip 10% of the bill. Taxi drivers are tipped depending on the length of the transfer, whether 'touring' took place or for extra stops, BZ$2-10.

Tour operators

Australia and New Zealand
Intrepid, T1300-018 871,
www.intrepidtravel.com.

Belize
Also see tour operators listed in the What to do sections in individual chapters.
Belize Travel Services, T1-877 445 2012 (toll free US/Canada), T822-3272, www.belizetravelservices.com. Arranges multi-country packages including all Central America.

UK and Ireland
Abercrombie & Kent, T0845-485 1471, www.abercrombiekent.co.uk.

Belize Revealed, T020-8404 9299,
www.belizerevealed.co.uk.
Geckos, T0845-863 9723,
www.geckosadventures.com.
Journey Latin America, T020-3432 9392,
www.journeylatinamerica.co.uk.
Last Frontiers, T01296-653000,
www.lastfrontiers.com.
Naturally Belize, T020-8274 8510,
www.naturallybelize.co.uk.

US and Canada
Apple Vacations, T800-517 2000,
www.applevacations.com.
Belize Tradewinds,
www.belizetradewinds.com.
Belize Travel Points,
www.belizetravelpoints.com.
Belize Trips, T561-210 7105,
www.belize-trips.com.
Ian Anderson's, T1-866 822 2278,
www.adventuresinbelize.com.
Island Expeditions, T800-667 1630,
www.islandexpeditions.com.
Slickrock Adventures, T800-390 5715,
www.slickrock.com.
To See Belize, T1-877-222 3549,
www.toseebelize.com.

Specialist companies
Live-aboard diving
Dedicated divers will get the best value and
maximum possible dive time over the finest
dive sites by booking a multi-day dive cruise
with a live-aboard dive boat. Two companies
offer this service in Belize.
Aggressor Fleet, T+1 706 993-2531 (US),
www.aggressor.com. This company cruises
Turneffe and Lighthouse in the *Belize
Aggressor III*, a 110-ft-long boat which visits
the same locations as the boats owned by
Dancer Fleet (see below) and has similar
facilities. Prices start at around US$2700
for 7 nights' full board (including local
alcoholic drinks), transfers from/to Belize
International Airport, 5½ days of diving
and up to 5 dives per day.
Dancer Fleet, T+1-305 669 9391 (US), www.
dancerfleet.com. This company cruises the
reefs and atolls on one of its largest and
best-equipped boats, the *Sun Dancer II*, a
138-ft-long vessel with a big covered and
open sun deck, a/c lounge and rooms, which
have private bathrooms and flatscreen TVs
with DVD players. Some have ocean view
windows. The boat sails from Belize City
and operates around the northern cayes
and atolls. Dive sites include the Blue Hole,
Half Moon Caye Wall, Turneffe Elbow and
sites around Long Caye in the Lighthouse
Atoll. Prices start at around US$2200 for 7
nights' full board (including alcoholic drinks),
transfers from/to Belize International Airport,
5½ days of diving with up to 5 dives per day.

Neither company visit Glover's Atoll, the
South Water Caye Marine Reserve or the
southern cayes. However, it is possible to
do so on a bespoke live-aboard sail cruise

with **Belize Sailing Vacations** (T664-5300, belizesailingvacations.com).

Wildlife and birding tours
Belize Birding Tours, T1-877 571 0653 (US), www.belizebirdingtours.com. Pretty much the only international birding tour operator specializing in Belize and offering 2 standard trips both visiting the best birding locations, but one staying in more comfortable lodgings. Standard trips offer far more variety and visit Crooked Tree, Community Baboon Sanctuary, Hummingbird Highway, Cockscomb, Hopkins, Blue Hole National Park (inland), Mopan River, Mountain Pine Ridge and Xunantunich. The more upmarket option visits Chan Chich and Rio Bravo, Chaa Creek and Xunantunich. Both have optional Tikal extensions. Tours are led by owner-operator Jon Friedman who has a degree in biology and has been guiding bird tours since the 1980s.
Exotic Birding, T1-877-247 3371, www.exoticbirding.com. US company run by Jim Wiittenberger, who has a PhD in zoology, and photographer Laura Fellows. Visits the standard locations: Crooked Tree and Blue Hole National Park (inland), as well as the north and some of the cayes.
Naturetrek, T01962-733051, www.nature trek.co.uk. The largest wildlife tour operator in the UK runs 2 tours to Belize (including Tikal), visiting reef and rainforest. Experienced guides.
Paradise Expeditions, T610-5593, www. birdinginbelize.com. Based in San Ignacio, Belize, with 20 years of birding experience in Belize. Visits selected sites from Lamanai, Crooked Tree, Community Baboon Sanctuary, Caracol, Macal River, Guanacaste National Park, El Pilar, Mountain Pine Ridge, Aguacate Lagoon, Crystal Paradise, Cockscomb, Mayflower Bocawina and the Blue Hole National Park.
Wildside Nature Tours, T1-888 875 9453, www.wildsidetoursinc.com. One of the larger wildlife and birding companies in North America, offering a range of Belize tours including birder-focused trips, more general reef and rainforest trips and combinations with Tikal in Guatemala. Birding tours visit Crooked Tree, Cockscomb, Lamanai, Monkey Bay, Blue Hole National Park (inland), Dangriga and Mountain Pine Ridge, with an optional extension to Tikal.

Tourist information

The quality and quantity of tourist information in Belize varies greatly. In the popular centres of the cayes, Placencia and the developed sections of Cayo, there is a steady supply of information available. Away from these areas, the information is less reliable. Contact the **Belize Tourism Board** ⓘ *64 Regent St, Belize City, T227-2420, www.travelbelize.org*, also with an office in the Tourism Village in the city, for information on hotels, parks and reserves.

There is an ID card system to validate official tourist guides, which works well in the popular areas. Off the main routes there is less government checking of guides so a more ad hoc system works.

Conservation organizations
Belize Audubon Society (**BAS**), 12 Fort St, Belize City, T223-5004, www.belizeaudubon. org. Daily 0800-1700. Both the equivalent of the US NPS (or the Australian NPWS) and the country's foremost conservation organization, BAS administers ATM, the Blue Hole National Park, Cockscomb Basin, Crooked Tree, Guanacaste National Park, Half Moon Caye, St Herman's Blue Hole, Tapir Mountain and Victoria Peak. They are a mine of information on flora, fauna and environment. You will need to approach them for permits to those parks closed to visitors (Victoria Peak and Tapir Mountain).
Programme for Belize, 1 Eyre St, Belize City, T227-5616, www.pfbelize.org. Similar to **BAS** but smaller, managing conservation and ecotourism in protected areas including Rio Bravo and the tourist camps at La Milpa and Hill Bank (see page 186). Contact them for information on the flora and fauna of Belize.

Useful websites

ambergriscaye.com is a mine of information on all things Belizean, from San Pedro restaurants to dive sites, sports fishing and the ruined Maya cities of the interior.
www.belizenet.com, **www.belize.net** and **www.belize.com** are reasonable general information sites.
www.belize.gov.bz is the official government website.
www.belizeexplorer.com is excellent for budget travellers, with extensive information on the sights and up-to-date practical information on public transport.

Visas and immigration

All nationalities need passports, as well as sufficient funds and, officially, an onward ticket, although this is rarely requested for stays of 30 days or less.

Visas are not required from countries in the EU, Switzerland, Australia and New Zealand, most Caribbean states, the US and Canada, Costa Rica, Chile, Guatemala, Iceland, Mexico, Norway, Uruguay, some African and Asian countries and most Commonwealth countries. Citizens of all other countries require a visa, including Israel, Brazil and Argentina.

If you need a visa, it is best to obtain one in Mexico City or your home country before arriving at the border. For more details, contact your local Belizean embassy or consulate. A list of these can be found on www.goabroad.com.

Weights and measures

Belize uses the imperial system, but Belizeans use the imperial and metric systems interchangeably, which is why we have included both in this guide.

Women travellers

Solo women travellers in Belize may encounter occasional unpleasant remark, overly attentive men and lots of invasive staring (particularly when you're in beachwear). Belize City is the most potentially problematic area, where men can be aggressive, especially if you respond to their wolf whistles with a put-down. It is best to ignore them. Never accept a lift from a new acquaintance if you are travelling alone and don't give your full name or the name of your hotel to a stranger. Be particularly wary of the friendly rastafarians on Caye Caulker. Most (but not necessarily all) are neither friendly nor rastas; they are professional hustlers who are known to locals for selling weed and visiting female tourists. There have been a number of incidents of their charm turning nasty, as any female hotel or business owner on the island will tell you.

Working in Belize

Visitors wishing to work in Belize require a permit. However, there are many voluntary work placements available, from teaching to working on wildlife and reef conservation projects. For example, Monkey Bay (see page 56) offers a huge range of environmental and ecological volunteerships, internships and educational projects and Belize Zoo (see page 54) occasionally accepts volunteers to help out around the grounds. Other organizations offering placements are:
Belize Audubon Society, see page 25.
Belize Travel Services, see page 39.
Beyond Touring, T+1-954 415 2897, www.beyondtouring.com.
Birds Without Borders/Aves Sin Fronteras, T+1-414-258-2333, www.zoosociety.org.
Green Reef, T+501-226-2766, www.greenreefbelize.org.
IZE (see page 174).
King's Children Home, T+501-822 20211.
Personal Overseas Development, T+44-1242 250901, www.podvolunteer.org.
Programme for Belize, see page 25.
ProWorld, T+1-877 429 6753, www.proworldvolunteers.org.
Teachers for a better Belize, T+1-314 822 1569, www.tfabb.org.

Contents

Footprint features

Belize City & District

At a glance

⊖ **Getting around** The main sights in Belize City lie within walking distance of each other. Consider basing yourself in Burrell Boom and taking organized day trips. Places beyond the city are accessible by bus, cab or with a tour company.

◕ **Time required** Allow 3 or 4 days to explore Bermudian Landing, Crooked Tree, Belize Zoo and Altun Ha.

☼ **Weather** It's warm and dry at around 15- 30°C Jan to May with cooler nights. It's more hot and humid May to Oct, with the possibility of hurricanes. Nov to Dec is warm with occasional colder spells of 13-15°C.

✖ **When not to go** May-Oct is hurricane season; Sep-Nov can be grey and overcast.

The country's largest city and the Belize district capital sits on a bubble-shaped promontory jutting out into the Caribbean Sea. Like all Belize's towns, the capital is a tiny place. Streets are lined with huddles of weatherboard houses gathered around the old Victorian colonial centre, which focuses on an Anglican church plucked straight from an English market town. You can see everything Belize City has to offer, including the collection of Maya artefacts in the National Museum, in a long afternoon.

Many travellers choose not to stay in Belize City at all. Everywhere in Belize District is no more than 30 minutes' drive away, and the district itself holds far more attractions than its capital: pristine wildlife sanctuaries with superb birding at Crooked Tree and Spanish Creek; the towering ruined Maya city of Altun Ha nestled in forest; the Belize Zoo with its collection of native animals, and the howler monkeys, toucans and crocodiles of the old Belize River, which can be seen so close you can almost touch them in the sleepy hamlets of Bermudian Landing or Burrell Boom. Many visitors base themselves in the latter, which has one of the best small hotels in the country and is just 15 minutes' drive from the capital and less than 10 minutes from the airport.

Belize City

Belize City is the only town in the country with a set of traffic lights and a population in excess of 20,000. It has been the country's de facto capital since it was founded by log-cutting ex-buccaneers in the 18th century. Almost everyone who comes to Belize will pass through here at some point – usually between the airport and the cayes, which are reached from the city's muddy Caribbean waterfront. The city has enough tourist draws for half a day, but its streets and buildings are redolent with Belize's fascinating history, and its citizens offer a microcosm of this ethnically and culturally diverse country.

Many visitors arrive in Belize City nervous; the city has a tawdry reputation, enhanced by the dubious glamour of documentaries made by people such as Ross Kemp, which have portrayed the city as one of the most dangerous on the planet. "Belize City," proclaims Ross Kemp in his gangland documentary, filmed here in 2008, "is the sixth most likely place on the planet for someone to die of a gunshot wound."

Those expecting to see thugs bristling with bling and homicidal hardware will be surprised to discover that Belize City is, in reality, a small, sleepy town. Ramshackle streets of clapboard wooden houses fronted with bougainvillea and topped with red iron roofs swelter either side of the sluggish Haulover Creek. Fishing boats bob up and down in the water next to the old iron swing bridge, and the air throbs with Jamaican soca and reggae and the calls of petty hustlers.

After dark things get edgier, especially on the south (and poorest) side of the creek, but unless you're looking for trouble, wandering recklessly around George Street or Kraal Road at night, or flashing cameras and expensive watches, you're unlikely to see anything rougher in Belize City than a stray dog or a petty tout. Between 2009 and 2010, the British consulate dealt with only one case of assault on a British tourist and, according to the UN's international crime statistics, Belize is safer than almost all of its less crime-hyped Central American neighbours.

➤➤ For listings, see pages 35-42.

Arriving in Belize City ➔ *Colour map B3. Population 65,042.*

Getting there
Belize City is the principal entry point to the country, both by air and sea.

Air International and some domestic flights arrive at **Phillip SW Goldson International Airport** ⓘ *IATA code BZE, Northern Highway, Ladyville, T225-2045, www.pgiabelize.com*, 10 miles from Belize City; see also page 7.

Taxis into Belize city cost around BZ$50. Licensed and legitimate cabs have green number plates. Some hotels will arrange pickup for an equal or cheaper price. **Belize Shuttles** ⓘ *Belize International Airport, Ladyville, T631 1749, USA T757-383 8024, Canada T647-724 2004, www.belizeshuttlesandtransfers.com*, offer transfers to and from Belize City, to many other parts of the country, and to Cancún in Mexico and Flores in Guatemala (for the ruins at Tikal). Transport is in US-style air-conditioned minivans and cars. Prices are very reasonable: for example, to Belize City, municipal airport and boat docks (11 daily coinciding with flight arrivals, BZ$30 per person and BZ$10 for each additional passenger), San Ignacio (BZ$50-70 per person and BZ$10 for each additional person), Placencia via Dangriga and Hopkins (BZ$70 per person and BZ$10 for each additional person). It is also possible to walk from the airport turn-off to the Northern Highway itself (about two miles), and flag down a bus to the city centre or main bus terminal (BZ$2).

Most domestic flights, including the island hops operated by **Maya Island** and **Tropic Air** arrive at the pocket-sized **Belize City municipal airport** ① *IATA code TZA, 2 miles north of the city centre on the seafront*. A taxi to the city centre will cost around BZ$20. ▸▸ *See Transport, page 39, for further details.*

Boat Belize City has three water taxi terminals serving the cayes; see Transport, page 39. Taxis to the city centre from the San Pedro marine terminal cost around BZ$16. A number of Caribbean cruise ships, including those operated by **Carnival Cruise Lines** (www.carnival.com) and **Royal Caribbean** (www.royalcaribbean.co.uk), call at Belize City **Brown Sugar Terminal**. Tours are whistle stop.

Bus The main bus station is on West Collette Canal Street in the west of town, half a mile from the Swing Bridge. It is possible to walk but advisable to take a cab – the area is sketchy and especially unsafe after dark, particularly for travellers carrying bags. There is a taxi rank outside the station; cabs to the centre are approximately BZ$10. It is also possible to book a **Belize Shuttle** (see above) to pretty much anywhere in the country from Belize City.

Getting around and orientation
Belize City sprawls north and south of Haulover Creek, which is known to almost all the locals as the Belize River, even though it is in reality a tributary of that stream. The northern part of town is the wealthiest, the safest and the least interesting to tourists. The administrative and commercial buildings, most of the mid-range and lower-end hotels and all the sights of any consequence lie south of the river, across the metal Swing Bridge, which spans Haulover Creek and which marks the city centre. Most are focused in a small grid of streets around St John's Anglican Cathedral, an area easy to negotiate on foot and just a 10-minute walk from the Swing Bridge itself.

Safety
Tourist police in dark green uniforms patrol the city centre in an attempt to control crime and give advice. By day Belize City is usually pretty safe, though it is always sensible to be careful with cameras and bags, and to be wary of conmen posing as guides and feigning racial offence in an attempt to intimidate. Official guides have to be licensed and should carry a photo ID. If you're going beyond the city centre, take a taxi. Some of the city's outlying streets are undesirable. And do not walk for more than 100 yds after dark, even for supper; take a cab. Leave a car in guarded car parks. Security guards at hotels with secure parking will usually look after cars for a few days while you go to the cayes, for a tip.

Tourist information
The helpful **Belize Tourism Board** ① *64 Regent St, T227-2420, www.travelbelize.org, Mon-Thu 0800-1600, Fri 0800-1600*, has plenty of information, including the latest bus, boat and aeroplane timetables. Their website is comprehensive. There is also a tourism booth in the Tourist Village, see below.

Background

Belize was a village long before it was a colony or a country. Mostly Scottish buccaneers came to Haulover Creek in search of dye-wood in the 17th century. They founded a camp

Don't miss ...

here and, as the camp became a village, the buccaneers became settlers and began to call themselves Baymen. Protracted battles with the Spanish saw the settlers flee, return and flee again, finally establishing Belize as a permanent settlement in the 19th century after the battle of St George's Caye, where a handful of enslaved Africans and tawdry British colonists saw off a bonsai Spanish Armada.

Aside from St John's Anglican Cathedral, whose ballast-block construction dates from 1812, little of colonial Belize City remains today. Fire, cholera, rioting by troops and several hurricanes have ravaged the city since then. The Belize Hurricane razed it to the ground in 1931 in the biggest natural disaster in the country's history. Over 10% of the population were killed. The city was built again, only to be destroyed once more by Hurricane Hattie in 1961, after which plans were drawn up to move the capital inland. However, by the time Belmopan was ready, Belize City had been reconstructed. Today, its tin-roof, rickety houses and tumbledown streets remain vulnerable, waiting for another storm.

Places in Belize City

Belize City's few sights can be visited in a languid afternoon. All are clustered in the couple of square miles crowding around Haulover Creek and Bird's Isle.

North of Haulover Creek: Fort George

The cape area immediately north and east of Haulover creek, between the little canal next to Queen Street and the Atlantic, is known as Fort George. Until the 1920s this was a swampy island that had been the site of the small wooden fort of St George, erected on the shoreline in 1803. After the land was filled, Fort George became the city's most distinguished neighbourhood, with streets of handsome wooden mansion houses and civic buildings, a handful of which stand today. They include the **Mexican Embassy** (Park Street at Marine Parade) and the **Great House Hotel** (see page 35). There are a few sights of interest.

The **Swing Bridge**, across Haulover Creek at the end of Queen Street, is the pivotal point of the city, so to speak. It is said to be the oldest working manual swing bridge in the world, a fact of historical curiosity more interesting than the bridge itself, which is little more than two 50-m long girders with a strip of asphalt between. Opening the bridge has been a morning ritual for well over half a century. Just after dawn, a team of men arrive to insert a jack in the keyhole beside the road and manually swing the road through 90 degrees on its perfectly balanced pivot allowing boats to enter the upper portion of Haulover Creek.

Just east of the Swing Bridge are two adjacent small museums: the **Coastal Zone Museum** ⓘ *North Front St s/n, Mon-Fri 1000-1700, free*, and the **Maritime Museum** ⓘ *North Front St s/n, Mon-Fri 1000-1700, free*, both with meagre exhibits devoted to marine life in Belize waters and the country's maritime history. More interesting than either is the **Image Factory** ① *91 North Front St, T223-1149, www.imagefactorybelize.com, Mon-Fri 0900-1700, free*, sitting next door to the **Caye Caulker Water Taxi Association** terminal. This is the best contemporary art gallery in the country, serving as a temporary exhibition space and a showroom for up-and-coming Belizean artists. These include Pen Cayetano (who paints village scenes in a faux-naif style reminiscent of Gauguin), Gilvano Swasey (who paints brilliantly coloured organic abstracts) and Pamela Braun (an expat from San Antonio who renders everyday scenes and images iconographic through striking colour and distorted perspective). The gallery has a decent gift and bookshop.

The Belize City **Tourist Village** ① *Fort St s/n*, some 200 m east of the bridge out towards the open sea, is the main point of entry for the increasing numbers of cruise ship passengers visiting Belize every year and is usually open only when ships are anchored offshore. The 'village' comprises a kind of waterfront mall, with a cluster of small shops, pharmacies selling cheap prescription drugs and waterfront restaurants, almost entirely purged of local charm and character. It is shut off from the city itself – to keep both the locals out and the cruise ship passengers' wallets within. Cruise ship excursions to attractions throughout Belize begin and end here. Non-cruise ship passengers wishing to enter the village can get a temporary pass at the gates, on presentation of photo ID. It is currently undergoing expansion and 'improvement'. Little money spent here goes into the hands of those that need it in Belize City. Be wise; for the best time and the best deals, catch a cab elsewhere and fix up a shore break through local operators.

Fort Street continues to the city centre's easternmost point, overlooking the open Atlantic, and graced with the **Fort George Lighthouse** and the adjacent **Baron Bliss memorial**, the tomb of Belize's ill-fated benefactor, Edward Bliss (see box, page 38). A performing arts centre named after the Baron lies on South Waterfront (see page 38).

Marine Parade stretches north around the cape of Fort George from the lighthouse past tiny Memorial Park and the Mexican Embassy to Gaol Lane. Belize City's former prison sits here. It's a surprisingly stately mock Palladian mid 19th-century building set in lawned gardens and now houses the city's top attraction, the **Museum of Belize** ① *Gabourel Lane s/n, T223-4524, www.nichbelize.org, Mon-Fri 0900-1700, BZ$10*. The museum has two floors. The lower floor combines preserved sections of the old gaol house, with galleries devoted to telling the story of the colony, through documents, etchings and prints, photographs and artefacts, which include a complete run of British Honduras and Belize postage stamps, the earliest of which are extremely valuable. There is also an exhibit of preserved Belizean insects, which include some magnificent, if pinned, morpho butterflies. The upper floor is entirely devoted to the Maya and was completely revamped in 2011 in preparation for the Maya celebrations in 2012 marking the completion of the long count (see box, page 201). Pre-Columbian artefacts sit alongside displays showcasing the lives of the modern Belizean Maya. The highlight of the gallery is a series of magnificent jade ornaments and carvings, the most spectacular of which is the Kinich Ahau jade head (see box, page 48). The Kinich Ahau is often on temporary loan to other museums, during which time it is replaced with a fibreglass replica. The gallery also preserves a number of beautifully intact ceramic bowls, plates and vases. Look out for the Buenavista vase, whose carvings depict the mythical Maya Hero Twins dancing in victory over the Lords of Xibalba, a story recorded in the *Popol Vuh*, the text of a Guatemalan Maya creation myth (see box, page 200).

South of Haulover Creek

Since the early 20th century, south Belize has been a divided neighbourhood. Handsome administrative buildings line the shore and the southern city's main thoroughfare,

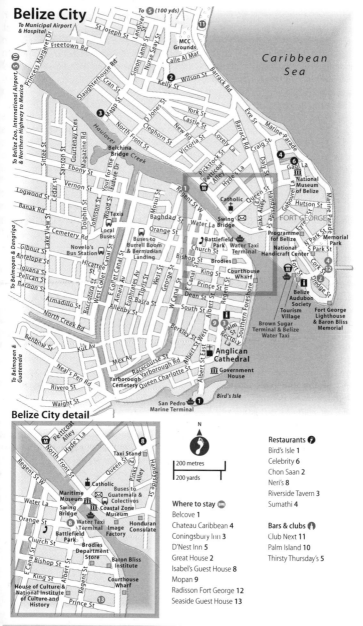

Belize City

To Municipal Airport & Hospital

Caribbean Sea

To Belize Zoo, International Airport, & Northern Highway to Mexico

To Belmopan & Dangriga

To Belmopan & Guatemala

St Joseph St
Landivar
Freetown Rd
Princess Margaret Dr
Slaughterhouse Rd
Cran St
Krapp
North Front St
Haulover
Belchina Bridge Creek
Out for the Future Dr
Magazine Rd
Courtenay Cres
Ebony St
Vernon St
Dolphin St
Johnson St
Woods St
Mosul St
Baghdad St
Regent St W
Water La
Catholic
Orange St
Taxis
Local Buses
Buses to Burrell Boom & Bermudian Landing
Hicattee St
E Collet Canal St
West Collet Canal St
Amara Av
Euphrates Av
Tigris St
Basra St
Allenby St
Armadillo St
Kut Av
North Creek Rd
Benbow St
Neal's Pen Rd
Rivero St
Waight St
Sittee St
Sarston St
Cedar St
Logwood St
Banak Rd
Lake View St
Cemetery Rd
Gibnut St
Antelope St
Pelican St
Iguana St
Racoon St
Simon Lamb St
Nurse Seay St
Kelly St
Wilson St
Barrack Rd
York St
Castle St
New Rd
Cleghorn St
Victoria St
Lovely La
Eve St
Marine Parade
Craig St
Daly St
Gaol La
Hutson St
Pickstock St
Pinks Alley
Handyside St
Gabourel La
Queen St
Hyde's La
Petticoat Alley
Swing Bridge
Battlefield Park
Water Taxi Terminal
Church St
Bishop St
Brodies
King St
Courthouse Wharf
Prince St
Dean St
South St
Berkley St
Regent St
Albert St
W Canal St
E Canal St
George St
West St
Southern Foreshore
Palm St
Rectory La
Mex Av
Racecourse St
Yarborough Rd
Queen Charlotte St
Albert St East
Albert St West
Anglican Cathedral
Government House
Bird's Isle
San Pedro Marine Terminal
MCC Grounds
Calle Al Mar
National Museum of Belize
FORT GEORGE
Programme for Belize
National Handicraft Center
Cork St
Gabourel La
Eyre St
N Park St
S Park St
Memorial Park
Belize Audubon Society
Tourism Village
Brown Sugar Terminal & Belize Water Taxi
Fort George Lighthouse & Baron Bliss Memorial

Belize City detail

Petticoat Alley
Hyde's La
North Front St
Regent St W
Queen St
Pinks Alley
Handyside St
Taxi Stand
Catholic
Maritime Museum
Swing Bridge
Coastal Zone Museum
Buses to Guatemala & Colectivos
Honduran Consulate
Image Factory
Water La
Orange St
Water Taxi Terminal
Battlefield Park
Church St
Brodies Department Store
E Canal St
Bishop St
Albert St
Baron Bliss Institute
King St
Regent St
House of Culture & National Institute of Culture and History
Courthouse Wharf
Prince St

N

200 metres
200 yards

Where to stay
Belcove 1
Chateau Caribbean 4
Coningsbury Inn 3
D'Nest Inn 5
Great House 2
Isabel's Guest House 8
Mopan 9
Radisson Fort George 12
Seaside Guest House 13

Restaurants
Bird's Isle 1
Celebrity 6
Chon Saan 2
Neri's 8
Riverside Tavern 3
Sumathi 4

Bars & clubs
Club Next 11
Palm Island 10
Thirsty Thursday's 5

named Regent Street, in emulation of that prosperous London boulevard. But behind them, immediately to the west, is a labyrinth of higgledy-piggledy dirt streets lined with ramshackle wooden houses that have peeling paint and wonky and weather-worn wooden terraces. This is Belize's gangster land, the tawdry terror of which was much romanticized by Ross Kemp in his BAFTA-winning series *Ross Kemp on Gangs*, but whose reality is poverty and desperation. More than anywhere in Belize City, the south is an area to visit with caution, especially at night.

Take a taxi from Haulover Creek to **St John's Anglican Cathedral** ① *East Albert St at Regent St, T227-3029, belizeanglican.org, daily 0600-1800, free*). This small, brown ballast-brick building with a castellated faux-Saxon tower and handsome arched windows sits in a grassy churchyard and looks like it has been transposed from a modest English city suburb. It is the oldest building in the city. There's been an Anglican church in Belize since the first minister arrived here in 1776. The first priest was a stalwart missionary, Reverend Shaw. The second, an evangelical called Reverend Stanford, was fond of more than just the Holy Spirit, being at one time reputedly too drunk to bury a visiting seaman. Nonetheless, he and his successor managed to found a mission to further-flung reaches of the colony, a publicly funded school (which had some 100 boys by the 1830s) and St John's itself, which was the first Protestant Church to be established in Central America when it was built by slaves (from 1810), and finally consecrated by the Bishop of Jamaica in 1826. Britain's staunch allies in the wars against the Spanish, the Mesquita kings from the Mosquito Coast (in modern-day Nicaragua) were crowned and baptized here. The adjacent **Yarborough cemetery** ① *open daily 24 hrs*, is a fascinating place for an historical wander. Its gravestones offer glimpses into the country's past; look out for graves of the early Baymen and British buccaneers and of the many Belizeans who lost their lives fighting for the British Army in Iraq during the Second World War.

The handsome porticoed clapboard mansion sitting opposite the cathedral and next to the seafront is the former seat of colonial power, Government House. The building and attractive gardens were refurbished at the turn of the millennium and opened to the public as the **Government House of Culture** ① *Regent St s/n, T227-3050, www.museoscentroamericanos.net, Mon-Fri 0900-1600, B$10*, one of a network of arts centres-cum-museums around Belize given over to temporary exhibitions, cultural shows and displays of Belizean life. The building is worth a visit in itself for its sweeping wooden *Gone With the Wind* staircase, its state rooms – where Queen Elizabeth II once stayed – and its displays of historical photographs and curios. Look out for the replica of Baron Bliss's dinghy, used to ferry his body ashore (see box, page 38), and the painting of Belize City at the turn of the 19th century, before most of the old buildings were devastated by the 1931 hurricane. Allow a little time for the gardens, particularly if visiting in the late afternoon, when the trees are a alive with tanagers and hummingbirds.

Belize City listings

For hotel and restaurant price codes and other relevant information, see pages 11-12.

Where to stay

As Belize City is usually more of a transit point than a tourist destination in its own right, it offers a poor choice of hotels. Some of the apparently grander establishments are in a sorry state of repair and are not included here. Some of the simpler guesthouses are shoddily run. Be sure to take a cab to a restaurant or bar at night. It is sadly not advisable to walk, especially alone. This is particularly true south of Haulover Creek. Those intending to use Belize City as a base to explore the region should also consider staying a little out of town at Burrell Boom or Crooked Tree.

Belize City *p29, map p33*
$$$$ Great House, 13 Cork St, T223-3400, www.greathousebelize.com. This lovely old timber frame mansion is one of the few left from Belize City's halcyon days in the prosperous 1920s. Rooms are spacious (at least twice the size of those in the adjacent **Radisson**), bright, decked out with lush polished wooden floors, painted eggshell blue and decorated with big period mirrors and prints. Beds are king sized and the bathrooms have tubs as well as showers. The best rooms are those on the higher floors, with a sea view, wraparound balconies and separate living and bedroom areas. Buy bread in the small bakery next door, which serves a reasonable latte. There is no lift. Be prepared to carry bags up at least 1 flight of stairs. There's Wi-Fi, cable TV, a restaurant and bar. Continental breakfast included. Credit cards accepted.
$$$$ Radisson Fort George, 2 Marine Parade, T223-3333, www.radisson.com. The city's only big brand hotel is one of the tallest buildings in the country, overlooking the water in the Fort George area north of

Haulover Creek. The hotel is secure, sitting in its own complex with a decent-sized pool, bar and 3 restaurants (see Restaurants, below), and service is friendly and welcoming. The best rooms are in the tower club wing and have ocean views. Colonial rooms also have sea views and balconies. Villa rooms are cheaper. Room decor is US country club-anonymous, with chunky armchairs, dark wooden desks, faux-marble or carpeted floors and flatscreen TVs (with cable TV). Staff do not encourage guests to leave the premises at night; allow yourself to do so but in a taxi. For a small surcharge, non-guests can use the pool and gym. There's Wi-Fi and breakfast is included. Book online for discounts. Credit cards accepted.
$$$ Chateau Caribbean, 6 Marine Parade, Fort George, T223-0800, www.chateau caribbean.com. This stately, romantic, timber-framed build is in a great location, right on the waterfront. Staff are warm and welcoming, and rooms are big and breezy. The best have wonderful sea views and all have big desks and dressers, queen-sized beds, plenty of closet space and en suites with a tub and shower. But they are shabby and some need new a/c units, while the corridors need new carpets and the restaurant needs fresh wallpaper. The hotel restaurant serves decent lobster, seafood and a delicious lemon chicken curry. There's Wi-Fi and cable TV. Credit cards accepted.
$$$ D'Nest Inn, 475 Cedar St, Belama Ext, PH 2, 2½ miles out of town on the Northern Hwy, T223-5416, www.dnestinn. com. The handful of rooms in this family-run guesthouse are themed by bird names and individually decorated. Hummingbird nest is chintzy and faux-Victorian; Kiskadee dominated by a huge 4-poster with carved fleur-de-lis; Dove nest has mock Tiffany lamps and big windows, and Parakeet is simpler, with lush green walls and flower prints. The hotel has a lovely garden, with brightly coloured tropical flowering plants

and busy with hummingbirds in the early morning and late afternoon. Excellent breakfasts and very friendly owners.

$$ Belcove Hotel, 9 Regent St West, T227-3054, www.belcove.com. This 3-storey hotel sits right over the water at Haulover Creek, a stone's throw from the Swing Bridge and within walking distance of the bus terminal and the island boats. The best rooms are on the upper floors, have a/c, shared balconies, with wooden deckchairs and a view. Some need renovating so look at a few first. There is cable TV. Staff are helpful with tours and transfers, and can organize an airport pickup. Be careful in the area at any time and especially after dark.

$$ Coningsby Inn, 76 Regent St, T227-1566, www.coningsby-inn.com. A/c rooms are plain and simple in this homely guesthouse, with white walls, tiled floors but cable TV, functional writing desks and a space to hang clothes. The worst are a little gloomy, while the best has a sea view. En suite bathrooms have a tub with shower and the hotel has a communal sitting area with a tiny bar, which is a pleasant spot to relax with a book. Breakfasts (around BZ$12 extra) are big enough to last until the evening. BZ$10 per extra person make this guesthouse good value for groups. There's Wi-Fi and a launderette. Credit cards accepted.

$$ Isabel's Guest House, 3 Albert St (access via the alley behind), T207-3139. This tiny guesthouse sitting up 2 flights of stairs above the **Matus Store** right near the Swing Bridge (a great location for the island boats), has just 3 double rooms and a big triple room. All are fan cooled but spotlessly clean, and have fridges and en suite shower rooms. Isabel and her staff are welcoming and friendly, and a guard dog ensures that the guesthouse is safe after dark. There is a disco nearby which can be noisy at weekends.

$$ Mopan, 55 Regent St, T227-7351, www. hotelmopan.com. Rooms in this small family hotel are very simple and a little scuffed, with tiled floors and en suite bathrooms (some of which have dripping taps), but

they are good value, especially for small groups. The hotel charges BZ$20 for an extra person and has rooms with space for up to four. There's cable TV, Wi-Fi and a bar. Breakfast is included. Credit cards accepted.

$ Seaside, 3 Prince St, T605 3930, seasidebelize@gmail.com. This tawdry, tumbledown timber house is Belize's City's backpacker favourite. Beyond its bargain basement price and cheap meals (not always available), it's hard to see why. From the ramshackle communal downstairs kitchen to the boxy little dorms and doubles, with their spongy mattresses and grungy sheets, everywhere is in need of a great deal more care and attention. Owner Mitch has a big Alsatian guard dog, Crystal; intimidating perhaps by day but needed at night in what is a decidedly sketchy area.

⊘ Restaurants

Belize City *p29, map p33*
You won't find fine dining in Belize City. Food here is either Belizean (big plates of meat/chicken/fish served with rice and beans) or US-orientated comfort cooking of the kind you'd expect in **TGI Fridays**. The best restaurants are at about the level of a **Sizzler Steakhouse**. Seafood and steaks are generally the better options, though it's wise to avoid shellfish. The sea in Belize City's environs, whilst fairly clean, is not as limpid as the waters off the country's other coastal towns and cayes.

$$$ Riverside Tavern, 2 Mapp St, T223-5640, facebook.com/riversidetavernbelize. Belize's upper crust gather at the over-the-water deck in their Ralph Lauren's to eat what are reputedly Central America's best burgers. The beef comes from the Bowen's farm in Gallon Jug. Inside, big screens show North American sports and some European football matches. The restaurant offers free pickup from the jetty.

$$$ St George's, Radisson hotel (see page 35). Business people and families on a day out eat in this tropical-themed a/c restaurant. The menu offers US-style dishes, such as burgers and chips, steaks and rich seafood. There's a popular lunchtime and breakfast buffet (the former on Thu and Sun, the latter with an omelette bar). The hotel has 2 other restaurants: the **Stonegrill ($$$)** next to the pool has meat and fish grilled on super-heated volcanic stones, at your table; **Le Petit Café ($)** has pastries, snacks and juices. Food is also available at the hotel's bars.

$$$-$$ Chon Saan, 1 Kelly St, T223-3008. The best Chinese in the city, attracting Belizean business people and families who come to eat chow mein, chop suey, crispy duck and other Chinese standards, as well as sushi and steaks, in the big a/c dining room. They'll also deliver to your hotel.

$$ Bird's Isle, 9 Albert St, T207-2179. No restaurant in Belize City has a better location than this one. It sits right over the water at the end of a short unpaved road that runs to the waterfront from St John's Anglican Cathedral. The crowd is a mix of locals and tourists. The menu is eclectic, with good ceviche and Belizean dishes like fried fish, rice and beans and steaks, all made from fresh ingredients and served in large portions. But be prepared to wait a while. Service can be a little slow when a cruise ship is in town and the dining room is busy.

$$ Celebrity Restaurant, Volta Building, Marine Parade s/n, T223-7272, www. celebritybelize.com. It may advertise itself as the most romantic restaurant in Belize, but this big and rather gloomy restaurant attracts people in love with sports. The dining area is dominated by huge flatscreen TVs showing live NBA and NFL games and, occasionally, Premier League football. The menu and the portions are huge, dishes are well prepared and, whilst you'll find nothing gourmet here, there's decent steak, burgers, filleted catch of the day, Caesar salads to eat-in or takeaway (no delivery service), ice-cold beers and a modest wine list.

$$-$ Sumathi Indian Restaurant, 190 Newton Barrack's Rd, T223-1172, www.sumathi.2get2u.com. The city's finest Indian offers tandoori and north Indian options, which, whilst having plenty of flavour, will seem light on spice to those used to British or Indian subcontinent curry houses. Takeaways and deliveries.

$ Neri's, Queen St at Daly St, T223-4028. This small family-run diner in the heart of town offers some of the best Belizean cooking in town. The menu has the usual rice and beans, together with jerk chicken, soups and generous breakfast options, and at lunchtime there's always a very reasonably priced 'special'.

Bars and clubs

Belize City p29, map p33
Be careful going out at night in Belize City and take a taxi back to the hotel rather than walking. The safest night spots are on the north side of the river. The **Radisson** bars (see page 35), **Bird's Island** (see above) and **Riverside Tavern** (see above) are popular pre-club venues at weekends. **Bird's Isle** turns into a karaoke bar at weekends after 2300.

Club Next, Princess Hotel, Newtown Barracks s/n, T223-2670. Both the club (and the hotel) have seen better days, but it still attracts a lively crowd at weekends who come to dance to DJs spinning Caribbean and international sounds.

Palm Island, Mile 2 Northern Highway, T223-0604, www.palmisland.bz. Mon-Wed until midnight, Thu and Sun until 0200, Fri and Sat until dawn. The city's most popular club, playing US hip hop, R'n'B, Jamaican ragga, Trinidadian soca and punta.

Thirsty Thursday's, 164 Newtown Barracks, T223-1677. **Thirsty's** started out as a restaurant but, whilst they still serve decent Jamaicanan and Caribbean food, the establishment has changed to become Belize City's most popular pre-club bar. Locals pack the 2 floors and gallery area Thu to Sun to drink One Barrel rum and Belikins and dance to Caribbean and punta from Ross and other local DJs. There's usually a Happy Hour in the early evenings, and things get liveliest after 2130.

All for the love of fish

Edward Bliss, an Edwardian oil magnate and self-styled 'Baron of Buckinghamshire and Portugal', had one overwhelming passion in life: fishing. Hearing from friends in the Caribbean that the waters around what was then British Honduras were swarming with fierce fighting tarpon, bonefish, permit and jack, like no other location in the British Empire, he wrote to the colonial authorities in Belize City in 1925, asking if the reports were exaggerated. In reply, a colonial official boasted that although he was a novice, the writer had caught 12 tarpon right off the city quay in a single afternoon.

Bliss had found his paradise and, without setting foot in the place, he became obsessed with Belize. In 1926 he left Europe, and took his luxury steam yacht *Sea King* through the Caribbean to the colony, intending to settle in Belize for good. But after calling in at ports in the Caribbean, Bliss contracted an illness and, within sight of the Belizean shore, he died suddenly in his cabin on 9 March.

Before dying he made a hurried and astonishing will. Despite never fishing off or becoming acquainted with the country, and even though he had only heard of it the previous year, he bequeathed his considerable fortune to Belize through the Baron Bliss Trust. The trust money was used for infrastructure projects, which included construction of the Western Highway, a water supply for Belize City and the Bliss Institute of Performing Arts (see below). The day of his death, 9 March, is celebrated as Baron Bliss Day. It was renamed National Heroes and Benefactors Day in 2008 but few Belizeans know it as this.

Entertainment

Belize City *p29, map p33*
Beyond the bars and clubs listed above there's little in the way of entertainment in Belize City. The country's solitary cinema is housed in the **Princess Hotel** (Newtown Barracks s/n, T223-2670). It's in decided need of refurbishment. The hotel has a casino too, with a BZ$70 minimum to kick off gambling.

Cultural centres
Baron Bliss Institute of Performing Arts, Southern Foreshore s/n, T227-2110. Mon-Fri 0900-1700, free. The country's premier performance venue shows plays and live music. It's also Belize's most prestigious arts venue and houses the nascent national art collection in the Bliss Centre Gallery. Its pieces include George Gabb's famous *Sleeping Giant*, a sculpture that you can see watermarked on the BZ$5 bill.
Image Factory Art Foundation, 91 Front St, www.imagefactorybelize.com. Mon-Fri 0900-1800. Has exhibitions of contemporary art.
National Institute of Culture and History, Government House, House of Culture, Regent St, T227-0518, www.nichbelize.org. Mon-Fri 0830-1700. Administers most of the country's Mayan sites as well as the Museum of Belize (see page 32) and the Institute of Creative Arts (which runs the Baron Bliss Institute, see above, and coordinates artistic events and performances around the country). Its useful website has details of performances organized by the ICA and information on archaeological sites. Contact them about filming and permits for the Mayan sites. The House of Culture can be visited for its art exhibitions and historical displays. It also stages concerts and plays.

Festivals

Belize City *p29, map p33*
Feb/Mar Carnival. The weekend before Mardi Gras (Shrove Tue) every year. Modest

street celebrations, but things are livelier on the cayes, especially in San Pedro.

4-10 Mar La Ruta Maya Belize River Challenge. A multi-day canoe race from San Ignacio to Belize City along the Macal and Belize Rivers. This was once the only link between the two cities. Colourful and used as an excuse to celebrate, especially over the weekend.

9 Mar Baron Bliss Day. Horse and cycle races and a yacht regatta off the lighthouse celebrate the life of the great benefactor of Belize, Edward Bliss (see box, page 38).

Apr Cross Country Classic Bicycle Race. Usually held immediately after Easter weekend, this race between San Ignacio and Belize is the premier cycle event in the country. Belizeans love the sport and there are always big crowds of participants, including international cyclists.

Sep St George's Caye Day. Celebrations to mark the day when the British and the Baymen saw off an Armada of Spanish ships from the Yucatán. Processions, sporting events, a fire engine parade and live music.

◎ Shopping

Belize City *p29, map p33*
Belize City offers little in the way of tourist shopping.
Brodie's, 16 Regent St, T227-7070, www.brodiesbelize.com. The city's one-stop shop stocks everything from groceries and clothing to woodcarvings. It is also the only bookshop in the city.
National Handicraft Center, 2 South Park, T223-3636. A modest array of crafts from around Belize, including jippi jappa baskets, custom jewellery, dolls, music, T-shirts, ziricote and rosewood carvings and music.

◎ What to do

Belize City *p29, map p33*
Helicopter rides
Astrum Helicopters, Cisco Base Mile 3.5, Western Highway, T222-5100, www.astrum

helicopters.com. If you splurge on one excursion in Belize District, make it a flight out over the reef with **Astrum**. Belize's Barrier Reef and atolls look at their most spectacular from the air. Bring a polarizing filter for your camera and leave plenty of space on the memory card.

Tour operators

San Ignacio hotels and tour operators (see pages 111 and 118), as well as dive companies in San Pedro (see page 81) or Caye Caulker (see page 95), will organize pickups from Belize City to coordinate with one of their tours.
Belize Travel Services, T822-0413, www.belizetravelservices.com. Organizes hotel bookings, packages, flights and transfers throughout Belize and are very efficient and reliable.
Black Orchid, see page 49.

◎ Transport

Belize City *p29, map p33*
Air
International There are flights to **New York** twice weekly with **United**, to **Miami** twice daily with **American**, and to **Houston**, which has 2-4 daily with **United**. Tropic (www.tropicair.com) fly once daily to **San Pedro Sula**, Honduras, and twice daily to **Flores**, Guatemala. There are no flights connecting Belize with Mexico.

Domestic Maya Island (www.mayaisland air.com) and **Tropic** have many departures daily to **Caye Caulker**, **Ambergris Caye**, **Dangriga**, **Placencia**, **Punta Gorda** and charters available to **Hidden Valley** in Mountain Pine Ridge or **Sarteneja**. There are no flights to San Ignacio, Orange Walk, Corozal or Belmopan. Flights leave both from the international airport and from the municipal airstrip (see page 30).

Boat

Belize City remains the principal access point for boats and water taxis to the country's

International buses

Even though it is not on any international borders, Belize City is a major international arrival and departure point for buses. Mexico buses leave from the **Belize Bus Terminal** (known as Novelo's), but Guatemala buses use the **Belize City Water Taxi Terminal** on North Front Street near the Swing Bridge. The official agents in Belize for these bus lines are **Shammi Travel** and **Mundo Maya**, both located inside the Water Taxi Terminal, though there are plenty of booths offering tickets outside on North Front Street. These booths also sell minibus (*colectivo*) tickets to destinations in Guatemala and Mexico, which tend to leave when full.

Mexico

There is a Mexican ADO (Autobuses De Oriente, www.ado.com.mx) bus daily between **Cancún Airport** and Belize City, leaving Cancún at 2215 and arriving in Belize City at 0600, BZ$80. The bus calls at Playa del Carmen, Tulum, Corozal and Orange Walk en route. The bus returns from Belize City at 1930, arriving at Cancún airport at 0430.

There is also an ADO bus between **Mérida** in Mexico and Belize City, leaving Mérida Alta Brisa terminal at 2100, calling only at Corozal, and arriving in Belize City at 0600, BZ$79. The bus returns from Belize City at 1900, arriving at 0500.

You cannot buy a return bus ticket when you arrive in Mexico. You are obliged to pay for the Belize–Cancún journey in Belize. You should pay your fare in Belizean dollars if leaving from Belize or Mexican pesos if leaving from Mexico. US dollars incur a surcharge. When leaving from Belize City you pay BZ$19 to the gate agent and then you have to leave the bus at Bacalar to pay the other BZ$60. Be sure to have the right change.

When coming from Belize, at Santa Elena on the border you leave the bus, fill in the immigration form and pass through customs. At night there are rarely people

most popular cayes, including Ambergris Caye (San Pedro) and Caye Caulker. There are 3 main boat terminals and boats sail at different times, between around 0700 and 1730 each day, so as long as you check schedules beforehand you are never more than 30 mins from a boat during the day.

The dock for **Water Jets Express** (T226-2194, www.sanpedrowatertaxi.com) and the **San Pedro Marine Terminal**, lies on Bird's Isle at the far end of Albert Street in the south side of Belize City, just beyond St. John's Cathedral. The company has services 4 times daily to **Caye Caulker** (BZ$24 single, 30-45 mins) and **San Pedro** (BZ$36 single, about 60-80 mins); 1 service daily continues on to **Chetumal** in Mexico (BZ$70 from San Pedro and BZ$80 from Caye Caulker, both single). The company is also an official agent for Mexican **ADO** buses and can book bus tickets from Chetumal or all along the Riviera Maya to Cancún, and connections beyond.

Belize's other 2 boat terminals both lie on North Front St, about 200 yds southeast of the swing bridge in the city centre. Both terminals have areas where you can leave a bag and the **Caye Caulker Water Taxi Association Terminal** has a few shops and cafés. Booths outside the latter sell onward bus tickets to destinations throughout Belize and beyond to Mexico and Guatemala.

Closest to the swing bridge is the **Caye Caulker Water Taxi Association** terminal (T226 0992, www.cayecaulkerwatertaxi. com) with a 4 times daily service to **Caye Caulker** (BZ$20 single, 45 mins) and **San Pedro** (BZ$30 single, 1½ hrs).

A little further on up the same road is the cruise ship tourist facility in the **Brown Sugar Terminal** and the **Belize Water Taxi** around and you may have to push the button at the customs desk. If you get red, wait to have your bags searched; if green, just walk on. You then have to walk from here to the bus, which waits across the border next to a late-night fast food place. The procedure is similar when coming from Mexico. The buses have the a/c turned up very high and get chilly. Bring a fleece and jacket and try and secure a seat away from the toilet at the back.

There are frequent buses running between Belize City and **Chetumal** on Mexico's southern Quintana Roo border next to Corozal town; about 15 daily each way, roughly every 30 minutes, starting at 0500 until 1800, four hours, BZ$10. Express buses from 0600 stop at Orange Walk and Corozal only, BZ$20, three hours. It is possible to change buses in Chetumal for Cancún (5-6 hours), Merida (6-7 hours), Campeche (5-6 hours) and destinations throughout Mexico.

Guatemala
Linea Dorada (lineadorada.info) operates one bus daily between **Flores** (the nearest town to Tikal) and Belize City, departing Flores at 0700 and returning from Belize City at 1300. San Juan Express runs two services departing Flores at 0500 and 0730 and arriving in Belize City at 1000 and 1430. These buses return at 0930 and 1230, BZ$45. The journey time is around six hours. There are daily buses between Belize City and **Guatemala City**, with a stop at the border crossing at **Benque Viejo/Melchor**, were you must leave the bus, collect your bags and pass through immigration and customs, rejoining the bus on the other side of the border. It is also possible to take any bus from Belize City to **Benque Viejo** and cross the border from there. The last possible bus connection to Flores leaves the border at 1600, but it's better to get an earlier bus to arrive in daylight. Many buses leave the border for **Melchor de Mencos**, 0600 1030.

(Brown Sugar Market Sq, 111 North Front St, T223-2225, http://belizewatertaxi.com). They have the same number of sailings to the same destinations as the **Caye Caulker Water Taxi Association**, for the same price and also continue once daily to **Chetumal** in Mexico (BZ$70 from San Pedro and BZ$80 from Caye Caulker, single).

Bus
Local Buses within the city operate on a hop-on, hop-off basis. They are very informal and the driver will always tell you where you are going and where to leave the bus. Most are old US school buses. They cost BZ$1 per journey and BZ$2 for a/c (**Arrowline** buses). There are many different operators. You can catch them into town from Cemetery Rd at West Collett Canal St. R Line or McFadzean buses for **Burrell

Boom and **Bermudian Landing** leave from the corner of Amara and Cemetery St or Euphrates at Cemetery at 1200, 1220, 1530, 1600, 1700, 1720, 2000 and 2100, BZ$3 , 1 hr. There are 2 buses back to Belize City, at 1530 and 1600. Any Northern Highway bus (between Belize City, Orange Walk or Corozal, about every 30 mins, BZ$3) will stop or can be flagged down at Burrell Boom. A pickup from Burrell Boom junction to Bermudian Landing will cost around BZ$50 (15 mins) and from the airport around BZ$80 (40 mins). The **Black Orchid Resort** can organize trips to the **Community Baboon Sanctuary** by car or river boat.

Long distance Buses are the main mode of transport for almost all Belizeans and, as Belize City is the country's main transport hub, you will find regular buses to most major towns from here. Buses operate from **Belize City Bus Terminal** (commonly known as **Novelo's**), 0.4 miles west of the Swing Bridge on West Collett Canal St. Whilst you can walk from here to the city centre by day (allow 40 mins), the area around the terminal and along the canal is unsafe after dark. If arriving at night, make sure you've reserved a hotel and take a taxi. There are also some services from the Water Taxi Terminal on Front St. For international buses, see box, page 40.

North: to **Corozal** and the **Santa Elena border to Chetumal** (3 hrs, BZ$15) via **Orange Walk** (90 mins, BZ$8), BBDC operates 21 buses daily, **T-Line**, **Tillet** and **Gilharry** start first at 0530, last at 1930. Gilharry have more buses. To **Sarteneja** 4 daily with **Sarteneja Bus** line from the water taxi terminal at 1030, 1200, 1600 and 1700, 3-4 hrs, BZ$12.

West: to **Benque Viejo** and **San Ignacio** via **Belize Zoo** and **Belmopan**, more than 40 daily, 24 hrs, BZ$10, 2-3 hrs, with **National Transport Services**, **Belize Bus Owners Coop**, **Middleton's**, **D&E**, **Shaw** and **Guerra's**.

South: to **Dangriga** via **Belmopan**, 18 daily with **James** (T702-2049), **Williams** and **G-Line** (James has the most buses), first at 0515, last at 1815, 3 hrs, 10 James buses continue to **Punta Gorda** (5-5½ hrs) via **Independence** (for **Placencia**) or you can change in Dangriga and catch a bus with **Ritchie's**. You will also need to change in Dangriga for **Hopkins**. To **Crooked Tree**, Mon-Sat 1055 (from a stop in front of Mike's Club on Regent's St West) and 1715 (leaving from the Novelo's), 90 mins, BZ$4.

Car
Car hire starts at BZS$150 plus insurance of around BZ$30 a day. Most rental firms have offices in Belize City and opposite the international airport terminal building, see belizeairportcarrental.net for details and links to all the major companies, which include **Auto Europe** (T203-5429,

www.autoeurope.com), **Avis** (T203-4619, www.avis.com), **Budget** (T223-2435, www.budgetbelize.com), **Thrifty** (T207-1271, www.thrifty.com) and **Zoom** (T222-4190, zoomrentalcars.com).

Taxi
Official cabs have green licence plates (drivers have ID cards) but no meters so agree the fare before getting in to the car. The standard fare for short trips in Belize City is BZ$5-7 per taxi (not per passenger). There is a taxi stand on Central Park, another on the corner of Collet Canal St and Cemetery Rd, and a number of taxis on Albert St, Queen St and around town. Outside Belize City, it costs BZ$5 per mile, for up to 4 passengers. Belize City to the resorts in Cayo District costs approximately BZ$250 for 1-4 people.

Directory

Belize City *p29, map p33*
Embassies and consulates
The Guatemalan embassy, 8A St, King's Park, T223-3150, 0830-1230, will not issue visas or tourist cards here; will tell you to leave it till you reach the border.

Medical services
Hospitals Karl Heusner Memorial Hospital, Princess Margaret Dr, T223-1548, www.khmh.bz. The best in the country.
Pharmacies You can purchase UK and US prescription medicines over the counter in Belize. Most brands are North American or European. Prices are about 25% higher than the US and 50% higher than Europe. Pharmacies at **Brodies** (see Shopping, page 39) and **Wilmac's**, Central American Blvd s/n, T663-1061.

Post
The main post office is at Queen St and North Front St, 0800-1700 (1630 Fri). Beautiful stamps for collectors around the corner on Queen St.

North of Belize City

Belize City sits on a round promontory that sticks out into the Caribbean Sea like a pimple. Its hinterland barely extends back into the main body of the country; heading north along the Northern Highway, things begin to feel suburban just three miles from Belize City centre, and by the time you get to the airport 10 miles away in Ladyville, it's positively rural. Beyond here, Belize is semi-wild. Tiny Burrell Boom is closer to the airport than the capital and is a far more salubrious place to base yourself. Jaguars have been spotted on the banks of the Belize River at the lovely Black Orchid resort, and you'll see howler monkeys in the hotel gardens every morning. A few miles away in Bermudian Landing, there's a community project devoted to protecting the primates. It's one of several wildlife reserves within 30 minutes' drive of Belize City, which include Spanish Creek and the extensive bird-filled wetlands at Crooked Tree. There are Mayan ruins too; Altun Ha is one of Belize's most impressive, though it can be busy with tourists when a cruise ship is in town. ▸▸ *For listings, see pages 49-51.*

Burrell Boom and the wildlife sanctuaries → *For listings, see pages 49-51.*
Colour map B2.

The sleepy hamlet of **Burrell Boom**, some 20 miles west of Belize City off the Northern Highway, is almost as close to Belize's international airport as the capital itself, and is a far more pleasant location to stay overnight before a flight, or to use as a base for an exploration of Altun Ha and the attractions of southern Orange Walk district. The hamlet straddles the **Belize River** at a point where logwood and mahogany were bundled together for shipping to Europe and the US. Mexican black howler monkeys are a common sight along the river's length and are best seen on a boat trip taken from the **Black Orchid Resort** (see page 49) or at the Community Baboon Sanctuary, see below.

Community Baboon Sanctuary
ⓘ *Bermudian Landing, T660-3545, www.howlermonkeys.org. Standard tours BZ$15 per person; river tours BZ$45 per person, minimum 2 people; night hikes BZ$25 per person. The Black Orchid Resort, see page 49, organizes trips to the Community Baboon Sanctuary by car or river boat.*

Some 10 miles west of Burrell Boom in the tiny village of Bermudian Landing, this sanctuary preserves 10 to 15 family groups of Mexican black howlers (the baboons), together with other threatened wildlife in the nearby forests and along the banks of the Belize River. It is a model ecotourism project, with the local community involved at every level. More than 240 local landowners grouped together to create the 20-sq-mile reserve. The sanctuary headquarters and museum are staffed and run by the local women's group and all the guides come from the surrounding villages. The wildlife-watching is superb. Wild black howlers come within a few feet of visitors in the forests, and Morelet's Crocodiles, spiny-tailed iguanas and numerous bird species can be seen around the Belize River.

Standard tours begin at the small museum, where there are information panels on Belize wildlife, including howler monkeys, and the sanctuary's work. These tours take 45 minutes to an hour and include a guided walk through the nearby forest, where sightings of black howlers are pretty much guaranteed. River tours involve a two- to three-hour canoe trip along the river and offer the best chance of seeing wildlife in large numbers. They are best first thing in the morning and in the late afternoon. Night hikes are 2½-hour nocturnal walks through the forest and adjacent savannah. They offer an almost guaranteed chance of seeing kinkajous, armadillos and opossums, as well as howlers, and a fair chance of seeing rarer animals like tayra or ocelot. For more on howler monkeys, see box, page 45.

Spanish Creek Wildlife Sanctuary → Colour map B3.

ⓘ *Rancho Dolores Environmental Centre, Rancho Dolores Village, 17 miles west of Burrell Boom, T220-2191, www.spanishcreek.org, no set opening hours but usually Mon-Fri 1000-1700, Sat and Sun 1000-1600, tours from BZ$45. Leonard Russell (T610-5164) runs a bus between the corner of Euphrates Av and Cairo St in Belize City at 1700 Mon-Fri and Sat 1300, returning at 0500 Mon-Sat, BZ$4 one way. Alternatively, Black Orchid (see page 49) organizes trips. Cyril Smith (T606-4627) owns the only local taxi.*

This 6000-acre wildlife sanctuary straddling five miles of languid Spanish creek was created in 2002 to preserve riverine wildlife and lowland tropical forest. It forms a vital ecological corridor between the Rio Bravo Conservation and Management area (see page 185), the Crooked Tree Wildlife Sanctuary (see below) and the Community Baboon Sanctuary (see above). The reserve is managed by the Rancho Dolores Environmental Center in conjunction with local villagers, a small community some 200-strong, who show visitors around. Like the Baboon Sanctuary, the reserve is a community-based ecotourism project.

Spanish Creek is rich in flora and fauna. Howler monkeys are a common sight, and can always be heard at dusk and dawn. There are still abundant white-lipped and collared peccary, red brocket deer and tayra. Jaguar, puma and Baird's tapir all breed here. The river itself has plentiful Morelet's crocodile.

Infrastructure is limited, and the village is so small you can walk across it in a few heartbeats. The centre can organize river tours, horse riding, walks and, with a bit of notice, simple homestay accommodation. There are no banks, restaurants or bars in the village. River trips are conducted in modern kayaks or, for something a little more special, in a genuine Belizean dory, a dug-out canoe hewn from a single log. There are also volunteering opportunities.

Crooked Tree Wildlife Sanctuary → Colour map A2.

ⓘ *3 miles off the Northern Hwy and 35 miles from both Belize City and Orange Walk. Daily 0800-1630, BZ$8. You have to go to the helpful Visitor Centre by the lakeshore in Crooked Tree village (daily 0800-1630) to register and pay the entrance fee. Crooked Tree and Bird's Eye View lodges, see page 49, can organize pickups from the city or airport (around BZ$100-150).*

This 16,400-acre wetland reserve just 30 minutes west of the international airport was the first government-protected wildlife reserve in Belize. It is a Ramsar site, and one of the top birdwatching locations in Central America. It is an important haven for endemic birds, a resting spot for migratory species and a key preserve for terrestrial and aquatic mammals, reptiles and amphibians and for large stands of logwood forest. The reserve comprises a series of lakes, lagoons, marshes and the labyrinth of creeks and waterways that connect them. The best way to explore the reserve is with a stay of one to two days at the **Crooked Tree Lodge**, see page 49, with early morning and mid-afternoon to early evening trips on the lagoon and the 20-plus miles of waterways, and trail walks in the surrounding terra firma forest and bush land and on the 500-m boardwalk. Guiding from the lodge is excellent.

More than 275 species have been recorded at the sanctuary, with new species encountered every other month. There are tens of thousands of individual birds here at any time and they congregate in profuse number in the dry season (February-May). The sanctuary protects globally endangered or threatened species including yellow-headed

Howler monkeys

There is no sound quite like the deep, guttural, sustained roar of a male howler monkey. Those who first hear it, unaware of its origin, wake with a fright at dawn, or sleep uneasily, with nightmares of jaguars leaping through the flimsy mosquito nets that cover the jungle lodge windows.

Fear not. The monkeys themselves are cute little creatures, barely as large as a poodle, with plaintive deep brown eyes, though don't stand beneath them when they're agitated as they defecate on assailants. They make their roar with a specially adapted and enlarged mouth and larynx fitted with a unique extended lingual bone.

In Belize they're known as baboons, but they have none of the physical power or aggression of these fearsome African primates. Howler monkeys are gentle, leaf-eating creatures, whose roar is most decidedly worse than their bite. Howlers rarely if ever come to blows. Dominant males just bellow at each other from neighbouring clumps of trees, uproariously asserting their territorial rights.

Howlers are unique to the tropical and subtropical Americas. There are 15 species, most of them living in Brazil. Belize has just one, the Guatemalan black howler (*Alouatta pigra*). The best places to see or hear them are the Black Orchid Resort (see page 49) or the Community Baboon Sanctuary.

parrot, sungrebe, Central American river turtle (hickatee), Morelet's crocodile and Mexican black howler monkey. Elusive birds like grey-necked wood rail, plain-breasted ground dove, olive-throated parakeets, Yucatán and lineated woodpeckers, Yucatán flycatcher, Yucatán jay, black-crowned tityra, spot-breasted wood wren and black-headed trogon can be spotted here. Crooked Tree is also the most important nesting site for jabiru stork in Central America; see box, page 46.

Crooked Tree village, which sits on an island within the reserve, has a long history. It was founded in the mid-18th century for the exploitation of logwood (which is still abundant in the reserve), making it perhaps the earliest inland European settlement in Belize. It's a sleepy, friendly place, and so quiet day or night that you can hear a hummingbird's wings as it passes, except in May when Crooked Tree celebrates the Cashew Festival; see page 50. There is a long boardwalk with tiny observation towers stretching out over the swamp around 1¾ miles north of the village. This skirts the *varzea* forest which fringes the lagoon and cuts into the swamp. It's a superb birding spot in the mornings and late afternoons and can be reached by boat or canoe in the wet and on foot or by car in the dry.

The small post-Classic Maya site of **Chau Hiix** ① *reached by boat from Crooked Tree Lodge, see page 49*, lies on the southwestern corner of Crooked Tree's Western Lagoon. What looks like a low hill is in reality a central pyramid of just over 30 m. Excavations by Dr Anne Pyburn of Indiana University (who named the site after the Maya word for jaguarundi) have unearthed a ball court, ceramic flasks, jewellery, obsidian knives and ornaments.

Altun Ha → *For listings, see pages 49-51. Colour map A2.*

① *Old Northern Hwy, T609-3540, daily 0800-1700, BZ$10.*

This medium-sized Maya site is one of the most attractive in Belize, and with such close proximity to Belize City and the cruise ships, one of the most extensively visited. The city comprises some 450 to 500 structures, spread over 2.3 sq miles, but as with most of the

Jabiru stork

Belize's national bird is the largest flying bird in the Americas. Jabirus are found throughout the American tropics. They are unmistakeable – huge white birds on twig-thin legs, with black, bare heads, grotesque bills and a red neck ruff. You'll see them in large groups in wetlands and on river banks from Argentina to Belize. Look out for their huge untidy nests in large trees near water. Australians and Asians sometimes mistakenly call their smaller black-necked stork, jabiru, but these birds are of an altogether different genus. Latin America can rightfully claim the stork and its name as their own. Jabiru is an indigenous Brazilian animal name. The word jabiru is a corruption of *iambyrú*, meaning swollen throat in Tupi, the language of much of pre-Columbian coastal Brazil.

Large male jabirus may stand as much as 1½ m tall and have a wingspan only marginally less than the Andean condor – at 3 m. Jabirus are opportunistic feeders, ploughing their huge bills through the water in search of small fish and crustaceans. They'll eat rodents too, and the storks can occasionally be seen snapping up mice in agricultural fields. Jabirus are protected in Belize. They can most easily be seen between late May and late July at Crooked Tree, where they nest.

Mayan sites in Belize, only a handful have been excavated. Most of these are 0.4 sq miles around two key plazas, prosaically called Plaza A and Plaza B, which are grassy lawns flanked with moss and lichen-encrusted stepped pyramids which back onto thick tropical forest.

Visiting Altun Ha
Tickets can be bought at the visitor's centre at the site entrance, which offers modest information on Altun Ha, and has a small gift shop with a few souvenirs. Bring insect repellent and a sunhat.

Getting there Despite being the most visited Mayan site in Belize, Altun Ha is almost impossible to reach without taking a tour or your own hire car. The site lies on the old Northern Highway, which divides from the new Northern Highway at Mile 19, after the turn-off to Burrell Boom and Bermudian Landing.

The easiest way to reach Altun Ha is to take a tour. These can be organized through **Belize Travel Services** (see page 39), **Black Orchid**, or any of the main resorts and hotels in Belize. Expect to pay around BZ$150-180 for a full six-hour day trip from Belize City or Orange Walk and about BZ$80-100 for trips from Burrell Boom or Crooked Tree. Trips from San Pedro tend to arrive by boat up the north river, a lovely route cutting through wetlands and gallery forest. A taxi from Belize City airport to Altun Ha will cost around BZ$80 for the round trip.

If you want to travel there independently, the **Maskall** bus leaves Belize City at 0500 (90 minutes, BZ$4) for **Lucky Strike Village** which is three miles from Altun Ha and 32 miles from Belize City. The bus returns to Belize City at 1830. You might be able to persuade the bus driver to drop you all or part of the way to Altun Ha, otherwise it is possible to walk or hitch a ride to Altun Ha from the village.

Background
Altun Ha has a long history. Whilst the oldest significant building at the site (the unimpressive Structure F-8 or Reservoir Temple) dates to 100 AD, archaeologists believe

that the city was a major population centre as early as 200 BC, making it contemporary with very early Classic Mayan sites such as Tikal in Guatemala and Palenque in Mexico. What you see today is a conglomerate of buildings (the Maya built their temples one on top of another) and dates in its earliest form to around 300 AD. At that time Altun Ha would have been a city of some 8000-10,000 people. It was probably involved in trade between larger Mayan cities in the highlands of Belize and further inland in modern-day Guatemala and cities further to the north in Mexico. By 900 AD Altun Ha's population had sharply declined and whilst there were Maya living here in the Postclassic up until the arrival of the Spanish in Mexico, they were small in number and did not, it seems, construct any new buildings.

The site

Visitors usually enter **Plaza A** first, as it lies closest to the visitor centre at the north of the archaeological site. Plaza A is dominated by a grassy mound at its northern end, with a thin stone stair case running up the middle. It is known as structure A-6 and was probably a residential or ceremonial complex. Climb to the top of the building for an overview of the Plaza and Altun Ha as a whole. The lawn which stretches in at your feet was the ceremonial centre of Altun Ha when the city was at the height of its power in the early Classic period. The buildings facing the plaza would have been painted bright reds and blues, and they and the plaza floor itself entirely coated in plaster. Immediately to your east is Structure A-1, the **Temple of the Green Tomb**. It is one of the most important buildings in the city and was built over at least seven construction phases, which began in the sixth century. You can see

Altun Ha

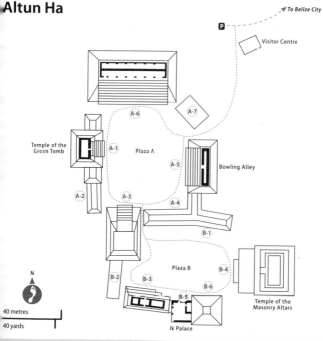

Kinich Ahau jade head

In 1968 whilst digging at Altun Ha, Dr David Pendergast of the Royal Ontario Museum of Canada chanced upon one of the greatest finds as yet discovered in the Maya world. After days of careful excavation, the archaeologist broke through a wall into a dusty seventh-century tomb below the stair block on the Temple of the Masonry Altars (Structure B4) and found the desiccated corpse of an elderly man who had clearly been one of the city's powerful elite. Around the corpse were some 40 ritual objects, including an exquisitely carved jade head of Kinich Ahau, a Mayan god of the Sun.

Only a handful of jade heads and death masks have been discovered in the Maya region, notably at Calakmul and Palenque, but none of them are as magnificent as the Kinich Ahau. Weighing almost 4½ kg and standing some 15 cm high, the head is the largest carved jade object so far discovered in Meosoamerica.

The carving is superb; it was carried out with stone tools, on a single massive block of jade, which is one of the hardest of all gemstones. The process would have taken months, if not years. The jade came from the Motagua River Valley region of Guatemala, showing that there was extensive trading between Altun Ha and the Guatemala Mayan cities. Jade was the most precious gemstone for the Maya, associated with life and rebirth, its green colour reflecting water (a gateway to Xibalba, or the Underworld) and maize (from which human beings were made by the creator God). The head is now preserved in the Museum of Belize (see page 32).

In the Maya pantheon, Kinich Ahau was closely associated with the creator god Itzamna ('itz' meaing life force in Yucatec Maya), and with jaguars. One of the chief ruling lords of Tikal, Curl Snout was apotheosized as Kinich Ahau, and it may be that the Altun Ha buried ruler was attempting to achieve similar status through death.

remnants of the first temple around the building's base – which is unusual in a Maya city. Excavations of a tomb inside the temple by Dr David Pendergast in 1968 unearthed some 300 spectacular jade objects and the remains of several smashed codices, or Mayan books. This find almost doubled the total number to have survived the bonfires of the Spanish priests. Sadly, the books were so badly damaged that they may never be pieced together. Opposite the temple of the Green Tomb is Structure A-5, also known as the **Bowling Alley**, after its very narrow single roof chamber. Archaeologists guess that it was used for ceremonial purposes. Opposite A-6 on the south side of the plaza is Structure A-3, a small tiered temple with a broad stairway flanked by the crumbling remains of stone and stucco masks.

Altun Ha's tallest building towers behind Structure A-3 off to the southeast in Plaza B. This is the 20-m Structure B-4 or the **Temple of the Masonry Altars**. Like Structure A-3 the temple is faced with masks. Look closely and you will see four, flanking the main staircase, with open mouths and large rectangular earrings. The temple is one of the most extensively excavated in Altun Ha. Prendergast's team removed two badly damaged outer layers to expose what you see today: a largely Classic-era Mayan temple, constructed sometime between AD 600 and 650. It hides an even earlier temple. A series of stone altars (again built one on top of another) at the top of temple give the building its name. Prendergast's excavations on B-4 unearthed one of the most spectacular finds so far discovered in the Maya world, the **Kinich Ahau jade head** (see box, above). The other temples around laza B were badly damaged by looters before excavations began. Structure B-3 on the ar southwestern corner of the plaza is topped with the shells of ceremonial or residential ooms. Structure B-5, next to this building and to the east probably served a similar purpose. preserves some original Mayan ventilator shafts in the shape of a T or, in Maya, an *ik*.

North of Belize City listings

For hotel and restaurant price codes and other relevant information, see pages 11-12.

Where to stay

Burrell Boom and the wildlife anctuaries *p43*

$$ Black Orchid, 2 Dawson Ln, T225-9158, JS T1866-437 1301, www.blackorchidresort. om. This riverside retreat run by the warm nd welcoming Thompson family is perhaps he best place to base yourself whilst xploring the Belize City region. It is around miles from the international airport and ewer than 20 mins' drive from Belize City, et is infinitely preferable to any hotels in he city itself. The location is very pretty, in a allery forest visited by toucans and howler nonkeys morning and evening and right n the banks of the Belize River. A/c rooms re very comfortable and well appointed, vith tiled floors and en suite shower athrooms. The best, next to the pool and verlooking the river, are very spacious and ave big wardrobes and large desks. There re self-catering villas for longer stays and ne of the best restaurants in the region see page 50). Staff are professional and

friendly and offer tours throughout Belize. Be sure to take a river trip with knowledgeable owner, Doug. These are great trips for wildlife, for learning about the history and politics of the country and for all-round good conversation. Tours are also arranged to the Community Baboon Sanctuary, see page 43, by car or river boat. There is also a pool, Wi-Fi and cable TV. Breakfast is included. Credit cards accepted.

$$ Community Baboon Sanctuary, see page 43. The sanctuary can organize homestays with families in and around Bermudian Landing. Prices include food.

Spanish Creek Wildlife Sanctuary

$$ Rancho Dolores Environmental Centre, see page 44. The centre can organize very simple homestay accommodation in the village given a few days' notice. Prices include food.

Crooked Tree Wildlife Sanctuary

$$$$-$$$ Crooked Tree Lodge, Crooked Tree Village, T626-3820, www.crookedtree lodgebelize.com. This Anglo-Belizean family home and wildlife lodge sits nestled in wild country right on the shores of the

Crooked Tree Lagoon. Solid wooden cabins with front terraces are set in a lawned garden shaded by dozens of flowering and fruit-bearing tropical trees. Each has simple a/c rooms decorated with pretty wildlife and landscape paintings. Hosts Angie and Mick Webb (a former British Army helicopter pilot) and their 2 young sons, Cory and Zach, offer warm hospitality and excellent food, and the wildlife, guiding and birdwatching in and around the lodge are excellent. Budget travellers can camp in the grounds for BZ$20 and use the pool and Wi-Fi. There is a restaurant and cable TV. Credit cards accepted.

$$$-$$ **Bird's Eye View Lodge**, Crooked Tree Village, T225-7027, www.birdseyeview belize.com. 20 homely rooms right on the edge of one of Crooked Tree's long lakes. The best rooms on the 2nd floor have balconies and sweeping views over the water. All have desks, wardrobes and small en suites, and are decorated with batik hangings and pictures of Belizean birds. There's a delicious smell of freshly baked bread every morning from the guesthouse kitchen. The food and guiding are excellent, especially for wildlife and bird lovers, and they offer tours throughout Belize. There's a pool, restaurant, cable TV and Wi-Fi. Credit cards accepted.

Altun Ha p45

$$$$ **Maruba Resort and Spa**, Old Northern Hwy Mile 40.5, T225-5555, www. maruba-spa.com. These faux-Maya cabins, with rich mahogany 4-poster beds, mosaic tile floors, Tudor windows and phalluses for loo paper holders either look like luxurious tribal chic, or a cheesy soft porn film set from the '70s, depending on your disposition. Either way it's fun to stay a night here if only for curiosity's sake and for a massage and treatment in the hotel spa, which is one of the best in Central America. The resort offers expensive airport pickups, trips to adjacent Altun Ha and other tours in the area. There's a pool, restaurant and bar, and Wi-Fi. Credit cards accepted.

🍴 Restaurants

Burrell Boom and the wildlife sanctuaries p43

$$$ **Black Orchid**, see page 49. Some of the best Belizean and international cooking i Belize District, with excellent seafood, steaks, pasta (try the delicious chicken fettucine), burgers for the kids and puddings, including brownies and home-baked cheesecake.

🎪 Festivals

Burrell Boom and the wildlife sanctuaries p43

May Cashew Festival, Crooked Tree, with live music, dancing, story-telling sessions and all manner of cashew produce on sale: from stewed cashew fruit, cashew wine, jams, syrup, biscuits and sweets, cake and fudge to the nuts themselves.

🕐 What to do

Burrell Boom and the wildlife sanctuaries p43

Whilst none of the places to stay have designated tour operators except **Black Orchid** (see page 49), all listed resorts organize trips and can arrange ones further afield in Belize.

For the **Crooked Tree Wildlife Sanctuary**, boats and guides are available through the guesthouses at Crooked Tree Wildlife Sanctuary (see under Where to stay, above) or in advance through the **Belize Audobon Society** (www.belizeaudubon.org), who manage the reserve in conjunction with the local community. Boat trips start at around BZ$140, canoes are complimentary at the larger lodges or can be rented in advance through the Audobon Society for BZ$30 per hour. Lodges can also organize horseback rides.

Black Orchid, see page 49. The most reliable tour operator in the Belize City area offers trips throughout the country in comfortable a/c cars, vans and boats.

Destinations include areas off the beaten track, such as Shipstern, as well as all the Mayan sites in Belize, Mountain Pine Ridge, snorkelling and diving on the cayes and light adventure activities, such as cave tubing and zip lining.

Cricket

Bermudian Landing is cricket crazy. **Conway Young**, conway.young1@yahoo.com, or **Kim August**, in the visitor centre, can slot you into a game given a bit of notice.

⊖ Transport

Burrell Boom and the wildlife sanctuaries *p43*
Bus
There are 2 buses back to **Belize City** at 1530 and 1600. Any Northern Hwy bus

(between Belize City, **Orange Walk** or **Corazal**, around every 30 mins, BZ$3), will stop or can be flagged down at Burrell Boom. A pickup from Burrell Boom junction to **Bermudian Landing** costs around BZ$50 (15 mins) and to the **airport** around BZ$80 (40 mins). **Jex and Sons** buses run to **Belize City** Mon-Sat from the turn-off to Crooked Tree Lodge at 0630 and 0700, taking 90 mins, BZ$4.

⊙ Directory

Burrell Boom and the wildlife sanctuaries *p43*
Banks
There are no banks in Burrell Boom or Bermudian Landing, but US$ can be exchanged at the **Black Orchid Resort** (see page 49).

South of Belize City

South of Belize City things thin out pretty quickly too. Beyond the small theme park of Old Belize, the landscape reverts to swamp and mangrove and the wilds of the Burdon Canal and the Sibun Forest Reserves near the Kriol village of Gales Point. ▸▸ *For listings, see page 53.*

Old Belize

ⓘ *Cucumber Beach Marina, Mile 5 Western Hwy, T222-4129, www.oldbelize.com, Sun-Mon 1000-1600, Tue-Sat 0800-1600, B$15, children half price. To get here take any Belmopan- or Dangriga-bound bus (around 15 mins) or a taxi from Belize City (10 mins, B$$20).*

Belize's half century of history is précised, polished-up and packed under one roof for cruise ship passengers in a hurry at this museum of living history. In a 45-minute tour they're whisked through a Belize of theme park reproductions. There's a reconstructed plastic rainforest (complete with stalagmite-filled limestone caves and waterfalls) where you'll learn about the country's flora and fauna. This is followed by a whistle-stop tour of a mock Mayan temple and contemporaneous village, with accompanying piped music. Belize's industrial past is showcased with genuine colonial era iron tools recovered from the forest. They include a hulking steam-powered sugar mill used to process sugar in the 1800s. You'll learn about the importance of logwood (for dye) and mahogany (for banisters in Victorian houses in Britain and the US) to the Baymen settlers in early Belize and how, until the rise of the modern petrochemical industry, chewing gum (introduced into the US in 1890) was made from *chicle* harvested from Belize's forests. The tour concludes with a jaunt around a replica of Belize City, recreated in its full late-18th century glory, complete with clapboard houses and models dressed as Belizean Kriols and Garinagu.

The ticket price also includes entry to the adjacent Marina (where there's a bank and a string of restaurants) and **Cucumber Beach**, an artificial triangle of powdery sand jutting into the Atlantic and surrounding a little purpose-built lagoon. The sea is so calm here that even a toddler can paddle with no fear, whilst adults and older children can whizz down the **Slippery Conch**, a 30-m-long water chute, ride a zipline into the sea or browse the gift shops.

Burdon Canal and Sibun Forest → *For listings, see page 53. Colour map B2.*

The Coastal Road (aka Manatee Highway), a mere dirt track pocked with puddles and pot holes, runs south from the tiny town of La Democracia in the far west of Belize District, eventually reaching Stann Creek district and Dangriga. Along the way it cuts through some of central Belize's roughest and remotest country, a marshy coastal hinterland dominated by a series of large brackish lagoons, linked by shallow waterways to the Atlantic, rising in the west to the Maya mountains. Much of the region is taken up by the Burdon Canal and Sibun Forest reserves.

Visiting Burdon Canal and Sibun Forest
Trips into Burdon to see both manatees, water birds and, in season, nesting turtles are easily organized in Gales Point Village (see below), where a government-sponsored ecotourism project is seeking to train local guides. It may be possible to hire a Gales Point villager to take a trip into Sibun Forest, but this will just be to get you in and out, without any proper wildlife guiding. Organized visits to Sibun are only possible on a bespoke tour with **Belize Travel Services**, see page 39.

The reserves
Burdon Canal Nature Reserve covers some 5255 acres of lagoons and wetlands and is probably the most important breeding ground in the world for West Indian manatees, an important migration stopover for water birds and a nesting site for hawksbill and green turtles. Morelet's crocodiles and green iguana are abundant.

The Sibun Forest Reserve stretches from the lowland marshes around the lagoons in Belize District south into Stann Creek and west into the foothills of the Maya Mountains in Cayo. With 106,393 acres, it is one of the largest protected wilderness areas in central Belize and an important natural reserve for larger mammals like jaguar, puma and Baird's tapir, as well as a proliferation of birds.

Birdwatching
The reserves' diversity of habitats make them a great place quickly to up a bird count. Burdon's extensive rivers and wetlands are home to most of Belize's waterfowl species, including agami herons and jabiru storks, whilst the broad leaf and pine forests in Sibun have abundant common species (like keel-billed toucans, collared aracari, white-fronted and red-lored parrots, long-billed hermits, rufous-tailed hummingbirds, acorn woodpeckers, rufous-capped warblers and eastern bluebirds) as well as rarer birds like white-tailed kites, stygian owls and orange-breasted falcons. In spring and autumn the Central American subspecies of hepatic tanager migrates here. The best time for birding is February to May when migratory species flock in.

Gales Point Village
Settlements are few and far around Burdon Canal and the Sibun Forest, with a scattering of tiny hamlets. The most interesting of these is the Kriol village of Gales Point which spreads

along a 3-km-long, 300-m wide appendix-shaped sliver of land stretching into the inky waters of the Southern Lagoon. It's a tranquil place to hole up for a few days, with little to do but take a boat out onto the lagoon to look for turtles and manatees or while away the hours with a book and a Belikin. There are currently no buses to Gales Point. A taxi from Belize city will cost around BZ$120.

The town was probably settled by fugitive slaves and its Kriol culture still retains strong African elements. The town is an important centre for drumming and is unique in Belize in having a traditional Kriol drumming school and drum-making workshop, **Talla Walla Vibrations & Maroon Creole Drum School**. This is run by percussion virtuoso Emmeth Young. Be sure to see hear him play before you leave town. Emmeth's school strives to keep traditional Kriol percussion techniques alive. He offers classes, and visitors can make their own drum from raw materials, a process which takes four days and costs BZ$250.

Gales Point is one of the few communities in Belize that still celebrates traditional fire **sambai**, a Kriol rhythm and associated dance that has been performed since the days of the early slave exodus. Enslaved Africans came from a diversity of different nations, with no more in common than the nations of contemporaneous Europe. When they met in Belize they sought to preserve their cultural identities through rhythm and ritual. Gales Point sambai strongly resembles Brazilian samba de roda danced by the descendants of West African Bantu people, but in Belize it is more strongly associated with fertility. As in samba de roda, sambai dances see a group forming a large circle. One person at a time enters the middle of the circle to dance whilst drummers play. Nowadays the dance takes place around a campfire, at each cycle of the moon and at weddings and birthdays. It is always danced during Christmas and New Year.

☉ South of Belize City listings

For hotel and restaurant price codes and other relevant information, see pages 11-12.

☐ Where to stay

Gales Point Village *p52*
As well as the upmarket option below, the village corner shop and local bar, **Gentle's Cool Spot**, offers simple rooms (**$**) and you can camp on the waterfront.
$$$$ Manatee Lodge, T220-8040, www.manateelodge.com. Rooms in this hotel sit right over the water of Gales Point lagoon, perfectly poised for spotting manatees. Each is decked out in luxurious polished hardwood and come with en suites and mosquito screening. The lodge organizes boat trips and tours. Rates

include a round-trip transfer from Belize City, all meals and tours, making the lodge a far more economical option than it seems from our price code.

☉ What to do

Gales Point Village *p52*
It is easy to organize a trip out onto the lagoon from Gales Point. All hotels and guesthouses can book a boatman for manatee watching, turtle nesting sites or night-time Morelet's crocodile spotting. Some hire canoes. One local resident, Mr Andrewin, offers hourly windsurfing lessons. There is easy but spectacular caving at remote Ben Loman's cave on the northwest shore of the Southern Lagoon.

West of Belize City

The Western Highway runs from Belize City to the border of Guatemala at Benque Viejo passing through Hattieville (where there is a notorious prison, open to voyeuristic tourists, and even with a gift shop) and the capital, Belmopan. The road is one of Belize's main highways but is rarely crowded. Within Belize City district, there are only a couple of sights of interest en route. » *For listings, see page 56.*

Belize Zoo and Tropical Education Centre → *For listings, see page 56.*

ⓘ *Mile 29 Western Hwy, T220-8004, www.belizezoo.org, daily 0830-1630, BZ$30, children BZ$10. Allow 1 hr to drive from Belize City centre. Buses running between Belize City and Benque, Belmopan, Dangriga, Punta Gorda or Placencia will drop you off. A cab from the airport costs around BZ$100.*

Belize Zoo began life in the 1980s as a collection of animals, left over from a film shoot and has evolved to become a delightful small zoo, very much in the spirit of Gerald Durrell's Zoological Park and Conservation Trust at Les Augres on Jersey. Anyone interested in Central American wildlife should make a stop here if passing, or if they have time to spare in or around Belize City, just over an hour away. The zoo preserves most of Belize's important mammalian species in its collection, has some magnificent birds and, perhaps most importantly, the animals are well-cared for, live in semi-natural grounds set in attractive dry forest and seem happy and content.

The zoo's director, Baltimore-born Sharon Matola, is a force of nature and what you see today is largely the result of her tireless work, enthusiasm and dogged determination. Sharon built much of the zoo herself, still personally tends to many of the animals and coordinates or co-runs myriad conservation, education and research projects. These include captive breeding programmes and important initiatives to protect or reintroduce into Belize species like the harpy eagle and scarlet macaw, details of which can be found on the excellent website. Sharon runs an important programme aimed at re-integrating jaguars with livestock that is one of a mere handful in the world (the others being in the Brazilian Pantanal). Belize Zoo has done much to change once superstitious attitudes to wildlife in Belize. Some 15,000 Belizean children visit the zoo annually, free of charge and, over two generations, their attitudes towards wildlife have begun to turn the country into one of Central America's top ecotourism destinations. In 2011 Sharon received a Meritorious Service Award in recognition for her work, presented by Belize's prime minister, and was honoured as a Belize patriot.

The zoo was badly damaged by Hurricane Richard in late 2010, but sterling work by a legion of volunteers (the US Ambassador was busy with a spade when we visited) has seen an almost miraculous recuperation. Visitors can offer their services as volunteers, with advance notice.

The collection

All animals in the zoo are native to Belize. They are orphans or their offspring, gifts from other zoos, or were rescued or rehabilitated from private collectors. They are housed in enclosures set along a woodland trail running through 29 acres of land. Environments change along the path to mimic those you will find in the Belizean wild, such as rainforest, pine woodland, lagoons and river forest. Animals at the zoo include a beautiful young aguar, Junior, ocelots, jaguarundi and margay, harpy eagles, king vultures, scarlet macaws, a couple of Baird's tapirs called Ceibo and Navidad, tayra, kinkajou and paca (known in Belize as gibnut) and Morelet's crocodile.

Keepers will allow you to get far closer to the animals than in most zoos, handling tarantulas, entering an inner chamber of the jaguar enclosure, or touching the tapirs. This is best experienced on the great guided nocturnal tour, when the animals are at their most active. The zoo also runs nature walks, birdwatching tours on high platforms, and caving and kayaking trips on the Sibun River, all bookable at the Tropical Education Centre or zoo reception.

It can get very hot at Belize Zoo and there are often plenty of mosquitoes. Toilets are primitive and the small gift shop only sells snacks and a limited selection of drinks. Try and come at the beginning or the end of the day, and bring water and a sun hat. Without advanced notice, Belize Zoo does not welcome even amateur photographers with professional-looking gear, tripods or monopods. They will be charged extra or asked to leave their equipment at reception. The zoo runs a small research centre across the road where there are simple cabins set in the forest (see page 56).

Monkey Bay Wildlife Sanctuary and National Park → For listings, see page 56.

ⓘ Mile 31 Western Hwy, T820-3032, www.monkeybaybelize.org. See under Belize zoo for how to get here.

This private sanctuary-cum-environmental education centre and adjacent national park make up a 3320-acre wilderness area connecting the Maya mountains and the lowland forests around the Sibun river, which form the core of the Central Biological Corridor of Belize.

The sanctuary and national park are home to a broad spread of Belizean fauna and flora. Most of the animals you see in captivity in Belize Zoo (see above) two miles away live in the wild in Monkey Bay. This includes large mammals, such as tapirs, pumas, jaguars and peccaries, more than 250 species of birds and Morelet's crocodiles on the Sibun river. There are Mayan ruins in the park and little-explored ceremonial caves.

Indian Creek Hike

The sanctuary is an active supporter of the Mesoamerican Trails System, a network of routes through pre-Columbian Central America which brings hikers in close contact with the region's pristine wilderness. Through Monkey Bay visitors can trek the Indian Creek Trail, a 16-mile, three-day hike running along the Sibun River and Indian Creek, through Manatee Forest Reserve. The hike is a great wilderness walk, cutting through rainforest, passing rushing clearwater creeks and caves littered with Mayan remains and ending at the beautiful Five Lakes National Park. Sleeping is in hammocks in the jungle. Monkey Bay supply guides and all camping equipment. Prices depend on group numbers but are good value. Contact the sanctuary for details.

Cox Lagoon Crocodile Sanctuary

This long inland lake surrounded by varzea and gallery forest sits at the heart of some 30,000 acres of unspoilt privately protected wilderness. The whole area is replete with wildlife, including abundant jaguars, tapirs and jabiru storks, and the lagoon itself teeming with Morelet's crocodiles. The best access is by canoe and the trail, both of which can be organized through Monkey Bay.

Volunteering at Monkey Bay

Monkey Bay runs a number of interesting conservation programmes that welcome volunteers. These include a green iguana captive-breeding programme (which you can visit), research work in the Mesoamerican Biological Corridor and the Sibun river watershed and a Wildlife Care Centre (WCC), where orphaned and abandoned wild animals, many of which are former pets are rehabilitated. The latter is not open to the public but offers training programmes and internships for conservationists.

The sanctuary specializes in hosting study abroad programmes, mostly from the US but welcomes short-stay visitors and offers a series of individual internships and volunteer programmes both at this principal Sibun River site and at field stations in the mountains at Mountain Pine Ridge and on the Cayes at Caye Caulker.

◉ West of Belize City listings

For hotel and restaurant price codes and other relevant information, see pages 11-12.

◍ Where to stay

Belize Zoo and Tropical Education Centre *p54*
$$ Belize Zoo Jungle Lodge, see page 54. Very simple dorms and doubles in stilted and mosquito-screened wooden huts. Basic comfort food available.

Monkey Bay Wildlife Sanctuary and National Park *p55*
Double rooms in the field research station, see page 55, dorm accommodation in the wooden bunkhouse and camping either on a lawned clearing or under *palapa*-thatched roof shelters. Simple food and a range of tours (including kayaking, trekking and birdwatching) in the reserve.

◉ Transport

It's 1 hr to drive to **Belize City** centre from either Belize Zoo or Monkey Bay. Buses running between **Belize City** and **Benque**, **Belmopan**, **Dangriga**, **Punta Gorda** or **Placencia** can pick you up. A cab to the airport costs around BZ$100.

Contents

San Pedro & the northern cayes

At a glance

⊜ **Getting around** The cayes are accessible by boat and plane; once there, the cayes are small enough to travel around on foot or by bicycle or golf cart. A single or multi-day dive cruise is recommended for the atolls.

⬤ **Time required** Allow at least 2-4 days to explore Ambergris Caye and/or Caye Caulker and 5 days to a week for a full dive or fishing trip from San Pedro or the atolls.

☼ **Weather** It's warm and dry at around 15- 30°C Jan-May with cooler nights. It's more hot and humid May-Oct, with the possibility of hurricanes. Nov-Dec is warm with occasional colder spells of 13-15°C.

✖ **When not to go** San Pedro is good at any time but will be busiest and most expensive in Dec and Jan. May-Oct is hurricane season. From Sep-Dec there are more sand flies on the cayes.

The shallow seas off Belize are dotted with islands for the entire length of the country, but by far the most accessible of these lie to the north of Belize City. This is largely because of the popularity of Ambergris Caye and its busy beach capital, San Pedro, which is the most visited destination in Belize. Its narrow beach is lined with three miles of hotels, bars and restaurants, mostly used by US package tourists.

Caye Caulker, a little to the south, has simpler accommodation spread along a handful of sandy streets. Bars play lilting reggae music and the island retains a village feel. Most visitors are independent travellers, many of them en route to or from Guatemala or Mexico. Smaller cayes like Palm Island or Spanish Lookout have space for little more than a single resort and are ideal for families.

There are two atolls in the northern cayes: Lighthouse and Turneffe. Lighthouse is one of the remotest and most beautiful stretches of reef in the Atlantic. It forms the centrepiece of the Belize Barrier Reef Reserve, a protected area and UNESCO World Heritage Site. Divers come here for the pristine coral, huge shoals of fish and the Blue Hole, a 100-m-wide circular fissure that drops into inky depths and a labyrinth of coral-encursted caves. Lighthouse also has its own cayes, including Long Caye, which has accommodation. The other atoll, Turneffe, has some of the best bone fish and tarpon fishing in the world.

Ambergris Caye

Belize's largest island, Ambergris Caye, is not really an island at all. It's the tip of a Mexican isthmus stretching down from Quintana Roo state and separated from the Mexican villages of Xcalak and Mahajual only by a thin and mangrove-choked canal, Boca Bacalar Chico channel. This was dug by the Maya before Columbus. Now it marks the caye's northernmost extremity, which remains largely wild and covered in forest, where ocelots and ospreys hunt undisturbed. The centre and south of the island are far busier, home to San Pedro and its hinterland spreading along the coast in a tourist strip 10 miles long and just a few hundred yards wide.
➤ *For listings, see pages 70-83.*

Arriving in San Pedro → *For listings, see pages 70-83. Colour map A3.*
Population: San Pedro Town 11,510.

Getting there

Flights to San Pedro leave from **Phillip SW Goldson International Airport** (a cab ride outside Belize City, see page 29) or from the municipal airport (on the waterfront in Belize City centre). If connecting with an international flight, book San Pedro flights from Philip Goldson Airport and not the municipal one. The airport is less than 10 minutes' walk from central San Pedro. Golf cart taxis are easy to catch just outside the terminal, and most hotels will send a rep to meet you given notice. The **Water Jets Express Terminal** and pier is located at the lagoon end of Black Coral Street next to the football pitch (soccer field), immediately west of the airport. The **Caye Caulker Water Taxi** arrives at their pier at the eastern end of Pelican Street. **Belize Water Taxi** boats arrive at the 'front dock', or Black Coral Street pier, which is ocean side and next to **Wahoo's Bar & Grill**. There are frequent daily boats to Ambergris Caye from Belize City (via Caye Caulker), run by three companies (see page 39 and page 83). There are also daily services to/from Corozal (see page 194) and Chetumal in Mexico. ➤➤ *For further information, see Transport, page 82.*

Getting around

There are no cars on Ambergris Caye; tourists whip around on golf carts or pedal bikes. San Pedro town centre is easily negotiable on foot.

Orientation

San Pedro is the only town on Ambergris Caye and has only one main street. The town spreads north and south along the beach. San Pedro has no formal addresses but you'll rarely have a problem finding services, as the town centre is tiny.

Tourist information

There are two **tourist offices** ① *next to the library, Mon-Thu 080-1630, Fri 0800-1600, and at the town hall, Mon-Fri 0800-1600.* The most useful source of information, however, is ambergriscaye.com, which has up-to-date details on everything from shopping and restaurants to dives sites and snorkelling. Also see www.belizeit.com. **Hot Card Belize** ① *http://hotcardbelize.com*, operates a discount card for many businesses in San Pedro.

San Pedro centre

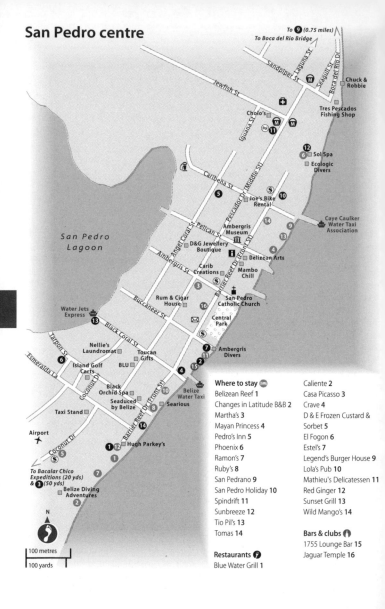

To ⑨ (0.75 miles)
To Boca del Rio Bridge

Sandpiper St
Laguna St
Seagull St
Boca del Rio Dr

Chuck & Robbie

Jewfish St

Cholo's
Ⓜ
Ⓟ ⑪
Ⓜ Ⓜ

Tres Pescados Fishing Shop

Iguana St

⑫ **Sol Spa**
⑥
Ecologic Divers

Caribena St
Pescador Dr (Middle St)

⑤
Ⓢ ⑩
Joe's Bike Rental

Pelican St
Angel Coral St

Ambergris Museum
⑭
D&G Jewellery Boutique
Belizean Arts
④
Caye Caulker Water Taxi Association
⑬

San Pedro Lagoon

Ambergris St
Barrier Reef Dr (Front St)

Carib Creations
Ⓢ ③
Mambo Chill

Buccaneer St

Rum & Cigar House
⑯
San Pedro Catholic Church

Water Jets Express
⑬
Black Coral St
Tarpon St

✉

Central Park

Ⓢ

Nellie's Laundromat
Toucan Gifts
⑥
Ambergris Divers
⑦
Island Golf Carts
BLU
⑪
②
④ ⑮

Esmeralda La

Black Orchid Spa
Seaduced by Belize
⑩
②
Belize Water Taxi
Searious
⑧ ⑭

Coconut Dr

Taxi Stand

Airport ✈

Ⓢ ⑤
①
①⑫ **Hugh Parkey's**

To Bacalar Chico Expeditions (20 yds) & ③ (50 yds)
⑦

Belize Diving Adventures
②

N
⚓

100 metres
100 yards

Where to stay 🛏
Belizean Reef **1**
Changes in Latitude B&B **2**
Martha's **3**
Mayan Princess **4**
Pedro's Inn **5**
Phoenix **6**
Ramon's **7**
Ruby's **8**
San Pedrano **9**
San Pedro Holiday **10**
Spindrift **11**
Sunbreeze **12**
Tio Pil's **13**
Tomas **14**

Restaurants 🍴
Blue Water Grill **1**

Caliente **2**
Casa Picasso **3**
Crave **4**
D & E Frozen Custard & Sorbet **5**
El Fogon **6**
Estel's **7**
Legend's Burger House **9**
Lola's Pub **10**
Mathieu's Delicatessen **11**
Red Ginger **12**
Sunset Grill **13**
Wild Mango's **14**

Bars & clubs 🍷
1755 Lounge Bar **15**
Jaguar Temple **16**

Don't miss ...

Background

San Pedro likes to think of itself as small. Forty years ago it was: an isolated hamlet of weatherboard fishermen's shacks in the forgotten corner of nowhere, with sandy streets shaded by palms and no traffic bigger than a donkey. Locals whiled away the hours between fishing trips snoozing in hammocks. Then, in the late 1960s, a few intrepid folk on the farther reaches of the traveller trail chanced upon the place and spread the word. The first guesthouses opened and backpackers began to trickle in to smoke weed and lie in the sun. In the late 1970s, they were followed by travel agents. Then, in 1987, Madonna dreamt of San Pedro and wrote a song about a mythical Spanish-speaking island, 'La Isla Bonita'. PR people from Alaska to Arkansas seized it as an anthem for the caye. What did it matter that the island wasn't Spanish and that the singer had never been there – Madonna was in love with San Pedro, and you should be too. Couples flocked in on honeymoon, and Ambergris Caye never looked back. By the mid-1990s it was a full-blown resort. Nowadays it's a lynchpin of the Belizean economy.

Places on Ambergris Caye

San Pedro

Compared to Playa del Carmen or Cozumel in Mexico, San Pedro still feels small, tranquil and low key. Resorts are low rise and limited to a thin strand which spreads along the beach. Spring breakers and big multinational brands are notable by their absence. The day-trip diving is arguably the best in Central America, making San Pedro a good base for dive or snorkel trips on the atolls or in gorgeous Hol Chan and Bacalar Chico reserves. Like all resort towns, however, San Pedro offers little home-grown culture. The modern town is the home of expats, mostly North American retirees. Many hotels or bars have cover bands playing the Eagles. Hawkers from the Caribbean make dubious commerce out of Bob Marley and mythological Jamaican cool. Mexicans come here for work, and Spanish now dominates the back alleys and grocery stores.

Ambergris Caye's sights are almost all natural, except for the **Ambergris Maya Jade and History Museum** ① *opposite the town hall, Barrier Reef Dr, T226-3311, ambergrisjade@ aol.com, daily 0800-1300 and 1400-2000, BZ$5*. It has a few tiny displays devoted to the history of the island, with some examples of Maya ceramics found on Ambergris, flint tools, bottles, coins and ammunition from the 17th-century pirate settlers. It also has some relics from 19th-century refugees fleeing the Caste Wars in the Yucatán. There's a small gift shop.

Beyond San Pedro

Ambergris Caye's **beaches** are pretty but narrow and are washed by tiny waves from a shallow lagoon filled with eel grass. When the tide is high, the beaches all but disappear.

Ambergris Caye

2 de Abril Point   To Xcalak (1 mile)   Santa Cecília

Chelem Caye   Boca Bacalar Chico

Bacalar Chico Canyons

MEXICO

Chac-balam

Bacalar Chico Marine Reserve   Ises Bowl

Visitor's Centre   Franco Canyon

San Juan

BELIZE

Cantena Lagoon   Rocky Point

Pesata

Robles Point

Basil Jones

Lemon Point   Basil Jones Canyons

Deer Caye

Santa Cruz Lagoon

Santa Cruz

Robles Point

Tostada Caye (Swab Caye)   Iguana Caye

Azul Point Canyons

Little Iguana Caye Bird Sanctuary

Caye Francés   Caye Francés Lagoon

Blackadore Caye (Cayo Negro)

Palmero Point

Palmero Canyon

Ambergris Caye

Mexico Canyons

Rosario Caye   Mexico Beach

Mexico Rocks

Mosquito Caye

Moto Lagoon

Mata Rocks Cut

Entrada de Mato

Piedras de Mato

Cayo Espanto

Arena Point

Pescador Tunnels

Buena Vista Point

Buena Vista Canyons

San Pedro Lagoon

Tres Cocos

Paradise Canyons

Tackle Box Canyon & Christ of the Abyss

San Pedro

Tuffy Rocks

Dardanelles Cut

Sailsports   Entrada San Pedro

Romero Caye   Victoria Tunnels

Cypress Canyons

Boca Ciego Caye   Boca Chica Canyon

Sandbar

Marco González

Hol Chan Cut

Hol Chan Marine Reserve   Pillar Coral

Shark & Ray Alley

Cangrejo Caye

Caribbean Sea

Barrier Reef

Caye Caulker Marine Reserve

Caye Calker Canyons

N

Caye Caulker (Caye Corker)

2 km
2 miles

Caye Caulker   To Caye Chapel (5 miles) & Belize City (21 miles)

Where to stay

Azul 1
Caye Casa 2
Cayo Espanto 3
Coral Bay Villas 4
El Pescador 5
Hotel del Rio 6
La Perla 7
Matachica 8
Portofino 9
Tides 11
Tranquility Bay 12
Turtleman's House 13
Victoria House 14
Xanadu 15

Restaurants

Hidden Treasure 1
La Palmilla 2
Le Bistro Portofino
  & Green Parrot 3
Legends Burger
  House 7
Palapa Bar & Grill 4
Rendezvous
  & Winery 5
Rojo Lounge 6

Floating gold

Ambergris (a corruption of the French for 'grey amber') is a dull-coloured, flammable substance with a musky smell that has been used as incense since the time of the Egyptian pharaohs. It's found washed up and smoothed into waxy pebbles on warm ocean beaches from Belize to Brazil, the Moluccas to Madagascar. Ambergris sells for over US$20 a gram and, as lumps weighing as much as 20 kg have been discovered on beaches, it is popularly known as floating gold. Ambergris is used as a base for perfumes and for flavouring in haute cuisine kitchens by star chefs like Heston Blumenthal.

For centuries, ambergris' origins were unknown. The Chinese called it dragon's spittle, and they weren't far off the mark. We now know that ambergris comes from sperm whale stomachs. Ejected initially as a thick bilious liquid, reeking like fishy faeces (and often coating sharp objects eaten by the whale, like squid beaks), it congeals and turns sweet and musky, after years of exposure to ocean salt and sun. Ambergris Caye has a poetical ring to its name; Whale Vomit Caye, less so.

The broadest sections are in the south of the caye near the **Victoria House** hotel. Immediately to the north of the town centre the beach has been appropriated by golf carts that chug along its now flattened sand on the way to hotels. Beyond the narrow creek known as **Boca del Rio** (river mouth in Spanish), which marks the end of the town proper, the beach road begins to cut further inland until it runs behind the resorts. It then runs north until about 2½ miles beyond the **Portofino** resort (see page 74) where it becomes an increasingly impassable dirt track. Beyond here, it is possible to pick your way along the coast, which is largely completely deserted, for four miles to the **Sueno del Mar** resort (where you can get a boat back to your golf cart or to town). The end of Ambergris caye, at **Bacalar Chico National Park** (see page 67), is three miles beyond **Sueno del Mar**. The coast here is wild and the beach is broken with mangroves. The Mexican border lies beyond the **Bacalar Channel**, immediately to the north of Bacalar Chico, five miles' walk away. From here it's a three-mile walk to Xcalak village, from where there are buses north to the Riviera Maya and Cancún. However, it is not possible officially to enter Mexico this way and there are no border posts. See also Boat, page 83.

Swimming and snorkelling

The **reef**, and the open ocean beyond it, lie over one mile offshore. In most parts of the island you have to wade out for about 400 yds through the eel grass beds to reach water deep enough to swim in. Or you can jump off the end of the numerous jetties. Swimming is safe everywhere, although swimming from San Pedro town can be hazardous because of the heavy boat traffic. It's possible to snorkel off Ambergris Caye beach but it's a long swim of about a mile out to the reef, through shallow sandy water and eel grass beds from San Pedro, and a third of that in the north of the caye. There are usually plenty of fish gathered under the wooden jetties (some hotels attract fish there by feeding them) and there are a number of other good snorkelling spots along the length of the island.

The **Mexico Rocks**, six miles north of San Pedro town (20 minutes by boat) and halfway to Bacalar Chico, are an ideal spot for novice snorkellers, as they are sheltered from strong currents and waves and are at a shallow depth of a few metres. Fish life is less abundant than in Hol Chan but there are plenty of common reef species, including grunts, parrot fish and wrasse, and a large variety of coral. You are more likely to see larger fish further north still at one of the dive sites (see below) or on a boat trip to one of the atolls.

Dive sites

Ambergris has many dive sites to the north and south of San Pedro that rank among the best in the Caribbean. Those to the south are generally more visited. It is important that you have a clear idea of where you will be going when you book a trip; some dive operators like to go to the well-swum sites, and it's not much fun sharing a dive (or snorkel) with half a dozen other boats. In general, the further north you go, the fewer the divers and snorkellers and the more pristine the coral. Hol Chan (see page 68) probably has the most abundant underwater life, as fishing has been prohibited there since 1987. Bacalar Chico is also excellent (see page 67) Dive masters are always discovering new locations, so ask around. The following list offers selected highlights of what are currently the best dives. See also Ambergris Caye map, page 62.

Bacalar Chico Marine Reserve ⓘ *Current: none. Depth: 20-35 m. General visibility: 30 m. Dive level: beginner-intermediate. Location: 25 mins north from San Pedro.* The most popular dive sites in the reserve are the Basil Jones Canyons (see below), Rocky Point and Robles Point. The former canyons cut through the reef where it meets the land, offering spectacular swim-throughs and abundant fish and crustaceans. The dive is often taken in conjunction with the Mata Rocks (see below). Rocky Point and Robles Point both lie in the current free waters of the inner reef and have abundant marine life and some of the most pristine coral on Ambergris Caye. Rocky Point has a tarpon hole and spur-and-groove formations cut with shallow canyons. Robles is mostly canyons. Turtles and eagle rays are common sights at both.

Basil Jones Canyons ⓘ *Current: none. Depth: 18 m. General visibility: 30 m. Dive level: beginner. Location: 20 mins north from San Pedro.* These plunging spur-and-groove canyons lie in the far south of the Bacalar Chico Reserve in the north of Ambergris Caye, away from the reach of the fishing boats, so there is a good chance of seeing large schools of fish here and even some pelagics.

Cypress Canyons ⓘ *Current: none. Depth: 15-35 m. General visibility: 30 m. Dive level: beginner. Location: 5 mins south from San Pedro.* This dive site is similar to Victoria Tunnels (see below), but is less challenging. The reef is particularly rich in multi-hued coral (with staghorn, lettuce and boulder alongside the usual elkhorn), sponges and invertebrate life, making this a great spot for macro photography. The steep but shallow canyons lead to a low swim-through and some impressive large stands to orange and white elkhorn coral swum by inquisitive snappers.

Hol Chan Marine Reserve: Hol Chan Cut ⓘ *Current: none to strong. Depth: 6-9 m. General visibility: 15 m. Dive level: intermediate-advanced. Location: 15-20 mins south from San Pedro.* The Cut is one of the most popular dive sites. The dive's sporadic strong currents and poorer than usual visibility are more than made up for by a wealth of marine life. The strong current has led to a profusion of filter feeders encrusting the canyon walls, including sea fans, gorgonians and many sponges. The fish life is prolific, and no species is diver shy. Huge black and Nassau groupers come within a few feet, great barracudas hover, there are big shoals of common reef species like grunt, schoolmasters and tang, and dozens of green morays.

Advanced divers can drop through the deep canyons in the reef and swim all the way to the outer inky blue drop-off, where there are some spectacular corals and invertebrates. Night dives here are great-too-with octopus, lobsters and flaming scallops common sights. There are numerous other dive sites in Hol Chan for all levels of expertise.

Hol Chan Marine Reserve: Pillar Coral ⓘ *Current: none but strong wave surge. Depth: 12-21 m (40-70 ft). General visibility: 15 m. Dive level: beginner. Location: 15-20 mins south from San Pedro.* This spur-and-groove reef dive is made impressive by the towering pillar corals sticking above the spurs and the large numbers of fish. These include big shoals of the common Caribbean reef species as well as lots of barracuda, bar jacks and yellowtail snappers. Eagle rays are a common sight and there are some 15 tame black and Nassau groupers living around the spurs.

Mata Rocks Cut ⓘ *Current: none to gentle. Depth 2-5 m. General visibility 15 m. Dive level: beginner. Location: 20 mins north from San Pedro.* This shallow dive offers the chance to see plenty of fish including eagle rays and nurse sharks, as well as the wreck of a small barge covered in soft corals and sponges. The area around the barge is sandy, with many conches and stingrays as well as eel grass meadows. The reef itself is brilliantly coloured and forms canyons and tunnels.

Mexico Rocks ⓘ *Current: none. Depth: 2-4 m. General visibility: 15 m. Dive level: beginner. Location: 20 mins from San Pedro.* This cluster of coral heads inside the barrier reef is one of the most popular combined dive and snorkel sites. It's a great spot for novice divers or those who haven't used tanks for a while and feel nervous. The heads support plenty of small fish and invertebrates. Morays and lobsters shelter in the crevices, there are shoals of common reef fish and the occasional visiting eagle ray, turtle or Nassau grouper (particularly close to the reef wall).

Paradise Canyons and Christ of the Abyss ⓘ *Current: none. Depth: 5-25 m. General visibility: 15 m. Dive level: beginner-intermediate. Location: 5 mins from San Pedro.* Shallow reef filled with elkhorn and plate corals leads to a series of narrow canyons with almost sheer walls encrusted with soft corals and sponges. Nurse sharks and stingrays rest in the sand grooves, and there are plenty of common reef fish in large shoals. The much-photographed Christ statue, which looks like a heavy set miniature version of Rio's famous Cristo Redentor, sits in 20 m of water on the top of the reef.

Sandbar ⓘ *Current: none. Depth: 15-20 m. General visibility: 30 m. Dive level: beginner. Location: 10 mins south from San Pedro.* This is one of the shallowest barrier reef dives on the island. There are plenty of colourful corals near the surface of the coral ridges, with large sections of boulder, staghorn (scarce on Ambergris) and mustard hill coral offering ample crevices for invertebrates and morays. The canyons separating them are swum by small shoals of common coral fish, whilst huge groupers can sometimes be seen hiding in the caves at the bottom of the reef canyons.

Tackle Box Canyons ⓘ *Current: none. Depth: 20-40 m. General visibility: 30 m. Dive level: intermediate. Location: 5 mins from San Pedro.* A narrow canyon whose upper walls are covered with boulder, elkhorn and brain coral (with abundant fish) leads to a gloomy coral-encrusted cavern which has little fish life but which makes a great swim through and posing spot for underwater photographs. There is decent snorkelling at the nearby **Tuffy Rocks**, which attract big shoals of grunt, solitary snappers, jacks and parrot fish.

Tres Cocos ⓘ *Current: none. Depth: 5-40 m. General visibility: 30 m. Dive level: beginner. Location: 5 mins north from San Pedro.* An easy beginner dive with deep canyons and gullies covered in numerous soft corals and sponges. There are at least 50 fish species, including large snapper, barracuda, Atlantic spadefish, various angels, jacks, parrot fish, trigger fish and, at deeper levels, large groupers. Turtles are abundant. The reef walls with their soft corals and sponges are home to morays and many invertebrates like octopus, brittle stars, colourful nudibranchs and spiny lobsters.

Victoria Tunnels ⓘ *Current: none. Depth: 10-30 m. General visibility: 30 m. Dive level: beginner-intermediate. Location: 10 mins south from San Pedro.* Some 100 groove canyons and tunnels with swim-throughs are encrusted with a decent variety of soft and hard corals and swum by large shoals of Atlantic spadefish, grunts and tangs, as well as abundant barracuda, trigger fish, jacks, morays, parrot fish, angel fish, groupers, snappers and nurse sharks. Turtles are a common sight and there are groupers at depth. Look out for the iconic crucifix on the seabed at around 20 m depth.

Birdwatching

Birdwatching is great throughout the caye, especially in the north of the island and in the Bacalar Chico Reserve. Commonly seen birds include white-tailed and swallow-tailed kites, white-collared seedeaters, yellow-throated and yellow-rumped warblers, yellow-headed parrots, ospreys, tricoloured, great Blue and yellow-crowned night herons, ruddy turnstones, magnifcent frigatebirds and elegant terns. There are numerous reported sightings of bumblebee hummingbirds, though the species has not been formally catalogued on the caye. Close to San Pedro to the south, the **Caribbean Villas Hotel** (caribbeanvillashotel.com) has a small private birding reserve, with a birding tower and abundant fruiting trees, due to open to the public in 2012 (contact the hotel for the latest details). This is a great spot to while away an early morning or late afternoon. Ambergris birds, such as white-eyed and Yucatán vireo, chacalaca, great kiskadee, black catbird, yellow-bellied elaenia, white-collared seedeater, golden-fronted woodpecker, black-headed saltator and hooded oriole are easily seen here. See also What to do, page 80.

Fishing

Whilst not as legendary amongst anglers as the Turneffe Flats (see page 87), or the permit flats and tarpon-filled waters of the South Water Caye Marine Reserve (see page 144), Ambergris Caye nonetheless offers great fishing. Some of the richest tarpon feeding grounds in the western Caribbean lies just 20 minutes offshore from San Pedro, there is superb fly fishing for bonefish and permit in the flats to the north of the caye, close to the border with Mexico, and the blue water fishing is so good that the caye regularly hosts international tournaments. Although there is good fishing all year round, the best season on the metre-deep flats around Ambergris is between May and November. The huge size of the flats – which extend for 50 miles – means that you will never feel crowded out. Even in high season you'll struggle to find other anglers, and the tarpon are so abundant and still so unused to sport fishermen that they will aggressively attack any properly presented fly. See also What to do, page 82.

At 26,440 acres, this reserve 17 miles north of San Pedro is one of the largest protected areas in the Belizean cayes. It is one of the seven special sites which make up the UNESCO World Heritage-listed **Belize Barrier Reef Reserve System** (see box, page 69). The reserve was founded in 1996 under pressure not from the residents of San Pedro, but from those of Sarteneja village in Corozal (see page 190), who recognized the large lagoon that dominates the reserve as an important spawning ground for fish and a crucial habitat for marine turtles and manatees.

Visiting Bacalar Chico Marine Reserve

You can visit Bacalar Chico on a guided tour from San Pedro or Sarteneja, see pages 80 and 188. **Turtleman**, see page 76, charges BZ$30 each way from San Pedro for guests staying at his lodge. The **Green Reef Environmental Institute** ① *100 Coconut Dr, San Pedro, T226-2833, www.greenreefbelize.org*, organizes volunteer tourism in Bacalar Chico; see their website for details of their tours and their volunteer projects. **Bacalar Chico Expeditions** ① *100 Coconut Dr, San Pedro, T226-2833, bacalarchico.org*, which work in partnership with Green Reef and share an office, run full day tours from San Pedro for BZ$180 with a minimum of four people. **Sarteneja Adventure Tours Expeditions** ① *c/o Sarteneja Tour Guide Association, Sarteneja town, T669-4911, www.sartenejatours.com*, offer tours of the reserve for BZ$170, or cheaper for groups of over four; prices include lunch and snorkelling gear. Once in the reserve, there is a **visitor centre** (T226-2833), at the San Juan ruins. For more on Bacalar Chico, see www.shipstern.org.

The reserve

The marine reserve comprises the shallow (1-2 m deep) Bacalar Chico lagoon, fringing coral reef, extensive sea grass beds and large areas of littoral forest, and mangrove. The reserve extends west into Chetumal Bay. Within the reserve is **Rocky Point**, the only place in Belize where the barrier reef meets the coastline.

The reserve is dotted with Mayan sites, many of them little explored. They include **San Juan**, in the park's northwest corner (where pottery shards litter the beach and a sea wall is visible under the water), along with **Chac-balam**. Both are partially excavated. The Bacalar Chico channel, which separates Ambergris Caye from the Mexican mainland, was dug by the Maya.

There are beautiful beaches too, including some of the broadest on Ambergris Caye. Snorkelling in the glassy clear, fish-filled waters or kayaking around the mangroves is a delight. However, fish poaching and plundering the mangroves for firewood is rife.

Bacalar Chico is an important Caribbean wildlife refuge for nursing fish, including tarpon, spadefish and permit, alongside some 120 other species of coral reef fish. Manatees graze on eel grass in the lagoon. American crocodiles breed in the refuge. Robles Point and Rocky Point are among the most important nesting sites for loggerhead and green turtles on the Central American Atlantic coast and the entire area is important for 187 species of resident and migratory birds. Jaguars, ocelots, pumas and margays live in the forests alongside 35 other mammal species, 58 reptiles and 22 amphibians.

Hol Chan, Yucatec Mayan for 'little channel', is the oldest marine reserve in Belize and the most popular day snorkel and dive destination for both Ambergris Caye and neighbouring Caye Caulker.

As its name suggests, the reserve is centred on a narrow cut in the reef some 23 m wide and 9 m deep. The park spreads around this cut, stretching north to the southern tip of Ambergris Caye and south towards Caye Caulker. It is divided into four principal habitat zones: the cut itself, a shallow lagoon with abundant eel grass, seven tiny cayes covered with white and black mangrove forest and the shark ray alley. Together they offer a couple of days' worth of attractions. See also page 64.

Visiting Hol Chan Marine Reserve
Guesthouses and dive shops on Ambergris Caye can organize a boat trip to Hol Chan. Expect to pay between BZ$40 and BZ$50 for a trip, including mask, snorkel and fins and a snorkelling guide. The trip is safe for children, who pay half price. There is an additional fee of BZ$5 per adult to admission to Hol Chan Reserve, collected at the reserve. Most trips last about three hours, visiting a fraction of the reserve. Try and go early morning or mid-afternoon to avoid the biggest crowds and the worst sunburn; guides discourage use of sun protection so bring a T-shirt to swim in.

The reserve
Currents are strong in the **cut** itself, making it a popular spot for safe drift diving or snorkelling. Boats drop you at one end and you float with the movement of the water past coral walls encrusted with sponges and elk- and staghorn coral and through large shoals of reef fish; see page 64. The **lagoon** covers the largest area of the reserve and is dominated by large fields of *Thalassia* and *Syringodium* sea grass (a favourite food of West Indian manatees). The Boca Ciega Blue Hole, a gathering point for large schools of fish in the northwestern portion of the lagoon, offers gentle cave diving, whilst Neptune's Garden, a mixed sponge and algae bed in very shallow water, offers perhaps the best snorkelling. It is an important site for nursing fish. *Eucheuma isoforme*, one of the dominant algal species here, is used to make the chlorophyll-rich Belizean seaweed smoothies. The **cayes** are also important nursing grounds for juvenile fish as well as roosting spots for myriad sea birds; they are a great spot for a sea kayak. Fishermen used to clean their catch at **Shark Ray Alley**, luring nurse sharks, southern stingrays and larger reef fish such as greater barracudas and groupers. They still congregate around any visiting boat in search of fish scraps, and snorkellers and divers are invited to swim with them in the shallow water. This can be an unnerving experience; currents are strong and the fish come very close, making touching or even standing on one difficult to avoid.

Fauna and flora
Fishing has been prohibited in Hol Chan since 1987 and there is abundant marine life. The cut has extensive sections of elkhorn coral, brain corals, boulder corals, and many sea fans and soft corals. There are big shoals of blue tangs, atlantic spadefish, permits and grunts and plenty of solitary great barracudas, nassau and black groupers, various snappers, nurse sharks, triggerfish and hogfish. Black-tipped reef and hammerhead shark, large tarpon and turtles are occasional visitors. Beyond the cut, the Hol Chan outer reef is rich in coral and sponge species, with a particularly impressive grouping of pillar corals

Belize Barrier Reef Reserve

The Belize Barrier Reef and coastal hinterland, inscribed on the UNESCO World Heritage list in 1996, is the largest barrier reef in the northern hemisphere, with atolls, hundreds of cayes, mangroves, lagoons and estuaries. UNESCO state that 'the system's seven sites illustrate the evolutionary history of reef development and are a significant habitat for threatened species, including marine turtles, manatees and the American marine crocodile.' The seven protected sites taken together make up a total area of 237,962 acres. The largest is **Glover's Reef Marine Reserve** (76,108 acres), followed by **South Water Caye Marine Reserve** (73,400 acres), **Sapodilla Cayes Marine Reserve** (31,380 acres) and **Bacalar Chico National Park and Marine Reserve** (26,440 acres). The remaining three areas – the **Blue Hole, Half Moon Caye Natural Monument** and **Laughing Bird Caye National Park** – are all around the same size, covering around 10,000 acres.

In recent years, environmentalists have become increasingly troubled about damage and resort development within the reserve. Belize's leading newspaper *Amandala* reported in March 2009 that there had been dredging for resort development in the South Water Caye Marine Reserve, dynamiting of the reef and substantial damage inflicted by large ships. The report also said that those eager to protect the reserve were deeply concerned about the possible construction of two new 'eco-resorts' within the South Water Caye Marine Reserve, **Yum Balisi** and **Chrysalis**. In 2009 the Belize Barrier Reef World Heritage Site was placed on the In Danger Red list, where it remains.

which mark a popular dive stop. Spotted dolphins are occasional visitors here. Bottlenose dolphins and West Indian manatees are visitors to the lagoon, which is always filled with young fish. There is also a large population of queen conches. The mangrove roots provide shelter for scores of juvenile reef and pelagic fish, together with seahorses and crustaceans. The roots themselves are encrusted with myriad tunicates, anemones and brittle stars. Look for large flocks of terns, frigates and other migrant and resident sea birds in the trees.

◉ Ambergris Caye listings

For hotel and restaurant price codes and other relevant information, see pages 11-12.

◉ Where to stay

Most hotels on Ambergris Caye can organize dive or snorkel trips and tours to the sights around the island and to locations on the mainland like Altun Ha or the ATM caves. As with everywhere in Belize, hotels generally adopt the US practice of not including tax in their rack rates. This can push the bill up considerably. Taxes can (and often do) amount to 9% room tax and a further 10% sales tax. They sometimes also involve an additional service charge of 10%, and another 5% on top of that for paying by credit card! Enquire before booking. Prices below include tax. Almost all hotels and guesthouses offer internet access.

San Pedro town's bargain bucket hotels are by and large an undesirable, tawdry bunch. Budget travellers should consider splurging on Ambergris Caye, pre-booking a bargain through **Tripadvisor** or using Caye Caulker or a mainland beach for their reef experience. They should also be aware that the cheapies do not always honour reservations.

There are very few options for environmentally conscious travellers. The best by far is the wonderful **Turtleman's House**, where environmental impact (and modern amenities) are minimal. But there are signs of change. In 2011 the Belize Sustainable Tourism Programme (www.sustainabletourismbz.org) announced that 3 very low density resort hotels were being planned outside Bacalar Chico National Park. To 'minimize the impacts on the environment, the areas chosen have been previously disturbed' and that 'small low-density new developments' would be built off the main road leading north from San Pedro.

The **Central American Collection** (www.centralamericacollections.com) offers good prices on luxury accommodation on Ambergris Caye as part of a package in Belize.

San Pedro *p59, map p60*
$$$$ Phoenix, 500 yds north of the town centre on the beachfront between Sandpiper and High School sts, T226-2083, T1-877 822-5512 (US), www.thephoenix belize.com. This 3-year-old resort is ugly on the outside, with unprepossessing, blocky architecture and concrete and stone paving around the huge pool. However, the suites are modern, very spacious and breezy, and come with living areas with US cable TV, kitchens and large bedrooms and bathrooms. Most have wrap-around balconies with a lovely ocean view. Service is mostly excellent, though staff can be snooty to local Belizeans, and the hotel organizes tours and dives. There is no beach out front. There's a gym, spa, restaurant, Wi-Fi and cable TV. Breakfast is included. Credit cards accepted.
$$$$ Ramon's, 550 yds south of the town centre near the airstrip, T226-2071, T1-800 624 4215 (US), ambergriscaye.com/ramons. This is one of the best-appointed resorts on the island. The grounds are lovely, with thatched-roof *cabañas* set in a lush garden near a pretty pool, and the dive shop is one of the better resort dive shops on the island. It's in a great location – perhaps the best of the mid- to upper-end resorts close to the town centre – so restaurants in town are easily accessible. A/c rooms are a little small and plain compared to others in the same price bracket, with hardwood or tiled floors, cream walls and a small patio. It's worth splashing out on one of the mini-suites. There's a spa, library, tours, restaurant, business centre and Wi-Fi. Credit cards accepted.
$$$$-$$$ Sunbreeze, 500 yds south of the town centre next to the airstrip, T226-2191, T1-800 688 0191 (US), www.sunbreeze.net. With long cloisters of concrete cubes and uninspiring decor, this beachside block

Bugged off

Persistent complaints by visitors about mosquitoes and sandflies in San Pedro and Long Caye in the Lighthouse Atoll (which are no worse than in Cancún to the north or any other tropical beach destination) has led to widespread use of insecticide on the islands. Carts patrol at dawn, spraying unpleasant chemicals, particularly around hotel grounds. This is very bad for biodiversity and particularly for butterfly, bird and small mammal life, which is already showing signs of suffering. If you are troubled by this, let your hotel and the tourist board know. And use insect repellent, Johnson's So Soft or jojoba oil instead.

feels more like an urban **Comfort Inn** than a holiday retreat. It's great if you use it as the former, if you plan to be out all day on tours or diving and want a central hotel with a pool near town. The hotel's dive shop, **Hugh Parkey's**, is one of the best in Belize (see page 81). Guests get attractive rates on pre-booked dive packages. See the website for full details. There's a recommended restaurant, massages, Wi-Fi and cable TV. Credit cards accepted. Similar deals are also available at their sister hotel on Barrier Reef Dr, the **Sunbreeze Suites ($$$$)**, T226-4675, sunbreezesuites.com, which offers spacious suites for 4 people (using sofa beds), kitchenettes and tired decor. Avoid those overlooking the cemetery.

$$$$-$$ Belizean Reef, on the beachfront, 1 block south of the airport, T600-3579, T1-310 438 7368 (US), ambergriscaye.com/bzreef. These big seafront condos are great value for families or couples travelling together, especially for stays of at least 5 nights. Even the simpler 1-bedroom suites have separate bed and living areas, the latter with 2 futons, bringing what would otherwise be a more pricey mid-range hotel into the upper budget bracket. Book online for the best rates. Suites are large, well appointed and have fully equipped kitchens, bedrooms, living areas and patios leading onto a shared lawn. The airport is close, so keep windows shut to avoid early morning flight noise. Wi-Fi and cable TV. Credit cards accepted.

$$$ Changes in Latitudes B&B, 36 Coconut Dr, 900 yds south of San Pedro centre next to the airport strip, T226-2986, T1-800 631 9834 (US), ambergriscaye.com/latitudes. Book early at this friendly, family-run B&B a block from the beach as there are only 6 a/c rooms. Each is very small but well furnished with plenty of storage space and en suites with hot showers, and there's a pleasant private courtyard. The **Belize Diving Adventures** office is right outside the hotel making this a handy option for divers. Guests can use the pool at the next door **Yacht Club**. Breakfast is generous, with oatmeal pancakes and syrup, ample fruit, juice and tea or coffee, and is included in the price. Complimentary bikes. Credit cards accepted.

$$$ Mayan Princess, beachfront between Pelican and Caribena sts (next to **Tio Pil's**), T226-2778, T1-800 850 4101 (US), mayan princesshotel.com. Rooms with terraces at this seafront hotel have wonderful reef and lagoon views, whilst dive shops and bars and restaurants are on the doorstep. Rooms are spick and span. Suites have kitchenette breakfast areas and separate bedrooms. Many are newly renovated. Although the hotel is quiet, the strip outside can get noisy at night and in the early morning, so bring earplugs. There are attractive dive packages run with their onsite dive shop, **Amigos Del Mar**. There's internet (lobby only), tours and cable TV. Credit cards accepted.

$$$ San Pedro Holiday Hotel, T226-2014, T1-713 893 3825 (US), sanpedroholiday.com. Accommodation is very simple and a little tatty in this beachside hotel, with pink and cream concrete walls, beds with chintzy spreads, closet-like en suites, wicker chairs and a tiny telly. Some have rickety doors and flimsy locks, so check a few. However, it's in a decent location right near the airport strip downtown and in easy reach of many dive shops and restaurants. The best rooms are on the 2nd floor and have terraces. Some have sea views. Those nearest to the street can be noisy. There's a dive shop and a restaurant. Credit cards accepted.

$$$-$$ Spindrift Resort Hotel, seafront between Buccaneer and Black Coral sts, T226-2174, T1-888 705 9978 (US), ambergriscaye.com/spindrift. This bright pink beachfront building bang in the centre of town offers very simple but well-kept 1- or 2-bed a/c or fan-cooled doubles or apartments with patio or beach views. Furnishings are few and modest but include a desk, small TV and tiny fridge. The best rooms share a terrace area with great views out over the lagoon. Like any hotel in central San Pedro, it can get noisy at night. Wi-Fi and cable TV. Credit cards accepted.

$$ Conch Shell Inn, 11 Foreshore St, between Caribena and Sandpiper sts, T226-2062, conchshellinn@gmail.com. This big pink-and-white weatherboard beach house in the heart of San Pedro offers some of the best-value ocean-view accommodation in town. A/c rooms are bright, airy and spotlessly clean. The best are on the upper storey and share a big shaded terrace (decked out with beach chairs) and a wonderful view over the lagoon. Wi-Fi and cable TV. Credit cards accepted.

$$ Martha's, T206-2053, Pescador Dr at Ambergris St, ambergriscaye.com/marthas. Rooms are as cheap and basic as it gets in San Pedro: small, scruffy wooden boxes with en suites and only a bed and a fan. The central location is excellent though, with easy access to restaurants, dive shops and bars.

$$ Ruby's, beachfront between Tarpon and Black Coral sts, T226-2063, ambergriscaye. com/rubys. This big white weatherboard family home has been here since San Pedro was a fishing village. It's the best budget

option in town and is usually full, so try and get here early and reserve a room. Internet bookings are not reliable. Estel keeps her place spick and span and offers towels and soap. All rooms but one are fan cooled and some have a sea view. But they sit over the **Early Bird Café**, so bring earplugs. Some rooms have en suites, some have balconies and the hotel has a pleasant lounge deck, a restaurant and internet. Restaurants, bars and dive shops are on the doorstep.

$$ San Pedrano, Barrier Reef Dr (Front St) between Pelican and Caribena sts, T226-2054, sanpedrano@btl.net. This waterfront hotel is another survivor of San Pedro fishing village. It's one of the better budget options. Like its counterparts, the fan-cooled rooms are basic, with not much more than a bed, cable TV, small table and chair and optional a/c unit (for BZ$20 extra per night). But whilst small, they are half as large again as rooms in the other old family-run hotels, generally cleaner and the paint and decor is less tired. There's also a terrace on the top floor with views out over the ocean. As with all the central hotels, it can be noisy at night. Credit cards accepted.

$$ Tio Pil's (formerly Lily's), beachfront between Pelican and Caribena sts, T206-2059, www.tiopilshotel.com. It's cash only at this tiny budget beachfront hotel which has been attracting backpackers since the early 1970s. Little has changed since then. The green clapboard house still doubles up as a family home. There are just 6 simple rooms with barely enough room for a fridge, bed, cable TV and rickety a/c unit (all with shared bathrooms), and 2 apartments (with space for 2 couples, each with separate living and bedroom areas). It's very basic and, for now, decoration is tired (though there are plans to redecorate in 2012), and it can be noisy outside at night and early morning, but beachfront in Ambergris Caye doesn't come much cheaper than this. There's a restaurant and Wi-Fi.

$$ Tomas, 12 Barrier Reef Dr, T226-2061. A tiny family home and hotel a block

rom the beach. It has somehow survived
n the town centre through decades of
development, despite having just 7 simple
but airy) a/c or fan-cooled rooms.

$-$ Pedro's Inn, next to the airstrip,
206-3825, backpackersbelize.com. The
self-proclaimed cheapest accommodation
option on the island has 2 buildings: a rough-
and-ready simple hostel with fan-cooled
wooden rooms as small as a railway carriage
sleeper cubicle (and partitioned from each
other with plywood), and an equally basic
larger hotel with 32 more spacious a/c rooms
with en suite bathrooms (for 50% more).
Things can get noisy when the hostel is full
rooms are very close to the bar) and when
the morning planes take off and land on the
adjacent airstrip. There's a bar, restaurant,
pool and tours. Credit cards accepted.

Beyond San Pedro p61, map p62

$$$ Azul, www.azulbelize.com. There are
only 2 villas in this US$500-plus per night
resort, set in 10 acres of palm groves, tropical
gardens and Yucatec dry forest fronted by
00 ft of beach. The open-plan villas are
vast, covering an astounding 3000 sq ft,
dominated by huge areas of white that
catch the warm natural light and are offset
by lush tropical hardwoods. 20 ft above
the raw stone floor, huge honey-coloured
nylady beams hold up the teak wood
roofs; windows and doors are carved from
caramel-brown jabin, and beds, furniture
nd bathroom cabinets from dark zericote.
The villas sit next to their own infinity pools
ight on the beach. There are hammocks in
every shady glade, jacuzzis on the rooftop
patio and, despite the resort's tiny size, it
as its own excellent restaurant, bar and
our service, as well as cable TV and Wi-Fi.
reakfast is included. But this is not for
hose who don't like dogs free of leads,
s the resort has 8. Credit cards accepted.

$$$ Cayo Espanto, private island 3 miles
est of San Pedro, T1-888 666 4282 (US),
mbergriscaye.com/cayoespanto. If a
rivate beach just isn't enough, then, with

this place, you can rent your own private
island. Or so it would seem from the hotel's
website. What you get is undoubtedly
luxurious: a beautifully appointed private
villa constructed from a forest of gorgeous
tropical hardwood, with superb ocean and
night sky views, your own butler and full
room service including in-house dining.
What you don't get for your US$1400-plus
(full board) is your own private island. Cayo
Espanto is a small caye, and there are 6 villas,
each with their own tiny beach space. And
San Pedro is a boat ride away, so it's hard to
pop down the road for a change of scene
or menu. There's a spa, restaurant, Wi-Fi and
cable TV. Breakfast is included. Credit cards
accepted; 4-night minimum stay.

$$$$ El Pescador, 2½ miles north of San
Pedro about 500 yds north of San Pedro
River, T226-2398, T1-800 242 2017 (US),
www.elpescador.com. As the name would
suggest, **El Pescador** (the fisherman) is
aimed at those who come to Belize for its
world class tarpon and bonefish. The resort
offers some of the best fishing tours on the
island, along with fly-fishing classes, and
has the only Scientific Angler Mastery Series
Fly Shop in Belize. Rooms are split between
the main lodge building (lush wood floors,
bright colours, shared balconies) and 8
larger, more luxurious private villas, with
big sun decks. All rooms have ocean views.
The lodge has introduced modest measures
towards sustainable tourism. It offsets
carbon, has cut down on use of plastics
and plants native flora in its grounds.
There's a pool, a gym, dive shop, massages
available, Wi-Fi and cable TV. Breakfast is
included. Credit cards accepted.

$$$$ La Perla, 6 miles north of San Pedro,
T226-2885, T1-866 290 6341 (US), www.
laperladelcaribe.com. The tasteful interior
decor in these handsome beach houses
is understated mock-hacienda meets
Morocco. Some have large terracotta floor
tiles, walnut and wicker sofas, heavy wood
tables and kelims on the floor, with colourful
bedspreads and bathroom tiles. Others have

lush wood and muted tones or are decked out with diaphanous drapes, Mediterranean blues and raw cotton sofas. The hotel does a great job of integrating with rather than imposing upon the landscape. The few amenities include free kayaks, a pool, tours, Wi-Fi and cable TV. There is no restaurant but other hotels are within 10 mins' walk, or you can self-cater or take a water taxi into town (BZ$40 round trip). Credit cards accepted.

$$$$ Matachica, 5 miles north of San Pedro centre, T223-0002, www.matachica.com. Rooms are housed in large palm thatch *cabañas* set in a shady, palm-filled garden on the waterfront. Each is elegantly furnished and decorated in rustic chic, with whitewashed walls, wicker furniture, hardwood tables and folk art and crafts. Beds are mattresses on concrete platforms (watch you don't bump your knees at night). Service is good, and amenities include complimentary kayaks. This is a spot for those wanting relaxation by the pool, bar (if you don't mind the piped music) or on the beach. The restaurant is decent but expensive. For a break, head to San Pedro or the nearby Portofino. There's a gym, massages available, tours, a dive shop, Wi-Fi and cable TV. Credit cards accepted.

$$$$ Portofino, 6 miles north of San Pedro centre, T226-4272, T1-253 660 0145 (US), portofinobelize.com. This luxury boutique hotel sits on a quiet stretch of the coast to the north of San Pedro. It's a great hideaway for couples. Rooms are housed in large palm-thatched *cabañas* overlooking the sea and *casitas* gathered around a lovely jewel-like pool. All are tastefully furnished and decorated with 4-poster beds and rustic rugs. The master suite is one of the loveliest on the island, with wonderful views from a series of huge glass windows; you can watch the sun rise over the lagoon from bed. The hotel restaurant is one of the best on the island, and there's a good, intimate little bar. The Belgian owners are warm and welcoming. Complimentary boat transfer for guests. There's a dive shop, massages available, tours,

restaurant, Wi-Fi and cable TV. Breakfast is included. Credit cards accepted.

$$$$ Victoria House, 2 miles south of San Pedro centre, T226-2067, T1-800 247 5159 (US), www.victoria-house.com. One of the premier luxury resorts in Belize, sitting on one of the broadest stretches of sand in San Pedro, and popular with honeymooners. Buildings and decor are tasteful and blend well with the natural surrounding, service is excellent, and the hotel has one of the finest resort restaurants in the country. Rooms range from beach villas with a sea view and their own private plunge pools, to duplex *casitas* with vast bedrooms and bathrooms and a living room/kitchen. Excellent facilities include a lovely, large pool and deck set in shady gardens, good dive shop, a gift shop, free bike rental, cart rental, massages, watersports and a tour agency. Wi-Fi and cable TV. Breakfast is included. Credit cards accepted.

$$$$ Xanadu, 1½ miles south of San Pedro, T226-2814, T1-866 351 4752 (US), xanaduislandresort.com. Rooms in palm-thatched well-appointed *cabañas*, set in a garden shaded by coconut palms around an attractive pool. Rooms range from studio suites to large 2- and 3-bedroom suites. The best have terraces with reef views. There is no restaurant but the hotel has courtesy bikes and kayaks, rents carts for trips into town, offers tours and has a dive shop. It is one of the greenest of the luxury lodges, conserving some water, using wind-powered electricity, composting waste, preserving wildlife on the grounds and employing local people. Wi-Fi and cable TV. Breakfast is included. Credit cards accepted.

$$$$-$$$ Coral Bay Villas, 1 mile south of the town centre beyond the airstrip, T226-3006, www.coralbaybelize.com. This is one of the smaller resorts close to town, with just 6 functional condo rooms, giving it an intimate boutique feel. These are housed in a big balcony-fronted mock-hacienda mansion looking over the water. What they lack in design flair or luxury, they more than make up for in space, intimacy and convenience. The resort is so small that even when it's full the pool and Jacuzzi never feel crowded. When other guests are out on trips you can have it to yourself. Restaurants and bars are within easy reach on the complimentary bicycles yet far enough away not to disturb. Sharing a condo and taking advantage of online discounts make prices very reasonable. Wi-Fi and cable TV. Credit cards accepted.

$$$$-$$$ Tranquility Bay, 12 miles north of San Pedro, www.tranquilitybayresort.com. Remoteness is both a plus and a minus in Tranquility Bay. The resort borders the Bacalar Chico Reserve, so the beach and water are pristine, the lagoon sees very little boat traffic and the reef is a fairly easy swim away. Life is as quiet and laid-back as the resort's name suggests. But San Pedro is a long way away. Distance and the hotel's poor shuttle service mean that you will have no choice but to eat and socialize here. Rooms are pretty, housed in traditional brightly painted Belizean weatherboard shacks, rustic without but functionally smart within, with dull decor and furnishings but attractive polished wood roof beams, internal balconies and balustrades, a kitchen and plenty of lounge space. Suites and simple budget rooms are available and there are ocean views from most of the chic shacks. The restaurants serve attractively prepared comfort food with a Mexican twist. Breakfasts are generous and there is a dive shop, complimentary kayaks on the beach and Wi-Fi. Credit cards accepted.

$$$ Caye Casa, beachfront 220 yds north of San Pedro centre, 100 yds south of the river, T226-2880, T1-800 936 3433 (US), www.cayecasa.com. This small boutique hotel with friendly staff and a great tour operator offers small but spotlessly clean rooms with separate living areas and bedrooms and more spacious villas for 4; the latter are good value if you're travelling in a group. The best accommodation is in the palm-thatch oceanfront *casitas*, with lovely views and balmy breezes, and the top-floor classic rooms, which have the most privacy. Town centre restaurants and bars are a stroll away. There's a miniscule pool, and the hotel offers well-thought-out bespoke tours and dive packages; consult font of all local knowledge, staff member Captain Boxter. Wi-Fi and cable TV. Credit cards accepted.

$$$ Tides Beach Hotel, beachfront 200 yds north of San Pedro centre, 150 yds south of the river, T226-2283, ambergriscaye.com/tides. This small hotel housed in a handsome old Belizean house offers a handful of rooms with shared ocean-facing terraces right near San Pedro town centre. Each is small, modest and sparsely furnished, with attractive honey-coloured wooden floors and bedside tables, bright coloured counterpanes and wall hangings and small en suites. The hotel offers some of the most competetive sleep and dive packages run with their dive shop, **Patajo's**.

$$$ Turtleman's House, 13 miles from San Pedro next to Bacalar Chico Reserve, T664-9661, turtlemanshouse.com. This thatched *cabaña* sitting on stilts over the water on the edge of Bacalar Chico is one of the best options in Belize for those looking for direct contact with pristine wilderness without the need for mod cons. The lodge is run by the Turtleman, a US marine biologist who has lived here for over 20 years, and his partner. The 1 room and loft are simple but decorated with delightful bric-a-brac collected from a lifetime's beachcombing: Portuguese glass, seashells, arty driftwood and sea urchin shells. There's no a/c, a

solar-heated shower and a compost toilet. Meals (which are extra) of spanking fresh fish and veggies are taken in the Turtleman's own home with his family and there are 2 resort restaurants and a bar within walking distance. Under 10s stay free, over-10s stay for BZ$20. The lodge runs manatee safaris, rents snorkelling gear and runs snorkelling and boat trips. They can also organize dive trips. Cash payment only.

$$$-$$ Hotel del Rio, beachfront 270 yds north of San Pedro centre, 90 yds south of the river, T226-2286, ambergriscaye.com/hoteldelrio. Like **Tio Pil's**, **Ruby's** and **Tomas**, this tiny wooden home was one of the island's first simple guesthouse hotels and has withstood the wave of building that has swept through San Pedro since its 'discovery'. Unlike the others, **Hotel del Rio** has expanded since and now has a choice of a/c rooms in big and breezy thatch-roof *cabañas* set in a garden, or cheaper fan-cooled rooms in the original wooden building. The former are duplex and with room for 2 couples (double bed downstairs and twin beds in the loft area), a big shared patio hung with hammocks, hot water showers and kitchenettes. The latter are very simple and boxy but have fridges. There is Wi-Fi, and tours can be organized. Credit cards accepted.

Restaurants

Bars double-up as restaurants, restaurants double-up as bars and most hotels have both. This makes it hard to list bars and restaurants separately, so we list them together here.

Most food here is hearty staple fare, served in large portions and catering to midwest US tastes. You'll find plenty of burgers, Tex-Mex (with dishes heavy on cheese and sauces), American-style pizza ba snacks like nachos with processed cheese, shakes and juices. Coffee is served weak in mugs. Genuine Mexican food is increasingly available in the cheaper Spanish-speaking restaurants in the back streets. Here you'll find Mexican staples like *huevos rancheros*, *huevos à la Mexicana*, quesadillas, tacos and *amales*. Beans are black, tortillas are made with maize and not wheat flour, and chillies are small, red and hot.

Fresh seafood dominates most of the better menus, which are generally in the upmarket resorts. The best are probably La Palmilla and Le Bistro Portofino.

Snack food and budget meals abound. Stalls around Central Park (on the waterfront between Buccaneer and Ambergris sts) sell tacos and suchlike for less than BZ$3. Various bakeries sell warm rolls and buns and Belizean cinnamon rolls. Cheap restaurants along the waterfront offer big breakfasts of eggs, bacon, jacks (deep-fried patties) and syrup.

All restaurants are open for lunch and dinner unless otherwise indicated. Most of those in the **$$$** category will organize a pick-up from your hotel, often included in the dining price. Sales tax and service charge generally are not included, and in the US-owned and run resorts, tips are expected.

San Pedro *p59, map p60*

$$ Blue Water Grill, **Sunbreeze Hotel**, see page 70. This unpretentious restaurant in an ugly resort has been serving excellent, uncomplicated grilled seafood and meat for over a decade. Some of the best chefs to work in Belize have cooked here. Much of the menu was created by Chris Aycock, current executive chef at **Yama** (in Vail, Colorado). There's a wide choice of grills, such as black-bean crusted snook and sesame butter-covered snapper, as well as pizzas, pastas and salads. The restaurant overlooks the beach.

$$ Casa Picasso, Stingray St, south of the airstrip near the lagoon, T226-4443, www.casapicassobelize.com. Open evenings only. This colourful, arty tapas eatery serves a global mix of fashionable bar food, such as chicken satay, seared scallops, ceviche and patatas bravas. Mains include lobster risotto

and cappellini in garlic olive oil. Excellent choice of cocktails.

$$$ Crave, Barrier Reef Dr at Black Coral St, T226-3211, www.cravebelize.com. The sister restaurant to **Hidden Treasure** (see below), this place has a menu created by the same chef, Juan Carlos Rosales. Whilst the latter offers intimate dining and specializes in Latin American dishes and seafood, **Crave** doubles up as a bar (with live music 3 times a week) and has a North American-influenced menu, with dishes such as rib-eye steak and barbecued ribs.

$$$ Red Ginger, Phoenix Resort, see page 70. The modish and mood-lit a/c dining room in this resort restaurant feels as much South Beach Miami as Ambergris Caye. In fact, much of its menu was designed by one of that city's better chefs, Andres Futo (formerly at **Cacao** in Coral Gables). Current chef José Torres offers mostly upscale versions of popular US, international and Caribbean dishes, including Tex-Mex enchiladas, grilled reef fish and honey-glazed ribs.

$$$ Wild Mango's, 42 Barrier Reef Dr at Tarpon St, T226-2859. In her 6 years here chef Amy Knox has twice won Belize's top culinary award, the Taste of Belize Chef of the Year. Her menu is one of the most creative and daring on the island. Starters include a 3-ceviche degustation with tropical, Thai and Ecuadoreno versions. Mains include Mexican lasagne with black beans and orange mojo grilled grouper with orange sauce and shaved coconut. There is no lobster or conch on the menu as Amy is concerned at the impact of overfishing on their numbers.

$$$-$$ Sunset Grill, 10 Black Coral St, on the lagoon side of San Pedro, T226-2600. You can feed fish as well as feed on fish at this informal seafood restaurant and bar overlooking the lagoon. The fish to feed are huge tarpon that congregate around the restaurant jetty. The fish to feed on include mango tango snapper (cooked with tropical fruit) and grilled grouper. As the grill's name suggests, the sun sinks over the lagoon right in front, making this a great spot for a sundowner.

$$ Caliente Restaurant and Pier Lounge, Spindrift Hotel see page 72, www.caliente belize.com. Closed Mon. This waterfront restaurant serves simple seafood (lobster fritters, grilled fish) and a mixed menu of Tex-Mex and Caribbean (ginger rum chicken) standards. On Thu the **Pier Lounge** hosts the 'Chicken Drop', an informal party attracting locals and tourists alike.

$$-$ Estel's, Buccaneer St at the beachfront, T226-2019, ambergriscaye.com/estels. Closed evenings. This is *the* place for a bumper budget breakfast on the beach in San Pedro. So much so that it can be hard to get one of the tables, which spill out of the shady dining room onto the sand. The food is cheap, cheerful and served in large portions. Much of it is fried, from big jonny cakes (fried cornmeal flat bread) to all manner of eggs (including *huevos rancheros* and eggy bread). The restaurant serves hearty lunches, with a huge menu featuring plenty of seafood options and American dishes.

$$-$ Lola's Pub, 8 Barrier Reef Dr, opposite **Belize Bank**, T206-2120, www.facebook. com/lolaspubbelize. This lively drinks and snack bar serves US and British fast food favourites – big burgers with a range of toppings and fillings, fish and chips, bangers and mash – and perhaps the broadest range of alcoholic drinks of any bar on the island. There's live music most nights and a rowdy crowd after 2100 in high season.

$ D & E's Frozen Custard and Sorbet, Pescador Dr between Pelican and Caribena sts. It's worth swinging by this little ice cream parlour on a hot afternoon to sample the huge range of hand-made exotic ice creams (aka frozen custards), sorbets and juices. These include creamy soursop (guanabana), Belizean dark chocolate, banana and Ben 'n' Jerry-style mixes like cookies and cream.

$ El Fogon, immediately north of the airstrip at corner of Tarpon St and Airstrip Ln, T206-2121, ambergriscaye.com/elfogon. Lunch only. At this tiny place local Belizean Patty Arceo serves cheap Creole and Spanish Belizean food cooked over a wood-fired open-hearth (*fogon*). There are just 5 chunky wooden campsite tables. The menu is based on rice and beans, which come with a slab of fried or grilled chicken or fish, stewed pork, stewed fish or stewed chicken, conch fritters or fish balls. Portions are hearty, and all slips down easily with a cold beer or juice

$ Mathieu's Delicatessen, Pescador Dr, T670-3354, www.facebook.com/mathieus delicatessen. Gunter Mathieu runs the best fast food eatery in central San Pedro. Breakfasts of fresh pastries, home-made muesli and apple cinnamon French toast set the tone for a lunch and evening snack menu of upmarket sandwiches, pizzas and home-made pasta.

Beyond San Pedro *p61, map p62*
$$$ Hidden Treasure, 2 miles south of San Pedro centre on the coastal road, T226-4111, hiddentreasurebelize.com. Ruben and Elvi Muñoz serve a mix of Latin American favourites (strongly influenced by Mexico and traditional Mayan cooking) at this award-winning restaurant. The dining room sits under a palm-thatched *cabaña* in a small tropical garden. The food is elegant and unpretentious, with dishes like *mojarra à la Lamanai* (Mayan-spiced snapper cooked in banana leaf) and blackened fish (catch of the day marinated in lime juice, olive oil and balsamic vinegar). Service is excellent; you get cooling hand towels soaked in eucalyptus water on arrival and the restaurant offers courtesy hotel pick-up and drop-off.

$$$ La Palmilla, Victoria House resort, see page 74. This place combines one of the most adventurous menus on the island with great service and a wonderful location. Chef José Luís Ortega is one of the best chefs in Belize and honed his skills at **Hugo's** in Houston. The best dishes are contemporary Latin American seafood and include starters like conch ceviche (served with avocado and sweet, mild *guajillo* chilli peppers) and wonderfully succulent pan-fried scallops served with tiny fish cakes, and mains like oven-roasted snapper in ginger-lime sauce and cashew-crusted grouper. There are also international dishes like Angus fillet steak. Unless it's breezy, opt to eat intimately by candlelight next to the pool.

$$$ Le Bistro Portofino, Portofino resort, see page 74. Belize meets Europe in an elegant fusion of tropical Belizean ingredients and Franco-Belgian cooking at this relaxed little bistro. On the upper deck of a lovely thatch-roof *cabaña* restaurant, it has wonderful ocean views. Dishes include beef sautéed in blue cheese and a delicious seafood platter. The restaurant is loveliest in the evening. Ask for a table in the open-sided part of the restaurant and arrive before sundown for cocktails in the **Green Parrot** bar downstairs.

$$$ Rendezvous Restaurant and Winery, beachfront 3½ miles north of San Pedro, 226-3426, ambergriscaye.com/rendezvous. If you're tired of burgers, beach bar snacks and seafood, sample some Thai and French cooking here, washed down with the restaurant's own Rendezvous Estate Belizean Wine, one of just a handful of wineries in the American tropics.

$$ Rojo Lounge, Azul resort, see page 73. This place offers chic-shack dining under an open-sided *palapa* overlooking the water at one of the island's swankiest resorts. Cooking is comfort food not fine dining. Come with a hearty appetite and expect rich sauces and strong flavours. Record producer-turned-chef Jeff Spiegel tours the world with his menu and creates his own fusions, from lobster pasta with arugula pesto to guava-glazed ribs with peanut slaw.

$-$ Legends Burger House, 500 yds north of the Boca del Rio bridge north of the town centre, T226-2113, legendsburgerhouse.com. Belizeans and tourists alike come from all over the island to eat and party in this burger restaurant housed in a handsome, big, blue stilted weatherboard mansion. There's a

huge choice of burgers, said to be the best in Belize. All are huge and come with plain or spicy Cajun chips (fries). Those with bottomless stomachs can attempt the King Kong challenge: 2.5 kg of burger, cheese and bacon with 3 fried eggs and 500 g of chips, to be eaten in 30 mins. Those who complete the challenge eat for free and get their picture on the Wall of Fame. Unsurprisingly, the wall is currently empty. **Legends** draws a buzzing crowd and live music most nights, but things get busiest on Tue from 1900 when local musicians come here to jam.

$$-$ Palapa Bar and Grill, 1½ miles north of San Pedro, T226-2528, www.palapabarandgrill.com. Closes at 2100. This self-proclaimed 'world famous' bar and grill sitting on stilts over the water closes very early for a dinner restaurant or buzzing night spot. Come during the day to snorkel around the pier and then sit at the palm-thatch bar in your swimwear and sip an ice-cold Belikin.

Bars and clubs

Most bars are listed with restaurants above.

San Pedro *p59, map p60*
1755 Lounge Bar, on the beach between Buccaneer and Black Coral sts. Draws a mixed gay and straight crowd.
Jaguar Temple, Barrier Reef Dr, between Buccaneer and Ambergris sts, www.jaguarstempleclub.com. A full-on dance club in a mini-warehouse with 600 capacity.

Festivals

Feb International Bill Fish Tournament.
Feb-Mar San Pedro Carnival. Usually weekend before Mardi Gras (Shrove Tue)
Jun Dia de San Pedro. A 3-day festival honouring the patron saint of the town. Live music from Kriol, Garifuna and Mayan marimba bands and ceremonies with the blessing of boats.

O Shopping

San Pedro *p59, map p60*
You won't find piles of bargain-priced gorgeous arts, crafts and textiles in San Pedro. The numerous gift shops in the centre mostly sell the predictable tourist tack you might expect to find in small beach town Florida. But there are some exceptions.

There are supermarkets and convenience stores throughout San Pedro town centre. **Richie's** and the **Island Supermarket** are the largest. Check your change in all shops.

Art
Belizean Arts, in the shopping arcade behind **Fido's**, T226-3101. This arcade has a few interesting shops of a generally higher quality, including this one, which stocks original art and sculpture from a number of the country's leading artists, including Pen Cayetano, Piva, Leo Vasquez and Nelson Young. Look out for Piva's haunting images of elderly Maya, Vasquez's impressionistic landscapes and Eduardo Garcia's figures in tropical forest scenes reminiscent of *Le Douanier* by Rousseau.

Cigars and liquor
Rum & Cigar House, Pescador Dr between Buccaneer and Ambergris sts. Americans hankering after domestically prohibited Cuban cigars should visit this shop, which also stocks Belizean and Caribbean rums and Guatemalan coffee.

Clothing and accessories
Caribe Creations, Barrier Reef Dr between Buccaneer and Ambergris sts, T226-3803. Stocks a broad range of colourful flowing dresses and skirts, Hawaiian shirts and vivid ties.
Mambo Chill, in the shopping arcade behind **Fido's**. Elegant beachwear (Belizean and imported), hippy chic jewellery and leather and reed sandals.

Fishing gear
Tres Pescados Fly Fishing Shop, Barrier Reef Dr at Sandpiper St, next to **Sun Breeze Suites** hotel, T226-3474, www.belizefly.com. Closed Sun. Bait, tackle, equipment and advice.

Handicrafts
Mexicans from the Yucatán and Chiapas sell their wares in the square around San Pedro Catholic church. Prices are higher than in Chiapas or Mérida, but if you aren't going to either you can pick up embroidered Mayan *huipil* shirts and Mérida cotton hammocks here.
Orange Gifts, Coconut Dr, T226-4066, www.orangegifts.com. This company has been making some of the most beautiful turned bowls and vases in Belize since the late 1970s. They also produce contemporary art nouveau metalwork, Guatemalan-inspired leather accessories, and jewellery.

Jewellery
Ambergris Museum gift shop, see page 61. Sells jade jewellery.

O What to do

Birdwatching
Elbert Greer, T226-2405, elbertgreer@fast mail.fm. Early morning birding tours (pickup at 0530, return 1000), including a visit to an offshore caye with many water birds. See also page 66.

Boat tours
A number of companies on the island run boat tours to nearby cayes with stops for snorkelling, diving and beach picnics along the way. It is also possible to organize a glass bottom boat trip for around BZ$50, meaning that you can see the beauty of the reef even if you can't swim.
Reef Runner, 49 Barrier Reef Dr, T602-0858, www.ambergriscaye.com/reefrunner. 2 tours daily to Hol Chan Marine Reserve and

Shark Ray Alley leaving at 0900 and 1400 in a 7-m- long boat (with a viewing glass 50 cm wide and 5 m long), which has been in operation for over 15 years. A wooden roof offers shade or serves as a sunbathing platform. Departure points vary. Bookable through any hotel.

Seaduced by Belize, Vilma Linda Plaza, T226-2254, www.seaducedbybelize.com. Sailing and snorkelling trips in a 12-m-long Athena catamaran around the caye and further afield to Caye Caulker.

Searious, beachfront between Tarpon and Black Coral sts, T226-2690, seariousadventuresbelize.com. Sailing around the caye, including a sunset cruise, and full day trips to Caye Caulker.

Diving

There are numerous dive shops on the island offering packages around Ambergris Caye and further afield to many other cayes and atolls in northern Belize on half- and full-day excursions. Prices depend on distance, with shorter trips like Mexico Rocks or Tres Cocos being cheaper. Pricier ones go further afield, to Turneffe Atoll (see page 87), Lighthouse Reef, including the Blue Hole (see page 89), and Glover's Atoll (see page 145). Lunch and drinks are included.

Unless you're staying in a hotel with its own dive shop and buying a room and dive package, book your dives directly with the dive operators. Otherwise you will probably have to pay a surcharge. Also see dive cruise boats, page 24. Some of the best dive sites are close to town but not all are (see page 64). The best dive shops should ask you what you are looking for, such as maximum marine life, a drift or night dive or a remote site. Bespoke dive trips cost more than scheduled runs to the Blue Hole or Hol Chan.

Ambergris Divers, Ambergris Divers pier, beachfront at Black Coral St or at the **Banana Beach Resort**, T226-2634, ambergrisdivers. com. This company is strong on local

knowledge and is one of the longest established San Pedro-owned Ambergris dive shops. They offer scuba instruction to Advanced Open Water level (including Discover Scuba), snorkel trips and dives to a wide choice of sites around the island and further afield to Lighthouse and Turneffe.

Belize Diving Adventures, next door to **Changes in Latitude B&B**, T226-3082, www.belizedivingadventures.net. A well-run, responsible small operator offering trips around Ambergris Caye and to Turneffe and Lighthouse for attractive prices. Instruction up to Advanced Open Water and tours to the sights on the mainland.

Chuck & Robbie, T610-4424, www.ambergris cayediving.com. Chuck and Robbie specialize in Ambergris Caye itself (rather than the outer atolls) and have one of the most extensive menus of local dives, from more remote sites on the Mexican border to Hol Chan or around the Mexico Rocks.

Ecologic Divers, on the pier next door to **Phoenix Resort**, T226-4118, www.ecologic divers.com. One of the largest and best-equipped dive companies on the island, with the usual gamut of trips around Ambergris Caye (including Basil Jones Canyons in Bacalar Chico), as well as dives further afield to Lighthouse and Turneffe. Longer trips are taken on sailing catamarans. The company also runs an extensive range of PADI courses up to and including Nitrox, Emergency First Response, Rescue and Divemaster levels. The company is very popular and the large dive boats are usually full.

Hugh Parkey's, on the beachfront in front of **Sunbreeze** hotel (see page 70), T220-4024, www.hpbelizeadventures.com. Although this company is relatively new on Ambergris Caye, it's been operating from Spanish Lookout Caye for many years and is well respected in Belize for its good boats, reliable equipment and excellent instructors and dive masters. They offer dives around Ambergris Caye and further afield to Lighthouse and Turneffe. Tours also available.

Fishing

Fishing licences are obtainable from the **Coastal Zone Management Authority and Institute** (www.coastalzonebelize. org). There is an online form or the licences can be obtained through **El Pescador,** the best resort for fishermen on the caye (see page 73) or **Tres Pescados** fishing shop, see above. Most dive shops and hotels can also organize fishing trips. Expect to pay BZ$250-350 per person for a full day's fly, reef or deep-sea fishing trip with bait and tackle, beer, soft drinks and lunch. See also page 66.

Belize Fish Finder, www.belizefishfinder. com. An online resource for fishing off Ambergris Caye, including fly, blue water, night fishing and annual tournaments. You can also charter a boat through the site.

El Pescador, see page 73. Offers the best options for fishing holidays, with attractive packages just for anglers or for the whole family.

Tres Pescados Fly Fish Tours, Barrier Reef Dr at Sandpiper St, next to **Sunbreeze Suites** hotel, T226-3474, www.belizefly.com. Some of the best trips on the island using some of Belize's most professional fishing guides. BZ$700 for the day for 2 anglers in a skiff with fuel, tackle, ice and refreshments. They also have a shop supplying everything you need to go fishing on Ambergris Caye.

Spas

Black Orchid Spa, Vilma Linda Plaza, T226-3939, blackorchidspa.com. Smart spa offering all manner of treatments including wraps, facials and scrubs as well as aromatherapy, Thai and Swedish massage.

Sol Spa, Phoenix Resort, see page 70. Maya abdominal, aromatherapy and reflexology massage, yoga, facials, wraps and treatments.

Watersports

Sailsports, seafront next to **Caribbean Beach** hotel, T226-4488, www.sailsportsbelize.com. Organizes windsurfing, kitesurfing and sailing

in 17-ft Getways and 14-ft Hobie Waves, with guides and/or instruction.

TMM, T226-3026, T1-800 633 0155 (US), www.sailtmm.com. Yacht and catamaran hire. Contact before arriving in Belize.

⊖ Transport

Air

The airport is tiny and can only receive small propeller planes. **Tropic** (www. tropicair.com) and **Maya Island Air** (www. mayaislandair.com) both fly to **Belize City** more than 6 times daily, 20 mins, BZ$85 one way, BZ$150 return. Tropic also flies to **Corozal** 6 times daily, 25 mins (BZ$110 one way, BZ$190 return), 4 of them via **Sarteneja**, 10 mins; to **Belmopan** 3 times daily, 50 mins BZ$190 one way, BZ$333 return; to **Caye Caulker** on request to cities throughout Belize (via Belize City); to **Guatemala City** and **Flores**, for Tikal. Maya Island also flies to **Caye Caulker** and **Caye Chapel** and cities throughout Belize through connections in Belize City.

Bicycle and golf cart hire

Bikes and golf carts can easily be rented through hotels. Some even include use of the former in their accommodation rates. There are bicycle rental companies dotted throughout the town centre. They include **Frederick's** (Boca del Rio s/n, T206-2013) and **Joe's** (Pescador Dr s/n near Caribena, T226-4371). Expect to pay around BZ$15 for a half day and BZ$20-25 for a full day. Both **Cholo's** and **Island Golf Carts** have 4- and 6-seater carts.

Cholo's, Jewfish St, behind the fire station, T226-2627, http://ambergriscaye.com/ cholos. This company is about 10% cheaper than **Island Golf Carts** for hourly rates, the same price for daily rentals and more expensive for weekly rates. They charge extra for drop-offs.

Island Golf Carts, Coconut Dr s/n, T226-4343, www.islandgolfcarts.com. Rent carts by the hour (minimum 2 hrs BZ$50), day (BZ$135), week (BZ$565) or month (BZ$2100), and will pick you up from the airport or drop a cart off at your hotel. Drivers must be 21 years of age with a valid driver's licence and need to present a credit card for security deposit.

Boat

Boats can be booked through hotels who can usually organize connecting transport. All boats travel via Caye Caulker during day light hours only. First sailings are around 0700.

Services to **Belize City** are run by 3 companies: **Caye Caulker Water Taxi Association** (T226-0992, www.caye caulkerwatertaxi.com) with boats every hour, 90 mins, BZ$30 one way; **Water Jets Express** (T226-2194), 4 times daily, 60-80 mins, BZ$36 one way; **Belize Water Taxi** (T223-2225, belizewatertaxi.com), which have almost the same number of sailings to the same destinations as the Caye Caulker Water Taxi Association, for the same price.

Caye Caulker Water Taxi Association boats depart from their pier at the eastern end of Caribena St. The **Water Jets Express** terminal and pier is located at the lagoon end of Black Coral St next to the football pitch (soccer field), and immediately northeast of the airport. **Belize Water Taxi** boats arrive and depart from Front Dock, at the other, oceanside end of Black Coral St.

Thunderbolt (T610-4475, thunderbolt travels@yahoo.com), runs boats to **Corozal** on the Mexican border daily at 1500, 2 hrs, BZ$50 one way, returning at 0700. They leave from the Back Dock, on the western lagoon side of San Pedro next to the football pitch (soccer field).

San Pedro Jet Express (Lagoon Dock, T226 2194, sanpedrowatertaxi.com) runs to the municipal pier in **Chetumal** (daily 0830 and 1000, returning daily at 1530 and 1700, BZ$85). **San Pedro Belize Express** runs a less reliable service (Ambergris Dock, San Pedro, T226-3535, Fri, Sat, Sun, Mon 0715 and 0930, returning from the municipal pier in Chetumal at 0300 and 0515, BZ$85). From late 2012 there will be a daily boat service to **Xcalak** in Mexico.

There is now also a **Coastal Express Water Taxi** running along the coast of San Pedro between the Amigos del Mar dock and Blue Reef roughly every 2 hrs at half past the hour 0530-0100.

❶ Directory

Banks Atlantic Bank (Pescador Dr s/n and Barrier Reef Dr s/n, T226-2195, www. atlabank.com) and Belize Bank (Barrier Reef Dr, T226-2482, www.belizebank.com) are both in the town centre, change money and have ATMs. There are additional ATMs dotted throughout San Pedro, including in supermarkets. Smaller restaurants will take US$ as readily as Belizean currency. Many smaller businesses will also accept Mexican pesos. **Medical services** San Pedro Polyclinic II, T226-2436. San Carlos Pharmacy, Pescador Dr between Pelican and Caribena. **Useful numbers** Tourist police, T206-2022.

Caye Caulker, smaller cayes and outer atolls

This laid-back little island of swaying palms and sandy streets lined with painted weatherboard houses has been a pit stop on the Central America overland trail since the 1970s. Independent travellers still flock here to snorkel or dive, dance to reggae and punta rock, sip Belikin beer next to the water at the Lazy Lizard bar, or to while away the afternoon doing nothing much at all as the sun sinks golden over the horizon. With the wealth of boat tours and waterfront watering holes and the rock-bottom hotel and restaurant rates, few travellers seem to mind that the caye has no beach, and many seem to end up staying here far longer than they'd anticipated. Two atolls further south, Lighthouse and Turneffe, have superb diving and fishing.

▸▸ For listings, see pages 91-96.

Arriving in Caye Caulker → *Population: 1300. Colour map A3.*

Getting there

The airport is a sandy strip between the mangroves with a weatherboard shack doubling up as airport terminal and waiting room. Caye Caulker's airport lies at the far south of town beyond the cemetery, around 15 minutes' walk, or five minutes in a golf cart taxi. Most hotels will send a cart to meet you given notice. You'll have to walk to the guesthouses.

Boats from Belize City and San Pedro with the **Caye Caulker Water Taxi Association** arrive at their boat pier off Avenida Hicaco (Front Street) at Calle al Sol. **Belize Water Taxi** boats arrive at the pier on Avenida Hicaco at Pasero Street (near the Police Station) and **Water Jets Express** boats (including those from Chetumal) arrive at 'Back Dock' – the lagoon side dock, on the other side of the island from Avenida Hicaco.

Getting around

There are no cars on Caye Caulker, and precious few golf buggies. The island's only town is so small it takes less than 30 minutes to walk it end to end, from the Split to the airstrip. Bikes are easily hired through guesthouses.

Tourist information

The local municipal authority runs the **Caye Caulker Belize Tourism Industry Association** (**CCBTIA**), which has no office but does have a useful website, www.gocayecaulker.com.

Safety

Be wary of the professional rastas who loiter around Caye Caulker. Very few are locals, though many are locally renowned, usually for their predatory behaviour towards female travellers and for making money from tourists rather than tourism.

Flora on Caye Caulker

The tiny size of Belize's cayes makes their terrestrial ecosystems particularly vulnerable to destruction. This is especially true of plants. Yet whilst the plants of mainland Belize have been fairly extensively catalogued, the cayes are as yet little explored by botanists. Caye Caulker, whose forests are increasingly being felled for holiday homes and hotels, is one of the few cayes whose plants have been inventoried as part of a project carried out by the island tourist board (the CCBTIA), see Tourist information, above. And, despite the island's

Caye Caulker

tiny size, the diversity of species the CCBTIA have so far discovered is astounding.

This is perhaps fitting as the island is named after a bush. 'Caulker' is a corruption of the Spanish *hicaco*, the name for the coco plum (*Chrysobalanus icaco*), a salt-tolerant fruiting shrub with leathery leaves used in the Caribbean to prevent beach erosion. You can still see plenty of the bushes along Hicaco Street. Look out for the small, white, waxy flowers (which appear in late spring) or the apricot-coloured summer fruits. These are very tart but make good jam.

The coco plum is one of a number of unusual flowering shrubs you will see on the island. Others include the pretty red maiden berry (*Crossopetalum rhacoma*), a plant usually associated with Florida and not found anywhere else in Belize but here; the sea grape (*Coccoloba uvifera*), a relative of buckwheat producing purplish fruit in grape-like bunches; and the highly toxic poisonwood (*Metopium browneii*), which can induce a rash just by standing in its shade; and its antidote, the gumbo-limbo (*Bursera simaruba*), a hurricane-resistant tall tree adapted to calciferous soils that grows in amongst the mangrove forests. Sea beans (*Mucuna* and *Oromosia* sp), whose 'horse eye' or 'hamburger' seeds are a common sight on beaches throughout the tropical Americas, are fairly abundant

Where to stay 🏠
Barefoot Caribe 1
Blue Wave Guest House 2
Caye Caulker Plaza 5
Caye Reef 3
De Real Macaw 4
Edith's 8
Ignacio Beach Cabins 9
Iguana Reef Inn 10
Island Magic 6
Lazy Iguana 11
Mara's 7
Miramar 12
Pancho's Villas 16
Rainbow 18
Sea Dreams 20
Seaside Cabañas 21
Tree Tops 25

Tropical Paradise 13
Tropics 23
Yuma's House 24

Restaurants 🍴
Glenda's 1
Julia's 2
Rainbow 9
Rose's Bar & Grill 10
Sobre Las Olas 3
Syd's 4
Tomboy 5

in the north of the island. All these plants sit alongside abundant red, white and black mangroves, coconut palms, bougainvilleas, amaryllis and hummingbirds (which despite their name are native to Southeast Asia, where they are used to flavour coconut curries).

Places in Caye Caulker

The five-mile-long Caye Caulker was one island until it was literally blown apart by Hurricane Hattie in 1961. The northern portion is all mangrove and wild forest. The inhabited southern half of the island begins at the point of divide, known locally as The Split. **The Split** is a convex dirt- and sand-floored promontory, fronted by small harbour wall and shaded by a few palms. This is the nearest thing Caye Caulker has to a beach.

There are no sights on Caye Caulker beyond this reserve, the reef, the remnant forest and pretty little **Caye Caulker village** itself. Unlike San Pedro this still retains many of its original weatherboard wooden buildings, as well as a laid-back island lifestyle. The village stretches south of the Split and takes up less than half of the inhabited side of the island. Avenida Hicaco (aka Front Street) is the main drag: half a mile or so of small waterfront hotels and weatherboard homes. Hicaco's middle reaches are fronted by a sandy path, optimistically called Playa Asuncion, although it's barely a beach at all. Most of the action takes place on the streets in the middle of town a few hundred yards to the south: Pasero, al Sol, Aventurera and Estrella streets. The two-acre **Caye Caulker Mini-reserve** ① *just north of the airstrip between Mangle (Back) St and the beach, daily 24 hrs, self-guided tours free, visitor centre with books and pamphlets daily 0800-1200, free, www.gocayecaulker.com*, preserves some of the plants listed in the Flora section above.

Caye Caulker Forest and Marine Reserve → *Colour map A3.*

Some 100 acres of the northern section of Caye Caulker have been reclaimed from coconut plantations grown before the arrival of Hurricane Hattie and are now wild and protected as a forest reserve. This comprises extensive stands of red, black and white mangrove forest broken with shallow lagoons and dotted with terra firma forest. Gumbo-limbo, buttonwood, strangler fig, poisonwood, coconut palms and invasive casuarina grow in the latter and the reserve. It is ringed with eel grass beds, which run out to the reef half a mile offshore. There is plenty of wildlife. Scaly-tailed iguanas laze in the trees, American crocodiles wallow in the shallow lagoons, turtles and manatees graze in the eel grass beds and mangrove warblers flit around the undergrowth. And there are abundant other birds, including some species difficult to see elsewhere, such as white-crowned pigeons, rufous-necked rails and black catbirds. Beyond a simple visitor centre there is little infrastructure in the reserve, but visits can be arranged through hotels or Caye Caulker tour companies (see page 95).

The **Caye Caulker Marine Reserve** protects the eel grass lagoon in front of the Caye Caulker Forest Reserve and the **Belize Barrier Reef** (see box, page 69) that runs parallel to the entire caye, extending to about a mile beyond the reef wall. It covers most of the snorkel sites (see below).

Diving and snorkelling

Caye Caulker does not have the same level of infrastructure as Ambergris Caye or that island's diversity of dive sites. But like Ambergris Caye, Caulker is in close proximity to the Hol Chan Marine Reserve and Shark Ray Alley (see page 68), and it has a number of excellent dive shops, see page 95, which visit both locations as well as Turneffe and Lighthouse reefs.

Along Caye Caulker itself the water is shallow and the reef has been damaged in places by clumsy boat manoeuvring and mooring. The outer wall offers spur and groove diving, with a few deep canyons, swim-throughs and fissures in the reef, and most dives are beginner or intermediate.

However, Caye Caulker is one of the best cayes for **snorkelling**. The water is shallow, warm and has abundant life, and the many companies offer some of the best-value boat trips in Belize. The inner reef is excellent for novice snorkellers. The water is seldom more than a few feet deep and there's plenty of variety. Many snorkel trips also visit Hol Chan and Shark-Ray Alley, and, as these are designated snorkel trips, snorkellers have their own guides and will not feel like a tag-on to a dive trip, as they would visiting from Ambergris Caye.

Smaller cayes → *For listings, see pages 91-96. Colour map B3.*

The tiny island of **Little Frenchman's Caye** – with a pearly beach washed by shallow, turquoise water, a lovely reef for snorkelling and a group of adjacent mangrove islets visited by manatees – is devoted entirely to a low-scale resort, the **Royal Palm** (see page 93). It's a lovely spot for families and is an easy 20-minute boat ride from Belize City. Like Little Frenchman's Caye, nearby **Spanish Lookout Caye** is home to a resort, see page 93, one of Belize's longest established dive centres and not much else. The beach is far smaller than Little Frenchman's and there is a small area of protected mangrove forest. **St George's Caye** was the first capital of Belize and the site of the battle which finally saw off the Spanish (see page 205). There is little tourism on the island, just one dive resort, the **St George's Caye Resort** (**$$$$**, www.gooddiving.com), some wooden residential homes and, in the south, a protected mangrove reserve. **Swallow Caye** (www.swallowcayemanatees.org) is a wildlife reserve protecting West Indian manatees; it can be visited with a Caye Caulker tour company, see page 95. **Little Iguana Caye** and **Rosario Caye** are two tiny wildlife sanctuaries managed by **Green Reef** (see page 67). They are a short boat ride from San Pedro, and are excellent places to spot water birds including roseate spoonbills and reddish egrets.

Turneffe Atoll → *For listings, see pages 91-96. Colour map B3.*

This 300 sq mile archipelago enclosed within the largest atoll in the Atlantic is one of the wildest and most biologically diverse ecosystems in Belize and a popular destination for divers and fishermen seeking pristine marine wilderness. The atoll is made up of nine different marine habitats. As well as fringing reef, coral beds and shoreline there are more than 200 mangrove islets, which serve as a natural nursery for a wide variety marine animals including reef and pelagic fish species, American crocodile (who live in the atoll in large numbers) and reef sharks. The reefs themselves have abundant eagle rays, large green morays, huge jewfish, nurse and grey reef sharks, trunkfish, groupers, snappers, permits, horse-eye jacks and whitespotted toadfish, which is endemic to Belize. Dolphins and turtles are a common sight and the atoll is one of the best places in the Caribbean for fishing bonefish, tarpon and permit. It is an important refuge for marine birds, both on the principal 16 acre island and on the bushy islets themselves. There are many frigate birds, boobies and a large resident osprey population.

There's an impressive diversity of plant species too, including extensive palmetto thickets and savannas, as well as mangrove, beach thickets, cocal, and cave forest. There are also small Mayan sites on the atoll.

Atolls

Atolls are circular, oval or horseshoe-shaped rings of coral, sometimes forming low sandy islands, surrounding a central lagoon. It was Darwin who first postulated how they are formed: when coral grows in the waters around volcanic peaks, often sticking up out of deep water. As the volcano cools and becomes denser, these peaks erode or sink, with only the coral ring remaining. The ring persists over millions of years as new corals grow on top of the old, often resulting in plunging, near-vertical walls at the edge of the atoll as it falls into deep ocean. Scientists have drilled over 1400 m through coral limestone before striking volcanic rock on large Pacific atolls.

Atolls vary enormously in size. Most are found in the Pacific and Indian oceans. It is often said that there are just four atolls in the Atlantic, three of them off Belize. This is not the case; there are between 10 and 30, depending on the geologist undertaking the count, including Glover's, Lighthouse and Turneffe off Belize, the Banco Chinchorro off the Yucatán in Mexico and the spectacular isolated Atol das Rocas in the Southern Atlantic off Brazil.

The atoll's fragile and unique ecosystems are under increased threats from improper tourist development which includes dredging the shallows for boat passage, clearing and deforestation of the smaller back reef cayes (resulting in erosion to the atoll), pollution from hotel rubbish and environmentally insensitive over-water development. For more information on how you can help and what you should avoid see www.turneffeatoll.org.

Visiting Turneffe Atoll

Access to the atoll is only available on day trips or by private transfers, either through one of the two tourist lodges on Turneffe (see page 93) or as part of a day's dive trip from Ambergris Caye, see page 81, or Caye Caulker, see page 95.

Diving

The southern end of the atoll, known as The Elbow, is the most commonly used dive site and almost all dive boats come here. Turneffe is the largest of Belize's atolls and the only one with extensive tracts of mangrove, which fringe the vast areas of shallow flats in the interior of the atoll. Most diving takes place at the southern end of the atoll, making other sites exciting as they are little visited and the marine life remains relatively undisturbed. Fish, invertebrates and corals exist in a variety and abundance unmatched in the Caribbean. Deep water and a substantial distance from the mainland mean excellent underwater visibility, normally in excess of 30 m and often up to 50 m. Large pelagics, rays, turtles, eels, and schools of snapper, jacks and permit are common sights.

Whilst the west of Turneffe is dominated by spur-and-groove formations, the entire eastern shoreline is fringed with a continuous vertical reef 37 miles long. From this reef's highest point, a narrow ledge drops over some 100 m to reach an average depth of 18 m where the drop-off begins. Along this ledge are a number of spur-and-groove formations which are host to abundant fish communities. At around 45 m there is a horizontal ridge followed by another at 75 m. These ridges extend throughout the length of the reef.

Turneffe has numerous dive sites, full details of which can be found on ambergriscaye. com. They include **Majestic Point** (15 m, intermediate), a small promontory in a huge coral buttress hanging over a deep drop-off; **Lefty's Ledge** (15 m, intermediate) with abundant shoals of jacks and permits; **Myrtle's Turtles** (30 m, intermediate), a deep dive with spectacular ridges and schooling tuna and mackerel; **The Elbow** (30 m, advanced), where there are strong swells but abundant large pelagics including large sharks and dozens of eagles rays; **Permit Paradise** (18 m, beginner), with brain and boulder corals and many permits; **Triple Anchors** (12-18 m, beginners), with beautiful coral formations and impressive sponges; **Hollywood** (15 m, beginner), with brain, lettuce and boulder corals and abundant common reef fish; and the **Wreck of the Sayonara** (15 m, beginner), a former cargo boat sunk in 1985 and covered in huge sponges.

Lighthouse Reef → *For listings, see pages 91-96. Colour map B3.*

Belize's remotest and most easterly atoll sits 43 miles offshore. From above it seems like an opal of turquoise, pearly whites and dark blues set in an inky Atlantic. The atoll is only slightly smaller than Turneffe (at 240 sq miles) and unlike Turneffe its shallows are coloured with coral gardens and sandy flats with great diving, and perforated by the Blue Hole, a deep round fissure as dark as the pupil of an eye and set in opal and aquamarine-coloured iris of water. Lighthouse is dotted with six tiny sandy cayes.

Dive or snorkel trips to the Blue Hole usually include a trip to the pretty little coral island of **Half Moon Caye**, which as its name suggests is dominated by a sickle-shaped white-sand beach. It's one of the most photogenic in Belize and is also a wildlife sanctuary. Trails lead through the scrubby forest to a viewing platform from where you can observe a big colony of some 4000 red-footed boobies, the smallest members of their seabird family (with a wing-span of around 1 m). Although the birds are found widely in the tropics this is thought to be their only nesting site in the Western Caribbean. The island is home to two rare reptiles: the island leaf-toed gecko, which is endemic to Belize, and Allison's anole.

Diving

The Blue Hole (30 m plus, intermediate-advanced) Belize's most famous and photographed tourist attraction is a perfectly circular perforation in the reef whose dark water contrasts with the turquoise of the surrounding reef. At 100 m across and 145 m deep, it's the largest oceanic sinkhole so far discovered (though not the deepest). It looks spectacular from the air and, whilst its anoxic waters harbour little life, the hole is encrusted with spectacular rock formations and caverns and is one of Central America's most celebrated dive sites.

Like other blue holes, Belize's Blue Hole is a vertical cave or sinkhole formed when the roof of a cavern previously on dry land collapsed under the weight of sea water after it was flooded by the Atlantic. The Blue Hole's sheer walls drop into murky blue for 35 m before the hole opens up to reveal massive overhangs which lead into the original cave, and scores of flowstones, stalactites and stalagmites, some almost 10 m tall. The water is glassy clear (with visibility of up to 50 m). There's almost no current and, because of the anoxic nature of the water, very little marine life, except the occasional lazy, undulating reef or hammerhead shark. The bottom of the cave is still a dizzying 100 m below and at this depth, when nitrogen intoxication begins and in the vast blue, it's easy to get disorientated or lose one's buoyancy control.

The Blue Hole has been protected as part of a small marine reserve since the late 1970s. There are abundant reef fish and crustaceans in the coral gardens which ring the Hole's mouth; look out for Pederson's cleaning shrimp around the ringed and knobby anemones –

they will even clean your hand if you hold it out for them – and the brilliant neon gobies, angelfish, butterfly fish, trangs and groupers. Elkhorn coral and purple sea fans grow around the rim, the latter waving in the gentle current and reflected in spectacular colour in the mirror of the surface of the sea.

Half Moon Caye Wall (15 m to unlimited, beginner) This is the atoll's most celebrated dive after the Blue Hole. A sheer ridge of coral cut with spurs and grooves drops directly into the oceanic abyss to a depth of over 2000 m. Sandy coral gardens with huge corals set on a white-sand bottom and with abundant garden eels lead to spur-and-groove canyons encrusted with myriad corals and some of the most spectacular sponge formations in the Caribbean and cut with swim-throughs. Large pelagics and turtles hover in the deep water off the drop-off's edge.

Hat Caye Drop-off (15 m to unlimited, beginner) and **Long Caye Ridge** (12 m to unlimited, beginner) These offer a similar experience to the Half Moon Caye Wall. Hat Caye Drop-off has a very shallow reef leading to a deep drop-off. There are some huge yellow tube sponges here, plenty of unusual coral and many fish. Long Caye Ridge is a promontory jutting into the ocean encrusted with hundreds of sponges.

Tres Cocos (9 m to unlimited, beginner) Just off the atoll's largest island, this is famous for its beautiful coral arches, sponges and soft corals and is one of the most popular spots in Belize for visiting professional dive photographers.

Silver Caves (12 m to unlimited, intermediate) This is named after the silverside minnows which are abundant here, and is one of the few spots where nocturnal reef fish and animals can be seen during the day.

For hotel and restaurant price codes and other relevant information, see pages 11-12.

◉ Where to stay

Many resorts on the cayes and outer reefs offer complete Belize packages including jungle trips and Mayan ruins. You are better off avoiding these, staying on the cayes or atolls for diving and staying at a designated rainforest resort for your inland Belize trips. You'll get better value this way and won't have to spend so much time on long boat trips in and out of Belize City.

Caye Caulker village *p86, map p85*
$$$$ Caye Reef, T226-0382, www.caye reef.com. Bright, tastefully decorated and well-appointed apartments in a big, ugly lemon-coloured concrete block overlooking the water. Each has its own sitting room (with a sofa bed), kitchen and bedroom, private balcony (with breakfast table) and is decorated with colourful paintings from local artists. There is a rooftop sun lounge area with a hot tub and staff offer attentive service. There is a pool, bar, tours, Wi-Fi and cable TV. Breakfast is included. Credit cards accepted. **Island Magic** is very similar but better value.
$$$$ Seaside Cabañas, far northern end of Playa Asunción next to the water taxi jetty, T226-0498, www.seasidecabanas. com. Despite its name, this mock-hacienda feels more mini-resort than beach *cabaña*. The bulk of the rooms are in long motel-like wings overlooking a small pool, bar and deck. A few are in larger, thatched-roof duplex cabins, next to the pool. Interior decor is mock Mexico-meets-Marrakech with rich lemon yellows, scatter cushions and Moorish lamps. Discounts on longer stays. No children under 10 years old. There are tours, Wi-Fi and cable TV. Credit cards accepted.
$$$$-$$$ Iguana Reef Inn, T226-0213, next to football pitch, www.iguanareefinn. com. One of the better hotels on the island

with large, brightly decorated, cheerful a/c rooms with fridges, comfortable beds and en suites with tubs. Some have porches and sea views. The hotel is in a quiet area on the lagoon side of the caye. There is a pool, bar, tours, Wi-Fi and cable TV. Breakfast is included. Credit cards accepted.
$$$$-$$$ Sea Dreams, at north end of the island, T226-0602, www.seadreamsbelize. com. There is a wealth of rooms to choose from in this waterfront hotel, from expansive houses and apartments with space for a family or 2, to small but cosy courtyard rooms. 10% of profits go to a community school established by co-owner Heidi Curry. Special prices on fishing packages. There are complimentary canoes and bikes, as well as tours, Wi-Fi and cable TV. Breakfast is included. Credit cards accepted.
$$$ Caye Caulker Plaza, Av Langosta s/n, T226-0780, www.cayecaulkerplazahotel. com. Together with **Island Magic**, this is the plushest, but not the priciest, hotel on the island. Rooms are large, well appointed and comfortable, with effective a/c units and bathrooms with powerful hot-water showers. Welcoming and efficient service. Yoga and massage. There are tours, Wi-Fi and cable TV. Credit cards accepted.
$$$ Island Magic, Av Hicaco s/n, T226-0505, www.islandmagicbelize.com. This beachside pile with a lovely pool and bar has some of the most upmarket rooms in Caye Caulker. They are bright, with quality bedlinen and curtains, flatscreen TV with cable, kitchenettes and balconies with sun loungers. The huge honeymoon suite is *the* room with a view on Caye Caulker – with wonderful ocean views from a big airy balcony and acres of space. There are tours and Wi-Fi. Credit cards accepted.
$$$ Lazy Iguana, Almina Dr s/n southwest side of the village, a block from the cemetery, T226-0350, www.lazyiguana.net. This carefully crafted B&B has just a handful of large, attractive rooms decorated with

Belizean art and furnished with wooden tables and chairs and queen-sized beds. There are great views from the rooms and the roof deck. The hotel collects and uses rainwater, rents kayaks and offers massages for guests. There is also a pool, tours, Wi-Fi and cable TV. Breakfast is included. Credit cards accepted.

$$$-$$ Pancho's Villas, Pasero St s/n, T226-0304, www.panchosvillasbelize.com. There are great views of the island from the rooftop sundeck in this blocky little hotel set away from the waterfront. There are suites only, with separate bed and living areas and kitchenettes. The largest are on the upper floors with space for up to 3 couples, making this hotel great value for groups. There is Wi-Fi and cable TV. Credit cards accepted.

$$$-$$ Tree Tops, T226-0240, www.tree topsbelize.com. With its pillared balconies and faux-lattice work, this welcoming hotel feels like it belongs in the southern US or Australia. A/c rooms and suites are stark but well kept and spacious. White walls are decorated with tribal art, hats, fans and ceramics. Most come with sea views and en suites. No children under 10. There are tours, cable TV and Wi-Fi. Credit cards accepted.

$$$-$ De Real Macaw, Av Hicaco s/n, T226-2459, www.derealmacaw.biz. This small beachfront establishment has a choice of wooden or tastefully designed concrete duplexes set in a shady garden. All have macaw-themed decor right down to the bed linen. Rooms are either a/c suites or a/c or fan-cooled doubles. Bathrooms are a little pokey. There is Wi-Fi and cable TV. Credit cards accepted.

$$ Barefoot Caribe, Av Hicaco, T226-0161, www.barefootcaribe.com. Big, colourful rooms with en suite bathrooms that have tubs. Some are a/c, some fan cooled, some have private balconies with sea views and a handful have space for 2 couples. Discounts are available through their website. There is also a restaurant, tours, Wi-Fi and cable TV. Credit cards accepted.

$$ Mara's, Split at Hattie St, T206-0056. Wooden *cabañas* in a good location overlooking the waterfront at the Split, near the **Lazy Lizard** bar. All are fan cooled and simply furnished, with hot-water en suites and small porches slung with hammocks.

$$ Rainbow, Av Hicaco s/n, T226-0123, www.rainbowhotel-cayecaulker.com. A big, sky-blue building on the waterfront with elegant, cosy rooms newly painted in warm yellows, all with sea views and verandas. Rooms have spacious en suites with hot water but lack storage space. There is also a restaurant, Wi-Fi and cable TV. Credit cards accepted.

$$ Tropical Paradise Hotel, 1 Luciano St, T226-0124, www.tropicalparadise-caye caulker.com. Recently renovated a/c or fan-cooled rooms in brightly painted wooden beach shacks, plus annexes of rather tired, boxy rooms. The best by far are the deluxe a/c *cabañas*, with private terrace, coffeemaker and more privacy and space. All rooms are en suite. The sister hotel, **Tropics** (same price, 18 Hicaco St, T226-0374, www.thetropicshotel.com), offers similar, though tatty, rooms. Both have attractive online discounts (minimum 2-night booking). There is also a tour operator and cable TV. Credit cards accepted.

$$-$ Blue Wave Guest House, T206-0114, www.bluewaveguesthouse.com. Simple but well-kept fan-cooled or a/c rooms in a small hotel just a short stroll from the waterfront. The cheapest rooms have shared bathrooms. Wi-Fi and cable TV. Credit cards accepted.

$$-$ Yuma's House (formerly **Tina's**), T206-0019, www.yumashousebelize.com. The fan-cooled rooms at this bright wooden hostel are simple. They range from large dorms to brighter doubles with shared balconies. Avoid dorm room 6 next to the stairs as it can get noisy. The hostel is in a great location a few steps from the waterfront and is run with stern hospital matron efficiency by the owner who keeps things squeaky clean and ensures that guests do not make too much noise or get drunk on the premises. There's a restaurant and Wi-Fi.

$ Edith's, C Langosta s/n, T206-0069, http://edithshotel.blogspot.com. This bright yellow wooden hostel and guesthouse owned and operated by local islander Tina Abel has long been a backpacker favourite. It offers 12 very simple but clean wooden rooms, with shared cold-water showers. All share a terrace and there is a communal kitchen. The owner also runs **Frenchies Diving** and offers dive package discounts.

$ Ignacio's Beach Cabins, T226-0175, facebook: Ignacio's Beach Cabins Caye Caulker. Very simple and small fan-cooled grape-coloured wooden huts on the beach just outside town to the south. The cheapest rooms have no hot water, all are in need of fresh paint, but the location is quieter than budget options in the heart of town. Book exchange, Wi-Fi and kayak and bike rental. Credit cards accepted.

$ Miramar, Av Hicaco s/n, T206-0357. Rooms in this 30-year-old timber building have few frills, being fan cooled with plain tile floors, wooden walls and tiny en suites. But the owner, Melinda, is friendly and helpful and the location next to the boat dock jetty couldn't be better. There's also a shared patio slung with hammocks.

$ Sandy Lane Guest House, Chapoose at Langosta, no phone. Rooms in this guesthouse are divided between a big central wooden building and white weatherboard huts clustered together in a sandy courtyard. All are well maintained and furnished with queen-sized beds and wooden tables and chairs. Some have shared bathrooms (with hot water) and a handful of the huts have cable TV and a kitchenette. Credit cards accepted.

Smaller cayes *p87*
$$$$ Hugh Parkey's Dive Resort, Spanish Lookout Caye, T220-4024, belizeadventure lodge.com. Attractive weatherboard cabins on stilts are connected by a boardwalk sitting over shallow clear-water flats. The dive centre is one of the longest-established in Belize, covering all the atolls and many of the best dives sites from here and from their dive shop in San Pedro (see page 81). Decent comfort food in the café restaurant.

$$$$ Royal Palm Island, Little Frenchman's Caye, T822-3344, T621-6762, www.royalpalm island.com. This lovely little family resort has an entire caye, beach and lagoons to itself. Accommodation is in simple weatherboard *casitas*, of the kind found on the Opal Coast in France. All have 2 bedrooms, sitting rooms and terraces with superb views over the ocean. Prices are good value – with all food, transfers and some excursions included. Kids under 6 stay for free and there's a dive shop, tours, spa, restaurant, bar. Breakfast included. Credit cards accepted.

Turneffe Atoll *p87*
$$$$ Turneffe Flats, T220-4046, www. tflats.com. The emphasis at this small

island resort set in the heart of the atoll is on watersports, with excellent facilities and guiding. Accommodation is in simple but elegant weatherboard a/c cabins, the best of which look out over the ocean. All rooms have decks and sit over the narrow but pretty island beach. There is a pool, dive shop, restaurant and tours. Prices are full board. Credit cards accepted.

$$$$ Turneffe Island Resort, www.turnefferesort.com. This large, US-run resort sitting on its own island in the atoll has large wooden cabins sitting on a white-sand beach, with outdoor showers and screened sun decks. All have wonderful ocean views and the most private sit on the edge of the resort furthest from the main lodge building (housing a restaurant and bar). Prices are full board. Fishing and diving trips can be organized through the lodge. Credit cards accepted.

Lighthouse Reef *p89*

$$$$ Huracan, Long Caye, T603 2930, www.huracandiving.com. It's hard to get remoter and wilder than this well-run, friendly diver resort right out on the outer reef. Sunsets and sunrises from the beach on the tiny island are unforgettable, with views over miles of ocean and, at night, the stars are as bright as moonlight. Accommodation is in fan-cooled smart wood-panelled rooms in a small chalet set in the forest. Prices are good value as they include full board (with delicious cooking from owner Ruth), transfers from Belize City, marine park fees and 8 dives, in a string of the best dive locations in Belize, including the Blue Hole. Minimum 4 nights. Credit cards accepted.

🍴 Restaurants

Caye Caulker village *p86, map p85*
As in most locations in Belize, bars double-up as restaurants and restaurants double-up as bars.

$$$-$$ Rainbow, Av Hicaco in front of the Rainbow hotel, T226-0281. Generous portion of fresh seafood served at rustic tables right on the water. Try the fillet of snapper or whole fried fish served with beans, rice, salad and coleslaw and washed down with juice or Belikin beer. Busy with day trippers at lunchtimes, more intimate in the evening.

$$$-$$ Rose's, C al Sol at Av Hicaco, T226-0407. One of Caye Caulker's most popular dinner spots, with tables spread out on a shady rustic wooden deck and ultra-fresh seafood, much of which is laid out in front of the shop in a colourful display.

$$$-$$ Sobre las Olas, in the Barefoot Caribe hotel, see page 92, T226-0161. Serves standard seafood options: grilled fish, lobster and ceviches, as well as great Caribbean coconut chicken and breakfasts of pancakes or burritos.

$ Glenda's, Aventurera St at Av Mangle, T226-0148. Open early. This bright blue weatherboard café with lino-covered wooden tables and a blackboard menu has a loyal host of regulars. They usually come for breakfast to eat omelettes, fresh cinnamon rolls and bread and fried jacks.

$ Julia's, Av Hicaco s/n. It's worth hunting down this little stall if only to stock up on litre bottles of freshly squeezed ice-cold juices – including cantaloupe, tamarind and watermelon – and the organic fruit and veg.

$ Syd's, Av Langosta at Aventurera. Decent fresh seafood and everyday Belizean fare like rice and beans and jacks. Popular with locals as well as tourists.

$ Tom Boy, Estrella St at Av Hicaco, T226-2991. Popular Indian dishes including *aloo ghobi*, *dhal* and *chana masala*, alongside fish, lobster and shrimp curries and burgers. Dishes are served at simple tables in an equally plain wood-walled dining room. As with most Belizean Indian cooking, curries are mild. Big and great value breakfasts.

○ Shopping

Caye Caulker village *p86, map p85*
Celi's Gift Shop, Av Hicaco s/n. This tiny boutique stocks a decent range of local and Caribbean music, including Garifuna records, featuring singers like Andy Palacio and Aurelio Martinez, from Stonetree (see page 210).

○ What to do

Caye Caulker village *p86, map p85*
Diving
Dive shops here offer a similar quality of diving to San Pedro but at a slightly cheaper price. Dive trips to Hol Chan Marine Reserve and Shark Ray Alley are slightly cheaper than from Ambergris Caye; BZ$90-100 for a 2-tank dive, and a similar price to Turneffe and Lighthouse, BZ$300 for a day trip with 3 dives. Divers tend to be younger independent travellers. There are just a handful of dive shops on the island.
Big Fish Dive Center, T226-0450, www.big fishdivecenter.com. Diving off Caye Caulker in Hol Chan, off smaller cayes including St George's and Sergeant's cayes and the Turneffe and Lighthouse atolls. PADI Open and Advanced open-water courses.
Frenchies, www.frenchiesdivingbelize. com. Room and dive discounts available in conjunction with **Edith's hotel** (see page 93).

Huracan Diving, see page 94. Dive packages are offered at this diver resort. Recommended.

Sailing
See also **E-Z Boy Tours**, below, for sailing trips.
Raggamuffin Tours, T226-0348, www.ragga muffintours.com. Offer a fun sunset cruise, BZ$60 per person, with drinks and music on a sailing boat, as well as a 3-day all-inclusive sailing tour to Placencia leaving Tue and Fri, BZ$800 per person, minimum 8 people including all food and 2 nights' camping on Rendezvous Caye and Tobacco Caye. It beats travelling by bus and is an increasingly popular trip.

Tour operators
Prices are consistent across all operators, so find someone you feel you can trust. The main trip is snorkelling in Hol Chan Marine Park and visiting Shark Ray Alley and San Pedro, BZ$55, equipment included. Snorkel trips can be combined with a yacht cruise. Kayaks can be rented and some companies offer camping trips around Caye Caulker.
Further afield there are other snorkelling trips, river and Maya site tours as well as excursions to Goff's Caye (a paradise-perfect circular island with good snorkelling), BZ$150; fishing trips BZ$350. Sunset tours are popular with snorkelling until dusk, BZ$70, and almost all tour operators will take you to the Caye Caulker Forest Reserve.

It is also possible to organize fly and blue-water fishing, manatee-watching and sea-kayaking with most operators.

Anwar Tours, T226-0327, www.anwartours.com. Offers snorkelling trips to Hol Chan, Shark Ray Alley, night snorkelling and trips to smaller cayes, including Swallow Caye (to see manatees) and the Coral Gardens at Caye Chapel, and crocodile- and seahorse-spotting tours. The manager Javier Novelo is recommended as a snorkelling guide.

E-Z Boy Tours, Av Hicaco, T226-0349, www.facebook.com/pages/EZ-Boy-Tours-Caye-Caulker/141314189258430. As well as the usual snorkelling tours, this company offers a seahorse-spotting, Maya archaeology and crocodile-spotting tour. It also runs sailing trips.

Raggamuffin Tours, see above. Tours to the Caye Caulker Marine Reserve and Hol Chan. They can also arrange fishing tours with local fishermen, full day, BZ$700 for 2 anglers.

⊖ Transport

Caye Caulker village *p86, map p85*
Air
All flights between **Belize City** and **Ambergris Caye** (**San Pedro**) will stop at Caye Caulker if there are passengers for the island. **Tropic** (www.tropicair.com) and **Maya Island Air** (www.mayaislandair.com) both fly the route between **Belize City**, Caye Caulker and **San Pedro** (Ambergris Caye) more than 12 times each daily, 15 mins, BZ$85 one way and BZ$150 return.

Caye Caulker flights to other destinations require a transfer in either San Pedro or Belize City. As with San Pedro, if you have an international connection, be sure that your flight arrives at **Phillip SW Goldson** and not the municipal airport.

Boat
Boats to **Belize City** are run by the same 3 companies as those from San Pedro, see page 83. All boats continue on to **San Pedro** on Ambergris Caye, 20 mins, BZ$15 one way.

Water Jets have a daily boat to **Chetumal** (Mexico) leaving at 0800 and returning from Chetumal at 1500, 2 hrs, BZ$80 one way. **Belize Water Taxis** sail to the municipal pier in Chetumal at 0700 (with a connection in San Pedro for immigration and customs) returning at 1530, 2 hrs, BZ$75 one way. See page 83 for contact details of both companies.

❶ Directory

Medical services There is no hospital on the island.

Contents

⁂Tikal

Cayo & the Maya Mountains

At a glance

⊖ **Getting around** The whole area is accessible by bus, taxi and hire car. Consider booking transport through a tour agency to minimize costs.

◉ **Time required** Allow 3 or 4 days to see Macal River or Mountain Pine Ridge, Xunantunich and ATM. If you want to explore the whole district, you'll need 5 days to a week.

☀ **Weather** It's warm and dry at around 15- 30°C Jan-May with cooler nights. It's more hot and humid May-Oct, with the possibility of hurricanes. Nov-Dec is warm with occasional colder spells of 13-15°C.

✘ **When not to go** May-Oct is hurricane season; Sep- Nov can be grey and overcast.

Cayo district is the heartland of wilderness Belize. Here the swampy plains rise into cave-pocked rainforest and then, higher still, into Mountain Pine Ridge, dripping with wispy waterfalls that fall onto canyon sides, pause in pools and fall again. Steep valleys are cut by rushing rivers and babbling brooks, and, in the far south, the forests of Chiquibul National Park stretch unbroken into Guatemala. Wildlife is abundant. Howler monkeys can be heard at dawn even in the towns and villages. There's a toucan on every other tree, and rare and endangered species, such as harpy eagle and jaguar, hunt in national parks.

The Maya are everywhere, living in myriad villages that speckle the district and spread into Guatemala. And they are remembered in ruined cities and unexcavated temples and tombs that rise in mounds from the forest. The district's capital, San Ignacio, is built around the ruins of their ancient city, Cahal Pech. Other magnificent temple cities lie nearby: at Xunantunich overlooking the Mopan river and, best of all, Caracol, one of the largest and least-visited Maya sites in Central America, sitting in the heart of pristine forest-covered wilderness. Sacred Maya caves are dotted around the hills: spectacular Crystal Cave in St Herman's Blue Hole National Park, with its tiny passages and vast caverns, and Actun Tunichil Muknal, where Maya skeletons lie melded into the flowstones in a natural temple of stalactites and stalagmites.

Despite its wilderness, Cayo is easy to visit. San Ignacio boasts the best selection of hotels and restaurants in inland Belize, together with a range of tour operators who can organize a trip anywhere in the country, or even to Tikal across in neighbouring Guatemala. And the forests of Mountain Pine Ridge and banks of the Macal river have abundant comfortable forest lodges and even a few options for budgeting backpackers.

San Ignacio and around

As the name would suggest, Belize feels more Hispanic in San Ignacio. Guatemala is a stone's throw away, and you'll hear melodic Central American Spanish spoken as often as thick Creole here. Highland Maya faces are more prevalent too, and many families living in the nearby villages have family just across the border.

San Ignacio is in reality two towns: San Ignacio itself and Santa Elena, which sits opposite, on the other side of the Macal River. Neither are of more than passing interest in themselves, but San Ignacio, which has all the tourist facilities, is an inevitable transit point and a comfortable base for trips into the rainforests and mountains nearby. It's the capital of Cayo district and the biggest city on the Western Highway. With a handful of decent restaurants, a few bars and a casino, it boasts the liveliest nightlife between the highlands of Guatemala and Belize City. San Ignacio is well connected with the rest of the country and with Guatemala, which lies 12 miles to the west at the frontier town of Benque Viejo. It is straightforward to arrange onward overland transport to that country from San Ignacio, and to organize a day or overnight excursion to the famous UNESCO-listed ruins at Tikal. ▶▶ For listings, see pages 111-120.

Arriving in San Ignacio
Getting there Buses arrive at Coronation Park in the centre of town.

Getting around and safety San Ignacio is easy to negotiate on foot. You can walk from the town centre to the outer suburbs in less than 30 minutes. Taxis to or from the edge of town or up the hill to Cahal Pech cost around BZ$8-10. The town is generally safe and trouble free.

Tourist information There are maps and pamphlets available at the **tourist information kiosk** ① *Mon-Fri 1000-1700*, on Coronation Park and at the visitor centre at Cahal Pech, see below.

Places in San Ignacio → *Colour map B1. Population 9925 (16,977 with the twin town of Santa Elena).*

Cahal Pech
① *www.nichbelize.org (click on Institute of Archaeology, then Archaeological sites & parks), daily 0600-1800, BZ$20, free for Belizeans on Sun. There is a visitor centre.*
The steep hill lying at the centre of San Ignacio is crowned with this crumbling ruined city of grassy plazas and stepped pyramids shaded by giant tropical trees. In the early mornings and late afternoons the ruins are visited by grazing *paca* (gibnut), which look like giant spotted guinea pigs, and myriad birds, including all three species of Belizean toucan. It's a wonderfully romantic location, particularly at a full moon, when the ruins are officially closed but easily seen from one of the neighbouring guesthouses. Despite the atmosphere and apparent exoticism of the name, Cahal Pech translates as 'the place of ticks'. They and their favourite prey of peccary and deer are long gone. So you can safely sit on the pyramids and gaze wistfully at the wonderful views, out over the surrounding forests and all the way into Guatemala on the western horizon.

Next to Caracol or nearby Xunantunich, Cahal Pech is tiny. But it's of great archaeological interest. Unlike both those cities, Cahal Pech preserves a large number of residential structures: corridors of rooms with stone beds all sitting under shady trees. And the site is far older than both Caracol and Xunantunich.

San Ignacio Hotel, Iguana Sanctuary and Butterfly farm
ⓘ *Western Hwy, T824-2034, www.sanignaciobelize.com, no set opening times, free.*
This small rehabilitation centre for green iguana and tropical butterflies is well worth a visit. It sits in pretty secondary growth forest planted with medicinal trees and bushes

San Ignacio

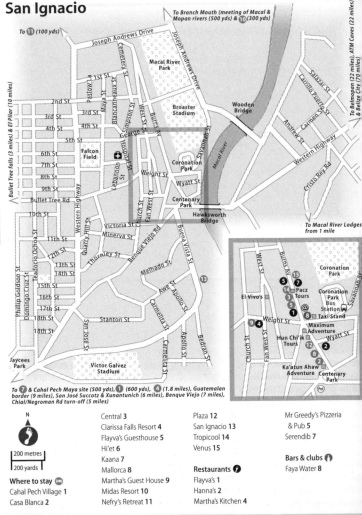

Where to stay ⬛		Central 3	Plaza 12	Mr Greedy's Pizzeria
Cahal Pech Village 1		Clarissa Falls Resort 4	San Ignacio 13	& Pub 5
Casa Blanca 2		Flayva's Guesthouse 5	Tropicool 14	Serendib 7
		Hi'et 6	Venus 15	
		Kaana 7		Bars & clubs ⬤
200 metres		Mallorca 8	Restaurants ⬤	Faya Water 8
200 yards		Martha's Guest House 9	Flayva's 1	
		Midas Resort 10	Hanna's 2	
		Nefry's Retreat 11	Martha's Kitchen 4	

Don't miss ...

within the extensive grounds of **San Ignacio Hotel** (see page 111). Visitors can handle green iguanas (wear long sleeves to protect your arms from the sharp claws), which are held prior to release in the wild in a large netted enclosure. They use the same building for butterfly breeding, and the air is filled with hundreds of electric blue morphos and tropical swallowtails, which float effortlessly through the air like falling petals.

A guide takes you through the enclosure and along the system of trails, explaining how the medicinal plants are used to treat ailments, as they have for centuries, according to lore developed by the Maya. Try and visit mid-afternoon, then stop at the hotel for drinks or dinner. The upper hotel terrace overlooks the forest and is a superb spot for birdwatching. Almost 200 species have been recorded here, including rare and endangered birds like the emerald toucanet and rufous-tailed jacamar.

Cristo Rey and Chiquibul roads → *For listings, see pages 111-120. Colour map B1.*

The **Cristo Rey Road** leaves San Ignacio town immediately to the south, dividing after around six miles. The south fork runs into the hills to Chiquibul and Mountain Pine Ridge (see page 129). The north fork is known as the **Chiquibul Road** and it doubles back to rejoin the Western Highway at Georgeville, the main road running between San Ignacio and Belize City. It's easy to drive the Cristo Rey and Chiquibul loop in a day, with time to stop off and see the handful of sights along the way. There are also some delightful places to stay.

San Antonio and Pacbitun

Stop off in this tiny Yucatec Mayan hamlet some three miles south of San Ignacio on the Cristo Rey Road to take a look at the exquisite wood and slate carving in the **Tanah Mayan Art Museum** ① *daily 0800-1700, BZ$8.* (It's easy to find, right on the main road; ask around.) They are carved by the Garcia Sisters, who are well-known in Cayo for the high quality of their work and whose pieces fetch quite a price. They are cheapest to buy here, either through the museum or in one of the village's gift shops. You can also purchase other Mayan handicrafts together with raw *copal* incense. San Antonio was the home of the late **Don Elijio Panti**, a shaman and medicinal plant healer who taught Heriberto Cocom (see page 119) and whose work was developed at Ix Chel Farms (see box, page 102). His home is now a small museum. A number of healers and shaman based in the village have continued Elijio's work. The museum is a good point of contact for them.

The Mayan ruin of **Pacbitun**, on the outskirts of San Antonio, is a medium-sized Maya site covering some 35 acres, but only a fraction of the buildings have been excavated. It's a wonderful place to wander around, particularly in the very early morning or late afternoon. It receives very few visitors apart from the local Mayan people and has a lovely atmosphere.

Ix Chel

This 35-acre farm and tropical research institute in San Antonio, owned and run by **Chaa Creek** (see page 115), was founded in 1981, by Rosita Arvigo, an alternative medical practitioner from the US with a strong interest in medicinal plants. She came to Belize to learn bush medicine from traditional Maya healers and settled in San Ignacio to study with 86-year-old Don Elijio Panti from San Antonio village. Don Elijio died in 1996, but Rosita and Ix Chel have kept his knowledge alive and applied it to modern medicine.

The Belize Ethnobotany Project run at Ix Chel has sent more than 2000 plants to the National Cancer Institute in the US for study and testing. Ix Chel also runs conferences and workshops for practitioners of natural healing and spearheads the Belize Association of Traditional Healers, an organization which runs Terra Nova Medicinal Plant Reserve, 6000 acres of plantations sown with pharmacologically active plants. Rosita also founded Rainforest Remedies, a cooperative manufacturing liquid herbal remedies; look out for their distinctive small bottles with Mayan designs throughout Belize.

It's possible to visit the **Ix Chel Tropical Research Center** and take a guided walk along the Elijio Panti medicinal plant trail, planted in the healer's honour. Trees and bushes are carefully labelled with descriptions of the plant and its historical and contemporary use. At the end of the walk, you can also visit a replica of Eilijio's home. For more information contact **Chaa Creek** (see page 115).

Like Xunantunich the core of the ruined city is made up of three plazas. Only one, Plaza A, has been excavated, and this is dominated by the site's biggest structure, a low mound which was once a fabulous pyramid over 15 m high. It is now excitingly named Structure 1. It is flanked by two further buildings (Structures 4 and 5); sitting opposite on the west side of the plaza is the far better preserved Structure 2, which retains a staircase and tiered sides.

Excavations of burial chambers at Pacbitun revealed the remains of two elite Mayan women, both buried with a series of beautiful but sadly broken musical instruments: ocarinas, flutes and drums all made from fired clay. The city dates from between the early pre-Classic (c 900 BC) and the late Classic (c AD 900).

Barton Creek Cave
① *Chiquibul Rd.*

Barton Creek is one of Belize's most fascinating caves, offering a similar experience to the better known ATM, but with far fewer visitors. Like ATM, Barton Creek is accessed through a large river cave, set in rocky hills in the heart of a forest glade. From a jewel-like jungle pool, the river stretches back into the hills for around four miles, spreading into a filigree of labyrinthine passageways and caverns, some of which are 100 m high. Mayan ruins and spectacular speleological formations line the corridors and, at one point, the way is curtained with a beautiful subterranean waterfall. Unlike ATM, there are no large, dry caverns.

Barton Creek is still in the early days of archaeological exploration, but artefacts so far recovered suggest that the Maya used the caves for various purposes, some grislier than others. They included ceremonial burial and agricultural rituals, possibly also fertility rites, ritual bloodletting and even human sacrifice.

Backpacker accommodation and camping is available at the **Barton Creek Outpost** (see page 113).

Calico Jack's

ⓘ *Mile 7, Chiquibul Rd, www.calicojacksvillage.com.*

Just off the Chiquibul road, this resort set in a private 395-acre wildlife reserve offers a mix of rainforest retreat and outdoor adventure activities. The latter include a great adrenaline-pumping canopy walkway tour, with a mix of precarious walkways and ziplines, a giant jungle swing suspended over an ersatz-Mayan pyramid, or slightly more sedate cave-tubing, caving, kayaking or horseback riding in the forest. The resort is open to day visitors but also has accommodation and a restaurant (see page 113).

Green Hills Butterfly Ranch

ⓘ *Mile 8, Chiquibul Rd, T834-4017, http://green-hills.net. Butterfly House 0800-1600, last tour 1530. Entrance fee plus guided tour is BZ$20, under-10s BZ$10.*

There is nowhere better in Belize to see those brilliantly coloured neotropical butterflies and huge, owl-eye moths than this lepidopteral centre and private conservation area. Swarms of tropical swallowtail, electric blue morpho, brush-footed and white and sulphur butterflies fill the 250 sq m landscaped flight area. Dozens more waft through the protected forest environs. The reserve also includes a botanical garden of flowering plants and cycads important for tropical butterfly conservation (all meticulously labelled) and some 100 acres of forest whose species are being rehabilitated. Jaguar, ocelot, paca, agouti and tayra have all been photographed at Green Hills.

Mountain Equestrian Trails

ⓘ *Chiquibul Rd, opposite Green Hills Butterfly Ranch, T820-4884, www.metbelize.com.*

This hotel and stables, lost in beautiful forest some seven miles from the village of Georgeville, offers horseback adventures in the Cristo Rey and Chiquibul region on bush trails within the centre's private reserve, and further afield to Mayan sites, caves and waterfalls. The centre can be visited as part of a day trip (book ahead for tours) or you can stay here overnight in one of their comfortable thatch-roofed cabanas (**$$$$**).

Macal River Valley → *For listings, see pages 111-120.Colour map B1.*

Immediately south of San Ignacio the rainforest-covered mountains that rise ever higher towards Mountain Pine Ridge are cut by a deep valley, scored by the bottle-green Macal River. There's abundant wildlife here, particularly birds, and plenty of opportunity for light adventure activities on and around the river, such as horseback riding, hiking, canoeing or, if you're not concerned about seeing animals, whizzing along forest trails on quad bikes. These are easily organized from one of the lodges listed on page 114.

The area offers a good alternative to San Ignacio town as a base for exploring the Cayo region. There are some excellent and very comfortable lodges, nestling on the steep-sided river banks and accessible along the Cristo Rey or Chial dirt roads. Most lodges lie off the road to Cristo Rey village, which runs parallel to the east bank of the Macal River. A handful lie on the west bank of the river, accessible via the Chial road, or its fork to the south, the Negroman road (the turn-off to Chial/Negroman lies five miles west of San Ignacio town; if driving, look for signposts to Chaa Creek). Some practise model sustainable tourism and all are set in pretty jungle surrounds rich in bird and mammal life.

As it is so close to town, many visitors choose to stay on the Macal river rather than in San Ignacio itself. We recommend you divide your time, spending a few days in both. The Macal river surroundings are undoubtedly more salubrious but, even though distances are short, getting back to the city is not easy or cheap without your own transport.

The rainforests around the Macal river are well preserved through a network of private reserves, many of them owned by the lodges themselves. Birdwatching is very good, with over 280 species and spectaculars, including ornate hawk eagles, orange-breasted falcons, white eagles, great black-hawks, grey hawks, laughing falcons, all three species of toucans, olive-throated parakeets, lineated and pale-bill woodpeckers, various trogons, king vultures, golden-hooded tanagers, purple-crowned fairies, and both the tody and blue-crowned motmot. Many of the lodges, such as **Black Rock** or **Crystal Paradise** cater well to birders.

Mopan River and around → *For listings, see pages 111-120.*

Meeting of the Macal and Mopan rivers
ⓘ *Take a taxi from the town centre, BZ$5 or walk (45 mins).*
Two of highland Belize's principal rivers converge at **Branch Mouth** in the suburbs of San Ignacio, 1½ miles from the town centre (along Branch Mouth Road), to form the Belize River which flows around 150 miles to the coast. Their confluence is a popular swimming spot. Locals bask on the river banks, or plunge into the flow from the wobbly 'hammock' suspension bridge spanning the water. The rivers are a delicious emerald green and set in bird- and agouti-filled forest. The bathing spot is only really busy at weekends. There is a simple snack bar near the bathing point.

Bullet Tree Falls
Whilst the Macal River begins in the highlands of Belize, the Mopan has its source just across the border in Guatemala. The river winds through the small town of Benque Viejo (see page 107) before cutting north into remote rainforest. Much of this part of the Mopan River Valley and its environs are remote and difficult to visit, but trips into the forest can be coordinated in San Ignacio or through the village of Bullet Tree Falls, three miles from San Ignacio and easily and cheaply accessible on a good road. The only way to the village is by taxi; a cab from San Ignacio to Bullet Tree costs around BZ$10 with waiting time.

Although it is wild upstream, the Mopan River in Bullet Tree itself is far tamer than the Macal River Valley. But there are a string of lodges here too, offering a cheaper alternative to those overlooking the Macal, with attractive forest and river scenes and plenty of birdlife, if less of a genuine wilderness feel (see page 116). There are also a few restaurants and bars in Bullet Tree itself.

In Bullet Tree it is also possible to organize a trip to the remote Mayan site of **El Pilar** ⓘ *7 miles north of Bullet Tree, daily 0700-1600 but unsupervised, BZ$20 payable in the visitor centre in Bullet Tree, taxi from Bullet Tree BZ$30 with waiting time.* Very few visitors make it to these small and only very partially excavated ruins, but it's a magical place. The temples are still earth- and tree-covered mounds; the ball court is overgrown with twisted roots and vines, and the air is so free of tourist guide patter that you can hear the beat of a toucan's wing above the perennial singing of cicadas.

Xunantunich → *Colour map B1.*

ⓘ *Western Highway s/n at San José Succotz, www.nichbelize.org (click on Institute of Archaeology, then Archaeological sites & parks), daily 0800-1600, BZ$20.*

Xunantunich is the biggest and most spectacular of Belize's easily accessible Maya cities and, after Altun Ha, probably the most visited. The city sits on a limestone crest above a curve in the Mopan river, just six miles from San Ignacio, making it an easy half-day trip. To beat the crowds (which are never large when compared to the Maya sites in the northern Yucatán or Tikal across the border), come early morning. But for the best views come in the late afternoon, when the stepped pyramids and stucco masks are bathed in a warm honey-coloured light, and the sun sinks low over the surrounding forests. Xunantunich (whose name roughly translates as 'Woman of the Rock') is photogenic, with wonderful views from the temple tops, out across the gently undulating hills and impressive stretches of forest.

Getting there Day tours to Xunantunich are easily organized in San Ignacio, either through one of the high-street operators or through a hotel or guesthouse. However, it's just as easy to visit under your own steam. Take a taxi (around BZ$10 one way, be sure to arrange a pick-up time or you may have to hitch a ride back) to the ferry at the

Xunantunich

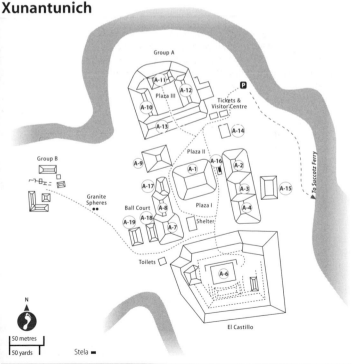

ruins' entrance, or an infrequent bus or *colectivo* taxi from Missiah street in San Ignacio to the Maya village of **San José Succotz**. The ruins themselves are accessed by a delightful wooden and wire-rope ferry, which crosses the Mopan river powered by hand-winch, and then a steep 500-yd road. San José itself is worth a peek; it's a sleepy settlement gathered around a small church, with a few craft shops, restaurants and a simple budget hotel.

The site Xunantunich, or to give the site its genuine, recently discovered pre-Columbian name, Ka'at Witz (Spirit Mountain), is a medium-sized Mayan site with a long history. Ceramics have been unearthed at the site dating to the late pre-Classic (100 BC-AD 100) and there is evidence of Mayan occupation as late as the Post Classic (shortly before the arrival of the Spanish), giving Xunantunich a Mayan history longer than that of the Roman Empire. The city's zenith was during the late Classic period, a time when the Maya of the Petén rainforest and environs were at the height of their power, with an empire of millions spread over hundreds of cities and settlements. Xunantunich is the largest site in the Belize valley, with some impressive, towering temples. But by the standards of the day it was a medium-sized place, a Newark to Caracol's New York.

As with most Mayan ruins, the city is far larger than the small portion you can see uncovered today. Excavated Xunantunich is made up of three principal plazas aligned south to north and prosaically named A1, A2 and A3, with A1 being the most southerly. Like the Zapotec city of Monte Alban in Mexico, the plazas are the product of an astonishing feat of manpower and manual engineering. An entire top of a ridge was removed to create them. The winding road up the ridge eventually emerges into the northeastern corner of Plaza A2, via the visitor centre. Go past a few modest Mayan buildings and some granite spheres and you'll eventually arrive in the heart of the plaza itself. Walk south past structure A1 (at the southern extremity of the plaza) and into the next plaza, A1, where you will see the jewel in Xunantunich's crown, the massive El Castillo temple, the tallest and largest building in Xunantunich, which dominates the plaza and which is topped by a roof comb. It's worth climbing to the top of structure A1 opposite El Castillo just to sit and admire the temple. A partially excavated stairway leads from the bottom of El Castillo to a ledge from where there is a path towards the summit of the building via a reconstructed Maya frieze on the east side. The frieze extended all around the building, but after centuries of root and soil erosion only this small portion remains, restored in a rather workmanlike fashion. The masks you see represent the moon and Venus. A wooden staircase leads from here to the top of the building, where you will find a series of chambers, and fabulous views over the site and across the rainforest into Guatemala.

Before leaving the site, be sure to step into the small museum where you will find a series of beautifully carved stelae.

Belize Botanical Gardens → *Colour map B1.*
ⓘ *10 miles west of San Ignacio, T824-3101, www.belizebotanic.org. Daily 0700-1700, guided tours 0730-1500. BZ$10, under-12s free, tour BZ$15. The only access is through private tour or taxi (around BZ$15 one way); be sure to arrange a pick-up time or you may have to hitch a ride back.*

Belize's sole botanical garden was founded in 1989 by Ken and Judy duPlooy (of the neighbouring **Duplooy's** (see page 115) to protect the floral biodiversity of Belize, and the bulk of the plant collection comprises only flora found within the country. The gardens and arboretum cover 45 acres, so you will need a long morning or afternoon to visit properly. As well as tropical trees and common flowering plants, there is a collection of more than 100 rare and exotic Belizean orchids, an exhibition on plants used by the

Maya, for ritual, medicine and daily living, and two miles of trails showcasing native and exotic fruits, palms, hardwoods and ornamentals. You can walk around with a self-guiding booklet, or staff offer jeep or horseback rides (which cost extra).

Benque Viejo → *Colour map B1.*

Most visitors see Belize's border town with Guatemala only briefly from the window of a bus, and there is little reason to stop here. Not that it's an unpleasant place, merely a residential one, with little to see or do. Despite the street names bearing the names of very English queens, the town has a distinctly Latin American feel, with Spanish spoken more widely than English and a large population of first and second generation Guatemalan Belizeans. For more on the border crossing, see box, page 119.

Parque Nacional Tikal → *For listings, see pages 111-120. Colour map A1. 44 km north of Flores and 135 km west of San Ignacio.*

ⓘ *Daily 0600-1800, US$19 per day, payable at the national park entrance, 18 km from the ruins (park administration, T7920-0025).*

After Chichén Itzá in Mexico, Tikal in Guatemala is perhaps the most famous and most instantly recognisable ruined Mayan city in the world. The image of its temple tops poking out of a seemingly endless sea of pristine rainforest has appeared on countless magazine covers, and the city has even featured in blockbuster movies – most notably as the rebel base on the jungle moon of Yavin in the first *Star Wars*. It is one of just a handful of Maya sites given four-star world-class status by Maya world authority Joyce Kelly, together with Chichén Itzá, Tulum, Palenque, Uxmal and Copán. Some 3000 separate constructions have been recorded here, including five temples 40 m high, myriad palaces and shrines, carved stelae and altars and paved Maya roads. The site lies in the centre of a 222-sq-mile rainforest park, replete with wildlife, including jaguar, tapir, peccary and more than 400 species of birds including scarlet macaws. A day trip, into Guatemala to see Tikal combines history with safari and archaeology with adventure, and is a unique, unforgettable experience.

Visiting Tikal

Getting there The best way to see Tikal from Belize is to take a day trip with one of the San Ignacio or Belmopan tour companies. **Hun Chi'ik** (see page 119), **Ka'tun Ahaw** (see page 119) and **Belize Travel Services** (see page 128) can all organize bespoke visits. These are far preferable to set group tours and it's worth paying the extra money as you will be able to choose when you leave and return and will have more liberty at the site. Be sure to leave Belize as early as possible (preferably around 0330-0400) to arrive at the park as it opens. An overall impression of the ruins may be gained in five hours, but you need at least a full day to see them properly and two days to absorb them at leisure. It is possible to stay at one of the park hotels (bookable through any of the operators listed above) as part of a bespoke tour. If you stay the night, it's possible to enter Tikal at 0500 once the police have scoured the grounds. This gives you at least a two-hour head start on visitors coming in from Flores (the nearest town to the site). At the visitor centre there is a post office, which stores luggage, a tourist guide service (see below), exchange facilities, toilets, a restaurant and a few shops that sell relevant guidebooks. Take a hat, mosquito repellent, snacks and plenty of water with you, as it's extremely hot, drinks at the site aren't cheap and there's a lot of legwork involved.

Best time to visit From April to December it rains every day for a while. The site is busiest November to January, during the Easter and summer holidays and most weekends. The best time for bird tours is December to April, with November to February being the mating season. Mosquitoes can be a real problem even during the day if straying away from open spaces. Use Citronella spray made to our Footprint recipe (see page 18).

Tourist information A guide is highly recommended as outlying structures can otherwise be missed. The official **Tourist Guide Association** offers tours of varying natures and in different languages. A private guide can be hired for US$60 or you can join up with a group for US$15 per person. Tours are available in Spanish, English, Italian, German and French. Bespoke guides can be organized through one of the Belize operators listed above. The

Tikal

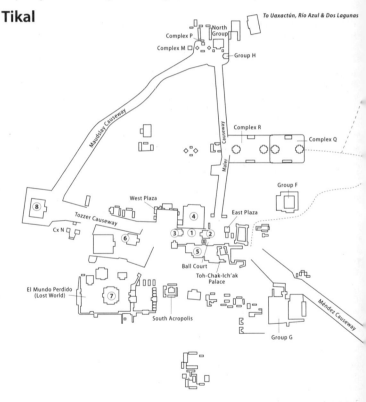

To Uaxactún, Río Azul & Dos Lagunas

North Group
Complex P
Complex M
Group H
Maudslay Causeway
Maler Causeway
Complex R
Complex Q
Group F
West Plaza
East Plaza
Tozzer Causeway
Cx N
Ball Court
Toh-Chak-Ich'ak Palace
El Mundo Perdido (Lost World)
South Acropolis
Group G
Méndez Causeway

200 metres
200 yards

Sights ○
Great Plaza **1**
Temple I (Temple of the Great Jaguar) **2**
Temple II (Temple of the Masks) **3**

North Acropolis **4**
Central Acropolis **5**
Temple III (Temple of the Jaguar Priest) **6**
Great Pyramid **7**

Temple IV (Temple of the Double-Headed Serpent) **8**
Temple VI (Temple of Inscriptions) **9**

guidebook *Tikal*, by WR Coe, in several languages, has an excellent map; or you can buy a reasonable leaflet/map at the entrance, US$2.50. Free transport around the site is available for elderly and disabled visitors, in an adapted pickup truck, with wheelchair access.

Background

Tikal is an old city whose story was almost as long as modern London's by the time Tikal fell into decline in the 10th century. It was first settled in 900 BC but rose to its full power after the decline of Mirador to the north, some 1000 years later. Its written history begins with a record of an extraordinary dynasty who would dominate the city state for longer than any other so far known to have existed in Mesoamerica. Inscriptions on temples and stelae throughout the site record their conquests and alliances. We know that the first of the dynasty was Yax Ch'akte-Xok and that he and the 38 dynastic rulers who followed him over almost a millennium called their city not Tikal, but Mutul, or Bird hair-knot. Tikal was in almost constant, prolonged warfare with neighbouring Mayan city states in the Early Classic period. Uaxactún, for example, was conquered by Tikal in a battle led by Toh-Chak-Ich'ak (True Great jaguar Claw) in AD 378; he died of battle wounds on the day of victory as an old man of well over 60. Uaxactún was united with Tikal, and the city-state saw the beginning of a golden era in which Tikal forged alliances with other city states, such as Naranjo (in Guatemala). In the sixth century Tikal was defeated in a protracted war with Caracol (see page 130) after which it fell into slow decline exacerbated by a military and economic hegemony led by another huge city state called Kan ('Snake'), which we now know to be Calakmul in neighbouring Mexico. The last recorded member of the dynasty is Hasaw Chan K'awill II, who ruled in the latter half of the ninth century AD.

The site → *The numbers in brackets relate to the map opposite.*

After buying tickets, a long forest-lined path takes you straight into the heart of the ancient city – the **Great Plaza (1)**, watched over by two of the site's tallest pyramids: the Temple of the Great Jaguar (Temple I) and the Temple of the Masks (Temple II), which face each other across the plaza. Like most of the buildings you see today, these date from the city's golden era between AD

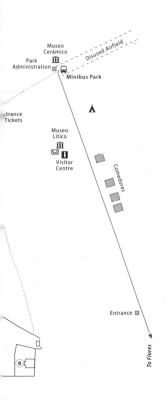

550 and 900. They've been restored, though not to their original state. It feels idyllically peaceful here, especially early in the morning before the tour buses arrive. Tanagers and cotingas flit from branch to branch, electric blue morpho butterflies float across the lawned plaza and howler monkeys call in the distant forest. But when the Maya ruled here, the trees would have been cleared, and the entire grassy area would have been paved with stucco and busy with hundreds of people. The temples and palaces themselves would have been faced with bright plaster covered in garish masks, and the temple roof combs decorated with coloured stucco figures.

Temple I (Temple of the Great Jaguar) (2), which dominates the Great Plaza, is named after a 1500-year-old, carved zapote-wood lintel found within the temple, still supporting not only the ancient stone structure, but the forest which had grown upon it. The lintel carving depicted the figure of a ruler seated on a jaguar throne. This was one of the city's greatest kings, **Jasaw Chan K'awiil I** (K'awiil who clears the Sky), who was later found buried within the structure. This seventh-century king defeated Calakmul in battle in AD 695, bringing a brief resurgence of power to Tikal. The **Temple II (Temple of the Masks (3)** opposite, across the Great Plaza is the Taj Mahal of the city, a great monument to love, built by Jasaw Chan K'awiil in homage to his wife Kalajuun Une' Mo (Lady Twelve Macaw), whose portrait was found on a lintel within the temple.

Flanking these two temples on the other sides of the plaza are two acropolises: the **North Acropolis (4)**, and in front of it on the plaza's south side, the **Central Acropolis (5)**. Both are honeycombed with spalted rooms and would have housed members of the ruling elite who governed the city state from here. Many of the city's rulers were interred in the North Acropolis. Clamber over the Central Acropolis and walk to its far eastern end to see the **Toh-Chak-Ich'ak Palace**, one of the most interesting buildings in the city. The palace was built by the great ruler whose conquest of Uaxactún had consolidated Tikal's regional supremacy. It was preserved as a shrine for some 600 years in honour of the great king, surviving the sack of the city by an alliance between Caracol and Calakmul in AD 562. Inside the palace you'll see a stone bench where Toh-Chak-Ich'ak probably held court. A pottery vessel found at Tikal depicts the king seated on a similar structure, attended by minions and entertained by musicians playing in the part of the room sitting beyond the outer wall.

Leave Tikal's heart from behind the Temple of the Masks to see highlights of the rest of the city. The first plaza you enter is the West Plaza. A skeleton adorned with a jade pendant (which was stolen from the site museum in the 1980s) was unearthed from under structure 5D II on the plaza's northwestern side. Shortly beyond this to the south you will see **Temple III (Temple of the Jaguar Priest) (6)**, named after a carved figure wearing a jaguar depicted on a lintel found within the temple. Some experts believe this figure is Ah Chitam (Nun Yax Ayin II, Ruler C), the grandson of Jasaw Chan K'awiil. Heading south from here you reach a group of structures known poetically as 'The Lost World' and congregated around a massive crumbling, flat-topped building flanked with stucco mask and more prosaically known as the **Great Pyramid (7)**. This group is thought to have been an astronomical complex. and it still has tremendous views. Head to the top of the great pyramid to see Temples I and II to the east and, behind you to the west, the tallest building in Tikal, the 70 m-tall **Temple IV (Temple of the Double-Headed Serpent) (8)**. You can reach it by heading west along the Tozzer Causeway. The Temple of the Double-Headed Serpent has been epigraphically and carbon-dated to the late eighth century and is thought to have been constructed in honour of Yik'in Chan K'awiil, son of Jasaw Chan K'awiil, who acceded to the throne in AD 734. There are wonderful views from the top of the building which is reached via a terrifying rickety wooden step ladder.

At the opposite end of Tikal and reachable along the Mendez Causeway (leaving from behind the Great Plaza and Toh-Chak-Ich'ak palace) is the **Temple of the Inscriptions (Temple VI) (9)**, which was discovered in 1951. The pyramid is only partially uncovered and it's a clamber to the top, up a rough dirt track and a series of boardwalks. From here you get the classic view of the city – as seen in *Star Wars*. The 12 m-high roof comb which towers above you is covered on both sides in the longest hieroglyphic text so far discovered at Tikal.

Before leaving Tikal be sure to visit the the **Museo Cerámico (Museo Tikal)** ① *near the Jungle Lodge, Mon-Fri 0900-1700, Sat and Sun, 0900-1600, US$1.30*, which has a collection of Maya ceramics, together with the exquisitely carved Stela 31 and the reconstruction of the tomb of Tikal's great ruler, Jasaw Chan K'awiil. In the **Museo Lítico** ① *inside the visitor centre, Mon-Fri 0900-1700, Sat and Sun, 0900-1600*, there are more stelae and photographs of the temples as they were originally found.

◉ San Ignacio and around listings

For hotel and restaurant price codes and other relevant information, see pages 11-12.

◉ Where to stay

San Ignacio *p99, map p100*

$$$$ Kaana, Mile 69 1/4, Benque Viejo Rd (Western Hwy), T824-3350, T+1(305) 735-2553 (US), www.kaanabelize.com. The plushest accommodation in San Ignacio comprises a series of luxurious cabins set in a lawned garden coloured with crimson heliconia flowers and situated in the forested outskirts of town. Each cabin is decked out in lush hardwood, has a huge king-sized bed and en suite bathroom with funky stone basins, huge mirrors and mood lighting. The larger villas have their own plunge pools. Service is excellent (with thoughtful touches, such as a complimentary mini dessert left in your fridge for when you return at night). The hotel restaurant (see page 117) is one of the best in Belize. There's also a pool, spa, , bar, cable TV and Wi-Fi. Tours organized. Breakfast included.

$$$$ San Ignacio Hotel, Western Hwy, T824-2034, www.sanignaciobelize.com. This small luxury hotel effortlessly blends a feel for the wilderness with urban comfort. The resort is set in its own 17-acre private reserve, which is contiguous with a far more extensive stretch of forest running over the surrounding hills. The pool patio, restaurant and suite balcony terraces look out over dense forest, cut by trails leading to the Iguana sanctuary (see page 100) and busy with birds early morning and late evening. A blackboard near the restaurant lists sightings of the day, which often include spectaculars like keel-billed toucans and collared aracaris, black-headed trogons and a host of tanagers. A/c rooms and spacious suites are well appointed and were redecorated in 2011. There's a decent spa, tennis court, a nightclub bar, one of the country's better restaurants, tours, Wi-Fi, cable TV and a convention centre. Breakfast is included and credit cards are accepted.

$$$-$$ Cahal Pech Village, Cahal Pech, T824-3740, www.cahalpech.com. There are sweeping views out over San Ignacio and the surrounding forests from the duplex cabins at this hilltop hotel. What the cabins lack in charm (decoration is plain and they look rather ungainly on their concrete stilts), they more than make up for in vast interior space and excellent location. The resort is a stone's throw from the Cahal Pech ruins. Family suites available (with separate rooms). Book the Kohunlich cabin for the best views. There's a pool, restaurant, bar, Wi-Fi, cable TV and tours. Credit cards accepted.

$$$-$$ Clarissa Falls Resort, Mopan River, Western Hwy Mile 70 (around 2 miles

west of San Ignacio), T824-3916, www.
clarissafalls.com. This simple resort on
a 900-acre estate sits in a shady garden
next to a pretty waterfall on the languid
Mopan River and within a stone's throw of
Xunantunich. You can see the ruins from
the faux-Mayan thatched-roof wooden
cottages. The garden is filled with birds,
from motmots and myriad species of
hummingbird to curassows and all the
Belizean toucans. Owner Chena offers great
food and a range of trips, including river
rafting and tubing, jungle hikes in search
of medicinal plants, horseback riding and
exploring the ruins at Xunantunich and El
Pilar. Camping and student discounts (more
than 50%) available. Restaurant and bar.
Credit cards accepted.

$$ Midas Resort, Branch Mouth Rd s/n,
T824-3172, www.midasresortbelize.com.
This riverside resort on the northern edge
of town has a series of large a/c cabins with
en suite bathrooms set in a pretty forested
garden, and a larger front building with a
luxurious pool. You can rent a kayak for an
excellent price (BZ$50) and paddle right
from the resort downstream or take a full-
day guided tour. There's also a spa, Wi-Fi
and cable TV. Credit cards accepted.

$$-$ Martha's Guest House, T804-3647,
www.marthasbelize.com. A handful of
cosy a/c rooms with chintzy furniture and
pretty en suite bathrooms, all scrupulously
well kept. There's a sister hotel a few mins'
walk away, if this is full, and their restaurant,
Martha's Kitchen, is downstairs. Laundry
service for guests and non-guests and tours
are available. Wi-Fi and cable TV.

$ Casa Blanca, 10 Burns Av, T824 2080,
www.casablancaguesthouse.com. Owner
Betty, who is a font of knowledge about
all things Belize, treats guests like family
members in her scrupulously clean
guesthouse. A/c or fan-cooled rooms are
simple (with tiled floors, solid wooden beds,
dressers and cable TV) but spacious and
spotlessly clean, and there is a communal
kitchen and living room. Good value triple

rates. There's Wi-Fi (BZ$3 per day) and tours.
Credit cards accepted.

$ Central Hotel, 24 Burns Av, T628-2361.
Accommodation is as basic and cheap as it
gets in San Ignacio in this old wooden house
on the town's main thoroughfare. Fan-cooled
rooms are spartan, mattresses spongy, sheets
old and frayed and bathrooms shared, but
the hotel is well kept and the owners friendly.
The hotel lies next door to **Flayva's** and
things can get noisy at weekends. Hot water
only in winter. Internet in the adjacent gift
shop. Credit cards accepted.

$ Flayva's Guesthouse, 22 Burns Av,
T804-2267. Rooms in this cheerful cheapie
are tiny boxes with bonsai windows and
barely enough storage space for a Barbie
doll's wardrobe. Only one is a/c but, whilst
the bathroom is shared, it is large, newly
refitted and has hot water. Can be noisy at
weekends when the restaurant-bar is in full
swing. The hotel operates a budget tour
operator called **Destiny Tours**, offering the
standard packages.

$ Hi'et, 12 West St, T824-2828. Not to be
confused with the **Hyatt**, this big wooden
building and adjacent newer annex in the
heart of town has very simple fan-cooled
rooms in need of some attention. Some have
a balcony, all are furnished with little more
than a bed. Half have shared bathrooms with
cold water. The best are in the annex.

$ Mallorca, 12 Burns Av, T824-2960,
www.mallorcahotelbelize.com. This
homely guesthouse is quiet, well run and
scrupulously clean. A/c or fan-cooled rooms
come with chintzy bed spreads, plenty of
storage space, towels, soap and en suites.
Beds have decent mattresses, and the family
will provide a small desk for those with
a laptop on request. Rooms for 4 (with 2
double beds) make particularly good value,
and there is a kitchen, laundry facilities,
Wi-Fi and cable TV. Credit cards accepted.

$ Nefry's Retreat, 2 Paslow Lane,
www.nefrysretreat.com. Run by a Belizean
family who have been offering well-priced
accommodation (which doesn't shirk on

omfort) for almost 20 years, this welcoming ttle guesthouse is one of the town's best-value places. A/c rooms are big, but cosy, very well looked after and come with large en suite shower rooms. Thoughtful little extras not usually offered by budget hotels include a water cooler, towels and soap. Occasional discounts on rooms for guests who book tours. Credit cards accepted.

$ Plaza, 5a Burns Av, T824-2040. Guest accommodation is integrated into the family home in this guesthouse, so time here feels like a homestay rather than a hotel. Rooms are surprisingly spacious and bright, especially at the front of the building, and they come with dressers, wardrobes and queen-sized beds. Those upstairs offer the most privacy and come with en suites and a/c. Downstairs are fan-cooled and with shared bathrooms.

$ Tropicool, 30 Burns Av, T804-3052. Fan-cooled rooms are barely as big as a bed in this small hotel tucked away behind the **Tropicool** shop. But they are well kept, painted a bright eggshell blue and come with towels and soap. The quietest are farthest from the street. Cable TV. Credit cards accepted.

$ Venus Hotel, 29 Burns Av, T824-3203, venushotel@btl.net. Very simple but bright, well-kept fan cooled or, for 10% more, a/c rooms in bright colours and with little work desks, big mirrors and wooden racks for hanging clothes. In a convenient location right in the centre of town. Streetside rooms on the lower floors can be a little noisy. Cable TV.

Cristo Rey and Chiquibul roads *p101*
$$$$ Calico Jack's, www.calicojacksvillage. com. This rainforest resort, with its zip lines, menu of adrenaline-pumping light adventure activities and American-orientated restaurant menu, is an option for families wanting to spend a night or two in the forest without getting too immersed in nature. Accommodation is in a/c Maya-themed concrete villas (some with mock roof combs

and all with kitchenettes and 2-3 bedrooms) or simple thatch-roofed cabins set in a rainforest garden. Unless you have your own transport, it's an expensive cab ride to San Ignacio, making the resort restaurant the only real option, and with tours and other extras the price can add up, so it's best to visit on a day trip or buy a pre-paid package through the website.

$$$$ Gumbo Limbo, Mountain Pine Ridge Rd, Mile 2, Georgeville, T650-3112, www.gumbolimboresort.com. There are only 4 cabins in this tranquil little lodge between Chiquibul and breezy Mountain Pine Ridge. They're set in a lawned garden and surrounded by forest. Each is very spacious and well appointed, with big French windows affording views out over the garden and forested hills. The remote location ensures good birdwatching and a real sense of peace. There's a pool, cable TV and tours. Credit cards accepted.

$$-$ Barton Creek Outpost, Barton Creek, www.bartoncreekoutpost.com. There's accommodation to suit every budget at this family-run lodge set in a big private forest reserve. You can pitch your own tent, sleep in the bunk bed-filled dorms or take a good-value, simple cabin set in the lodge's garden. Barton Creek Cave is within walking distance, the forest location is great for birding and seeing small mammals, and the helpful North American owners can organize tours throughout the region.

$ Chichan Ka Guest House, San Antonio Village, T669-4023, www.awrem.com/tanah/experience.html. The Maya of San Antonio built this 2-storey thatched roof lodge to give visitors the option of staying in the heart of the community. Guests can learn to cook Mayan food, walk medicinal trails, discover how the people use forest plants, learn to play marimba, and generally enjoy immersion in Maya village life without discomfort. Rooms in the lodge are simple, fan cooled but well kept, and those on the upper storey have good views out over the village and the surrounding forest.

Macal River Valley p103

Accommodation lies off 3 roads. Cristo Rey Rd, which leaves San Ignacio south from Santa Elena suburb, accesses the east bank of the river and has the bulk of the lodges. Chial Rd, which leaves the Western Hwy south just opposite the entrance to Xunantunich, accesses the west bank of the river, where there are 2 lodges. Negroman Rd forks off from the Chial Rd, running south. There is only 1 lodge off this road.

Be aware that these lodges are in the rainforest. Dirt tracks to them can be rough, especially in the wet. Many lodges have generator electricity which is not available 24 hrs so bring a torch (flashlight). Expect to see insects and arachnids. Whilst a number include half board in their price, most charge extra for food, which is usually a good deal more expensive than its equivalent in San Ignacio.

East bank (Cristo Rey Rd)

$$$$ Ek Tun, Mile 15 Cristo Rey Rd, T820-3002, www.ektunbelize.com. This remote lodge sits on a wild stretch of the Macal river below the craggy, forest-covered cliffs of the Vaca Plateau, a region famous not for its cows, as the name might suggest, but its myriad raptors. Accommodation is in simple but attractive palm-roofed *palapas* (some of which are duplex) in a tropical garden busy with butterflies, which merges with the surrounding rainforest. There's a lovely natural 'mineral water' pool and abundant birds. The communal restaurant serves decent Belizean-American comfort food. However, this is a lodge for adventurers. There is no electricity, nights are dark, and sleeping is not fan-cooled. Be sure to bring your own mosquito net and torch (flashlight). Be aware that the advertised prices don't include the 9% room tax and 10% sales tax required by the Belizean government, plus a service charge of 10%, and an extra 5% if paying by credit card. The restaurant is relatively pricey. No under 18s.

$$$$ Mystic River Resort, Mile 6 Cristo Rey Rd, T834-4100, www.mysticriverbelize.com. With their curved terracotta tiles, little chimneys and gravel paths, the cabins at **Mystic River** look like they belong in a Hansel and Gretel wood, especially in the twilight when the gravel paths are lit with fairy lights and the twitter of birds fills the air. The owners have put care and attention into the design: interiors are lush and comfortable with dark wood and beautiful heavy furniture. Huge beds are covered with thick velvety counterpanes and hung with mosquito nets, and there are even stone hearths. Private balconies offer glorious views of the Macal river and surrounding forest, as does the open-sided restaurant, where superior Franco-Belizean food is served from a menu designed by the French owner Nadege. There is a pool, Wi-Fi, a restaurant and a bar. Tours are available, including kayaking or canoeing on the river, horse riding or walking forest trails, and there are off-season special rates. Breakfast is included. Credit cards accepted.

$$$$-$$$ Table Rock, Cristo Rey Rd, T834-4040, www.tablerockbelize.com. **Table Rock** is an award-winning resort for travellers with an ecological conscience. US owners Alan and Colleen have done all they can to make their small resort a model for sustainable tourism. They work extensively with the local community, Cristo Rey Mayan village, run reforestation projects (particularly for mahogany) and follow best practice throughout their operations, from recycling rubbish and water to using renewable energy and organically growing most food for the restaurant. Fan-cooled palm-roof cabins set in the resort garden overlook the rainforest or the Macal river, on which the lodge offers self-guided kayak tours. Each is well-appointed and tastefully furnished with a mix of rustic and antique furniture, and decorated with flowers from the garden and locally sourced art and textiles. The restaurant serves excellent simple fare, and trips include jungle walks in their private reserve and birdwatching. Wi-Fi.

$$$-$$ Crystal Paradise Resort, Cristo Rey Village Rd, T820-4014, www.crystalparadise. com. Despite the name, this jungle hotel on the edge of Cristo Rey village caters to serious birdwatchers rather than to the New Age crowd. The lodge's open decks are often busy with birders scoping the surrounding forest or snapping away with 600-mm lenses. The lodge offers excellent birding guides (ask for Eric) and runs trips throughout the country, has a decent selection of birding books and a downloadable species list. Rooms are functionally comfortable, set in thatched a/c or fan-cooled roof cabins and cottages, with tiled floors and lemon yellow walls hung with colourful but kitschy local art. All have en suites.

$$$-$$ Macaw Bank, Mile 8 Cristo Rey Rd, T603-4825, www.macawbankjunglelodge. com. As at the plusher **Table Rock**, Ron and Al at nearby **Macaw Bank** strive to practise sustainable tourism, generating electricity from solar panels, composting, recycling and supporting local cottage industries amongst other ventures. Accommodation is homely and comfortable, with fan-cooled rooms in modest palm-thatched cabins that have mosaic floors and chunky faux-antique furnishings. Much of the food – which comes in hearty portions – is grown on site, and the lodge offer a range of tours and activities, including walks in the forest, horse riding, river trips and outsourced excursions to Tikal or Caracol. Discounts for students.

$$$-$$ Maya Mountain Lodge, Mile 0.75 Cristo Rey Rd, T824-2164, www.maya mountain.com. This US-owned hotel sits over the Macal river right on the edge of San Ignacio town in a 100-acre private reserve. It is too close to San Ignacio to have a true sense of remoteness but serves as a possible base for the town itself. Accommodation is in modest mock-Maya a/c cottages with palm-thatched roofs and whitewashed walls. Each comes with a little terrace slung with a hammock. There are also family suites. There's a pool, an overpriced restaurant, cable TV and the hotel organizes tours

(outsourced with a hefty surcharge). No alcohol unless you bring it yourself. Discounts for families. Credit cards accepted.

West Bank (Chial/Negroman roads)
$$$$-$$$ Chaa Creek & Macal River Camp, Chial Rd s/n, T834-4009, UK T+44-(0)20-7096 0329, US T+1-1877 709 8708 (toll free), www.chaacreek.com. **Chaa Creek** offers 2 jungle experiences. The Lodge is one of the most comfortable rainforest hotels in Belize, with a series of villas and cottages sitting in a lawned area overlooking the Macal river. All are luxurious and beautifully designed, most notably the treetop suites, whose rooms stand at canopy level and boast polished wood floors, near 360-degree windows offering a bird's eye view and interior spaces broken by Starckian cotton drapes. By contrast, the Macal Jungle Camp, 15 mins' walk from the lodge (and whose high price includes breakfast and dinner at the camp) has rustic canvas and pine wooden huts sparsely furnished with 2 single beds and with shared outside bathrooms. All accommodation is fan cooled and sits within Chaa Creek's private forest reserve of some 365 acres. Discounts online and for children. There's a pool, spa, Wi-Fi, restaurant, bar, cable TV, and tours are available. Credit cards accepted.

$$$$-$$$ Duplooy's, Chial Rd s/n, www.duplooys.com. **Duplooy's** sits in thick forest next to the Belize Botanic gardens (which they administer), see page 106, and opposite **Mystic River Resort**, 10 miles from San Ignacio. The lodge strives to practise sustainable tourism, generating its own electricity (not 24 hrs), planting trees and employing local people. It lies at the centre of a private 100-acre reserve filled with beautiful tropical fruit trees and flowering plants. The modest accommodation comes in all shapes and sizes, all in need of a little care and attention. The best is La Casita, a duplex bungalow for 4, ringed with a terrace and with light flooding into the lemon and white interior from ample sash windows and glass doors. The modest private bungalows have terracotta tile floors, slat windows and whitewashed walls. Their terraces have forest views and are reached by their own private mini-canopy walkways for optimum birdwatching. The best views are from the River House, a dorm house sitting high over the river and with room for up to 7 couples in 2 discrete suites. Simpler dorm accommodation is in the lodge garden. Reasonable comfort food is served in the restaurant. There are good facilities for birding, including guiding, and the owners are knowledgeable about neotropical flora. There are free canoes. Cheaper rates for groups, and under 12s are free; discounts are also available online. Breakfast is included. Credit cards accepted.

$$$$-$$ Black Rock Lodge, Negroman Rd s/n, T820-4049, www.blackrocklodge.com. This well-run, good-value conservation-conscious jungle lodge is nestled in a private 245-acre rainforest reserve on a curve in the Macal river. There are breathtaking views from many of the cabins and from the restaurant terrace out over a grassy slope to the rushing Macal river below. The lodge grows much of its own organic produce, recycles water and draws power from a hybrid of micro-hydroelectric and solar sources. Staff are local. Accommodation is in rustic wooden cabins of varying degrees of comfort topped with roof sheets and fronted by little hammock-strung terraces. Interiors are simple, but surprisingly airy and well designed, with attractive polished wood or stone tile floors, sturdy beds, writing desks and comfy wicker sofas. The best have gorgeous river views. Birding is excellent; there's a species list and good guiding. Discounts online. There are tours and a restaurant. Credit cards accepted.

Mopan River and around p104
Lodges in Bullet Tree offer a jungle experience, but, although staying here is certainly wilder and more peaceful than in San Ignacio, you're still in a village, so expect barking dogs, cockerels at dawn and even some urban noise pollution now and again. The village lies less than 15 mins' drive from San Ignacio, so it's easy to use the village as a base for the region and still dine in the city at night. Buses are sporadic. Book cabs at least 1 hr in advance.

$$$$ Mahogany Hall Boutique Resort, Paslow Falls Rd, Bullet Tree Falls, T664-7747, www.mahoganyhallbelize.com. With its grand Georgian-London-meets-Mexican-hacienda mansion house and rooms packed with charmingly kitschy pre-fab-Zorro decor, this plush resort feels like it should be in Coral Gables rather than the wilds of Belize. A/c rooms and the decent grill restaurant overlook the Mopan river and the firefly-filled forest. Suites come with jacuzzis, chunky hardwood furniture and shiny 4-poster beds as big as a Spanish galleon. Service is excellent, and the hotel can arrange all manner of tours, including to Guatemala, which lies just 5 miles to the west (though prices are often cheaper through tour operators in San Ignacio). Popular with honeymooners. Online discounts available. Kids under 6 share a room with their parents for free. There's a pool, restaurant, bar, Wi-Fi and cable TV. Credit cards accepted.

$$ Cohune Palms, Mopan River, Bullet Tree Falls, T824-0166, www.cohunepalms.com. This small resort offers simple but elegant fan-cooled mock-Mayan cabanas on stilts set in a pretty lawned garden on a bend in the Mopan river. Each has a hammock-slung terrace, polished wooden or tile floors, a palm thatch roof, small writing desk and Mexican and Guatamalan decorations: colourful rugs, mirrors and naïve art on the wall. Some are duplex. Melanie prepares hearty home cooking in the open-air restaurant, and there's a lovely yoga deck overlooking the river. Good-value triple room rates. Payment is cash only. Under-12s stay free. The resort can organize tubing and kayaking from their doorstep and visits to El Pilar. Other excursion prices (to Caracol etc) re cheaper booked through tour operators in town. Free pick-ups from San Ignacio. There's a restaurant and Wi-Fi.

$$ Parrot Nest, Mopan River, Bullet Tree Falls, T820-4058, www.parrot-nest.com. There's a profusion of birdlife here; you'll feel in the midst of it in the 20-ft tall stilted, thatched-roof treehouse cabins that reach into the lower canopy. The cabins cluster around towering Guanacaste trees, which themselves sit in an attractive rainforest garden filled with red heliconias and pink gingers. Fan-cooled treehouse rooms are small and simple, with a couple of single beds and mosquito nets. More down-to-earth, though less fun, options are also available, but whilst they come with hammock decks, internally they are equally simple – fan cooled, only a little bigger and like the treehouses all but 2 have shared bathrooms (en suites are 10% extra). Dining is communal and good value for the lodges (though a little more than cheap options in San Ignacio), with home fare served in generous portions. Tours include free river tubing and trips to El Pilar and all the Cayo sights. Under-14s stay free. Lots of cats and dogs. There's a restaurant and Wi-Fi. Credit cards accepted.

🍴 Restaurants

San Ignacio *p99, map p100*
There are plenty of restaurants to choose from. Most are strung along Burns Av. A handful are closed on Sun.

$$$ La Ceiba, Kaana hotel, see page 111. This resort restaurant vies with the Running W as the best in town. The menu mixes gentrified versions of traditional Belizean dishes, Latin American favourites (from ceviche to nachos) and superior comfort food like organic beef burgers, bespoke pizzas and home made ice cream. The wine list is the best in the city.

$$$ Running W Steak House, San Ignacio Hotel, see page 111. It's worth dining at the terrace restaurant in the San Ignacio

Hotel for the wonderful view alone. Come at around sunset for pre-dinner drinks, when toucans and tanagers flit around the forest in front of you, and then dine on some of the best steaks in Belize, or choose from a menu that includes pasta, fish and chicken dishes.

$$$-$$ Hanna's, 5 Burns Av, T804-2301. Open for breakfast, lunch and dinner. This very simple family-run restaurant has a huge menu of Belizean classics (chicken with rice and beans), Latin American standards (burrito and quesadillas) and more adventurous options such as ginger rum shrimp. There are burgers too and, unusually in San Ignacio, a number of vegetarian options. Much of the food is organic and the restaurant has a tiny wine list.

$$ Flayva's, see page 112. This lively restaurant and bar serves a broad range of popular snacks and meals in large portions and at attractive prices. Favourites include nachos, gibnut (*paca*) steak, chicken curry, fajitas and sandwiches. The bar plays reggae music and *soca* and serves decent industrial-strength cocktails. Try the sweet piña colada, Caye lime twist and the Margaritas.

$$ Mr Greedy's Pizzeria and Pub, 34 Burns Av, T804-4688. This little restaurant and bar is said to serve the best pizza in Belize. Owner Jonathan Caraiddi recommends his favourite, the Cubano, which comes with a garlic shrimp topping and in a portion big enough for 3 people.

$$ Serendib, 27 Burns Av, T824-2302. There's plenty of variety on offer in this elegant restaurant, which is housed in one of the city's few remaining 19th-century wooden buildings. The menu includes Sri Lankan curries, peppered steaks, lobster in butter sauce and chow meins. The best tables are under the shade of tropical trees in the attractive back patio.

$$-$ Martha's Kitchen, see page 112, T804-3647. Martha operates one of the most popular kitchens in town, offering generous home-cooked portions of dishes such as rice and beans, *escabeche* (fried vinegar-marinated chicken or fish) and Belizean snapper. The most coveted tables are outside on the small patio, but in the heat of the day it's cooler in the a/c dining room.

Macal River Valley *p103*
All the lodges have their own designated restaurants which are open to those not staying in the resort. The best cooking is at **Mystic River** (see page 114) and the **Chaa Creek** (see page 115). Both have a modest wine list.

Mopan River and around *p104*
$$-$ Cabañas del Sol, opposite the football pitch on Bullet Tree Rd, Bullet Tree. Basic Belizean fare, with a menu strong on both rice and beans. These are served with chicken or barbecued meat and washed down with water or Belizean beer. Karaoke and/or live music at weekends.
$$-$ Riverside Tavern, Bullet Tree Rd, Bullet Tree. A popular restaurant and bar serving Belizean standard dishes, pizza and burger. Lively at weekends when bands play and people flock in from San Ignacio.

West of San Ignacio *p105*
$ Benny's Kitchen, San José Succotz s/n, T501 823 2541. Just 10 mins' walk from the Xunantunich ferry, this Maya-owned restaurant is a popular pit stop for breakfasts and lunches. The kitchen serves simple fare – fried egg and toast, rice and beans and *escabeche* soup – and some game, including gibnut (*paca*). The limado lime shakes are deliciously creamy and refreshing; perfect after a hot morning trek around the ruins.

🍸 Bars and clubs

San Ignacio *p99, map p100*
Faya Wata, 34 Burns Av, T824-3070. San Ignacio's favourite watering hole has a beach bar feel, with rustic log stools clustered around a long bar next to the street, and long vinyl-covered tables in the main sitting area. There's rock music and a lively crowd of locals any night of the

week, here for beer and cocktails. And at the weekend there are soca and Caribbean dance parties in the big back room.
Stork Club, San Ignacio Hotel, see page 111. This a/c bar makes a welcome retreat from the summer evening heat and serves decent cocktails, wine and ice-cold beer. Live music most weekends.

🎉 Festivals

Mopan River and around *p104*
4-10 Mar La Ruta Maya Belize River Challenge. A multi-day canoe race from San Ignacio to Belize City along the Macal and Belize Rivers. This was once the only link between the 2 cities. Colourful and used as an excuse to celebrate.
Easter Sun and Mon Easter Fair. In Bullet Tree, soca and traditional hog head dancing and old British folk games, such as catching the greased pig and climbing the greasy pole, which are dying out in the home country, are followed by a canoe race from San Ignacio to the bridge at the **Riverside Tavern**. Partying continues into the night.

🏃 What to do

San Ignacio *p99, map p100*
Spas and massages
Most resorts have spa and massage services. **San Ignacio Hotel** and **Kaana** have designated spas.
Gretel's Beauty Care and Body Massage, 7 Far West St, T604-1126. This place offers a massage service in the town centre: Swedish/deep tissue massage, aromatherapy, hot stones and mud wraps.

Tour operators
There are a cluster of tour operators in central San Ignacio, all offering similar tours (to ATM or Tikal, mountain biking and rafting). Most charge roughly the same prices: ATM BZ$150, Barton Creek BZ$100, El Pilar BZ$100, Caracol BZ$150, horse riding in the forest BZ$150, Tikal BZ$240 (with an additional departure

Border crossing: Belize–Guatemala

Benque Viejo–Melchor de Mencos
This is a popular and well-used crossing for travellers heading between Belize and Tikal. Taxi rip-offs are common so bargain hard.
Currency exchange Good rates for quetzales, Belizean dollars and Mexican pesos on the street; or try Banrural at the border (0700-2000).
Belizean immigration Open 0600-2000.
Guatemalan immigration Open 0500-2100.
Onwards to Guatemala There are several buses a day from Melchor de Mencos to Sana Elena, two or three hours; colectivos 1½ hours.
Onwards to Belize Regular buses to Belize City. If you leave Santa Elena, Guatemala, at 0500, you can be in Belize City by 1200. Also direct buses Flores–Chetumal (Mexico) with Línea Dorado. You will be required to pass through Belizean customs on entering Belize, and Guatemalan customs on entering Guatemala, presenting bags for inspection in both cases.

---

ax of US$37.50), river tubing or kayaking BZ$150, spelunking BZ$150.

Only a few offer anything different or have a discernibly better level of service. They include those listed below.
Heriberto Cocom, book through **Cahal Pech Village Resort**, see page 111. Traditonal Mayan healer Heriberto Cocom, pupil of the late Don Elijio Pantí (see page 101) is one of the few remaining keepers of the traditional Mayan rainforest medicine. He runs guided day walks through the forest around San Ignacio, visiting unexcavated Mayan temples along the way and talking about different plants and their traditional uses. It's a fascinating tour.
Hun Chi'ik Tours, hunchiik.com. Run by a well-organized, efficient and irrepressibly enthusiastic Mayan family, **Hun Chi'ik** wins hands-down as the best all-round operator in Cayo. They visit all the standard sites, including ATM, Caracol and Xunantunich, but as co-owner Eduardo states: 'in Yucatec Maya Hun Chi'ik is the solitary *coati* which breaks from the pack to make its own path', and true to their philosophy, the company also offers more adventurous trips further afield, including caving in Crystal Cave (see page 125) and multi-day hikes in the heart of the Chiquibul rainforest (see page 132).

K'atun Ahaw Adventure, 10 Burns Av, T610-6477, www.belizeculturetours.com. One of the few companies in San Ignacio that is licensed to guide both in Belize and Guatemala (meaning you don't have to change driver and guide at the border).
Maximum Adventure, 27 Burns Av, T623-4880, www.sanignaciobelizetours.com. An enthusiastic young company offering a broad range of trips, including the standard tours to Caracol, Tikal and Mountain Pine Ridge, as well as to Barton Creek (see page 102), spelunking in a number of different caves and kayak trips on the nearby rivers.
Mayawalk Tour Company, 19 Burns Av, T824-3070, www.mayawalk.com. Trips to ATM, Barton Creek, Mountain Pine Ridge, Tikal and canoeing on the Macal River. Ask for Andrew, one of the best guides.

◉ Transport

San Ignacio *p99, map p100*
Buses and colectivos
San Ignacio lies 67 miles from Belize City, a drive of around 2 hrs. There are at least 40 buses daily to **Belize City** starting in Benque Viejo and passing through San Ignacio, with **Guerra's, D&E, Middleton's, Shaw** and **National Transport Services**,

the first at 0230, the last at 1830. Buses leave from from next to Coronation Park, heading east to Belize City (via **Belmopan**) and west to **Benque Viejo** and the **Guatemalan border** via **San José Succotz** (for **Xunantunich**). For **Dangriga** and **Punta Gorda**, change buses in Belmopan. For **Corozal**, **Orange Walk** and **Yucatán**, Mexico, change buses in Belize City. There are frequent *colectivo* minivans to Benque Viejo and the surrounding Maya villages, including **San Antonio**.

Taxi
Cabs are easy to come by. There is a taxi stand in the centre of town on Weight St near Coronation Park and the bus stands. In 2012 prices from San Ignacio were roughly as follows: Xunantunich (BZ$60 with wait time), Cahal Pech (BZ$5), Benque Viejo (BZ$20), Guatemala border (BZ$30), San Antonio (BZ$50), Macal River guesthouses (BZ$40-$60), Mountain Pine Ridge (BZ$150), airport (BZ$175), Belize City Marine Terminal (BZ$150), Tikal (BZ$375).
Manazenero's Taxi, T608-7629, www.mauricefield.net/belize/manztaxi. shtml, offers good rates further afield.

Benque Viejo *p107*
For transport to Guatemala, see also box, page 119.

Bus
Buses run to **San Ignacio**, **Belize City** and **Belmopan**, every 30 mins 0500-2300. There are also onward international buses to **Melchor** and **Flores** in Guatemala.

Taxi
A taxi to the border will cost around BZ$5.

❶ Directory

Banks These sit together at the southern end of Burns Av and have ATMs: **Belize Bank**, 16 Burns Av, T824-2031; **Atlantic Bank**, Burns Av s/n, T824-2347; **Scotia Bank**, Burns Av at River St. All change TCs, as does **Martha's Guest House**, see page 112. Change US$ into quetzales in Guatemala for best rates. **Medical services** Loma Luz Hospital, T824-2087 (private). La Sante Pharmacy, 106 Benque Viejo Rd, and **Codd's Drug Store**, both close at 2100 and are closed all day Sun.

Central and eastern Cayo

The Western Highway from San Ignacio to Belmopan is dull in itself, but a route to all manner of wonderful attractions, including Belize's most celebrated sight after the reefs and rainforests: the haunting Actun Tunichil Muknal or ATM caves. These lie at the edge of the Tapir Mountain Nature Reserve, one of several reserves – including Guanacaste National Park – that lie in the vicinity of the country's undistinguished capital, Belmopan. The latter city could serve as an alternative to San Ignacio as a base for exploring the region, just as Newark could serve as an alternative to New York, or Slough to London. Don't be tempted by geography, however. Belmopan has nothing for tourists; San Ignacio is the better choice. ▶▶ For listings, see pages 126-128.

Actun Tunichil Muknal (ATM caves) → For listings, see pages 126-128. Colour map B1.

From the moment you set foot in Belize you will hear about the ATM caves, so much so that it's easy to dismiss them as being too big a tourist draw not to feel unspoilt. But the ATM caves are special, imbued with mystery, an ancient Mayan sacred site that genuinely feels sacred, seems to demand reverence, and that will leave even the most hardened cynic impressed.

Visiting Actun Tunichil Muknal

The entry fee is BZ$50. The caves are only accessible with organized tour groups. **Hun Chi'ik** in San Ignacio (see page 119), whose guides are drawn from local Maya communities, offers some of the best. Their tours are BZ$150-330 including the entrance fee, depending on the size of the group. It's easy to join a group through the tour company if you email them a week or so before. A tour of the caves is not for everyone and you'll need to be reasonably fit to undertake it.

Background

ATM was first explored by Canadian geologist Thomas Miller in 1989, but wasn't explored by archaeologists until the late 1990s. It is now thought to have been used by the Maya principally in the Classic era (between AD 250 and 900). Stingray spines and obsidian blades found on the ledge above the stream indicate that Maya priests performed blood-letting rituals, probably in homage to the rain god Chaak, in the cave. And the remains of 14 individuals discovered crystallized into the floor of the main chamber, by calcites secreted from the flowstones and other speleological formations, suggest that young women and even children were sacrificed here. Child sacrifice to propitiate the gods of Xibalba (the Underworld) and the natural elements, particularly rain, were unpleasantly common throughout Mesoamerica, especially during times of agricultural or social crisis in the Post Classic and Colonial periods. Other artefacts discovered in the main chamber include musical instruments (*ocarinas*), tools (*mano* and *metate* mealing stones) and large storage vessels, all of which are associated with rituals for successful crop harvests.

The caves

The journey begins at the turn-off from the Western Highway, with a 20-minute bump over a dirt road cutting through maize fields to the edge of the vast **Tapir Mountain Nature Reserve**, a 6741-acre protected area open to scientific researchers only. A walking trail cuts into the lower reaches of this reserve, through low forest, tracing the course of a gentle mountain river. You'll have to ford the stream a few times in preparation for the big wade to come; after a 30-minute walk the river disappears into a gash in a sheer rock wall the gateway to ATM. From here you swim and then walk waist deep in the river itself, up a water-gouged passageway whose dimensions are hard to fathom in the inky darkness. After another 30 minutes or so you reach a rocky shelf. A clamber up and a tight squeeze brings you into a vast and stalagmite-filled cavern encrusted with glittering calcite, which glistens in the torchlight like a mithril vest.

When the Maya civilization was at its height, only priests were allowed in here. Even the brashest visitor seems quietened by the chamber, as if in a medieval cathedral. They call it a burial chamber, but it is nothing so prosaic. ATM is a temple to the gods of the earth, a place where the sacred and sacrificed were reunited with the court of Xibalba, the Maya underworld. Human bones melt into the shimmering crystal floor, giant earthenware pots over 1000 years old are coated in a sparkling carpet of crystallized stone, and ceilings and walls drip with twinkling flowstones and eerie speleological shapes: a shrouded man, a crouching woman, a swooping eagle. Taking pictures seems almost sacrilegious; it is certainly pointless. No camera can capture the sight, let alone the feel.

Belmopan and around → For listings, see pages 126-128. Colour map B2. Population: 13,351.

Even the most patriotic of Belizeans find their capital a little uninspiring. It seems half built and half deserted: a thinly spread sprawl of concrete, broken by couch grass, scrubby bush and untidy streets. By far the largest building is the US embassy, a concrete fortress shut behind huge steel fences with its own restaurants, bars and leisure facilities. Visit Belmopan out of curiosity, to say that you've seen the world's newest purpose-built capital city, to stay in a place within easy reach of anywhere, or perhaps to change bus. But don't come for the sights, as there are precious few to see.

For information and tours in the Belmopan region (and especially along the Hummingbird Highway), talk to the very helpful staff at the **El Rey Hotel** (see page 126) who run the best tour guide operation in town. See also www.belmopancityonline.com.

Background
Whilst Belmopan is principally visited for its excellent location (everywhere in Belize is so easy to reach from here), it's not much of a capital city. But it should have been. Belmopan's creation was a brave idea born of noble motives but withered inexcusably by Whitehall bureaucracy. The city began on paper in 1961 after hurricane Hattie razed 75% of Belize City to the ground, leaving devastation and a dire social problem in its wake. The colonial administrators of British Honduras went cap in hand to Westminster. 'We could rebuild Belize city', they said, 'but why not construct a new capital away from the hurricane coast and its floods and raging waves, on higher ground, in the interior'. They would call it Belmopan – celebrating the Belizean cultures of the coast and the (Mopan) Maya people of the interior. The British hummed – mumbling about how it was a great idea – and hawed, and eventually pledged far too little money too late. By the time the first concrete mixers had arrived in 1967, Belize City had been rebuilt by those who had lost their homes and had fostered a new generation. But the Belizean government moved nonetheless, or commuted from Belize City. Business and embassies would follow, they thought. However, it wasn't until 2006 that the United States relocated, deeming their previous handsome wooden headquarters in Belize City unsafe from terrorists. It remains to be seen if their presence will bring new life to Belmopan.

Places in Belmopan

Take a cab ride past the city's rather grey and grim **Government Buildings** ① *between Trinity Blvd and Constitution Dr*, which were built to evoke a Mayan city and are laid out in Mayan-style plazas. One even sports a kind of ersatz roof comb. Drop in to the **George Price Centre** ① *Price Centre Rd, T822-1054, www.gpcbelize.com, Mon-Thu 0800-1800, Fri 0800-1700, Sun 0900-1200, free*, a conference centre named in honour of the first prime minister of Belize and one of the most vocal advocates for Belmopan. Here you will find a small exhibition on the history of the city, through the life story of George Price: "the man behind the politician" who "by the Might of Truth and the Grace of God" led the young nation of Belize from a British colony to a strong, dynamic and independent country. It's rather hagiographic but it's a fascinating insight into the birth of one of the world's newest nations and includes some interesting national memorabilia and symbolic artefacts (including the first Belizean flag).

Belmopan

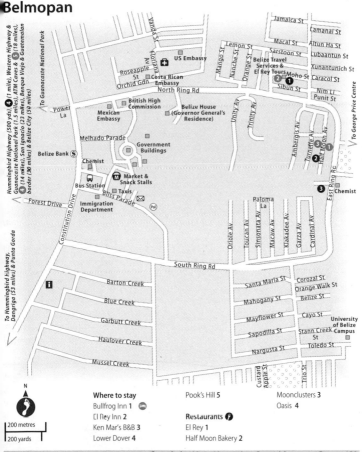

Where to stay
Bullfrog Inn **1**
El Rey Inn **2**
Ken Mar's B&B **3**
Lower Dover **4**

Pook's Hill **5**

Restaurants
El Rey **1**
Half Moon Bakery **2**

Moonclusters **3**
Oasis **4**

Guanacaste National Park → *Colour map B1.*

ⓘ *Western Hwy at the Hummingbird Hwy, www.belizeaudubon.org, daily 0800-1630, BZ$5 BZ$1 nationals.*

This 50-acre national park, just two miles north of Belmopan, was one of Belize's firs protected areas. With boardwalks, an informative visitor centre and easy access from the main road, it's one of the easiest to visit in the country, even with young children Despite its small size, the park boasts a diversity of plants and animals, including the black orchid (Belize's national flower), two young mahogany trees (Belize's national tree) and large stands of cohune palms. The park is named after its guanacaste or elephant's ea trees (*Enterolobium cyclocarpum*), known in Belize as tubroos. Guanacaste trees, which are among the largest in the Central American rainforest, have huge, widely spreading branches that support a wide variety of epiphytic plants, including orchids.

The park has numerous small mammals, including *paca* (gibnut), nine-banded armadillos, jaguarundi and kinkajou, all of which are fairly easily spotted, the latter two in the late afternoon. The **Belize Audobon Society**, which administers the park, has recorded some 120 bird species, including blue crown motmot, black-faced ant-thrush, belted kingfisher, smoky-brown woodpecker, magnolia warbler and red-lored parrot.

Hummingbird Highway → *For listings, see pages 126-128. Colour map B2. Population: 18,000.*

The road from Belmopan to Dangriga and coastal Stann Creek district, known as the Hummingbird Highway, is one of Central America's most beautiful drives. It passes through lush rainforest, skirts the foothills of the Maya mountains and cuts through limestone hills dripping with waterfalls and clear-water streams. The highway is beautiful merely as a drive, but it also serves as a route to a string of natural attractions, including a series of national parks and some wonderful caves.

St Herman's Cave and Blue Hole National Park

ⓘ *Hummingbird Hwy Mile 12, daily 0800-1630, BZ$8, BZ$2 nationals. The park has 2 entrances, for St Herman's Cave (where there is a visitor centre, gift shop and trail heads) and the Blue Hole itself. Both entrances have picnic areas. Ask any Belmopan–Dangriga or Hummingbird Hwy bus to drop you at the park entrance.*

Mexico's Yucatán Peninsula immediately to the north of Belize is famous for its caves and its cenotes: caverns filled with glassy clear water and connected to each other through a vast network of stalactite- and stalagmite-encrusted caves and passageways. The karst limestone mountains along the Hummingbird Highway support a similar, if smaller network of caves, cenotes and underground rivers. Like those in the Yucatán, they were sacred to the Maya. For the Maya, the physical actual world was imbued with sacred significance. Caves and cenotes were passageways to the underworld court of Xibalba, one of the three realms of the Maya universe. In St Herman's Cave and Blue Hole National Park, some 575 acres of protected forest rich in bird, small mammal and reptile life, is home to the Blue Hole, Belize's most famous cenote, St Herman's Cave and the Crystalline Cave.

St Herman's Cave and Blue Hole Begin a visit at St Herman's. Like ATM, this cave is decorated with speleological forms and littered with Mayan remains. To see them you'll need a guide, which you will need to book in advance either through the **Belize Audubon Society**, see page 25, **Belize Travel Services**, see page 128, or a tour operator in San Ignacio, see page 118. After a guided tour through the cave you can either clamber back out and walk to the Blue Hole for a dip, or float downstream through the caverns to the cave mouth.

The Blue Hole is linked to St Herman's Cave by an underground river. The Blue Hole is great place for swim, especially in the heat of the Belizean day. The hole itself is some 90 m across and drops around 30 m, and the cenote itself is a further 8 m deep. Like many cenotes, it is an underground river, exposed when the roof of a cave collapsed.

Crystalline or Crystal Cave The Crystalline Cave (aka Crystal Cave or Mountain Cow) is one of the most breathtakingly beautiful cave systems in Central America. The caves involve climbs, very narrow passageways and tight squeezes and can only be visited on a guided tour, with a company like **Hun Chi'ik** in San Ignacio, see page 119. The caverns in the Crystalline Cave system are huge and filled with enormous flowstones, stalactites and stalagmites and, like ATM, scores of Mayan artefacts and skeletons, all of them melded into the calcite; some are thought to be as much as 2000 years old.

Five Blue Lakes National Park
ⓘ *Hummingbird Hwy Mile 32, daily 0800-1630, BZ$8, BZ$2 (nationals).*
More of the Hummingbird Highway's beautiful limestone mountains, forests and caves are preserved in this 10-acre national park only a little further down the road from the Blue Hole. The park is dominated by an eerily cobalt blue lake, which sits jewel-like in thick forest. The surrounding hills are honeycombed with caves and, despite the park's small size, the whole area is an important habitat for dozens of species of bat, some of them very rare. They include nectar feeders, which pollinate a number of the park's larger plants, and the lesser dog-like bat, which can be seen roosting in the cave mouths. Birdwatching is good too, with some 220 species recorded, including sun grebe, white hawk and black hawk eagle (which soar around the cliffs above the caves), and the park is home to coatimundi, collared peccary, *paca* (gibnut), ocelot and agouti. Visitors can swim or canoe on the lake. Tourism in the caves is in its infancy, even though the system is said to be spectacular.

Billy Barquedier National Park
ⓘ *Hummingbird Highway Mile 16.5, billybarquediernp.webs.com, daily 0800-1630, BZ$8, BZ$2 (nationals).*
This large national park of some 1500 acres preserves large tracts of pristine lowland rainforest and mountain foothills, which are coursed by dozens of small rivers and filled with waterfalls. Trails lead through the forest, one to the small **Billy Barquedier Waterfalls**, which plunge over iron-coloured rocks into a clear-water swimming pool. The park is particularly rich in wildlife, including jaguars, Baird's tapirs, tayras and black howler monkeys, which are common. Birds include keel-billed motmots, great currasows, hawk eagles and myriad hummingbirds.

◉ Central and eastern Cayo listings

For hotel and restaurant price codes and other relevant information, see pages 11-12.

◉ Where to stay

ATM caves *p121*

$$$$ Dream Valley, Teakettle village, Western Highway, 8 miles west of Belmopan, T822-3344, www.dreamvalleybelize.com. This 2012 opening offers luxurious, well-appointed a/c cabins overlooking the river and set in a tropical garden within an extensive private reserve. The best rooms are the Dream Cabañas, with spacious rooms and enough accommodation for a family or small group, jacuzzis and a large terrace. The hotel has a spa, cable TV, restaurant, bar and tours including trail walking and biking, horse riding, kayaking and trips to sights in Cayo.

$$$$ Pook's Hill, Western Hwy between Belmopan and San Ignacio, southern turn-off at Teakettle Village, T832-2017, pookshilllodge.com. This is about as close as you can get to the beautiful unspoilt rainforests of the Tapir Mountain Nature Reserve. The lodge's luxurious, beautifully designed thatched roof cabins cluster around a Mayan ruin in a tiny ridge-top clearing. This sits in a vast swathe of forest that encompasses the private protected area of **Pook's Hill** and stretches into the Tapir Mountain Nature Reserve itself. There's great birdwatching, especially for forest species, and the lodge has a species list as well as equipment and a small library of field guides. There's a good chance of seeing some of Belize's larger mammals, including ocelot. The lodge runs tours to all the nearby sights and has a decent homely restaurant. There is a map of how to reach **Pook's Hill** on their website.

$$ Lower Dover, Western Hwy, northern turn-off at Unitedville village, www.lower doverbelize.com. This field station-turned-jungle lodge offers a simpler, cheaper alternative to **Pook's Hill**. Like that resort, **Lower Dover** is in a private rainforest reserve, has a Mayan ruin on its grounds and offers great bird and wildlife watching. And whilst **Pook's Hill** has a more spectacular setting (with wonderful views out over the forest and mountains), you will sleep and wake to the sound of rushing water at **Lower Dover**. The lodge is enclosed by rivers on 3 sides and sits a stone's throw from the Little Barton Creek waterfalls. Accommodation is in a wooden bunkhouse dorm or simple weatherboard cottages with terraces and hammock space. Both lie in a large lawned space from where trails lead into the surrounding forest.

Belmopan *p122, map p123*

Belmopan's better hotels are overpriced, bolstered by the diplomatic dollar. But there is one great and newly opened budget option. **$$$ Bullfrog Inn**, 25 Half Moon Av, T822-3425, www.bullfroginn.com. Belmopan's top hotel offers the same quality and comfort as a lower-end US brand name inn. Large rooms come with rather tawdry beige carpets, terraces, small desks and queen- or king-sized beds with colourful counterpanes and newly renovated en suites with tubs and shower heads. Some rooms are decidedly musty, so look at several. The best are 26, 27 and 28 on the upper floor. There is a restaurant, bar, cable TV and Wi-Fi. Credit cards accepted.

$$$ Ken Mar's, 22-24 Half Moon Av, T822-0118, www.kenmar.bz. Very simple individually decorated rooms and suites, brightly painted in egg-shell blue or brilliant white, and furnished with wardrobes, bedside desks and faux-antique hardwood beds. All have en suites, kitchenettes (with microwaves and fridges) and lounge areas. The included breakfast is a little meagre for the price. There is a restaurant and Wi-Fi. Credit cards accepted.

$$-$ El Rey Hotel, 23 Moho St, T822-3438, www.elreyhotel.com. This welcoming little guesthouse run by an Anglo-Belizean couple is the best option for independent travellers and makes a good base for explorations of the Hummingbird Highway. There are 3 room categories. A/c city rooms are bright and spacious and well looked after but simply furnished with a bed and cupboard space. Suites are larger, with lounge areas, coffee-making facilities and business workspaces. All rooms have en suite facilities with hot showers. The hotel also has a decent bistro restaurant and bakery serving Belizean and international food, a bar, an in-house tour operator and plenty of public space for relaxing or reading a book. The city centre and bus station are a 10-min walk or 2-min taxi ride. There is cable TV and Wi-Fi. Credit cards accepted.

Hummingbird Highway p124
Belmopan is a good base for the Hummingbird Highway.
$$$$ Ian Anderson's Caves Branch Jungle Lodge, Mile 41½ Hummingbird Hwy, T673-3454, T+1-866 357 2698 (US), www.cavesbranch.com. One of Belize's best wilderness lodges sits in some 60,000 acres of forest in the foothills of the mountains. The area is riddled with caves and cut with fast-flowing rivers, and the lodge organizes a range of activities and speleogical trips. They are one of the premier caving outfits in Central America. The lodge itself is very comfortable, with luxury hardwood and raw stone rooms set in cabins, some of which are as high as the forest canopy, with wonderful views of the surrounds and great birdwatching. Some have private jacuzzis on their terraces and all share extensive gardens, a pool and internet. There's a decent restaurant, they accept credit cards and they can arrange transfers.

🍴 Restaurants

Belmopan p122, map p123
$$ Moonclusters, Unit 6, Belmopan Shopping Centre, T602-1644. Belizean politicians come to this arty little café decorated with Saint-Exupery suns and moons to drink ice-cold *cholis*, frozen coffee, served with ice cream and cinnamon, and to eat huge 'flying saucer' quesadillas and other snacks.
$$ Oasis, Rivera Area, T822-3548, www.aguallos.com/oasisgrill. Come to this attractive *palapa* restaurant right next to the rushing Belize River for steaks, chicken, *escabeche*, decent grilled fish and a choice of 10 different tropical fruit juices.
$$-$ El Rey Hotel, see Where to stay. Open to non-guests for breakfast, lunch and dinner. Belizean comfort cooking with dishes like East Indian curries, chicken/beef with beans and rice, and big hearty breakfasts.
$ Half Moon Bakery, Half Moon Av s/n. Cinnamon buns, fried jacks, rolls, cakes and freshly baked white and brown bread. Very friendly staff.

⚙ What to do

Belmopan *p122, map p123*
Belize Travel Services, El Rey Hotel,
see page 126. One of the leading tour
operators in Central America. They can
organize excursions throughout Belize,
including to Ambergris Caye and the smaller
cayes. They also arrange diving and fishing
trips, hotel bookings, transfers and tours
into Guatemala and beyond. They also
have a full range of tours: along the
Hummingbird Hwy, to locations such
as ATM, and to lesser-known attractions
like the Blue Hole and Crystal Cave, plus
expedition excursions into Chiquibul.

Hummingbird Highway *p124*
For caving and jungle adventures,
see **Ian Anderson's Caves Branch
Adventure Company**, above.

⊖ Transport

Belmopan *p122, map p123*
Bus
Belmopan bus station (aka **Novelo's**,
Constitution Dr at Bliss Av) is one of the
busiest in the country. All buses from Belize
City heading south to Punta Gorda and
Dangriga or east to San Ignacio/Benque
Viejo pass through Belmopan. As you will
never have to wait long for a bus, Belmopan
is a good base for those travelling by public
transport. There are at least 2 buses to **San
Ignacio** and **Belize City** an hour, with more
frequent services in the early morning.
First bus 0300, last bus 1800, and hourly
buses south to **Dangriga** (change here for
Placencia) and **Punta Gorda** 0615-1930.

ⓘ Directory

Belmopan *p122, map p123*
Banks Atlantic Bank, Garden City Plaza,
T822-129; Belize Bank, Constitution at
Melhado Dr, T822-1291; Scotiabank,
1015 Ring Rd, T822-1412, all with ATMs.
Embassies For embassies and consulates
in Belize see http://embassy.goabroad.com.
Immigration New Administration
Building, T822-2662, www.belize.gov.bz,
visas and extensions. **Medical services**
Belmopan Hospital, T822-0666. City
Pharmacy, Novelo's Bus Terminal, T822-1299;
Cardinal's Pharmacy, Market Sq, T822-3065.

Southern Cayo

The crags and canyons of Belize's isolated Maya Mountains begin in earnest in southern Cayo, creating a landscape that contrasts markedly with the rest of the district. As you drive up into the hills, steamy jungle and meandering rivers give way to thin pine forest and a rugged, worn terrain cut by deep canyons and dripping with babbling streams and little waterfalls that drop in silky threads from the hills over such heights that the eye cannot take in their span in one gaze.

The Maya Mountains are quite different from other Central American highlands and are an altogether separate geological formation. There are no fuming volcanoes in Belize, no limpid mountain lakes. These mountains are unique to Belize and are far older than any other on the isthmus: a solid block of ancient granite, riven by deep fault lines and surrounded by rugged, limestone karsts honeycombed with water-worn caves. They reach a plateau at Mountain Pine Ridge, where there are a series of luxury lodges, and then climb high to the east into Stann Creek district to form Belize's highest peaks. To the west they drop into the thick rainforests of the Chiquibul Reserve, which spread like a green blanket into lowland Guatemala, and which hide in their depths one of the biggest and most mysterious Mayan ruins in Central America, Caracol. ▶▶ *For listings, see pages 133-134.*

Mountain Pine Ridge → *For listings, see pages 133-134. Colour map B1.*

The bumpy Cristo Rey dirt road leaves San Ignacio to the south, climbing up into the foothills of the Maya Mountains, then dividing to head one way to the cool sierra at Mountain Pine Ridge, and another to the monumental Mayan ruins of Caracol, lost in the steaming montane rainforests of the Chiquibul National Park (see page 132). The roads are rough and rutted, but the few hours of discomfort are more than made up for by the wild beauty of the scenery. Waterfalls nearly 300 m high plunge into steep ravines in the rocky hills of Mountain Pine Ridge, the air is crisp and glassy clear for tens of miles and the bird- and wildlife-watching are among the best in Belize.

Getting there

It's possible to visit Mountain Pine Ridge and even Caracol in your own hire car, but not advisable. The area is sparsely populated and there have been occasional armed hold-ups by Guatemalan bandits who've sneaked in across the border. Roads are dreadful and broken by potholes, maps are poor and there are very few signposts so it's easy to get lost. It's far better to base yourself at one of the excellent lodges in the area and explore the region with them at leisure on day tours. Or, if you simply don't have the time, join a day trip to the region leaving from San Ignacio with a tour company like **Hun Chi'ik** (see page 119).

Mountain Pine Ridge Forest Reserve

The crisp air, pine forests and cool rushing streams of Cayo's southernmost tourist area offer some respite from the sticky heat of Belize's beaches and rainforests and a complete contrast to the volcanic uplands of the rest of Central America. Mountain Pine Ridge is ancient, a carboniferous and permian landscape of crumbling canyons and weather-worn granite mounds, which peak at the 1016 m **Baldy Peak**. The region is sparsely covered with pine and evergreen oak forest, rendered sparser still by a blight of southern pine bark beetle, which denuded many of the trees in early 2000. Pockets of palmetto and lush tropical montane forest dripping with mosses and lichens line steep valleys cut by small brooks. These drop into rivers like the **Rio On** (which feeds the Macal river), or fall into deep canyons in cataracts that stretch over 500 yds, and which include the tumbling **Big Rock falls**, the more languid **Rio On pools** (where you can swim and explore a mossy cave), and Central America's highest, the spectacular **Thousand Foot Falls**. The entire region is populated only by a handful of rangers at the **Douglas da Silva Forest Reserve** guard hut and the staff of four top-end forest lodges. Birdwatchers flock to luxury wildlife lodges, such as the **Hidden Valley Inn** (see page 134) to see uncommon species like green jay, blue-crowned mot-mot, golden hooded tanager, orange-breasted falcon, king vulture and stygian owl.

Chiquibul National Park and Caracol → *Colour map C1.*

Chiquibul is Belize's wilderness frontier – a vast spread of pristine rainforest stretching into Guatemala and home to significant numbers of all of Central America's large mammals, including jaguar, puma and tapir. The forest is dotted with spectacular Mayan ruins, most notably Caracol, one of the Classic Maya's great metropolises, whose central pyramids are as imposing and impressive as any at Tikal or Chichen Itzá.

Getting there
Aside from a trip to Caracol which can be arranged with an operator in San Ignacio (see page 118), visiting Chiquibul is difficult, though not impossible. Currently **Hun Chi'ik** (see page 119) is the only operator offering trips to the rainforests and caves within the park. Cost depends on numbers, and it's best to contact them directly to get a price. Visitors should allow at least five days and be prepared to face the discomfort, physical strain and excitement of trekking through and camping in virgin rainforest.

Caracol
ⓘ *60 miles (2 hrs' drive) from San Ignacio. Daily 0800-1600, BZ$30. There is parking, a visitor centre, café-restaurant, toilets and a small shop. It's best visited on a tour, easily bookable through an agency in San Ignacio, or before arriving in Belize with Belize Travel Services (see page 128).*

Far more visitors to Cayo district take a day trip to Tikal in neighbouring Guatemala than visit Belize's largest and most spectacular Mayan ruins: Caracol. Perhaps it's because because Tikal is that much more famous. Perhaps it's because it's more vaunted by tour operators in San Ignacio, a puzzle in itself. It's hard to think of any other good reason. Caracol is fabulous: a romantic ruined city lost in thick rainforest and centred on an enormous, monumental stepped pyramid.

Whilst you'll coast along a smooth road, together with a host of other vans and buses, to reach Tikal; to get to Caracol you'll spend a couple of hours on a rutted forest track. Peccaries will probably trot out of the bush in front of your tour car. When you stop to negotiate a particularly deep pothole, all you'll hear is the hiss of cicadas and the shrill call of the screaming piha or guttural roar of howler monkeys far off in the canopy. You might see one or two other hardy vehicles, if you're unlucky. And once you reach Caracol itself you'll probably have the ruins entirely to yourself. Getting to Tikal was once an adventure; getting to Caracol still is.

Once you reach the city, you'll be equally amazed. Archaeological investigations over the last 20 years have shown that Caracol was vast: one of the largest cities in the ancient Maya world and probably the centre of the civilization that toppled Tikal and dominated the entire Petén region. The archaeological site covers an astonishing 34 sq miles, half as big again as Tikal and probably larger than Chichen Itzá in Mexico. And whilst both of those cities have been extensively unearthed and restored, visitors can see only a tiny fraction of Caracol's immensity: the cluster of plazas that formed the administrative and ceremonial centre of the ancient city. A wander around the site is an extraordinary experience. You feel like Frederick Catherwood, the 19th-century English artist who chanced upon the ruined cities of the Maya in the thick forests of the Yucatán and first brought them to the attention of the world.

Background Caracol reached the height of its powers in the Late Classic era, between AD 650 and 700, when it was a rainforest metropolis of some 36,000 buildings with a population over 10 times that of contemporaneous London. With some 150,000 people, Caracol would have been one of the largest cities in the world, greater even than Constantinople. After Caracol was abandoned in the late 12th century, it lay under the forest for some 850 years until it was discovered by Rosa Mai, a logger looking for mahogany in 1938. Shortly afterwards, Belize's Archaeological Commissioner, AH Anderson visited the site and named it Caracol (Spanish for snail) after the large number of shells he found here. We know now that the city's true name was Oxwitzá, meaning

Caracol

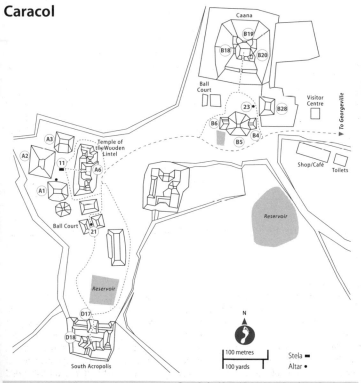

'three hills water'. A stucco text from Structure B-16-sub on the Caana pyramid records a 'star war' attack on the city, named as Oxwitza', by the 37th ruler of Naranjo in Guatemala. We know little more though, for whilst there are Mayan reservoirs all over Caracol (some still with their stucco lining), it is a mystery why the Maya built so vast a city in a location so far from rivers or lakes.

The site The tallest building in ancient or modern Belize, the great pyramid of **Caana** (sky palace), towering 43 m over contemporary Caracol, dates from this period. Caana lies at the heart of Caracol, crowning the principal plaza and topped by three separate pyramids (**B18**, **B19** and **B20**), each a respectable size in its own right. Excavations of Caana have unearthed vaulted passageways, corridors of rooms and numerous stone masks, altars and sundry artefacts. Climb to the top of the pyramid for unforgettable views out over the site towards interminable, gently undulating hills of rainforest beyond.

Five **sacbeob**, or paved Maya highways, radiate out into the city from the plaza at your feet, and beyond for a distance of at least 1½ miles. They probably extend far beyond that but archaeologists are yet fully to investigate. Directly opposite you across the lawned plaza are Structures **B4** and **B5**. These border the south side of another plaza. Climbing B5 (which was still in use in the late 12th century) gives the best views of Caana itself. Excavations on the temple have uncovered lintels depicting Witz-monsters (gaping-jawed mythical beasts representing the spirits of mountains and hills), jaguars and lily pads (used as symbols of the passage between life and death by the Maya).

Walk past B5 and you'll enter another plaza, prosaically called Plaza B. Look out for the altar next to the ball court, which has eroded carvings depicting two bound captives. Translations of the glyphs on the altar indicate that both are noblemen, one from Ucanal in modern Guatemala. Plaza A lies to the west of Plaza B. Structure **A2** on the plaza's west side is capped by a stela with 140 blocks of glyphic text, the greatest number so far found in Belize. Opposite A2 is the tallest building in the square, structure **A6**, or the **Temple of the Wooden Lintel**, a pyramid that was 1000 years old when it was finally abandoned in 1100, and whose wooden lintel was still holding up part of the structure when it was unearthed in the late 20th century. The best views of Plaza A are from the more modest pyramid that crowns the square at the north end: Structure **A3**. This is a good spot to sit and contemplate for a while. You're right up in the forest canopy here, on the edge of the excavated site and in a great location for spotting birds and primates; bring binoculars or a zoom lens and look out for emerald toucanets, mot-mots, assorted tanagers and howler monkeys in the nearby trees.

Assorted stelae and altars litter the ruins at Caracol. Most are very worn, but some have been deciphered and indicate that in the sixth century, the city and its ally Calakmul were victorious in a protracted war with Tikal (see page 107), coming to dominate this region of the Maya world.

Chiquibul National Park

Caracol sits in the heart of one of Belize's largest, wildest and least-visited national park: Chiquibul. The park preserves outstanding biological diversity and is a critical habitat for many endangered species, including large neo-tropical mammals, such as jaguar, tapir (see box opposite) and puma as well as the harpy eagle, the largest eagle in world. Covering 414 sq miles, Chiquibul is made up mainly of lowland tropical moist forest. This forest extends into Guatemala, forming the largest remaining contiguous block of tropical forest north of the Amazon. It is also a key segment in the internationally funded

Tapirs

The national animal of Belize is the Baird's tapir, known locally as the mountain cow. These shy, gentle animals, which are related to horses and rhinos, are the largest mammals in the Neotropics, weighing up to 300 kg. Like cows, they spend 90% of their waking hours grazing, pulling leaves from the trees and bushes with their odd little trunk-like noses, and sleeping deep in the bush or partially submerged in rivers.

Family groups live in a very small geographical area, but they are very seldom seen. Look out for their distinctive three-toed footprints in the mud next to rivers. Or listen for their loud foot stamps and whistles, made when the animal is startled or alarmed.

There are only four species of tapirs in the world, three of them in the Americas and one, the Malayan tapir, in Southeast Asia. All are endangered, victims to hunting and habitat loss. There are estimated to be 650-3300 Baird's tapirs in Belize, in all the national parks with the exception of Guanacaste and Rio Blanco, both of which are isolated from the surrounding forests by agricultural land and roads. Populations are particularly healthy in Cayo, particularly on the upper Macal River Valley and in Chiquibul National Park around the Upper Raspaculo River.

Mesoamerican Biological Corridor. In Belize alone it abuts on the Mountain Pine Ridge Forest Reserve to the north and the Cockscomb Basin Wildlife Sanctuary and Bladen Nature Reserve to the east and south. The park is home to the longest and most expansive cave network so far discovered in Central America: the Chiquibul Cave System. However, Chiquibul is increasingly threatened by illegal logging, poaching and agricultural activities, mostly by Guatemalans. In 2007 alone, over 1000 acres of the park were illegally cleared for cultivation. There is a Chiquibul-Maya Mountain Programme (mayamountains.org) campaign to protect and preserve the park; you can find out more about the park and how to help protect it through their site.

◉ Southern Cayo listings

For hotel and restaurant price codes and other relevant information, see pages 11-12.

◔ Where to stay

Mountain Pine Ridge *p129*
All the lodges in Mountain Pine have their own restaurants and organize their own tours. There is no public transport to Mountain Pine Ridge. Resorts will arrange transfers.
$$$$ Blancaneaux, T824-4912, www.coppolaresorts.com. Francis Ford Coppola's rustic chic mountain resort straddles a steep ridge near the Big Rock waterfalls in pine forest. Palm-roof cabins come with their own private plunge pools and the best have waterfall views. It's said that Mr Coppola himself favours number 7. Cabana Rooms are decked out in hardwood with high domed thatched roofs and kitted out with mod cons like iPod docks, but there are no TVs and no a/c; it's very much about immersion in nature. Tours are active and include hikes, horse riding and guided wildlife walks, and the resort grounds are steep and rocky so this is not a good location for the physically challenged. The 2 restaurants serve wood-fired pizzas and US-style Central American food, washed down with a selection of Coppola wines. There's a pool and a spa. Credit cards accepted.

$$$$ Hidden Valley Inn, T822-3320, www. hiddenvalleyinn.com. This romantic, intimate luxury wilderness lodge has a series of spacious, very comfortable cabins set in a flower-filled garden in one of the remotest and wildest stretches of Mountain Pine Ridge. Each is beautifully appointed with big hardwood beds, hearths with fireplaces and en suite bathrooms in lush wood and terracotta tiles. The resort offers a broad range of tours and excursions and has a lovely little mountain stream on its grounds, running through montane forest and dropping through dozens of falls. Guiding is superb, especially for those interested in wildlife and birds, and **Hidden Valley** has perhaps the best birding facilities in Cayo. The restaurant is one of Belize's best. Chef Natascha Xisto das Neves, who trained in South Africa and has worked with British Chef Ainsley Harriott, sources all her fruit and vegetables from local Mennonite markets, her seafood from the Belizean coast, and bakes all the bread on site daily. Her cooking fuses Belizean ingredients with traditional Maya techniques. There's a pool, tours and Wi-Fi. Credit cards accepted.

$$$$-$$$ Five Sisters Lodge, T834-4005, www.fivesisterslodge.com. The eponymous 5 sisters are 5 small mountain waterfalls that plunge into pools a stroll away from the hotel's wooden and palm-thatch cabins. Spacious luxury cabins are good for couples, with a romantic waterfall view, polished wood or tile floors and small sitting areas. Standard cabins are slightly smaller and simpler and come with 2 double beds but no waterfall views. There are larger family cabins and suites available too. All have (mosquito-screened) terraces with hammocks. Tours are offered in the Mountain Pine Ridge Reserve and beyond, including trips to Caracol. There's also a restaurant. Credit cards accepted.

$$$ Pine Ridge Lodge, T606-4557, www.pineridgelodge.com. Accommodation is simple but very elegant in this lovely lodge set on a ridge in a beautiful pine forest garden filled with Belizean orchids. Rooms come in large thatched-roof mock-Maya cabins. They have polished concrete floors, a double and 2 single beds (with modest price increases for extra guests), small screened verandas and private bathrooms. They are all built with sustainable materials and decorated with Maya and Creole art and Guatemalan Maya fabrics. The restaurant serves organic fruit and vegetables from the lodge garden and offers an international menu with a French twist. There are trails cutting through the lodge's private reserve to streams and waterfalls and there are tours organized in the vicinity and further afield, including options for birders.

Contents

Footprint features

Border crossings

Southern Belize

At a glance

⊕ **Getting around** There are buses, cabs, boats and hire cars. Some places are only accessible with transport organised with a tour operator.
◔ **Time required** Allow around 5 days to visit Stann Creek and the Cayes and a week to 10 days to explore the entire region at leisure.
☀ **Weather** It's warm and dry at around 15- 30°C Jan-May with cooler nights. It's more hot and humid May-Oct, with the possibility of hurricanes. Nov-Dec is warm with occasional colder spells of 13-15°C.
✘ **When not to go** May-Oct is hurricane season, Sep-Nov can be grey and overcast and there are more biting insects.

The country's two southernmost districts – Stann Creek and Toledo – show two sides of modern Belize. Stann Creek is home to one of Belize's fastest-changing resort towns, Placencia, and a peninsula lined with an increasing number of resort hotels and condominiums, intent on challenging San Pedro for the country's tourist crown. By contrast, the rest of southern Belize seems lost in time.

Both district capitals – Dangriga and Punta Gorda – remain Garifuna-speaking strongholds, hosting spectacular celebrations to celebrate the arrival of their people from Roatan every November. The rippling hills that stretch from southern Belize into Guatemala are dotted with dozens of indigenous American villages, where Mayan peoples preserve pre-Columbian languages and customs.

And, in between, are stretches of rainforest, cave-pocked hills and unspoilt coastline. The rugged Cockscomb Basin Wildlife Sanctuary is one of the best places to see jaguar in Central America; dozens of Morelet's crocodiles laze on the beaches of the Monkey River, and upland Toledo is honeycombed with spectacular caves. There are hundreds of cayes too: the Tobacco Cayes in the Southwater Caye Marine Reserve off Dangriga; Laughing Bird Caye National Park off Placencia (where there are abundant manatees); the Sapodilla Caye Marine Reserve and the Snake Caye archipelago off Punta Gorda, and, far out to the east, Belize's third atoll, Glover's Reef, with superb diving and snorkelling.

Outside Placencia, facilities in the south are less developed than in Cayo or San Pedro and herein lies the region's charm. Southern Belize's villages, cayes and forests offer an undiscovered Belize where, if tourists are not a surprise, they are still relatively few and far between.

Stann Creek District

Stann Creek District is the second largest in Belize, covering 950 sq miles, stretching between the mangrove and beach-lined coast and the Cockscomb Range in the foothills of the Maya Mountains. Its capital, Dangriga, is an untidy town, with little to recommend it but a lively Garifuna festival in November. But the coast south of Dangriga is one of the prettiest in Belize, lined with attractive beaches, particularly at Hopkins, a delightful, sleepy Garifuna village that is as yet unspoilt by resorts.

Beyond Hopkins the mangroves and beaches are broken by a long peninsula at Placencia, Belize's biggest beach resort town after San Pedro on Ambergris Caye. Just beyond Placencia is the Monkey River, on the border with Toledo province, which is a great spot to see manatees, Morelet's crocodiles and waterbirds. Inland, Stann Creek is covered in lowland rainforest, swamp and farmland. Much of the land is protected, though not all the national parks are readily accessible to visitors. Those that are include the Cockscomb Basin Wildlife Sanctuary, a designated jaguar preserve, the remote Bladen River Nature Reserve and the Victoria Peak Natural Monument, protecting Belize's highest mountain.

Stann Creek is well-served by flights (into Dangriga or Placencia) and by buses from Belize City along the Coastal Highway or Manatee Road, and San Ignacio via the Hummingbird Highway. None of these destinations are more than three hours' drive away, much the same distance as Punta Gorda in neighbouring Toledo in neighbouring Toledo district, to the south.
➤➤ For listings, see pages 146-155.

Dangriga → For listings, see pages 146-155. Colour map B3. Population: 9096.

Stann Creek's capital and southern Belize's largest settlement is a scruffy beachside town huddled around two sluggish rivers. Stann Creek, which gives its name to the district and sits in the centre of town, and tiny Havana Creek to the south. The town was named after Stann Creek until Independence, after which it was rechristened Dangriga, a name which sounds poetic in English, but which prosaically means 'fresh water' in the Garifuna language.

Dangriga is one of Belize's largest Garifuna towns, second in importance only to Punta Gorda, where the sacred Garifuna *dugu* or temple is found, see page 167, and host to one of the biggest Garifuna festivals in Belize: Settlement Day on 19 November (see page 152). Dangriga's population is made up largely of Garifuna people, descendants of the Carib people (who suffered so greatly under the Spanish and Portuguese) and West African fugitives from slavery; they have a fascinating history and culture (see page 214).

Arriving in Dangriga

Getting there The airstrip is at the north end of town next to the **Pelican Beach** resort and just under a mile from the centre. Taxis into Dangriga cost around BZ$10. Buses arrive in town along Stann Creek Valley Road, a turn-off from the Southern Highway just south of the junction with the Hummingbird Highway. Dangriga's bus station lies at the far south end of town at the junction of Stann Creek Valley Road and Havana Street (the continuation of the town's main street: Commerce Street/St Vincent Street). It is 50 yds south of Havana Creek and 500 yds south of the centre of town on Stann Creek. Buses from Hopkins arrive at a small bus stop on the south bank of Stann Creek immediately west of the **Riverside** restaurant. Boats from the South Water Caye Marine Reserve arrive at the quay on the south side of Stann Creek. ➤➤ See Transport, page 154, for further details.

Places in Dangriga

Despite its illustrious status, little happens in Dangriga outside festival season, and there is very little to see. Boats bob up and down in the creek. Locals wander along sleepy St Vincent Street, which bridges Stann Creek in the heart of town, changing its name to Commerce Street as it runs north. Whilst it's the biggest town in southern Belize, Dangriga is in fact tiny, made-up of just a handful of streets, lined with tumbledown shops and weatherboard houses, many of them barely withstanding the tropical heat and damp. The town is the main departure point for the South Water Caye Marine Reserve (see page 144), and a transit point for a bus to balmy Hopkins an hour to the south. But if you get stuck here, there are a couple of attractions to while away an empty afternoon.

The **Gulisi Garífuna Museum** ① *Stann Creek Valley Rd, 2 miles west of town, T669-0639, www.ngcbelize.org, Mon-Fri 1000-1700, Sat 0800-1200, BZ\$10*, has multimedia exhibits and information about the origins of the Garifuna, their customs, spirituality and their remarkable music. You can hear the beating of the *dugu* drums, which are the metaphoric heartbeat of Garifuna community life, and which are used in ceremonies to evoke archetypal spirits. And you can watch videos or listen to CDs of many key Garifuna and Punta musicians, such as Andy Palacio (see box, page 172) or Pen Cayetano (see box, page 212). There are arts and crafts too, and a physic garden of traditional plants and herbs. The museum is named after one of the first and most highly revered Garifuna people, Gulisi, who founded Punta Negra after being exiled from the island of St Vincent by the British and subsequently deported from Roatan along with her 13 children. To get

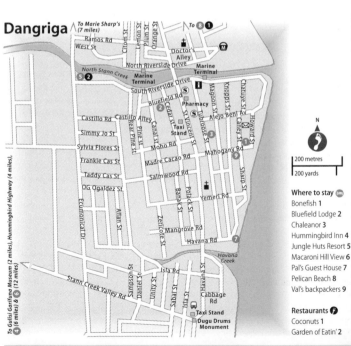

Dangriga

Where to stay
Bonefish 1
Bluefield Lodge 2
Chaleanor 3
Hummingbird Inn 4
Jungle Huts Resort 5
Macaroni Hill View 6
Pal's Guest House 7
Pelican Beach 8
Val's backpackers 9

Restaurants
Coconuts 1
Garden of Eatin' 2

Don't miss ...

to the museum take a cab (BZ$10 return) or any bus passing west along the Stann Creek Valley Road that connects to the Hummingbird Highway.

Belize's famous chilli sauce, is made at the **Marie Sharp Factory** ① *1 Melinda Rd, Stann Creek Valley, T520-2087, www.mariesharps-bz.com, free*, six miles outside Dangriga. You can visit for a tour of the farm and bottling plant. Alternatively, buy her produce in shops throughout Belize, including her main one in Dangriga at 3 Pier Street, T522-2370. Marie's spicy sauces are a real Belizean success story. She started her business in her home in the 1980s, with help from family and friends. Her factory now employs dozens of people and sells sauces, chutneys, jams and squashes for the national and international market. These are some of the tartest, tangiest and most torrid condiments you'll find anywhere, and make a great Belizean souvenir. Sauces come with distinctive names, describing their potency: 'Hot', 'Fiery Hot', 'Beware' and 'No Wimps Allowed'. The latter three blow tabasco right out of the water. All the ingredients come from plants grown on Marie's home farm.

A few miles further north near the airstrip there's a narrow **beach** backed by coconut palms and, at the opposite end of town, in the far south where Stann Creek Valley Road meets the far end of Commerce Street is an undistinguished **monument** to the sacred *dugu* drums of the Garifuna people, sculpted by Nigerian artist Stephen Okeke.

Hopkins → *For listings, see pages 146-155. Colour map B2. Population: 1600.*

This sleepy Garifuna village nestles between reef and rainforest next to one of the country's longest and most beautiful beaches. Life trickles along in the village pretty much as it has done for decades: at a snail's pace. And, outside the pretty little village of painted weatherboard huts, a handful of beach hotels offer guests the chance either to do absolutely nothing at all in hammocks, beach loungers and comfy air-conditioned rooms, or to go birdwatching in the rainforest, snorkelling or diving on the offshore cayes, or to visit Mayan ruins. Despite its tiny size, Hopkins has one of the best restaurants in Belize and some very comfortable rooms, making it a less touristy, more relaxed and rustic alternative to Placencia. But come soon, as developers have their eyes on Hopkins.

Arriving in Hopkins

Getting there Buses from Dangriga run along the village street and stop at the corner of the turn-off for the Southern Highway. Services from Belize City, Placencia and Punta Gorda arrive at the bus stop on the Southern Highway itself, six miles from Hopkins, from where it is usually easy to catch a ride into Hopkins village. ▶▶ *See Transport, page 154, for further details.*

Getting around and orientation Taxis and hire bikes can be organized through hotels and restaurants, but everywhere in the town centre is within easy walking distance. Hopkins has just one unnamed street, which runs parallel to the beach. Shops, restaurants and the few cafés and bars are spread along its length. There are no addresses. Most of the cheaper and more charming hotels lie in the village; larger resorts sit to the north and the south.

Places in Hopkins

The **Lebeha Drumming Centre** ① *T665-9305, www.lebeha.com*, preserves and teaches the sacred and ceremonial drumming styles that form the heartbeat of the Garifuna communities. The group was founded by local Garifuna drummer Jabbar Lambey and his Canadian partner Dorothy Pettersen in 2002 and now has a membership of a score or so of mostly young people from the Hopkins Garifuna community. They perform at the centre most Friday evenings, or on demand for a fee. There is simple accommodation at the drumming centre, see page 148.

Hopkins merges with the small **Sittee River Village**, made up of expat fishermen's homes, riverside guesthouses and Garifuna shacks a few miles south of the **Hamanasi** resort. There's little to see in the village itself, but the river is a great spot for bird- and Morelet's crocodile-watching, especially at the beginning and the end of the day. It's easy to organize a kayak or boat trip here through **Sittee River Marina** ① *T670-8525, www.sitteerivermarina. com*, or through a guesthouse in the village or in Hopkins itself (see pages 147 and 148).

The small **Possum Point Biological Station** ① *T523-7021, www.marineecology.com*, has room for up to 30 people (in cabins with a central dining hall-cum-classroom, **$$$**) and sits in its own private rainforest reserve a short boat ride from Sittee River village. The only access is by boat from Sittee River and, while it's only a one-mile ride, Possum Point has a real sense of remoteness. The reserve's little stilted weatherboard huts sit in a lawned area on the edge of rainforest, with plenty of bird and animal life, and the river in front is estuarine at this point, meaning that manatees, stingray and larger saltwater fishes like tarpon are a common sight, alongside Morelet's crocodiles. Run in conjunction with the **Wee Wee Caye Marine Lab** (see page 144) in South Water Caye Marine Reserve, Possum Point mainly hosts college groups but is open to other visitors who make reservations.

Hopkins

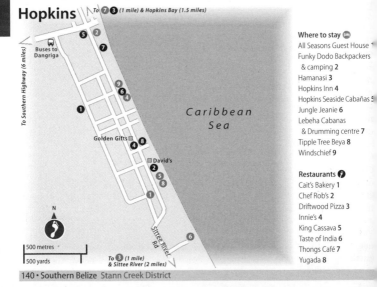

To ⑦ ❸ (1 mile) & Hopkins Bay (1.5 miles)

Buses to Dangriga

Caribbean Sea

Golden Gifts ▢ ❽

▢ David's

N

500 metres
500 yards

To ❸ (1 mile) & Sittee River (2 miles)

Sittee River Rd

To Southern Highway (6 miles)

Where to stay 🛌
All Seasons Guest House 1
Funky Dodo Backpackers
 & camping 2
Hamanasi 3
Hopkins Inn 4
Hopkins Seaside Cabañas 5
Jungle Jeanie 6
Lebeha Cabanas
 & Drumming centre 7
Tipple Tree Beya 8
Windschief 9

Restaurants 🍴
Cait's Bakery 1
Chef Rob's 2
Driftwood Pizza 3
Innie's 4
King Cassava 5
Taste of India 6
Thongs Café 7
Yugada 8

Mayflower Bocawina National Park → *Colour map B2.*

In the rush to Cockscomb or the reef, many visitors to Stann Creek overlook this delightful national park covering almost 7413 acres of pristine lowland and low mountain rainforest. The park is one of Belize's newest, established in 2001 to provide a biological corridor between the Maya Mountains and the coast. As it receives few visitors, you are unlikely to encounter other walkers, as you might in Cockscomb, and the bird and wildlife is relatively undisturbed.

Visiting the park The park lies just four miles off the Southern Highway, some 15 miles northwest of Hopkins and just north of Silk Grass village. There is a small **visitor centre** ① *daily 0800-1600, where you pay the BZ$10 entrance fee*, near the park entrance, which is often unstaffed. Maps of the trails and the Mayan ruins are available here. There are no buses to the park but taxis can be organized in Silk Grass village (ask at the local restaurant). Hotels and tour companies in Dangriga and Hopkins can arrange a visit or you can take a cab from Hopkins for around BZ$80 for the round trip with waiting time.

Wildlife, Mayan sites and waterfalls Like Cockscomb, Mayflower Bocawina has a healthy resident jaguar population (you will see tracks on many of the trails), as well as significant numbers of peccary, brocket deer, ocelot, coatimundis, tapirs and tayra. The park bird list has over 250 species. All three of Belize's motmots (blue-crowned motmot, tody motmot and the rare keel-billed motmot), all Belize's toucans, several species of trogons, crested guans, great curassows and ocellated turkeys can be seen here, and there have been reported sightings of scarlet macaws.

There are three Mayan sites in the park, all of which are still under excavation by the **Mayflower Archaeology Project**. One of the Mayan sites (**Mayflower**) lies just across the road from the visitor centre. The other two (**T'au Witz** and **Maintzunun**) are a short distance away and can be reached along a forest trail lined with giant heliconia flowers and patches of banana musa bush.

The park is also home to three beautiful waterfalls. **Bocawina Falls** and the **Three Sisters Falls** lie close to each other and at the end of an easy two-mile walk that initially cuts through flat rainforest before climbing steeply into mountain foothills. The 30-m-high **Antelope Falls** are more challenging to reach, lying at the end of the 2½-mile-long Antelope trail, which runs through Maintzunun before cutting steeply into the hills to the falls. At the falls there are breathtaking views out over the forest to the Caribbean, and a refreshing plunge pool where you can cool off. Be very careful on the trail after rain, as it can be very slippery.

Cockscomb Basin Wildlife Sanctuary and Jaguar Reserve → *Colour map B2.*

Central America's only designated jaguar preserve lies some 19 miles south of Dangriga off the Southern Highway to Placencia. Administered by the **Belize Audobon Society** (see page 50), the reserve covers some 21,000 acres and offers superb hikes through lowland tropical forest and the Cockscomb Range of the Maya Mountains.

Visiting the reserve The turn-off to Cockscomb is at Mile 14 on the Southern Highway, marked by an important Mayan community, focused on the **Maya Centre** (see below). Any buses travelling north or south along the Southern Highway will drop you at the Maya

Centre. The reserve's **visitor centre** ⓘ *daily 0800-1700, BZ$10*, is at the former settlement of Quam Bank, six miles west of the Southern Highway at the head of 20 miles of trails, one of which leads to the path to Belize's second-highest mountain, Victoria Peak (see below). The centre has interactive video displays, information panels, maps and helpful staff who can organize guides, kayaking and tube-floating. There is very simple accommodation and a camping area.

Wildlife It was founded in 1990 to protect an area inhabited by what was then thought to be the country's highest density of jaguars (this is now known to be in Rio Bravo, see page 185), and their smaller cousins. In descending order, these are pumas, ocelots, margays and jaguarundis, the last of which is black or tanned and about the size of a large house cat. Many other mammals share the heavily forested reserve, including Central American coatimundis, white-lipped peccaries, Central American agoutis, tamandua anteaters, Baird's tapirs and tayras. There are also red-eyed tree frogs, boas, iguanas and fer-de-lances, as well as over 290 species of bird, including king vultures and great curassows. The sanctuary is a good place for relaxing, showering under waterfalls, tubing down the river or listening to birds; hundreds of bird species have been spotted and there are several types of toucan, hummingbirds and scarlet macaws to be seen by early risers.

The Maya Centre ⓘ *Mile 14 Southern Hwy, T615-1313, nuukcheil@btl.net*. The cultural and community centre is in itself well worth a visit and its **Nuukcheil Cottage Cabañas** make a delightful place to stay when visiting the park (see page 149). The Classic era ruins of **Kuchil Balam** indicate that Maya people have lived in Cockscomb for over 2000 years, coming into conflict with mahogany loggers in colonial times and then forced out of the park itself when it was established in 1984. The Maya Centre, run by Mopan Maya, is one of the few places in Belize where it is possible to come into direct contact with Maya spiritual and medicinal traditions that have existed unbroken since pre-Columbian times. There is a small museum and an excellent little gift shop (where it's possible to by souvenirs including raw copal and copal candles), and staff here offer cooking lessons, healing consultations (using traditional Mayan rainforest medicine) and Mesoamerican herbal massages. They will also transfer guests in and out of Cockscomb, seven miles down the track, and offer the best guiding to the park, through village guides or **Cockscomb Maya Tours** (see page 153).

Victoria Peak Trail ⓘ *The trail is open only during Belize's dry season, 1 Feb-31 May. All hikers must be accompanied by a licensed tour guide (who can be hired from the Maya Centre, see above, or in advance through Belize Travel Services (see page 153)*. Stann Creek's Cockscomb Mountains rise abruptly from the sweltering lowlands of the coast in a rugged wave of green that reaches its zenith at the 1120 m **Victoria Peak**, Belize's second highest mountain. Hiking to the summit of Victoria Peak is one of Belize's most exciting wilderness adventures. But it's not for the physically unfit or those who cannot endure discomfort. The walk covers 15 miles of very rough, forest-covered terrain with steep elevations.

The well-marked and well-maintained trail begins at the Cockscomb Basin Wildlife Sanctuary park headquarters, following an old logging track for a long, flat stretch before crossing the Sittee River. You will most likely see jaguar and tapir footprints along the way. After a break for lunch, the hike becomes more difficult as you enter the foothills of the mountains. A series of climbs and drops eventually brings you to the steep, long climb at Heartbreak Hill and the first overnight stop. Like all the campsites along the way the site

The misery of macaws

Macaws unique to the Neotropics are the largest, longest lived and, arguably, the most beautiful parrots in the world. They are highly intelligent and wonderful imitators. And they are also among the world's most recognisable birds; Long John Silver's parrot is a scarlet macaw. It is not a surprise therefore that macaws have been among the worst-hit victims of the animal trade. The brilliant blue Spix's macaw, made famous by the children's cartoon *Rio*, is now extinct in the wild. At least three other species, including the magnificent turquoise glaucous macaw, are extinct altogether. There are now only 14 species left in the wild. And yet, even in the 21st century, if you search on the internet for information on macaws, the biggest hits are for sites offering the birds for sale.

Belize has just one kind of macaw, a rare subspecies of scarlet macaw: *Ara macao cyanoptera*. It is in urgent need of protection. There are fewer than 100 pairs in the country. They can be seen seasonally at Red Bank (see opposite), but they nest almost exclusively along a short stretch of the Upper Macal and Raspaculo rivers, on the border between the Mountain Pine Ridge Forest Reserve and Chiqiuibul National Park.

From late February to early March the birds excavate holes in quamwood trees, laying eggs shortly after and nursing chicks from July. Quamwoods have brilliant yellow blooms, so they are very easy for poachers to find. In 2010 all the chicks were poached or lost to predators, despite the efforts of monitors from the **Friends for Conservation and Development (FCD)** NGO and **Blancaneaux Lodge**.

If the situation persists, the rare Belizean scarlet macaws face extinction, like so many of their cousins before them. For information on how you can help protect them, see www.fcdbelize.org.

---

close to a water source – in this case a very pretty waterfall, and has a thatch *palapa* offering protection from the rain (where you can set up a small tent or hang hammocks), a campfire hearth, pit latrines and cooking equipment. There are no bins, so you will need to take all your rubbish with you.

The next day you leave your packs at the camp for the ascent to the summit, reaching the base of Victoria Peak itself in the late morning. There's a scramble here up a rocky stream into elfin and then cloud forest draped with dripping moss and lichens. Look out for the fiery-coloured, epiphytic *Epidendrum ibaguense* orchid, a species found only in Latin American mountains of this elevation. Peccaries and spider monkeys are a common sight. The final climb to the peak involves some easy rope work. The views from the top are stunning, out over the crinkled green folds of the foothills and the vast rainforest-covered wilderness of Cockscomb basin to the distant Caribbean.

Red Bank Scarlet Macaw Site → *Colour map C2.*

ⓘ *4 miles down a dirt road off the Southern Hwy some 30 mins' drive towards Placencia from Cockscomb. Red Bank is difficult to reach on public transport, but visits to can be organized through the Maya Centre (see page 142).*

This tiny Mopan Maya village is the seasonal home for scarlet macaws, which gather here between January and March in some of the largest flocks you'll find anywhere in Central America to feed on blood-red *urucum* berries (annatto, or *Bixa orellana*), which ripen at this time. The **Red Bank Conservation Group** ⓘ *T622-2233, BZ$35 for guided walks*, founded by local villager Geronimo Sho, is a community-based ecotourism initiative aimed at conserving the *urucum* trees and providing a limited infrastructure for tourists. Simple accommodation is available (see page 149), together with meals and handicrafts at the village shop, but as supplies are limited, it's a good idea to bring some snacks, a torch (flashlight), mosquito net and insect repellent.

Cayes off Dangriga and Hopkins → *For listings, see pages 146-155. Colour map C3.*

South Water Caye Marine Reserve

ⓘ *All non-Belizean tourists entering South Water Caye Marine Reserve must pay an entrance fee of BZ$10 per day for up to 3 days, BZ$30 for 4-7 days and BZ$36 for 8-10 days; students BZ$20 for 10 days. It's easy to organize visits through hotels in Hopkins or Dangriga. It is also possible to stay on one of the cayes. Most hotels will arrange transfers from Dangriga (with reps meeting guests off the plane or at the quay on Stann Creek). Alternatively, boats can be chartered from the quay next to the Stann Creek River in Dangriga.*

The largest marine reserve in south central Belize sits right offshore from Hopkins and Dangriga, covering some 117,800 acres of shallow reef, cayes, sea grass beds, Caribbean mangrove forests and nascent coastal scrub forest. It's the usual destination for snorkel and dive trips out of Hopkins. The reserve protects important habitats not only for marine invertebrates and fish but also for manatees and dolphins, both of which can often be spotted here, and sea birds. Man-o-War Caye is an important North Atlantic nesting site for brown boobies and magnificent frigate birds.

The archipelago feels a little like a Caribbean Maldives, with tiny beach-fringed islets set in shallow sea; a few have resorts, private homes or guesthouses squeezed in under the coconut palms, overlooking a tiny sliver of silver sand. A few days on one of the cayes, with nothing but the stars, the lapping waves and a few fellow travellers or local fishermen for company, is wonderful tonic for the urban soul; a week can begin to induce *cabaña* fever.

Tiny **Tobacco Caye**, nine miles off Dangriga to the north of the archipelago and covering less than one acre, has the bulk of the accommodation, with a huddle of backpacker and dive hotels under the coconut palms or on the meagre beach. The island sits opposite **Man-O-War Caye** (aka Bird Island, where there are hundreds of nesting magnificent frigate birds and brown boobies) and next to the mangrove-covered islets of the **Tobacco Caye Range**, a grazing ground for manatees. Look out for Marie Sharp's private island, which has hundreds of conch shells piled up as a wall against the encroaching sea, a testament to the short-sightedness of chopping down mangroves.

Privately owned **South Water Caye**, 12 miles off Dangriga, has just three hotels, but they feel squeezed in; an Olympian could throw a javelin from one end of the caye to the other. The tiny beach leads straight to shallow coral gardens and then, after less than 100 yds, there is a fringing coral wall, with glorious snorkelling. Many day trippers from Hopkins come here. Other islands include **Coco Plum Caye** (with one comfortable resort see page 150), **Thatch Caye** (with an eco resort, see page 150) and **Carrie Bow Caye** (where the **Smithsonian Institute** runs a Caribbean Coral Reefs Ecosystems Program).

The **Wee Wee Caye Marine Lab** ⓘ *T523-7021, www.marineecology.com*), is the sole occupant of a tiny islet in the marine park. It's a stunning little mangrove caye with, as its hosts put it, 'the textbook zonation of the mangrove species', making it an ideal place for scientific study by trainee biologists and college groups. It is these that make up most of the lab's guests, although the administrators are happy to receive other visitors. Permanent residents include several genera of land crabs, lizards and a healthy population of Central

...merican boa constrictors. The island has 7-m-long fibreglass boats for trips around the reserve and for transport to and from Dangriga, and has room for up to 30 people housed in simple weatherboard cabins, eating and taking classes in a central dining and lecture hut. Boardwalks between the cabins ensure minimum impact on the mangrove habitat. The surrounding sea is glassy clear, with extensive eel grass beds leading to fringing coral reef with very healthy marine life and excellent snorkelling.

Glover's Reef Marine Reserve

① Resorts in the atoll can arrange a transfer. Or visit on a guided snorkel or dive tour organized out of Dangriga or Hopkins (see page 153).

Belize's southernmost atoll, some 28 miles off the mainland, has the greatest diversity of reef types of all the atolls in the Caribbean. Unlike Turneffe and Lighthouse, it has a deep central lagoon (some seven miles wide, fringed by a 20-mile-long coral wall) studded with 850 patch reefs and pinnacles. The outer reef wall is broken in just three places, allowing water to flow between the lagoon and the open sea, but creating a sheltered habitat as well as excellent clear water with visibility of up to 50 m. The Glover's Reef Marine Reserve includes the entire atoll and a 100-fathom depth contour extending out from the reef wall. Together they make-up a total area of 86,652 acres.

The atoll wall rises to form a cluster of small cayes, the largest of which are **Northeast Caye** (where there are some Mayan middens), **Southeast Caye** (which is split by a narrow channel), **Long Caye** and **Middle Caye**. The last island is home to the headquarters of the **Wildlife Conservation Society (WCS)** ① www.gloversreef.org, who run the Glover's Reef Research Station and manage conservation in the atoll as a whole. WCS have divided Glover's atoll into four zones. The Conservation and Wilderness Zones are off-limits to almost all but scientists, whilst the Seasonal Closure and General Use Zones, where there are cayes with some simple resorts, can be visited by divers and snorkellers.

There are six resorts within the atoll. Unlike resorts on Turneffe or Lighthouse they are almost all ecologically sensitive operations using wind and solar power, recycling waste and conserving water.

Diving Diving at Glover's is about as good as it gets anywhere in the Atlantic. The sheer variety of dive sites beggars belief, as does the marine fauna. Whale sharks, manta rays, grey reef, hammerhead and black tip sharks and several species of turtle are relatively common sights, alongside pelagic fish like tuna, large schools of jacks and hundreds of barracuda. The northeastern end of the atoll preserves one of the largest grouper spawning sites in the Caribbean. A brief selection of the dives sites is given below; see also ambergriscaye.com

Long Caye Wall (9 m to unlimited, beginner): A swim out over coral gardens takes you to a huge drop-off covered with a bewildering array of corals of every size and colour, including some massive plate corals. These compete for space with towering sponges and, off the wall in the inky blue, it's common to spot large pelagics including Manta Ray and Grey Reef Sharks, as well as several species of turtle. This spectacular wall is easily reached from the beach on Long Caye.

Middle Caye Reefs (6 m to unlimited, intermediate): A remote dive site on the windward southern reef with a healthy array of coral formations and communities in a relatively small area. The reef wall is pristine, dropping in terraces through ultra-clear water and, on the drop-off, there are clusters of rare corals including meandrine brain, rare rose, giant brain, large flower and large cactus corals. These compete with sea fans, sponges and soft corals, and the marine forest is home to myriad invertebrates.

Southwest Caye Wall (15 m to unlimited, intermediate): This easy-access dive offer a spectacular drop-off covered in plate and boulder coral and swum by big shoals c common reef fish.

Shark Point (15-27 m, intermediate): This remote dive site (some nine miles from th nearest resort) sits in choppy seas and, whilst it can take an hour just to get here, diver are rewarded with mounds of reef visited by nurse, grey reef, blacktip, hammerhead an tiger sharks. The coral mounds themselves are home to hundreds of tropical fish an crustaceans, making this a great location for dive photography.

◉ Stann Creek listings

For hotel and restaurant price codes and other relevant information, see pages 11-12.

◑ Where to stay

Dangriga *p137, map p138*
$$$ Bonefish Hotel, 15 Mahogany St, on seafront near post office, T522-2243, www. bluemarlinlodge.com. An undistinguished but well-kept weatherboard hotel over-looking the sea. The best rooms are the a/c upper-floor doubles with rather garish furnishings: chocolate-coloured tiled floors, 1950s-style faux-satin caramel bedspreads and matching curtains, and heavy wooden bedheads. All have minibars, cable TV and sea views. There's a pleasant lounge and breakfast area and a decent though simple seafood restaurant. Staff are helpful and can organize fishing excursions. The hotel is twinned with the **Blue Marlin Lodge** on South Water Caye, see page 150, and offers all-inclusive fishing and diving packages with that hotel; see the website. Credit cards accepted.
$$$ Pal's Guest House, 868 A Magoon St, T522-2095, www.palsbelize.com. A big wooden hotel with a/c or fan-cooled rooms overlooking a rather unkempt beach. All have seen better days, but come with balconies, cable TV and sea views. The cheaper rooms in the main buildings have shared bathrooms. **Dangriga Dive Centre** operates from next door. Credit cards accepted.
$$$ Pelican Beach, T522-2044, www. pelicanbeachbelize.com. The smartest place in Dangriga, sitting right on the beach (which is clean and cleared of sea grass daily)

at the north end of town, some 10 mins' walk from the airstrip. The rooms are either in the mock-British colonial Whispering Pines wooden mansion or in the plainer, modern concrete Ixora annexe. The best rooms have sea views and balconies, and Garifuna artwork by artists like Ben Nicholas and Pen Cayetano hangs on the walls. There's a restaurant and tours can be arranged. Packages organized in conjunction with their sister hotel (also called **Pelican Beach**), on South Water Caye (see page 150), including visits to Cockscomb basin, Maya sites and diving and or snorkelling in the South Water Caye Marine Reserve. There's Wi-Fi and cable TV. Credit cards accepted. Discounts in low season and online.
$$$-$$ Hummingbird Inn, Mile 6, Hummingbird Hwy, www.hummingbird innbelize.com. Rooms in this family hotel, set in pretty gardens off the highway, are modest, well maintained and rather old fashioned, with polished white tiles and whitewash walls, small writing desks and plenty of wardrobe space. But the welcome from the owners is warm, the food (with plenty of vegetarian options) hearty and there are trips on offer throughout Belize, as well as transfers to South Water Caye Marine Reserve. Cable TV. Credit cards accepted.
$$ Bluefield Lodge, 6 Bluefield Rd, T522-2742, bluefield@btl.net. Rooms in this small hotel in the heart of town are small and sparsely furnished, but they are great value, bright and well looked after, and the owner Louise Belisle is very helpful and welcoming, and can organize tours and transfers. The

best rooms are on the inside away from the street; others can be noisy.

$$ Chaleanor, 35 Magoon St, T522-2587, chaleanor@btl.net. A hotel in a good location in the centre of town, offering unkempt but spacious a/c or fan-cooled rooms, some with TV and some with sea views, plus a rooftop restaurant. Unremarkable but very popular with tour operators.

$$ Jungle Huts Resort, 4 Ecumenical Dr, T522-0185. A pretty little family-run jungle lodge on the river bank a few mins' walk from the beach. A/c or fan-cooled rooms are elegantly simple, sprucely furnished with hand-made tables and chairs built by the owner Phil, but with mosquito screens and decent a/c. But what guests love here is the personal service; the owners are very helpful with organizing tours and dive trips and do all they can to make you feel a member of the family, especially at mealtimes in the restaurant which is open to non-guests. Dog lovers will enjoy a stay here.

$$-$ Val's backpackers, 1 Sharp St at Mahogany, T502-3324, www.valsbackpacker hostel.com. Fan-cooled 4-bunk dorms are very simple in this friendly hostel, coming with little to no furnishings beyond lockers. But all have hot-water showers, and the host Dana is warm, welcoming and overflowing with knowledge and tips about her town and the area as a whole. She can help to organize transfers to the cayes and trips around the region.

Hopkins *p139, map p140*

Resort hotels north and south of the village discourage their guests from leaving the premises, even going so far as to imply that Hopkins is not safe at night. Nonsense! They are merely keen to ensure that their guests don't spread their money to the deserving villagers. Hopkins is not only safe, but charming, and it has some excellent places to eat and sip a coffee or a beer.

$$$$ Hamanasi, T533-7073, www. hamanasi.com. The best hotel in Hopkins is just out of town to the south, sitting right on the beach. Stilted wooden bungalows are hidden in a forest garden fewer than 5 mins' stroll from the sea. The best come with tennis court-sized living areas, separate polished wooden bedrooms slung with mosquito nets and bathrooms you could park a Cadillac in. Trees shade the private verandas (which have their own jacuzzis) and the forest setting means that you wake to chirruping songbirds. There's a pool, cable TV, Wi-Fi and a restaurant and bar. The resort offers a bewildering array of trips: snorkelling or diving on the nearby Tobacco cayes or outer reefs, treks into the rainforest in search of jaguars, expeditions to the Mayan temples at Lamanai and Xunantunich, birdwatching or hiking in Cockscomb basin. Credit cards accepted.

$$$$ Hopkins Bay, nearly 1 mile north of Hopkins, T523-7284, www.hopkinsbayresort. com. Lumpy but very comfortable a/c villas, which, while not in keeping with their natural surroundings (they look like they belong in a Florida suburb), are great for a family, with space enough for up to 6. All have big granite kitchens with gas hobs and microwaves, dining rooms and TV lounges, and overlook a lawned garden with pools right next to the beach. There's Wi-Fi, cable TV and a restaurant. Credit cards accepted.

$$$ Jungle Jeanie, T533-7047, www.jungle bythesea.com. A series of varied fan-cooled wooden bungalows set in a coconut and coco plum garden next to the beach. All have colourful deck lounges slung with hammocks. Rooms are decorated with panache, with Santa Maria hardwood floors, writing desks built from a tree-trunk cross section, conches for lamps and spacious bedrooms with up to 2 beds. Some have an additional loft room with a queen size and 2 doubles. The more expensive cabins have sea views. Take a look at the beautiful Mayan marimba, which is played on the hotel's occasional marimba nights. Credit cards accepted.

$$$-$$ Hopkins Inn, T523-7283, www. hopkinsinn.com. The only B&B in Hopkins and one of the few in southern Belize. Accommodation is in very spacious and airy, if plain, concrete cabins right on the beach. Some have 2 beds, others 3, making this a good budget option for couples travelling together, families or small groups. Continental breakfast included. Tours arranged and there's cable TV. Credit cards accepted.

$$$$-$$ Sir Thomas at Toucan Sittee, in Sittee River Village, T523-7309, www. sir-thomas-at-toucan-sittee.com. One of the best birding spots in Stann Creek, this 18-acre riverside rainforest hotel sits in its own private reserve of wild and planted trees and shrubs. These attract all manner of forest birds, whilst trips on the river yield dozens of waterfowl species. Although birding is the lodge's speciality, they can also organize trips to the reef and sights throughout Belize. Accommodation is in 6 fan-cooled, palm-thatch bungalows with polished wooden walls, decent beds, hot water and fridges. The cheaper bungalows have shared bathrooms. All have room for up to 4 in double beds. There's a restaurant, bar and Wi-Fi. Credit cards accepted. Guests can also camp from BZ$40 per night, and the lodge rents kayaks and fishing equipment.

$$ All Seasons Guest House, T523-7209, www.allseasonsbelize.com. Rooms in this big red shutterboard house a block back from the beach come with en suites, coffee makers, cable TV and terraces overlooking a coconut-shaded garden. The hotel also rents out a beach house a little to the south, overlooking the water, and *cabañas* right on the beach about 1½ miles south of the town centre. Online discounts available. Credit cards accepted.

$$ Hopkins Seaside Cabañas, T665-9305, www.hopkinscabanas.com. Simple weatherboard cabins a stroll from the beach with attractive polished wood interiors decorated with local art. Some sleep up to 5 and have kitchenettes with fridges. Others sleep 3, making them good value for groups. All have balconies. The owners are helpful, and run excellent dive and snorkelling trips. There is free Wi-Fi, complimentary bike usage and credit cards are accepted.

$$ Windschief, T523-7249, www.windschief. com. Budget accommodation in shed-like shacks (with weatherboard sides and little inside besides a bed) right on the beach in a guesthouse run by windsurfing coaches Levi and Oliver. See page 153 for details of board rental and lessons. There's a bar, internet and tours arranged. Credit cards accepted.

$$-$ Glover's Guest House, T509-7099, in Sittee River Village, www.glovers.com.bz. Simple accommodation in private cabins, a block with rooms, dorms or camping. Meals are made with ingredients from the lodge's garden and are a very reasonable price. There are great wildlife tours on the river, complimentary kayaks and the lodge is the departure point for the Sun shuttle to the **Glover's Atoll Resort** (transfers BZ$120); see page 151.

$$-$ Lebeha Cabañas and Drumming centre, Hopkins village, T665-9305, www. lebeha.com. Very simple, scruffy fan-cooled *cabañas* with en suites and hot showers, and a handful of fan-cooled rooms with kitchenettes in a plot next to the beach at the north end of the village. The guesthouse is also home to a Garifuna drumming centre (see page 140), making stays here worthwhile for the night-time shows, despite the poor rooms. Wi-Fi. Credit cards accepted.

$$-$ Tipple Tree Beya, T520-7006, www.tippletreebelize.com. Spacious, well-maintained fan-cooled wooden cabins with kitchenettes, sofas and tables, en suites with cold water or in the cheaper rooms with shared bathrooms. A number of the cabins (even in the cheaper price ranges) overlook the sea. Rooms have plenty of storage space and most have hammocks hung outside. There's cable TV and tours arranged. Credit cards accepted.

$ Funky Dodo Backpackers Camping, T668-3852, wwwthefunkydodo.com. Rough-and-ready wooden and concrete dorms with outside cold-water showers and toilets, set a block back from the beach. The hostel has a communal kitchen, lockers and a small garden slung with hammocks.

Mayflower Bocawina National Park
p141

$$$-$$ Mama Noots Eco Lodge, T670-8019, www.mamanootsbelize.com. This lovely ecolodge sits right on the edge of the national park in its own 50-acre reserve. It's a great spot to hole up for a few days, especially if you want to watch birds; some 200 species have been recorded in the hotel environs. Jaguars have been spotted regularly nearby, howler monkeys call at dawn and dusk, and the hotel staff will take guests on hikes in the park. Rooms and pricier suites are fan cooled but surprisingly well appointed for the rainforest, freshly painted in light yellows and whites and with en suites. Netting on the windows keeps the insects out, but it's still wise to have your own net when staying anywhere in the rainforest. The lodge can organize transfers from Hopkins or Dangriga. For full board add another BZ$70 per day.

Cockscomb Basin Wildlife Sanctuary and Jaguar Reserve p141

$$$ Macaroni Hill View, Hummingbird Hwy Mile 12, Pomona, T502-0701, www.macaroniview.com. A family run lodge ideally positioned for Cockscomb Jaguar Reserve, with comfortable rooms in a 2-storey home right next to the highway. A/c rooms are spacious and colourful, with cherry red bedspreads and matching curtains. There's complimentary coffee and fruit juice all day and lovely views of the rainforest-covered hills from the back garden. The hotel offers a full range of tours throughout Belize, including a Garifuna settlement tour in and around Dangriga. Good food. Transfers from Dangriga cost BZ$60 or ask for any Hummingbird Hwy bus to drop you off. There's Wi-Fi and cable TV. Credit cards accepted.

$$-$ Nuukcheil cottage cabañas, Maya Centre, T615-1313, nuukcheil@btl.net. Simple rooms and dorms, with tiled floors and lemon yellow walls, are gathered in a lovely hummingbird- and bougainvillea-filled garden right on the edge of the forest at the Maya Centre. Some have en suites, others shared baths. Full board is available, with delicious Mayan food, including hand-made maize tortillas and locally grown coffee. There's a cultural centre and a gift shop on site, and villagers offer healing massage. Transfers to and from Placencia, Hopkins or Cockscomb, and guiding and birding in the park with the former park director, Ernesto Saqui.

Red Bank Scarlet Macaw Site p143

The village rents very simple weatherboard cabins (**$**), set on the edge of the forest. Be sure to ring in advance (see page 143), or organize stays or visits through **Belize Travel Services**, see page 153 or the **Cockscomb Maya Tours**, see page 153.

South Water Caye Marine Reserve
p144
Tobacco Caye

This tiny island has so many small hotels that it can feel crowded when full. It's a popular spot with backpackers.

$$$ Reef's End Lodge, T522-2419, www.reefsendlodge.com. There are 2 small terracotta-roofed *cabañas* and a more spacious honeymoon suite, all with balconies sitting right over the water, and a series of rooms in a 2-storey wooden block some 20 yds from the sea. The lodge has one of the island's better restaurants, sitting on a jetty with a lovely atmosphere, especially at night. The lodge runs dives all over South Water Caye, as well as to Gladden Spit with the whale sharks, Glover's Reef and the Blue Hole in Lighthouse Reef. Various dive, snorkel and fishing packages available. Price is for full board. Great value. Credit cards accepted.

$$$ Tobacco Caye Lodge, www.tclodge belize.com. Simple, brightly coloured, small wooden cottages on stilts have fans and sheet roofs (making them hot during the day). All are furnished with little more than a bed, and have small en suites. The lodge has a popular thatched-roof beach-bar restaurant right next to the water and can organize dive and snorkel trips. Prices include meals.

$$ Tobacco Caye Paradise, T520-5101.
Big, well-kept wooden cabins with balconies jutting out over the water, rooms in a block set back from the beach, and an equally simple restaurant serving pizza and grilled fish or meat with rice and beans.

$$-$ Lana's, T520-5036. One of the cheapest places on the island, offering very basic wooden rooms with foam beds and cold-water showers. Snorkel trips out on the reef and a basic restaurant.

South Water Caye

South Water is more upmarket and larger than Tobacco Caye, but it still feels tiny. There are 3 resorts.

$$$$ Blue Marlin Lodge, T520-5104, www.bluemarlinlodge.com. Like the other resorts on the caye, **Blue Marlin** offers accommodation based on all-inclusive packages with minimum stays of 3 nights. It offers some of the best fishing and diving tours in the reserve, as well as more family-orientated stays. Rooms are the best appointed on the caye and come in bizarre dumpling-shaped cabins, which look like something out of *Star Wars*, but are cool and comfortable inside, a weatherboard house and more traditional cabins. The best are close to the ocean, catching the breeze and with wonderful views.

$$$$ Ize Marine Biology Station and Lodge, T670-5030, www.izebelize.com. A US-run and administered research station and small hotel offering dorm accommodation and more comfortable private cabins, the latter facing both the breeze and the dawn. Food is simple, with grilled fish, prawns and rice and similar options, and the hotel has a small bar over the water on a jetty. Available only as part of a minimum 7-night package booked through **IZE** in the US (or their website), and including meals and tours. There's a pool and tours can be arranged. Credit cards accepted.

$$$$ Pelican Beach, T522-2044, www. pelicanbeachbelize.com. The sister of Dangriga's plushest hotel (see page 146)

has a series of pretty white weatherboard cottages with big wooden decks (furnished with heavy armchairs) set under coconut palms with views through the mangroves over the reef to the horizon. The resort has privileged access to the best beach on the island, a tongue of white sand shaded by palms and casuarinas. Prices are based on packages with a 3-night minimum stay and include full board, transfers from Dangriga, a half-day snorkel trip and park entry fees.

Coco Plum Caye

$$$$ Coco Plum Island Resort, www. cocoplumcay.com. One of the most luxurious island resorts in Southern Belize, with a handful of chic-shack a/c *cabañas* on white sand, shaded by casuarinas and mangrove trees and set around a central bar and restaurant area. The best rooms are furthest from the bar (which is never very noisy) and the more luxurious and newly built villa, which has its own private deck and steps right down to the water. Good diving and fishing excursions.

Thatch Caye

$$$$ Thatch Caye, T532-2414, www. thatchcayebelize.com. This comfortable eco-resort, near Coco Plum Caye and within kayaking distance of Laughing Bird Caye, offers breeze-cooled or fan-cooled *cabañas* set over the water and uglier concrete *casitas* set on a tiny island in pristine reef. The resort is one of the few in Belize that practises conservational tourism, recycling water, using wind- and solar-powered electricity and planting native vegetation to curb erosion. The island itself forms part of a private 10-acre marine park.

Wee Wee Caye

Wee Wee Caye Marine Lab Research Station (see page 144) is nominally open only to college/university groups but it's worth enquiring whether you can visit or join a research group. It's a beautiful place.

Glover's Reef Marine Reserve *p145*

$$$$ Isla Marisol, www.islamarisolresort. com. Shed-like a/c weatherboard huts with metal roofs are more attractive within than without, with cosy wood and eggshell blue walls and en suites. The best accommodation is in the pistachio and pink reef house, with enough space for 2 couples or a family and a 12 m-long veranda positioned perfectly for sunrise views. The resort is on Southwest Caye, which it shares with **Island Expeditions**, see below. This is a package-only resort aimed resolutely at divers and sports fishermen and is one of the few to offer Nitrox. Free kayak usage. Prices include transfers.

$$$$ Island Expeditions, T1-800 667-1630 (freephone USA), T0800-404 9535 (freephone UK), www.islandexpeditions.com. Run by a well-respected and environmentally responsible Canadian operator, this field camp has accommodation in large canvas tents set under the palms right on the beach on Southwest Caye, one of the smallest and most beautiful in the atoll. Trips include sea kayaking to deserted islets, snorkelling, diving and windsurfing. Guiding is very good. Packages only. Prices include transfers.

$$$$ Manta Resort, T01268-541732 (UK), www.global-travel.co.uk. This UK-based company operates the remotest and most comfortable resort on Glover's atoll, situated on gorgeous South West II Caye. Well-appointed a/c mahogany cabins have modern en suite bathrooms. The resort offers diving, snorkelling, kayaking and fly-fishing.

$$$$ Off the Wall Dive Center & Resort, T614-6348, www.offthewallbelize.com. The atoll's premier dive resort offers PADI certification dives and accommodation in attractive beachfront cabins on Long Caye, which the resort shares with **Slickrock**, see below, making the tiny island feel a little crowded in high season. Packages only. Prices include transfers.

$$$$ Slickrock Adventures Inc, bookable through the US only, T+1 435 259-4225, www.slickrock.com. Located on 800 yd-long, kidney-shaped Long Caye, which has one

very small beach, this US-owned adventure resort has accommodation in stilted palm-thatch cabins dotted around the perimeter of the island. Stays here are bookable only as packages which include all food and some activities. A range are on offer, including diving, snorkelling, sea kayaking, windsurfing and fishing. Prices include transfers.

$$-$ Glover's Atoll Resort, T532-2916, www.glovers.com.bz. Located on tiny, idyllic Northeast Caye with a pretty coconut palm-shaded beach is the only backpacker option in the atoll, with a range of accommodation from camping (with your own or their rented) tents, bunkhouse dorms or simple cabins with thatch roofs, the best of which sit on stilts over the water. Activities offered include scuba diving and PADI training, snorkelling, kayaking, sports fishing and sailing. The restaurant offers simple meals (fish/seafood with rice). Transfers from their resort on Sittee River (see page 148) cost BZ$750 per boat (up to 6 passengers) or you can take their weekly shuttle from the resort on Sun at 0900, BZ$120 per person. If you stay a week, the round trip is free.

🍴 Restaurants

Dangriga *p137, map p138*
With Chinese burger bars, greasy spit fried chicken, street stalls selling dodgy meat on wooden skewers and tired-looking cassava fries, Dangriga is a long way from a gourmand's mecca. **Coconuts Grill** aside, if you're looking for more than sustenance take a drive to Hopkins.

$$$ Coconuts Grill, Bar and Coffee Shop, Pelican Beach, see page 146. The best menu in Dangriga in the most salubrious surroundings. Dishes feature Garifuna food, such as fish in coconut milk, spicy chicken curry, fried jacks (a kind of doughy patty) and tortillas and beans. Try an ice-cold beer from the bar first or a cocktail, like the tangy house speciality, the Pelican's Sunrise.

$$$ Garden of Eatin', **Jungle Huts Lodge**, see page 147. Non-guests can sample the

Tex-Mex and international comfort cooking at this hotel restaurant, with standards like tamales, burritos and quesadillas, as well as fish, chicken and good old Belizean beans and rice. Great cooked breakfasts, too.

Hopkins *p139, map p140*

$$$ Chef Rob's, T670-0445. Don't leave Hopkins without sampling the best cooking in southern Belize, served in this gorgeous little chic shack, furnished with metre-wide faux-antique clocks, a huge still life in a rococo frame and beach furniture. The façade is painted in the creams and deep blues of the Dutch countryside. And the food is exquisite: a degustation of ceviches – conch, snapper and shrimp – is followed by a light and fragrant Thai king prawn red curry, served with aubergine rice and offset by a tangy, piquant mango and passion fruit sauce. Chef Rob Pronk is from the Netherlands and formerly cooked at the **Hilton** in Park Lane, London. But he's happier here in Hopkins.

$$ Driftwood Pizza, www.driftwoodpizza. com. This thatch-roofed *cabaña* just back from the beach boasts the best pizza in Belize, which isn't really saying a great deal as pizza is rarely seen in the country. They're up to European standards, though, served light crispy or deep pan in a variety of pick-your-own or ready-made flavours (try the delicious driftwood veggie with aubergine, courgettes, sun-dried tomato and white cheese). Made using a secret recipe that, before they headed south, earned the chefs the accolade of 'best dough in the French Quarter of New Orleans'.

$$ King Cassava, T503-7305. This restaurant-cum-bar-cum-nightclub has been a Hopkins institution for years. Garifuna superstar Andy Palacio played here shortly before he died, and there is live music or drumming most weekend nights. The food is good, too, with hearty plates of beans and rice served with chicken, fish or occasionally game meat (like paca/gibnut) and assorted international dishes.

$$ Taste of India. This locally owned curry house offers simple Belizean East Indian chicken, fish or beef curries, which are thick on gravy and thin on spice compared to those you'd find in Bangalore or Brick Lane.

$$ Thongs Café, T662-0110. A colourful café restaurant serving fruit juices, milk-shakes, breakfast of French toast, *huevos à la Mexicana*, bacon and eggs, and comfort food like burritos, fajitas and spaghetti carbonara throughout the day. The café has free Wi-Fi and a small book exchange.

$ Cait's Bakery, T664-4942. Cait bakes a whole range of delicious breads and buns at her home just a block back from the main drag in Hopkins (everyone knows her, so ask for directions). Her specialities include multigrain and wholemeal loaves, US-style muffins and slices of sumptuous banana, pumpkin and carrot cake. She also makes her own veggie burgers, sold with or without a bun, to cook back in the hotel kitchen.

$ Innie's, T503-7333 (next door to **Golden's Gifts**). One of the best traditional Belizean and Garifuna restaurants in Stann Creek district, serving breakfasts of eggs, beans and burritos and lunches of delicious Garifuna cooking, such as *bundigu* or *hudutu* (mashed plantain with coconut milk, fish or meat and herb-infused gravy) as well as fresh juices and cold beer.

$ Yugada, T503-7255. A cosy, homely restaurant serving Belizean standards like chicken/fish, rice and beans, jacks and home-made cassava bread (which you can learn to make with the owner if you ask). Very friendly and relaxed.

Cockscomb Basin Wildlife Sanctuary and Jaguar Reserve *p141*

Maya Centre, see page 142. Delicious Mayan breakfasts, lunches and dinners. Try their home-grown coffee and hand-rolled tortillas.

✪ Festivals

19 Nov Garifuna Settlement Day (see page 210) is celebrated in Dangriga and

Hopkins, with re-enactments of the boat arriving, draped in flowers. This is followed by drumming, with live music from top Garifuna acts (like Aurelio Martinez) and dancing until dawn

O Shopping

Hopkins *p139, map p140*
The **Hamanasi** resort (see page 147) has a small gift shop selling Rainforest Remedies (see page 102), T-shirts, music from Stonetree records (see page 210) and assorted arts and crafts.
David's, T667-4677, www.aguallos.com/davidwoodcarving. David's woodcarving shop sits in a little shack under luxuriant palms and vines. Inside you'll find rows of gorgeous, perfectly worked rosewood bowls and mahogany statuettes. Andy Palacio's wistful, melancholy Belizean blues-soul music echoes from a battered CD player and the owner greets all those who enter with a nod and smile from under his dreadlocks, as he chisels and whittles wood at the back of the shop, lit by shafts of rich orange sunlight.
Golden's Gifts, T662-4618. Good-value T-shirts, traditional Garifuna woven baskets, local coffee, hand-made dolls and Garifuna drums. The owner is a renowned local birding guide.

Cockscomb Basin Wildlife Sanctuary and Jaguar Reserve *p141*
Maya Centre, see page 142. The village gift shop sells clay figurines, weave-work, raw copal incense and copal candles.

O What to do

Most guesthouses and hotels in Dangriga and Hopkins can organize tours to the reef or rainforest. Most offer visits throughout Belize. For booking excursions in advance and in conjunction with hotel reservations, contact **Exotic Belize** (see page 165) or **Belize Travel Services**, www.belizetravelservices.com, who offer guided trips to

sights throughout Stann Creek and Toledo as a bespoke regional package or as part of a more general tour of the country, as well as hotel bookings, transfers and flights.

Hopkins *p139, map p140*
Birdwatching
Golden's Gifts, see Shopping, opposite. For birdwatching trips.

Diving
Hamanasi (see page 147) and **Hopkins Seaside Cabañas** (see page 148) both have excellent dive shops offering trips to South Water Caye and Glover's Atoll. The instructors and dive masters are some of the best in Stann Creek. Both offer dive and accommodation packages.
Hopkins Underwater Adventures, T633-3401, www.hopkinsunderwateradventures.com. Dives around South Water Caye Marine Reserve, Glover's Atoll and Gladden Spit with Irishman and master scuba diver, Declan Kelly.

Windsurfing
Windschief, Hopkins Village, T523-7249, www.windsurfing-belize.com. This windsurf school has around 25 boards to rent (for a modest price and a hefty safety deposit), and offers lessons for BZ$60 for individuals and BZ$40 for groups of 2-4. English and German spoken.

Cockscomb Basin Wildlife Sanctuary and Jaguar Reserve *p141*
Cockscomb Maya Tours and Birdwatching, Maya Centre, T660-3903, www.cockscombmayatours.com. Julio and Ernesto Saqui (former director of Cockscomb Basin) offer some of the best guided tours of the park, first class birding and a unique insight into the Mayan heritage, including medicinal plants. They will take you on trails to the waterfalls, wildlife watching, river tubing and to see the scarlet macaws at Red Bank. Other trips include a visit to the Mayan Cultural Centre and museum and various tour-and-stay packages available online or through

talking with Julio. He can also arrange pickups from Dangriga, Hopkins or Placencia.

South Water Caye Marine Reserve
p144
Reef's End Lodge, Ize Marine Biology Station and Lodge, Pelican Beach and Blue Marlin Lodge (see page 150) all offer diving and snorkelling throughout the South Water Caye Marine Reserve, Glover's Reef, the Blue Hole in Lighthouse Reef and Gladden Spit (to see the whale sharks), and have or can organize sports and fly fishing, especially for tarpon, bonefish and permit.

Glover's Atoll *p145*
All resorts have adventure activities ranging from snorkelling and kayaking to windsurfing and sailing. Slickrock, Off the Wall, Island Expeditions and Isla Marisol all offer diving around the atoll. See page 151.

⊙ Transport

Dangriga *p137, map p138*
Air
Daily flights to Belize City, Punta Gorda and Placencia with Maya Island and Tropic Air.

Boat
Boats to South Water Caye Marine Reserve and Glover's Atoll can be chartered from the Stann Creek quays in Dangriga centre; ask at the Riverside restaurant. There are no regular public services but it's usually possible to find a boat and other passengers to share with, especially first thing in the morning. Most lodges on the cayes will also arrange transfers. Expect to pay around BZ$50 to the South Water Caye Marine Reserve (Tobacco or South Water Cayes). All the Glover's Reef resorts include transfers except Glover's Atoll Resort; for details on how to get there see page 151.

To Honduras The Nesymein Neydy boat (T522-0062) leaves for Puerto Cortés in Honduras on Fri at 1100. Passengers should be at the dock at 0900 to pass through immigration and customs. The boat takes 2½-3 hrs, BZ$120. The boat returns from Puerto Cortés on Mon at 0900. It's also possible to charter a boat. See www. belizetohonduraswatertaxi.com for details.

There are boats to Puerto Cortés in Honduras via Placencia from the quay on the south side of Stann Creek, usually leaving on Sat, 3 hrs, BZ$150.

Bus
Buses operate north to Belize City and Belmopan, 18 daily, with James (T702-2049), Williams and G-Line (James has the most buses). Change at Belmopan for San Ignacio, Benque Viejo and the Guatemalan border.

There are 3 buses Mon-Sat south to Placencia with Ritchie's (T523-3806) at 1100, 1400 and 1640, and 1400 and 1640 on Sun, leaving from the bus station on Havana St just south of Havana creek. It is also possible to take any Punta Gorda bus with James (see below), get off at Independence and catch a launch to Placencia.

To Hopkins, 2 buses Mon-Sat at 1015 and 1330, leave from the road next to the quay opposite the Riverside restaurant, see page 118, returning at 0700 and 1400, 45 mins. Or take any bus to Placencia or Punta Gorda and get off at the Hopkins turn-off (4 miles from Hopkins), from where you can hitch (most people wait less than 30 mins).

There are 12 buses daily to Punta Gorda via the Hopkins turn-off and Independence at 0745, 0915 then every 15 mins past the hour until 1815. The last bus from Dangriga is at 1845. Journey takes 3 hrs.

Hopkins *p139*
To catch a bus to Placencia and destinations south, you will need to take the Dangriga bus or hitch to the junction of the Southern Hwy and await any southbound bus there. There is one roughly every hour.

◑ Directory

Hopkins *p139, map p140*
There are no banks or hospitals in Hopkins.

Dangriga *p137, map p138*
Medical services New Southern
Regional Hospital, T522-3832.

Placencia and around

Placencia is a peninsular village-turned-patch of paradise for vacationing foreigners and is in stark contrast to the rest of coastal Stann Creek. Instead of laid-back and low-key beach villages you'll find burgeoning condo-communities coursed by golf carts, a marina full of yachts and rows of beach hotels frequented by folk wearing sun visors and white sneakers. Outside San Pedro, nowhere in Belize is more touristy than here. But then, compared to resort towns across the border in Mexico, nowhere in Belize is touristy at all. Placencia still feels like the fishing community it once was, albeit with a holiday hinterland.

You will rarely feel crowded out of Placencia's narrow white-sand beach, even in high season, or have to queue for a table in one of the mood-lit restaurants. There are all manner of rooms, tours and tables to choose from, together with assorted conveniences including shops selling foreign newspapers and speedy internet. But come to Placencia soon before they put up the parking lot: building is underway on a mega-resort, with a new private airport (which will be the biggest in Belize), three-storey condo houses resembling those in Florida, a Dubai-style offshore marina, private hospital, gun range and one of the largest golf courses in Central America. The resort will occupy a substantial stretch of the entire peninsula north of Maya Beach.

Placencia is a good place to base yourself if you're craving a comfortable air-conditioned suite and a choice of different restaurants. And, you can still enjoy dipping your toes into the town's wild environs. On boat tours running south to Monkey River, Bugle Caye and Rocky Point, you can see Morelet's crocodiles, myriad water birds and that most elusive of marine mammals, the manatee. There's good snorkelling and diving offshore in Laughing Bird Caye National Park (home to a huge colony of rare sea birds) or further west in the Gladden Spit Silk Cayes Marine Reserve or at Glover's Reef. ⏵ *For listings, see pages 159-166.*

Arriving in Placencia → *For listings, see pages 159-166. Colour map C2. Population: 750.*

Getting there

The airstrip is 1½ miles north of town. Resorts will pick you up, or you can take a cab into Placencia village, BZ$10. There are always taxis awaiting flight arrivals. The turn-off for the Placencia Peninsula road is just under 10 miles south of the Maya Centre off the Southern Highway. Buses from Dangriga arrive at the petrol station at the far southern end of the Placencia Peninsula road. There are plans to introduce a free shuttle service along the peninsula in late 2012. ⏵ *See Transport, page 166, for further details.*

Getting around

A well-paved highway runs along the peninsula, past the village of Maya Beach and the Garifuna settlement of Seine Bight (see page 156), both of which are now well and truly incorporated into the Placencia conurbation, past Placencia's airport (the largest in the country after the international airport in Belize City) and, after around 12 miles, into the northern portion of the village itself, whereupon it becomes a sandy track. It takes less than 15 minutes to cross the village itself north to south or east to west. Most larger resorts offer complimentary (or rented) golf carts and bicycles. Enquire at the tourist office (see below) for other rental outlets.

Tourist information

Placencia Tourism Centre ① *T523-4045, www.placencia.com, Mon-Fri 0900-1700, closed public holidays and 1130-1300 in low season*, sits in Placencia Village Square, just south of the petrol station. Staff are very helpful and offer lots of useful information, maps and pamphlets. The centre also publishes a monthly newssheet, *Placencia Breeze*, www.placenciabreeze.com. There are internet cafés dotted around Placencia village, ATMs, a post office, laundries and some convenience stores.

Placencia Peninsula

Placencia sits opposite the mainland village of Independence, at the end of a 16-mile-long spit of sand, which separates from the coast just north of Maya Beach village. The sand spit forms a lagoon on its west side, which has now become a huge marina sitting behind a string of condominiums. The ocean side of the spit is fringed by a very narrow white-sand beach for its entire length.

The peninsula road enters **Placencia village**, reaching a crossroads that marks the town centre. The town's other main drag is the **Sidewalk**, said to be the world's narrowest street, only a yard wide in places. It's not really a street at all, however, but a sandy path running along the back of the beach and leading to holiday homes and a handful of hotels, restaurants and shops. Placencia's main jetty lies at its southern end.

Many visitors to the Placencia Peninsula are disappointed with the **beach**. The pictures show idyllic white sand, shaded by coconut palms, but don't show how narrow the strip of sand is (especially in the north around Maya Beach), or that the shallow sea is full of eel grass. The water is clean, clear and gently lapping, however, and the offshore kayaking, snorkelling and diving are some of the best in the Caribbean.

Two villages share the spit with Placencia. Furthest north is **Maya Beach**, a once soporific fishing community, many of whose residents have sold their land to property developers. It is now blighted by holiday homes most of which are utterly at odds with their low-key tropical surrounds. There's a convenience store, a couple of restaurants and a few decent beach hotels here (see page 159). Most are cheaper than Placencia, but if you want better restaurant options, you'll have to cycle or take a cab nine miles south to Placencia (BZ$30 each way).

Around 2½ miles south of Maya Beach and seven miles from Placencia is the Garifuna village of **Seine Bight**, a huddle of rather decrepit shed-like homes, small guesthouses and shops sprawling along the beach. The village has the reputation for being a Garifuna arts and crafts centre; see the paintings in **Lola's Art Gallery** ① *Seine Bight s/n, near the football pitch*, and the **Goss organic chocolate factory** ① *www.gosschocolate.com*. Like Maya Beach, Seine Bight is surrounded by condo homes and resorts, some of which offer decent accommodation (see page 159).

Monkey River

ⓘ *15 miles south of Placencia. Most easily reached by boat on one of the many day trips available in Placencia. It is also accessible by road via a very rough and rutted dirt track leaving the Southern Hwy 1 mile south of San Juan village.*

This is a Creole village at the mouth of the river of the same name, comprising little more than a few weatherboard shacks, a church and a couple of shops. It was once a big logging town, wiped out by the death of the logwood and chewing gum trade and a series of hurricanes. It is now home to fewer than 200 people. Many work in tourism, offering half-day boat trips upriver and in the aquamarine Caribbean Sea around the peninsula. The trips are very worthwhile, especially for birdwatchers and those keen to see manatees. They usually begin in the late morning (with lunch in the village), but it's better to schedule one for dawn or late afternoon when the birdlife on the river is at its most prolific. Despite

Placencia

To **13**, Airstrip, Seine Bight, Maya Beach & Southern Highway

Avadon Divers

Caribbean Sea

Hokey Pokey Water Taxi to Independence/ Mango Creek

Toadal Adventures

Joy Tours

BTL

Wallen's Supermarket

Secret Garden Spa

School

Caribbean Travel & Tours

Siripohn Spa

Medical Centre

Eagle Ray Tours

The Sidewalk

Isy Paradise

Sports Field

Trip 'n Travel

Nite Winds

Buses to Dangriga & Taxis

Fuel Dock

Sea Horse Dive Shop

Placencia Caye

N

50 metres
50 yards

Where to stay 🛏
Captain Jack's **1**
Chabil Mar **3**
Deb & Dave's Last Resort **2**
Inn at Robert's Grove **14**
Lydia's Guesthouse **5**
Miramar Apartments **15**
Paradise Vacation **6**
Seaspray **8**

Trade Winds **12**
Turtle Inn **10**
Yellow House **11**

Restaurants 🍴
De Tatch Café **2**
La Dolce Vita **8**
Mare **1**
Omar's **3**

Rumfish **14**
Secret Garden **15**
Siriphon **5**
Tutti-frutti Ice Cream Parlour **9**

Bars & clubs 🍸
Barefoot Bar **6**
Yoli's **7**

extensive logging in the late 19th and early 20th centuries, Monkey River sits at the heart of a large tract of healthy lowland rainforest centred on the **Payne's Creek National Park** (see page 171), so you can expect to see most of Belize's water fowl on Monkey River, together with Morelet's crocodiles and freshwater turtles, and plenty of rainforest species on a short hike through the park itself. On the way back to Placencia the sharp-sighted guides almost always spot a manatee, and the cayes in between the Monkey River and Placencia are home to nesting boobies, magnificent frigate birds and laughing gulls.

Cayes and faros off Placencia → *For listings, see pages 159-166. Colour map C3.*

The Belizean Barrier Reef changes at Placencia. North of the peninsula it is dominated by extensive flats made up of eel grass beds broken by coral gardens leading to drop-offs, deep ocean and the Belizean atolls. South of Placencia the eel grass flats deepen to an area pocked by sink holes, pinnacles and mini atolls or faros, such as **Laughing Bird Caye**, see below.

There are numerous dive sites with drop-offs around the faros, where it's often possible to see larger pelagics, eagle rays and turtles, coral gardens, pinnacles, extensive tracts of elk and staghorn coral, with large shoals of common reef fish, and myriad ridges and spurs.

The Gladden Spit Silk Cayes Marine Reserve, as well as Scipio and Colson Cayes – two tiny cayes set in shallow water near Gladden Spit – have excellent beginner diving and shallow snorkelling and are a prime location for diving with whale sharks. The **Bird Cayes** have a wealth of marine life among the mangrove roots, seagrass beds, coral pinnacles and drop-offs. Diving and snorkelling is easy even for absolute beginners.

Laughing Bird Caye National Park
ⓘ *www.laughingbird.org. Most boat tours from Placencia visit the caye, and all dive shops in Placencia (see page 165) can organize snorkel and dive trips. For a good birding guide, contact Carlos Franco, T626-0591.*

Some 10 miles offshore from Placencia, the Belize Barrier Reef rises into an isolated faro, a kind of mini-atoll comprising a small plateau of shallow, coral-filled water sitting between two deep ocean channels. The plateau is ringed by shallow sandy water, which becomes dry land to form Laughing Bird Caye itself. Both the marine environment – comprising shallow and shelving reefs, sandy shallows and eel grass beds – and the mangrove and scrub forests on the island have been protected since 1981 and are home to a wealth and diversity of animals.

The caye measures just 425 m by 20 m and gets its name from the laughing gull (*Larus artricilla*), which is easily seen on the island. It once bred here, but now nests on nearby islets after an increase in the number of tourist visits. Other residents and regular visitors include nesting double-crested cormorants, brown pelicans and green and tri-coloured herons, reddish egrets, melodious blackbirds and white ibis, as well as many other birds from the surrounding cayes and the mainland.

Snorkelling and diving around the caye is superb. The reef itself is made up of a barrier reef with an outer rim cut by coral spurs and sandy grooves, and a silty inner lagoon with patch reef and steep-sided coral heads. Snorkellers will find plenty to see in the coral gardens of the central lagoon and the elk horn beds on the west side of the caye, whilst outer wall dive sites, such as Brian's Drop-off Fall from 20 m to an unlimited depth, enabling sightings of pelagics, turtles and larger rays.

Gladden Spit and Silk Cayes Marine Reserve

This small conglomeration of cayes some 22 miles off Placencia offers excellent clear-water diving and is one of the best locations in the Caribbean for seeing whale sharks. They gather here over a 10-day period during full moons between March and June, when snappers and groupers come together to spawn off Gladden Spit, a promontory of a submerged atoll that sticks out of the deeper ocean like an elbow. The fish produce eggs and sperm in such vast quantities that it clouds the sea, attracting whale sharks who sweep up from the deep ocean to filter-feed in the water. The phenomenon was first observed in 1997 by a group of marine biologists working in conjunction with local fishermen. The spit and cayes became a marine reserve three years later. In 2002, Friends of Nature, now **SEA**, began to co-manage the reserve along with the Belizean government.

The reserve has excellent diving and snorkelling at any time (with some 30 species of fish) and is easily visited through dive shops in Placencia (see page 165).

Other cayes

Between Laughing Bird Caye and Placencia are the **Bird Cayes**: three small islets with abundant nesting brown pelicans, frigate birds and brown boobies, and excellent, easy snorkelling and diving. They can be visited through tour companies and dive shops in Placencia. Other islets near Placencia can easily be visited or even rented out. They include **Whipray** and **Tarpon Caye** (both with excellent fishing), **French Louie Caye**, **Robert's Grove** (a private island operated by the resort in Seine Bight) and **Ranguana Caye**. The latter two are similar to Laughing Bird Caye, though far smaller, with coral gardens studded with pinnacles leading to deep drop-offs.

◉ Placencia and around listings

For hotel and restaurant price codes and other relevant information, see pages 11-12.

◉ Where to stay

Placencia Peninsula *p156, map p157*
There are beach resorts all along the peninsula. All resorts can organize tours and dive trips and many in the upper price bracket have their own in-house operations. Much of the best high-end accommodation is 10 miles north of Placencia village in Maya Beach and Seine Bight. Guests tend to use hotel restaurants, as cabs into Placencia from Maya Beach or Seine Bight cost around BZ$30 each way and bus services are sporadic. There are plenty of mosquitoes and sandflies in Placencia. Bring repellent and a mosquito net and wear long trousers in the evenings. See also www.ctbelize.com.
$$$$ Chabil Mar, Placencia Rd, 1 mile north of the village, www.chabilmarvillas.com.

These comfortable copper-roofed duplex a/c condos wouldn't look out of place in Coral Gables. Each is privately owned and rented out when guests are not in residence. They're good for families, with a large living area, fully-equipped kitchen and 1-2 bedrooms. The best – Sea Front luxury villas – have beautiful views. And whilst the beach is narrow, the resort has 2 pools and lies within easy reach of Placencia village, 15 mins' walk along the sand or a 5-min cycle ride. Use of bicycles and kayaks is included; golf carts are extra. There's a restaurant, bar, gift shop, cable TV and Wi-Fi. Tours organized. Credit cards accepted.
$$$$ Green Parrot, 1 Maya Beach, T523-2488, www.greenparrot-belize.com. 8 single-storey and duplex cabins sit on the beach and blend in well with their surroundings. All have sea views, large decks with hammocks and en suites. The 6 'beach houses' have space for 4, with loft bedrooms and sitting areas

with sofa beds, as well as kitchenettes. The more intimate cabins have palm-thatch roofs and secluded outdoor showers. The resort administers some modest conservationist tourism practices. Online discounts and special rates for kids. The restaurant is one of the best-value ones in Maya Beach. Breakfast and the use of glass-bottomed kayaks are included. There's a bar and Wi-Fi, and tours are arranged. Credit cards accepted.

$$$$ The Inn at Robert's Grove, 4 miles north of the airstrip, Seine Bight, T523-3565, www.robertsgrove.com. Bright, spacious lemon-yellow rooms and suites housed in palm-roofed, mock-hacienda villas. Each has timber-frame ceilings, tiled floors and splashes of colour from Guatemalan knitwear on the beds and Seville tiles around the wash basins. There are views out over the resort pools and/or the beach. Some rooms need renovating. The quietest and most intimate have higher numbers and sit further down the beach from the main resort buildings. Robert's Grove does all it can to be all-inclusive, with a full range of tours and dive trips as well as bars and restaurants. Whilst all are adequate and the staff pleasant and helpful, you'll find better and better-value food in Maya Beach and Placencia village. There's a spa, dive shop, cable TV and Wi-Fi. Credit cards accepted.

$$$$ Laru Beya, 4 miles north of the airstrip, Seine Bight, T523-3476, www.larubeya.com. With their concrete and steel balconies, corporate design and patio garden denuded of local vegetation, these huge, 2- or 3-storey condos would look fine in Jupiter, Florida. They look clunky and out of place in low-key Seine Bight. But they're large enough even for big families with 1-, 2- and 3-bedroom villas, all with plenty of living and bedroom space and fully equipped kitchens. There's a big pool, mini-golf, spa, shop, restaurant, cable TV and Wi-Fi, and great views from the rooftop jacuzzis. Tours are arranged. Credit cards accepted.

$$$$ Placencia Hotel, Maya Beach, 12 miles north of Placencia town, T533-4110,

www.theplacencia.com. This big, ungainly and rather vulgar resort sits at the centre of a huge project to develop the Placencia Peninsula into a kind of mini-Florida resort town. Big terracotta-roofed mock-hacienda condo-style rooms with terraces look slick from the outside, though completely out of keeping with the Belizean surroundings. But this masks the musty interiors and poor fittings (badly fitted shower doors and fixtures) and the internet rates are exorbitant. There is little to do, shuttles into town are expensive and the beach grainy. Guests staying here have reported feeling pressured into buying condos. There's a pool, restaurant, bar, gift shop, cable TV and Wi-Fi. Tours organized. Credit cards accepted.

$$$$ Turtle Inn, Placencia Village, www.coppolaresorts.com. Francis Ford Coppola's faux-Balinese palm-thatch *cabañas* with airy and elegant minimalist interiors, clustered around a jewel-like pool next to the beach, offer the most stylish chic shack accommodation in Placencia. All the rooms are fan cooled; the 'sea front cottages' are cooler, breezier and brighter than those in the garden. Opt for one away from the pool and bar. C1 is the quietest and most secluded. There's a restaurant, dive shop, spa, cable TV and Wi-Fi. Tours organized. Credit cards accepted.

$$$$-$$$ Singing Sands, 30 Maya Beach Rd, Maya Beach, 6 miles north of the airstrip, T520-8022, www.singingsands.com. This laid-back and freshly renovated little resort has garden rooms set in a unit in a heliconia garden, a private family flat, and 6 palm-thatched *cabañas* dotted under shady palmetto and coconut palms right on the beach; these are the most relaxed and intimate option. Nos 1-3 are closest to the beach; *cabaña* 6 sits right next to the 'highway'. Bedrooms are fan cooled with optional portable a/c. The garden rooms can get hot, but a gentle sea breeze keeps the *cabañas* fairly cool. Garden rooms are simply furnished with a bed and wicker chairs and have en suites with wooden washstands and lovely bright blue-fired clay basins. *Cabaña* rooms are more rustic chic, with wooden floors, louvre windows and locally made wooden furniture. The resort has a decent grill restaurant. Tours organized, and there's a dive shop, pool and Wi-Fi. Credit cards accepted.

$$$-$$ Captain Jack's, Placencia Village, T628-6447, captainjacksbelize.com. 2-storey a/c wooden villas are set in a shady garden next to the lagoon in the heart of Placencia village. The largest are the spacious and well-appointed 2-storey villas, with living areas (furnished with wicker sofas, chunky coffee tables and huge flatscreen TVs), 2 bedrooms, kitchens, en suites and big balcony decks. Lush interiors are decked out with polished hardwood floors, chunky wooden beams and muted colours. Garden cottages are similar but simpler and smaller. Tours organized, and there's Wi-Fi. Credit cards accepted.

$$$-$$ Maya Beach Hotel, Maya Beach, 6 miles north of the airstrip, T520-8040, www.mayabeachhotel.com. Each of the 5 a/c rooms in this upscale beachfront guesthouse is homely, simple and bright, some in tile and whitewash with space for a family, others in lush, warm wood and with a more intimate, romantic feel. They sit alongside 4 private condos, each individually decorated. There are kayaks and bicycles for guest use and a full range of tours, including fishing trips, sailing and diving. The hotel restaurant is one of the best on the peninsula (see page 164). There's also a pool, dive shop, spa and Wi-Fi. Credit cards accepted.

$$ Blue Crab, 4 miles north of the airstrip, Seine Bight village, T523-3544, www.blue crabbeach.com. Simple a/c or fan-cooled thatch roof and weatherboard beach huts with homely, clean polished hardwood and whitewash decor and en suite shower rooms. Each room comes with a bar of free hand-made Belizean chocolate. Complimentary bikes. Very good Southeast Asian restaurant with dishes cooked by the Taiwanese owner, officially for guests only (who reserve ahead), though non-guests dropping in or ringing ahead might get lucky. Online packages and discounts. Tours organized, and there's Wi-Fi. Credit cards accepted.

$$ Paradise Vacation Hotel, Placencia village, at the end of the peninsula next to the piers, T523-3179, www.paradisevacation belize.com. A/c rooms in a big yellow weatherboard house sitting over the sea, 5 mins' walk from the beach. All are freshly decorated but most do not have windows; ask for an 'ocean-view'. There is also an adjacent, spacious condo for families. Whilst rooms are modest with little storage space, the hotel has good amenities; there's a hot tub with a view on the upper floor, a breezy rooftop terrace restaurant and bar, and the hotel has complimentary bikes and kayaks for guests. Cable TV. Credit cards accepted.

$$ Trade Winds Hotel, South Point, T523-3122, www.placencia.com/Members/Tradewinds.html. A cluster of very simple, colourful fan-cooled concrete beach huts and set in a large coconut grove on the beach at Placencia Point, in the village but on the far southeastern corner of the peninsula. Furnishings are limited to a bed, fridge, lounge chairs, hammocks and storage space for clothes. Each has a kitchenette. The coolest huts are right on the seafront.

$$-$ Mahogany Beach, Placencia Village, www.ctbelize.com. Sprucely furnished, breezy fan-cooled beach cabins with verandas. Furnishings are limited to a bed, a fridge and some chairs. Service is minimal, but the location is good and the price very reasonable. Credit cards accepted.

$$-$ Seaspray, Placencia Village, T523-3148, www.seasprayhotel.com. These brightly painted white and blue beach huts come in a range of prices, from basic, fan-cooled double or twin rooms 30 yds from the beach, with little more inside them than a bed and a fridge, to seaside cabins with veranda, cable TV, microwave and kitchenette. Friendly staff and a simple grill restaurant, **De Tatch**, on the beach. Credit cards accepted.

$ Deb and Dave's Last Resort, T523-3207, facebook: Deb & Dave's Last Resort Placencia. One of the better options for travellers on a budget: well-kept simple rooms with a shared bathroom and kitchen set in a little tropical garden. Guests can rent kayaks and bikes, and the couple running it own a decent adventure tour company, **Toadal Adventures**, see page 165.

$ Lydia's, Sidewalk, Placencia Village, T523-3117, www.lydiasguesthouse.com. 8 very simple but clean double rooms with tiled floors and shared bathrooms, and shared hammock and public spaces in a lovely old timber and weatherboard house set on a quiet part of the beach. Welcoming and laid back. Tours organized, and there's Wi-Fi. Credit cards accepted.

Flats and home rentals

All the flats listed below, and a whole host more, can be booked through **Caribbean Travel and Tours**, see page 165.

$$$$ Casa del Sol, www.casadelsolbelize. com. Like many resorts along the coast, this chunky mock-hacienda mansion with room enough for 11 looks like it would sit better on a Florida rather than a Belizean beach. But the villa is a good base for a group or a large family, with 4 a/c bedrooms, 2 kitchens, 2 living rooms and a pool. And it's in a good location on a quiet stretch of beach on the outskirts of Placencia village. There's Wi-Fi and cable TV. Credit cards accepted.

$$$ Miramar Apartments, T523-3658, miramarbelize.com. A big concrete Brighton rock pink ersatz colonial house on the beach with a series of modern, well-appointed suites. They range in size, but each is decorated in attractive polished wood and kitted out with kitschy furniture, full kitchens with eating areas and numerous TVs. There's Wi-Fi and cable TV. Credit cards accepted.

$ The Yellow House, T523-3481, www.ct belize.com. This big yellow house in the heart of the village is a great rental option for families or travellers in a group as it must be rented in its entirety. The house has 2 bedrooms with a shared bathroom, a big wooden-floor living area, kitchen breakfast area and big balconies.

Around Placencia p157

$$$$ Stepping Stones, South Englishtown, www.steppingstonesbelize.com. This delightful, intimate beach lodge set on a remote and genuinely wild stretch of coastline between Placencia and Monkey River (with access only by boat) is one of the best conservational tourism destinations in Belize. The traditional Belizean weatherboard terrace-fronted house is built almost entirely using locally sourced material (including driftwood). The entire resort uses collected rainwater and grey water run-off and is fed by solar power, with occasional generator backup when the weather is cloudy. Guests have their own open-plan kitchen, living room, bedrooms and bathroom. The 2nd-floor veranda has beautiful views out over the Caribbean, where the English owners run excellent angling and snorkelling trips out to the reefs and flats. Kayaks and snorkelling gear are available at the resort.

Cayes and faros off Placencia p158

$$$$ French Louie Caye Lodge, www. frenchlouiecayebelize.com. Simple, rustic accommodation is provided in colourful wooden huts on a tiny white-sand islet set in pristine, reef-filled seas. The lodge owners offer a great selection of first-class fishing, snorkelling and kayak tours, and when guests are not out in the wild, they can laze around with a book in one of the myriad hammocks which lie strewn between palm trees all over the island. The best rates are for longer packages (8 days/7 nights or 4 days/3 nights). Prices include all meals, lodging, round-trip transport from Placencia village, snorkel gear and kayaks. There is space on the island for 2 families, making it more economical to visit as a group. Credit cards accepted.

$$$$ Robert's Grove Caye and **Ranguana Caye**, www.privateislandsonline.com. Both these tiny cayes are managed by the **Inn at Robert's Grove** (see page 160) and offer similar simple cabin-based accommodation with an option to hire out the entire island or to share with other guests.

$$$$ Tarpon Caye Lodge, T523-3323, www.
tarponcayelodge.com. Like Laughing Bird
Caye, Tarpon Caye is a faro, or mini atoll, set in
deep water and with a small central lagoon.
The caye itself, lying 16 miles from Placencia,
is covered with low scrub and red mangrove
forest and has a small white-sand beach.
Accommodation is simple in stilted, fan-
cooled wooden huts with hammock terraces
sitting right over the water. But the emphasis
here is very much on the fishing, with some
of the best tarpon catches in Belize in the
deep central lagoon and permit fly fishing in
the flats all around. Prices are full board and
include fishing. Credit cards accepted.

$$$$ Whipray Caye Lodge, www.whipray
cayelodge.com. This family-run island lodge
on gorgeous, remote little Whipray Caye
is one of the best fishing lodges in Central
America. Guiding by owner Julian Cabral is
first class and the waters around the island
are packed with permit. The snorkelling off
the caye is great, too. Accommodation is
in weatherboard huts shaded by coconut
palms and cooled by a sea breeze. They are
simple though well maintained, but the
emphasis at **Whipray** is very much on nature
itself: the fishing, the reef and beautiful star-
filled nights. The lodge has some modest
sustainable tourism practices including water
conservation and solar-generated electricity.
Prices are full board. Credit cards accepted.

🍴 Restaurants

Placencia Peninsula *p156, map p157*
Most resorts have their own restaurants,
which are mainly nothing special, serving
familiar international standards (pasta, ribs
and pizzas), assorted grilled fish and Belizean
staple fare, such as jacks or chicken/beef/
fish with rice and beans. A few – such as the
excellent restaurant at the **Blue Crab**, see
page 161, are (officially) open to guests
only. There are other simple restaurants
around the village, too, and most of the bars
serve food, so there are plenty of options for
browsing. If you're looking for something

other than the standard beans and rice fare,
we list some of the better options below.
$$$ Bonefish Grill, see Singing Sands
hotel, page 160. Romantic open-air dining
right on the beach, with an eclectic menu
of uncomplicated dishes drawing on Asian,
North American and Belizean cooking, like
Korean noodles with shrimp, spicy griddled
pork, seafood platter, pasta and grilled fish.
Portions are large. The restaurant is most
intimate at night, but is open all day, serving
light food at lunch (including fish club
sandwiches) and generous breakfasts.
$$$ Danube, Main Rd, Seine Bight, next to
the football pitch, T610-0132, www.danube
belize.com. One of Placencia's few European-
owned restaurants offering Austrian dishes
with a Sydneysider contemporary twist,
including paprika chicken breast with
spaetzle (small dumplings), Wiener schnitzel,
goulash and meat fondue. There are also
vegetarian (and with advanced notice,
vegan) options available. For a romantic
meal, come for dinner served by candlelight.
$$$ La Dolce Vita, T523-3115, www.ladolce
vitaplacencia.com. Italian home cooking
from a genuine Italian chef, Simone de
Angelis, with a choice of antipasti like
mushroom and mozzarella crostini, excellent
and authentic Roman pasta (with ingredients
imported from Italy), seafood and gelatos.
These are complemented by a decent Italian
wine list. The restaurant is decorated with
stills from Fellini's iconic film, and dinner
comes with mood music from Italian tenors.
$$$ Mare, see Turtle Inn, page 160. Chef
Edwin Alvorado offers a menu which mixes
familiar comfort food (like wood-fired pizza,
steaks and ribs) with decent pasta dishes
and more refreshing fare, like ceviche and
gazpacho. Vegetables are sourced from
the organic kitchen garden at the **Turtle
Inn**, there's a decent wine list (strong on
Coppola's California reds) and the dining
area is open plan and semi-alfresco, under
a large, open-sided *palapa*. **Turtle Inn** has
4 other restaurants. The **Gauguin Grill**
offers a seafood menu and a more romantic

setting on the beach under the stars dining. **Auntie Luba's** is a Belizean restaurant overlooking the sea, serving dishes like curry chicken, coconut shrimp and beef stew. The other 2 restaurants are bar based and serve snack food.

$$$ Maya Beach Hotel Bistro, see Maya Beach hotel, page 161. It's well worth catching a cab from Placencia to enjoy an evening at one of southern Belize's best restaurants. The food here is as close as you'll get to gourmet in Placencia with dishes like peanut- and coconut-encrusted fish, spicy black beans or cacao pork chop with papaya-chipotle-coconut sauce. Reserve beforehand.

$$$ Rumfish, Village Sq, Placencia, T670-3293, www.rumfishyvino.com. This gastro bar set in a lovely terraced wooden house in the centre of the village was set up by a Californian couple who honeymooned in Placencia, fell in love with the village and relocated here. The menu consists of upmarket comfort dishes: gourmet burgers (with a tangy house sauce), lobster Reggiano, conch steaks and grilled fish. The wine (strong on Californian and Italian bottles) and cocktail lists (try the coconut mojito) are among the best in Belize.

$$ Secret Garden, next to the football pitch near **Wallen's** convenience store, T523-3420, www.secretgardenplacencia. com. This spa café offers a varied and eclectic menu of fresh, light, healthy fare. This changes regularly but usually includes an array of flavoursome salads, easy Thai dishes like *tom ka gai* and green curry, falafel and pasta. The café also serves big, wholesome breakfasts and US-style coffee.

$$-$ De Tatch, see Sea Spray, page 161. Simple Belizean fare such as grilled (and very fresh) fish with rice and beans, shrimp curry and coconut jerk snapper, and hearty breakfasts served in a big open-sided *palapa* right on the beach in the heart of town.

$$-$ Omar's, East Sidewalk. Reliable seafood (decent snapper and lobster), Caribbean Creole cooking (with dishes like fried Rasta Rice) and Tex-Mex (with refried bean burritos in tomato salsa) served in a laid-back setting on the beach.

$ Siripohn, opposite the **Barefoot Bar**, T620-8718. Fri lunchtime only. Thai food lovers should try the genuine article from Siripohn herself, a native Bangkokian whose delicious *tom ka gai*, *tom yam kung*, pad thai and assorted curries put all the ersatz Thai chefs in Placencia to shame. She will cook special orders on request too; contact her through the **Siripohn Spa**, see page 165.

$ Tutti Frutti, Village Sq, Placencia. Excellent, creamy Italian and US-style ice cream and sorbet in a vast variety of fruity and exotic flavours, including coconut, raspberry, peanut butter and Bailey's Irish Cream. Decent yogurt and passable cappuccino, too.

🎶 Bars and clubs

Placencia Peninsula *p156, map p157*
Placencia village has just a handful of nightspots.

Barefoot Bar, Main St, T523-3515. By far the most popular in town. Almost everyone staying or working in Placencia seems to grab a stool and a Belikin beer here at some point during their stay, and the bar is probably the best place in Placencia to meet a fellow traveller (outside one of the resorts) or a local. They serve simple food too.

J-Byrd's, next to the Placencia village dock, near the petrol station. Cover bands playing US AOR most nights in season.

Yoli's dock bar, next to the jetties at the south end of town. Another option worth checking out.

🎉 Festivals

Placencia Peninsula *p156, map p157*
Feb Sidewalk Arts Festival. Usually in the 1st or 2nd week. Placencia's long, narrow street is lined with arts and crafts stalls, from canvases of tropical scenes to jewellery, carvings, cosmetics and cakes. Kids take time off school to paint and draw in the kids' tent and Belizean musicians play shows at night.

Jun Lobsterfest. With fishing tournaments, raffles, sports events and lots of lobster. Usually in the latter half of the month.

O Shopping

Placencia Peninsula *p156, map p157*
Placencia isn't a shopping mecca, offering mainly ersatz Maya handicrafts, cheesy postcards and general tourist tat. One exception is listed below.

Isy Paradise, below the **Rumfish** restaurant, T523-3214. The best option for shopping is this French-owned boutique selling its own-brand jewellery, stylish papier mache gifts designed by **Firmin a Maya** in Chiapas and assorted knick-knacks.

O What to do

Placencia Peninsula *p156, map p157*
Diving
Avadon Divers, T503-3377, www.avadon diversbelize.com. Run by experienced and very knowledgeable Anne-Marie McNeil and offering the best choice of dives around Placencia using good equipment and boats. She also offers instructor-level training and Nitrox dives.
Sea Horse Divers, T523-3166, belizescuba. com. Offers PADI and NAUI instruction and diving throughout the Placencia area.
Splash Diving Center, T523-3058, splashbelize.com. One of the best-established dive operators in Placencia, specializing in dive training courses and offering trips around the entire region including Glover's atoll. A registered PADI centre. Good boats and equipment.

Spa and massage
Secret Garden, next to Wallen's convenience store, T523-3240, www.secretgardenplacencia. com. Swedish, Thai, hot stone and other massages from Japanese-trained US masseuse and chef Lee Nyhus. From BZ$100 per hr.
Siripohn Spa, next to **Caribbean Travel**, Sidewalk, T620-8718. You'd expect a Wat

Po-trained alumni of the illustrious Mandarin Oriental spa in Bangkok to offer a great massage. Thai native Siripohn offers what are arguably the best foot, essential oil and ayurvedic massages in Belize, together with body treatments, facials and wraps of the quality you'd receive in a top Asian spa, but at a fraction of the price: around BZ$130 per hr.

Tour operators
Caribbean Travel and Tours, Sidewalk, T523-3481, www.ctbelize.com. This great little agency is a one-stop shop for Placencia, organizing tours, transfers, flights and flat and hotel bookings. Owners Lance and Veronique McKenzie have many decades of experience working with tourism in Belize and are the best people in Placencia to arrange bespoke trips or standard tours.
Eagle Ray Tours, Sidewalk, T661-9516, placenciatoursbz.weebly.com. Tricia Hernandez and Rene Leslie offer tours throughout Belize from their little beach office in Placencia village. Trips are good value and very popular with budget travellers. They include trips around the cayes to snorkel and see the birdlife and manatees, to the rainforest in Stann Creek and Toledo (including the Cockscomb reserve) and to Monkey River.
Exotic Belize, T664-0309, www.exoticbelize. com. Basilio Mes organizes guided trips and tours in Stann Creek and Toledo districts, including Cockscomb and the Maya Centre, whitewater kayaking, Maya homestays, visits to Blue Creek Cave, Mayflower Bocawina and the Cayes.
Joy's Tours, T523-3325, www.belizewithjoy. com. An award-winning tour company offering trips throughout the Placencia area (including Cockscomb and Monkey River), to the cayes and around Belize.
Nite Winds, T523-3487. Snorkelling trips around Placencia and the cayes. Experienced and reliable.
Toadal Adventures, T523-3207, www.toadaladventure.com. Great light adventure trips throughout the Placencia

area, including multi-day sea kayak, jungle river and caving trips. Owner operator David Vernon has been guiding trips to remote areas in Belize for more than 20 years.
Trip 'n Travel, Village Sq, Placencia, T523-3205, www.placencia.com/Members/Tripntravel.html. Fly fishing tours throughout the Placencia area and one of the better tours to Monkey River, led by sharp-sighted local guides.

Placencia Peninsula *p156, map p157*
Air
Placencia is well-connected to the rest of Belize by frequent, regular flights. Maya Island and Tropic Air have 6 flights daily to **Belize City** via Dangriga, and to **Punta Gorda**.

Bus
Ritchie's (T523-3806) operates 3 buses Mon-Sat to **Dangriga** leaving from the petrol station in Placencia village. It is also possible to take a water taxi (Hokey Pokey, T523-2376, www.aguallos.com/hokeypokey), leaving every 30 mins 0630-1200 and 3 times in the afternoon, 10 mins,

BZ\$10, to **Mango Creek/Independence** on the Southern Hwy and from here catch any northbound bus (at least 10 daily) to **Belize City** via **Belmopan** and **Dangriga**. You can also catch buses to **Punta Gorda** (at least 10 daily, 60 mins) from Mango Creek/Independence. To get to **Hopkins** you will have to take a northbound bus and stop at the turn-off for Hopkins village.

Boat
The Belize–Honduras Boat, T632-0083, www.belizeferry.com, BZ\$120, runs a weekly speedboat service to **Puerto Cortés** in Honduras. The journey can be quite choppy. The boat leaves the dock near the petrol station at 0930 every Fri, passing Big Creek at 1000 to complete immigration formalities. It arrives in Puerto Cortés at around 1200. Buy tickets in the Placencia Tourism Centre. The return service leaves Puerto Cortés on Mon at 1100, arriving 1330.

Placencia Peninsula *p156, map p157*
Medical services The nearest hospital is in Dangriga. **Wallen's Pharmacy**, Wallen's Market, T523-3128.

Toledo District

That Belize's southernmost district is so little visited owes more to its lack of infrastructure than its attractions. Until just a few years ago even getting to Punta Gorda was a challenge, involving a long and bumpy drive with stops or, occasionally, complete halts at river crossings to take rickety ferries or negotiate precarious bridges. Toledo has, therefore, long been isolated from the rest of tiny Belize, and it could claim to be the country's least spoilt and most Belizean district. The rainforests in the foothills of the Maya mountains and the reefs around the Sapodilla Cayes are pristine and still rarely visited. As are the caves that honeycomb the hills and the Mayan ruins of Lubantuun and Nim Li Punit.

Whilst the Creole culture of the north is less prevalent in Toledo, Garifuna culture is strong. The country's most important and sacred dugu temple is in Punta Gorda and its most famous musical export, Andy Palacio, was born in a tiny village in the district's far south. There are large communities of Belizean East Indians and Belizean Chinese and Taiwanese. But if Toledo is arguably Belize at its most Belizean, it's also Belize at its most Central American. In Toledo the rest of the mini-continent makes itself most readily known. The district's interior is dotted with dozens of indigenous villages, populated by Maya peoples originally from neighbouring

Guatemala and Honduras, who have moved here over the centuries. It's possible to stay with them and sample village life. And on the building sites and buses of the district capital, Punta Gorda, you're as likely to hear Honduran Spanish as English. ▸▸ *For listings, see pages 172-176.*

Punta Gorda → *For listings, see pages 172-176. Colour map C1. Population: 5205.*

Toledo's capital is a neat and tidy bonsai-sized town of wooden houses, concrete convenience stores and few hotels nestled between the forest and the Caribbean. It's only a few streets deep and long, and it feels as sleepy and lost in time as the village in Laurie Lee's *Cider with Rosie*. Locals snooze in deckchairs in small lawned gardens pinked by bougainvillea and busy with bees and hummingbirds. But for the birds and breeze, the only noise is the clatter of the cars or pickups that occasionally pass through, or the clamour of children leaving or coming back from school. Little happens in Punta Gorda, or PG as it is known locally, and there's little to see or do. If you're intent on doing nothing at all, Punta Gorda's the town for you. Use it as a base and, when you're exhausted with the languor, take a boat from the docks to dip your toes into the coral-rich waters of the offshore cayes, clamber up a Mayan ruin – there are plenty here in the far south – or cave, trek or raft in the rainforest nearby.

Arriving in Punta Gorda
Getting there The Punta Gorda airstrip lies at the back of town to the northwest. Taxis wait for the frequent flights coming in from Belize City via Dangriga, but it's only a few hundred yards' walk to the town centre. Buses enter town along Front Street next to the sea (ask to hop off at any time) and come to a halt at the bus stop at the junction with King Street. Walk a block north on King and a block south on Main Middle Street and you'll

Punta Gorda

To ① (100 yds), Joe Taylor Creek & Garbutt's Marine (200 yds)

New Rd
North St
Alejandro Vernon St
Wattema
Airstrip ✈
King St
Queen St
Middle St
Main St
Ugaldez St
Far West St
West St
Prince St
Clemente St
Pampana St
Front St
Chocolate Factory
James Bus Line
Taxi Stand
Civic Centre
Tide Tours
Customs & Immigration
Taxi Stand
Taxi Stand
Marine Terminal
Caribbean Sea

To ③ (400 yds) & ④ (1.5 miles)

N
100 metres
100 yards

Where to stay
Beya Suites **1**
Charlton's Inn **2**
Coral House Inn **3**
Hickatee Cottages **4**
Inn at Joyful Garden **5**

Mahung's Inn **6**
Sea Front Inn **7**
St Charles **8**
Tate's Guest House **9**

Restaurants
Earth Runnins **1**
Gomier's Veggie Café **2**
Grace's **3**
Punta Pizza **4**

reach the main town square and a taxi stand. All the town hotels lie within 10 minutes' walk of here. Hotels and lodges out of town will usually meet you at the airport or the bus stop. ▸▸ *See Transport, page 176, for further details.*

Places in Punta Gorda

There is just one sight of any note in PG, the **Chocolate Factory** ⓘ *Front St, between King and North, Mon-Fri 0900-1600, free*, where you can see cacao beans being roasted, ground and churned to produce delicious chocolate. Bars are on sale here. Much of **Green and Black's** chocolate is sourced from Toledo.

Cayes and reefs → *For listings, see pages 172-176. Colour map C2.*

See What to do, page 175, for a list of tour operators that run trips to the cayes and reefs.

Sapodilla Cayes Marine Reserve

Belize's Barrier Reef thins out off the coast of Toledo, tapering to a point that stretches towards Roatan and the Bay Islands of Honduras, and breaking into fragmented islets as it does so. The reef here is little visited and is especially beautiful around this marine reserve, whose sandy islands fringed with coconut palms have a real Robinson Crusoe feel. It's expensive and time-consuming to reach the Sapodilla Cayes, which lie 30 miles offshore from Punta Gorda, a boat trip of at least two hours. Don't forget your snorkel and mask.

The reserve itself covers around 50 sq miles and protects 14 mangrove islets and sandy islands. These latter are some of the prettiest in the country, especially on **Hunting Caye**, where a sweeping half-moon beach is as often visited by nesting turtles as it is tourists, and is washed by shallow seas rich with eel grass beds and pristine coral gardens, whose heads are exposed at low tides.

Unlike the reefs off Ambergris Caye and the atolls, there are no dramatic coral walls. The coral gardens off the Sapodilla Cayes slope gently into deep blue and are home to large shoals of common reef species, as well as pelagics like jack and barracuda. Turtles and eagle rays are a common sight and, in the deep beyond, manta rays and whale sharks are frequent visitors. Whilst the Sapodilla Cayes are pristine for now, they are under increased pressure from day-tripper boats out of Livingston in neighbouring Guatemala.

Nicholas Caye, Hunting Caye and **Lime Caye** receive the most visitors and have simple facilities, including a ranger station on Hunting Caye where visitors pay a BZ$25 entrance fee. **Northeast Caye** has been set aside as a nature reserve. **Frank's Caye** has a great reef and a few shacks. If you're not on a dive excursion, think about staying here (see **Garbutt's**, see page 174), or bring a tent and camp out wild under the stars.

Port Honduras Marine Reserve

Not all the cayes off Toledo lie out on the reef. Port Honduras Marine Reserve lies just a over a mile north of Punta Gorda. The bushy, mangrove islands here sit in shallow water, rich in permit and bonefish, and the reserve is justifiably popular with fly fishermen. The reserve is also home to one of the greatest concentrations of Caribbean manatees in Central America. There are the partially excavated ruins of a Mayan saltworks, built from reef coral blocks on **Wild Cane Caye**.

Staying in Mayan villages with the TEA

The **Toledo Ecotourism Association (TEA)**, a cooperative of Q'eqchi, Mopan and Garifuna villagers based in Punta Gorda, organizes stays in their village-based guesthouses, which are simple wooden buildings with traditional thatched roofs offering dormitory accommodation. Meals of corn-flour tortillas, beans and fish or meat are eaten communally.

TEA uses an indigenous model for wealth distribution, which seeks to share the benefits of tourism as widely as possible throughout each participating village. Guides, food providers and entertainers are rotated among seven to nine families in each village. The chairman, treasurer and secretary are elected for each TEA village every two years, and TEA members appoint a village-run board, which oversees the running of the programme.

Q'eqchi and Mopan villages participating in the TEA scheme include Laguna, Blue Creek, Pueblo Viejo, San José, San Miguel, San Antonio, San Pedro Columbia and Santa Elena. It is also possible to stay in the Garifuna village of Barranco in southern Toledo (birthplace of Garifuna musician Andy Palacio, see box, page 172) or to stay longer as a voluntourist.

Expect to pay roughly BZ$65 per night per person for two meals, accommodation and a forest tour, and BZ$90 for full board, a forest tour, music (which includes Garifuna drumming in Barranco) and dancing. See www.teabelize.org for full details.

Inland Toledo → *For listings, see pages 172-176. Colour map C1.*

Mayan villages

Village names don't get much worse than **Dump**. This huddle of ugly houses sits at a curve in the Southern Highway around 10 miles north of Punta Gorda and just beyond ugly little **Big Falls** (where there's a decent restaurant and a feeble hot spring).

You'll inevitably pass through both villages on your way to Toledo's fabulous Mayan villages, which are reached via a dirt road running inland from Dump, to the west. This cuts up into the rugged karst limestone folds of the Maya Mountain foothills to a string of delightfully small mostly Q'eqchi and Mopan Maya villages. Their inhabitants still predominantly speak these Mayan languages, dress in colourful clothing and grow maize on long rectangular plots of land called *milpas*, much as their ancestors did at the height of the Maya civilization. Most of this part of western Toledo is theoretically set aside as protected indigenous-owned land, but in recent decades there has been increasing encroachment by farmers and loggers. Many villagers have turned to tourism to secure income and to increase awareness of their rights to their ancestral lands. A cluster of classic-era Maya sites lie within easy access of the villages.

A **homestay** with the Toledo Maya is a highlight of a visit to southern Belize. Stays in the villages are easy to organize and are either operated by **TEA** (see box, above) or are private homestays (see page 174).

Blue Creek and the caves

Blue Creek, a mixed Mopan and Q'eqchi Maya village of some 40 families a few miles north of Aguacate, takes its name from the beautiful clear-water river flowing through its centre. It is involved in the **TEA** programme (see box, above). This mountain stream rushes through gorgeous rainforest above the village, forming a series of aquamarine pools. Its source is a gash in a forest-covered wall of rock leading to a labyrinthine cave system, which is safe to explore only with a guide, bookable though the nearby **Blue Creek Forest Lodge** (see page 174). Blue Creek is one of a number of caves pocking the karst hills of Toledo. Others include **Tiger Cave**, set in thick forest hunted by jaguars and ocelot, a 90-minute hike from the village of San Miguel, and **Laguna Cave**, which has towering stalactites and stalagmites and is littered with shards of broken pre-Columbian property. All can be seen in a tour with **Hickatee Cottages** or **Sun Creek**, see page 172.

Rio Blanco National Park
This tiny park near the Maya village of **Santa Elena**, some 30 miles west of Punta Gorda, is a community-run and protected area of forests around the pretty Rio Blanco river falls, which drop into a very deep pool in a glade in the lush tropical forest. The park itself only covers around 100 acres, but there's plenty of bird and small mammal life, and guides from Santa Elena or Santa Cruz villages can be hired to walk the trails with visitors.

Lubaantun
① *Daily 0800-1700, BZ$10.*
This is by far the most impressive Mayan site in southern Belize and the only one with the same level of excavation and visual impact as those in the north of the country.

The city's name means 'place of the fallen stones', which was an accurate description of the site when it was first 'discovered' in 1924, as buried rubble under ancient rainforest, sitting in a dramatic location, high on a ridge between two tributaries of the Columbia river. It was a significant religious centre, as seen in its ceremonial precincts, which focus on 18 plazas along a north–south axis, covering 15 acres. They are surrounded by a residential and agricultural hinterland of almost 1.5 sq miles. The original buildings were significantly taller than those you see today. These crumbling pyramids were capped with tall buildings constructed from perishable materials, a style of construction also found at Nim Li Punit and Uxbenka, but recorded at very few other Classic-era Maya sites.

The site is reached via a cement footbridge, which crosses the eastern tributary of the Columbia River. A trail climbs from here into the site, entering **Plaza IV**. There is a **visitor centre** where visitors must register and pay the entrance fee. Plaza IV itself is enclosed by pyramids. **Structure 12** on the eastern side of the plaza is the second tallest building in Lubaantun at 9 m and offers a good vantage point over what was once the ceremonial centre of the city. The tallest pyramid, **Structure 10**, lies immediately to the south. The **ball courts** – where the Maya played the elaborate game which mimicked the interplay between our world and the Xibalba, the realm of the dead – lie directly to the north, in the adjacent Plaza V, and to the northwest, just beyond that plaza's limits. See also box opposite.

Other Maya sites
These following three sites are accessible only on an organized tour with **Hickatee Cottages**, page 172, or with your own transport. **Uxbenká** ① *no opening hours or entrance fee*, lies on the outskirts of Santa Cruz village, four miles west of Santo Antonio. Like Lubaantun, it occupies a dramatic position on the crest of a ridge. Although the site has some beautiful carved stelae, it has been badly looted and is little excavated. It was a ceremonial centre, though far smaller than Lubaantun. **Nim Li Punit** ① *daily 0800-1600, BZ$10*, which lies 35 miles south of the Independence junction near Indian Creek village, is also a minor ceremonial centre sitting on a ridge top and preserving a number of beautiful stelae, one of which is among the finest unearthed in Belize. The site hasn't been excavated much but is set in attractive, partially forested surrounds. **Pusilhá** ① *no opening*

The crystal skull

In either 1924 or 1927 (depending on which accounts you read), 17-year-old British schoolgirl Anna Mitchell-Hedges apparently discovered one of the most controversial of all Mayan artefacts, the **Crystal Skull of Lubaantun**. The skull, which is an almost anatomically exact replica of that of a female human, was unearthed in two parts – the cranium and mandible – which are both thought to have been carved out of the same piece of almost flawless, glassy clear rock crystal. It weighs 5 kg and is about 13 cm high, 13 cm wide and 18 cm long. Study of the skull by Hewlett-Packard laboratories in 1970 concluded that it had been carved without the use of metal instruments and against the natural axis of the crystal (a practice rarely undertaken by modern crystal sculptors, as it is likely to shatter the rock), using silicon abrasives and water. As such a technique is hard to date, they could not conclude if the skull itself was modern or pre-Columbian. Archaeologists remained sceptical of its Mayan origins, however, suggesting that Anna's adopted father, the journalist and amateur archaeologist Frederick Mitchell-Hedges, had planted the skull for Anna to find.

The Mitchell-Hedges skull is one of six supposedly Mesoamerican crystal skulls in existence. Another was allegedly sent anonymously to the National Museum of American History in 2008, apparently with an unsigned letter stating: "This Aztec crystal skull, purported to be part of the Porfirio Díaz collection, was purchased in Mexico in 1960 ... I am offering it to the Smithsonian without consideration." A subsequent study of this skull undertaken by the Smithsonian Institution itself using a scanning electron microscope concluded that the skull had been cut and polished with modern diamond tools and was not pre-Columbian. Another crystal skull of supposedly Mesoamerican provenance owned by the British Museum was also tested by the Smithsonian who concluded that it was cut and polished on a mounted rotating lapidary wheel and that the rock crystal used was probably from Brazil.

The Mitchell Hedges skull has not as yet been examined by the Smithsonian, and its provenance and supposed power continue to fire speculation and the imagination of artists and film-makers from Damien Hirst to Steven Spielberg.

---

hours or entrance fee, is remarkable principally for its remote setting – in lush forest next to the rushing Moho River right on the Guatemalan border – and for the large numbers of intricately carved stone tablets in eerie animal shapes, some of which still litter the ruins. There's also a walled ball court and a partially intact Maya bridge over the Moho River.

Paynes Creek National Park → *Colour map C2.*

ⓘ *Accessible only by chartered boat or with a tour operator like Tide Tours, see page 176.*
This park in the north of Toledo District protects just under 40,000 acres of moist lowland forest, mangroves and broken pine savannah. It's very rich in wildlife with healthy populations of jaguar, ocelot and jaguarundi, as well as howler monkeys, peccaries, tayras, nesting hawksbill turtles and, in the **Punta Ycacos Lagoon**, West Indian manatees who breed here. Some 300 species of birds inhabitat or migrate to the park, including jabiru storks, aplomado falcons and nesting white ibis. The pine forests, which have suffered heavy logging and fire damage, are the most threatened ecosystem within the park and are home to yellow-headed parrots and black-throated bobwhites. Archaeologists have

Andy Palacio's Wátina

Although he had been playing music for many years, Garifuna musician Andy Palacio burst onto the international music scene in 2006 with a stunning CD, *Wátina*, produced by Cayo-based master musician and founder of Stonetree records, Ivan Duran.

The CD was widely distributed, receiving lavish praise in magazines and supplements like *Songlines* and *Observer Music Monthly*. It was on myriad 'best of' lists for 2007 and won a BBC World Music and Womex Award, catapulting Andy Palacio, the Garifuna and Belize to worldwide musical attention. So, if you buy just one CD in Belize, make it *Wátina*.

Expect to be surprised. There is nothing Jamaican or Hispanic Central American about *Wátina*. This is gorgeous, gentle music, instilled with the melancholy of the sea and reverberating with the sway and swing of Africa. African languages still infuse the Garifuna tongue, together with Carib, French and Spanish influences. And on *Wátina*, the rhythms and the echoing women's chorus (both of which are based on traditional Garifuna tropes) belong far more to the oldest continent than the new. Whether they are gentle laments, warm, lilting ballads or funky, tight dances, each song on the CD feels far closer to Baaba Maal or Youssou N'Dour than Bob Marley or Buena Vista. The CD as a whole is a rare treasure that is as rich and multi-layered as it is easy on the ear.

discovered four very early submerged proto-Mayan sites in the Ycacos lagoon. These sites were recently excavated and evidence shows that some date back to 1300 BC. See also Monkey River, page 157.

Barranco and the far south → *Colour map C1.*

There are no roads south to the southern border with Guatemala along the Sarstún River. Nor are there any visitor facilities at present, except a simple **TEA** guesthouse in the Garifuna hamlet of **Barranco**, which is the access point to the thick forests and mangrove forests of the **Sarstoon-Temash National Park**. There are no guides to take you there, though you might be able to organize a trip in a dugout in Barranco itself. The village feels almost deserted, with most of its younger people long gone. A few have even found fame and fortune, including the late Andy Palacio (see box, above) who is buried here. Barranco is connected by dirt road to the rest of Belize via the village of Santa Ana.

◉ Toledo listings

For hotel and restaurant price codes and other relevant information, see pages 11-12.

● Where to stay

Punta Gorda *p167, map p167*
$$$$ Coral House, 151 Main St, T722-2878, www.coralhouseinn.com. A big neo-classical house offering 4 spacious, well-appointed a/c homely rooms decorated with local arts and crafts and with large, airy balconies and modern en suites. There's a pool, Wi-Fi and cable TV, and tours can be arranged. Minimum 3-night stays in high season and discounts for NGO workers and Belizeans. At the lower end of this price category. Credit cards accepted.
$$$ Hickatee Cottages, Ex-Servicemen Rd s/n, T662-4475, www.hickatee.com. Much

of the forest immediately northwest of Punta Gorda along the Southern Hwy has been felled for agricultural land. But there is plenty of forest immediately to the south of town around these cottages, making them the best place in Toledo to base yourself. It may be just a 10-min drive from PG but this delightful guesthouse feels a world away. Spacious, elegant wooden cottages with big bathrooms and bedrooms hung with mosquito nets and complete with living areas (and their own little libraries) sit in a lovingly tended semi-wild garden in lush rainforest. English owners, Ian and Kate, prepare full breakfast and teas served on the wooden balcony of the main building. It's enchanting to sip Earl Grey and watch hummingbirds and butterflies and hear the cicadas in the surrounding trees. Ian is a mine of knowledge on Toledo and all things Belizean and has a wonderful collection of rare Garifuna CDs. They organize some of the best tours in Toledo, including private homestays in Maya villages. There's a pool, Wi-Fi and a restaurant. Credit cards accepted.

$$$ Sea Front Inn, 4 Front St, T722-2300, www.seafrontinn.com. This ungainly 5-storey stone and concrete building with bizarre blue alpine roofs sits right on the seafront. Rooms are themed by marine animal names and come with private balconies and small stone bathrooms. A backyard is decorated with bright murals and ersatz Mayan artefacts. The East Indian and Mayan owners are friendly and helpful. Wi-Fi and cable TV, and breakfast is included. Credit cards accepted.

$$ Beya Suites, 6 Hopeville, San Antonio Rd, T722-2188, www.beyasuites.com. Spotless tiled rooms in this big, Brighton rock-pink, balcony-fronted building have en suites with powerful hot-water showers. Owner Lisa can organize trips to Blue Creek, Tiger Caves and the Cayes, as well as kayak rental and transfers. It's on the outskirts of town, right on the seafront. Wi-Fi and cable TV. Credit cards accepted.

$$ Charlton's Inn, 9 Main St, T722-2197, www.charltonsinn.com. The nearest thing PG has to a business hotel offers long corridors of boxy but well-maintained a/c rooms with space for 3 guests. Each room has a work desk, a tiny TV, a queen-size and single bed and chocolate-box paintings of Alpine views. Avoid the top floor, which sits under a tin-roof and gets too hot during the day for the a/c to cope. There's a restaurant, Wi-Fi and cable TV, and tours can be arranged. Credit cards accepted.

$$ Inn at Joyful Garden, Middle/Main St, T722-2111. A/c rooms in the guesthouse sit above a hardware shop on the northern side of the town's main square and come with tiled floors and en suites. The quietest are at the back. Most have balconies. If Joy is not there, ask in the shop downstairs or in the family's supermarket, **Supaul's**, 100 m south of the guesthouse and the main square.

$ Mahung's Inn, 11 North St at Main St, T722-2044, mahungsinn@hotmail. com. Rooms here are scruffy, with scuffed yellowing walls, spongy beds and pokey bathrooms with chipped tiles. But what they lack in comfort and sophistication, they make up for in price. There is nowhere cheaper than this in PG. Cable TV. Cash only.

$ St Charles, 23 King St, T722-2149, stcharles pg@btl.net. Climb the stairs above a hardware shop and you'll find this modest guesthouse whose no-nonsense a/c and fan-cooled rooms come with en suites, small desks and communal balconies hung with hammocks. Special single rates for solo travellers. There's Wi-Fi and cable TV. Credit cards accepted.

$ Tate's Guest House, 34 JM Nunez St, T722-0147, tatesguesthouse@yahoo.com. Simple fan-cooled or a/c rooms in this family-run guesthouse have stone tile floors and plain white walls, armchairs and beds with firm mattresses. En suite bathrooms are large with powerful showers. The guesthouse owner, Tate, is welcoming and very helpful in organizing tours both inland and out on the cayes. Grab a breakfast bite at **Corinne's Pastry Delights**, a small stall in front of the guesthouse open most mornings. There's Wi-Fi, cable TV and communal kitchenettes. Payment is cash only.

Cayes and reefs p168

Garbutt's, see page 175, can organize stays in simple wooden huts on the cayes, or you can camp. Bring lots of water, food and sun protection, and be sure to arrange a return pickup.

Inland Toledo p169

For details of the **TEA** guesthouse programme, see page 169. Alternatively, private homestays are available in Aguacate village in the Toledo highlands. These can be arranged through **Hickatee Cottages** (see page 172) or directly with **Louis**, Aguacate Village, T702-2973/633 9954, cucullouis@hotmail.com. Prices start at BZ$60 per night and guests must make their own way to the village which is served by bus from Punta Gorda on Mon, Wed, Fri and Sat at 1130.

$$$$ Belcampo Lodge, Southern Hwy 5 miles from PG, T1-888 299-9940 (USA), www.belcampoinc.com. This luxurious jungle lodge sits on a rainforest-swathed ridge above the Rio Grande River in a 15,000-acre private reserve. The rainforest canopy suites are among the most elegant rooms in Belize, with raw terracotta tile floors and exposed beams set against light cream walls hung with abstract ethnic art. Balconies offer magnificent views out over the tree canopy (making this a good spot for birdwatchers). **Belcampo** has its own kitchen gardens and farm, with a cacao plantation, and the food in the restaurant is fresh and full of flavour. It also has a spa. Tours arranged. Cheaper when booked as part of a package. Credit cards accepted.

$$$$ Cotton Tree Lodge, Ex-Servicemen Rd at the Moho River near Piebra, T670-0557, www.cottontreelodge.com. Rustic chic jungle *cabañas* are set in rainforest overlooking the Moho River. Each cabin has polished hardwood floors, hammock-strung verandas and partially open sides, screened against mosquitoes but with wonderful views. The restaurant is housed in a large faux-*maloca* (longhouse). Trips include kayaking through the forest on the Moho River, treks and visits to cacao farms.

The restaurant uses produce grown in the resort's organic kitchen garden. Wi-Fi, credit cards accepted.

$$$$ The Lodge at Big Falls, Big Falls, www.thelodgeatbigfalls.com. Rooms with a/c or ceiling fans are set in tropical gardens on the edge of the forest and next to a rushing mountain river. The most intimate are those in thatch-roof *cabañas*, which overlook the river and come with hammock-slung terraces and spacious bedrooms with en suite shower rooms filled with exuberant tropical plants. Birdwatching in the vicinity and guided birding trips in Toledo are excellent. There's a pool, restaurant and Wi-Fi. Credit cards accepted.

$$$$ Tranquility Lodge, T665-9070, www.tranquility-lodge.com. Comfortable a/c rooms with flatscreens, iPod docking stations and shared verandas in Maya-inspired buildings nestle in rainforest next to Jacinto Creek. Trees in the grounds are covered with epiphytic orchids that attract birds and butterflies, and the lodge offers good facilities and guiding for birdwatchers, including a species list. Good restaurant, and tours arranged. There's Wi-Fi and cable TV. Breakfast is included. At the lower end of this price category. Credit cards accepted.

$$$ IZE Blue Creek Rainforest Lodge, T1-508-655 1461 (USA), www.izebelize.com. This lodge is run by **International Zoological Expeditions**, a North American ecotourism company who offer package adventures to Belize with a conservational bent, and who also run a property in the South Water Caye Marine Reserve (see page 144). Accommodation in Blue Creek is in simple twin-share or dorm rooms housed in a rustic wooden building. There's a restaurant, and tours are arranged. Full-board packages only, bookable in advance. Credit cards accepted.

⑦ Restaurants

Punta Gorda p167, map p167

PG has very few restaurant options. The best food is probably at **Hickatee Cottages**, see page 172; ring ahead to see if they have space for non-guests.

$$ Earth Runnins, 13 Middle St at North St, T702-2007. Owner Giovanni has decorated his café-bar with bright tropical greens, reds and lemon yellows, murals of Heile Selassie, hieroglyphs and assorted bric-a-brac garnered from a life on the road. The menu of simple but well-prepared comfort food includes dishes like chicken roti, veggie pasta, burritos and club sandwiches, all served at chunky wooden tables. There's snack food too, including a delicious home-made mezze of baba ganoush, hummus and pitta, and hearty breakfasts. In the evenings, and especially at weekends, it turns into bar, with live reggae and jazz on the 15th and last weekend of every month, and a cocktail menu featuring a range of margaritas and refreshing lime and lemongrass daquiri.

$ Gomier's Veggie Café, Vernon St s/n (behind the **Sea Front Inn**), T722-2929. Opens early for breakfast. Usually closed on Sun. The menu in this vegetarian and wholefood restaurant wouldn't be out of place in Notting Hill or Williamsburg. Carefully prepared and flavoursome veggie lasagnes, curries and grilled dishes are complemented by a delicious range of tropical juices (try the Carambola and Golden Plum), soya milk ice creams and pastries.

$ Grace's, 19 Main St. This Belizean family restaurant serves big and filling lunches of beans and rice, Belizean curries and breakfast of jacks and eggs. Service can be a little slow, even for laid-back PG.

$ Punta Pizza, above **Cotton Tree Chocolate**. Decent Italian-style thin-crust pizza with seafood, meat and vegetarian options.

Inland Toledo p169
This area has very few restaurants outside the resorts.

$ Coleman's Café, Big Falls on the Southern Hwy, T732-4017. Tom, Perleen and their family offer big portions of Belizean East Indian dishes, including chicken curry, Kohun palm cabbage, dal, rotis and curried

shrimp, as well as Belizean plates like rice and beans and filleted fish. Desserts include their home-made ice creams, all washed down with one of their tangy tropical juices.

⊛ Festivals

Punta Gorda p167, map p167
May Cacao Festival. Throughout Toledo, usually towards the end of the month (see toledochocolate.com). Restaurants, shops and stalls celebrate chocolate with chocolate wine, drinks, cakes and sweets throughout Punta Gorda and Toledo, and the chance to learn how to make chocolate.
Late Nov Battle of the Drums. Garifuna drummers from all over Central America converge in Punta Gorda to play together and celebrate Garifuna culture and music. See www.battleofthedrums.rog.

Inland Toledo p169
May Maya Week. Held in Blue Creek, these week-long celebrations are in honour of Maya history and culture, including a Fire Ball Game in which men use clubs to hit a flaming ball down a field to score goals, and a ceremonial Torch Run between the village and Lubaantun, as well as music, dancing and arts events.

⊙ What to do

Punta Gorda p167, map p167
Tour operators
Splash Dive Centre (see Placencia) offers diving in the Sapodilla Cayes. Trips leave from Placencia.
Garbutt's Marine, Joe Taylor Creek, T722-0070, garbuttsfishinglodge.com. Snorkelling, diving and fishing trips in both the Sapodilla Cayes and Port Honduras Marine Reserve. They have simple fishing lodges on lovely Joe Taylor (great for tarpon, and for kayak trips) and on the cayes.
Hickatee Cottages, see page 172. Organizes some of the best trips in Toledo, including Mayan homestays, snorkelling or

Border crossing

Punta Gorda–Puerto Barrios/Livingston

Various boat services go from Punta Gorda in Belize to Puerto Barrios and Livingston in Guatemala. They include **Requena Water Taxi** (12 Front Street, T722-2070), departing from the dock opposite immigration. Schedules are changing and irregular; arrive as early as possible or better yet, arrange in advance. Bike and motorbike shipment difficult; no permits available in Livingston.

Currency exchange Money-changers at both sides, but better to buy quetzals in Guatemala. Nowhere to change traveller's cheques.

Belizean immigration Obtain stamps from the customs house near the pier on Front Street. Allow up to two hours for processing.

Guatemalan immigration If you arrive in Guatemala by boat, check into immigration immediately. Offices are in Puerto Barrios and Livingston, both open 24 hours. Exit fees to leave Guatemala by boat are US$10.

Onwards to Guatemala Highway connections from Puerto Barrios to Guatemala City and Flores.

Onwards to Belize Connections with southern Belize.

---

diving on the cayes and light adventure in the caves and rainforest.
Tide Tours, 41 Front St, T722-2655, www.tidetours.org. Kayaking, diving and snorkelling around the Sapodilla Cayes and Port Honduras Marine Reserve, and trips inland, including to the Maya sites, Blue Creek and Tiger Cave and the national parks and protected areas in Toledo.

Cayes and reefs *p168*
Voluntary work
Reef Conservation International, www.reefci.com. An international organization offering voluntary work on a number of marine conservation and monitoring projects throughout the Americas, including the Sapodilla Cayes.

⊖ Transport

Punta Gorda *p167, map p167*
Air
Several flights daily to **Belize City** via **Placencia** and **Dangriga** with Maya Island and Tropic. It's possible to charter a plane to fly to **Guatemala** or **Roatan** in Honduras; enquire at the airport.

Boat
Boats to **Guatemala** can be chartered through **Garbutt's Marine** (see above) or ask Ian at **Hickatee Cottages** (see page 172). For **Sapodilla Cayes** it is possible to hitch a ride through to **Livingston** in Guatemala from a dive boat. Be sure to leave Belize officially through immigration before you do so.

Bus
North to **Belize City** via Independence (for **Placencia**), **Dangriga** and **Belmopan**, 9 daily with **James** (T702-2049) 1550, BZ$22, 5-7 hrs; also 1 express service at 0600, BZ$24, 5 hrs.
To **Barranco**, Mon, Wed, Fri, Sat at 1200 with **Barranco's Bus**, BZ$3, returns following morning. **Crique Sarco** via **Blue Creek** and **Aguacate** on Mon, Wed, Fri, Sat at 1130 with **Chub's Bus**, BZ$2, returning the following morning very early.

⊕ Directory

Immigration Municipal dock, daily 0700-1600 (though not always reliably open) T722-2247. **Medical services** PG Hospital, Main St, T722-2026.

Contents

Footprint features

Border crossings

Northern Belize

At a glance

🟢 **Time required** Allow 5 days to explore Rio Bravo and/or Gallon Jug, Lamanai and Shipstern. If you want beach time in Sarteneja or a visit to Cerros, then give yourself a week.
🌤 **Weather** It's warm and dry at around 15-30°C Jan-May with cooler nights. It's more hot and humid May-Oct, with the possibility of hurricanes. Nov-Dec is warm with occasional colder spells of 13-15°C.
❌ **When not to go** May-Oct is hurricane season; Sep-Nov can be grey and overcast.

Beyond the cities, northern Belize remains largely wild. In Corozal District the tropical coast is broken by brilliant-blue brackish lakes and lagoons swum by manatees and nursing reef fish, and the flat, rocky land is covered with low-level Yucatec dry forest, cut by crystalline creeks and broken by sinkholes called cenotes that are filled with glassy-clear water. Wildlife preserves, such as Shipstern, near the sleepy fishing village of Sarteneja, are home to distinctively Yucatec bird species, as well as large numbers of semi-aquatic jaguar, and American and Morelet's crocodiles.

Orange Walk District is dominated by the steamy El Petén forests, which extend into southern Mexico and Guatemala. These are dotted with Mayan ruins, such as Lamanai, whose temples sit pretty on the banks of the winding and crocodile-filled New River, or La Milpa, still submerged by the trees in the forest park of the Rio Bravo Conservation Area. Large tracts of wild country in Orange Walk are protected as private land, notably at Gallon Jug, where Chan Chich Lodge offers some of the most enchanting rainforest accommodation in Belize.

Belize has astonishing cultural diversity for so tiny a nation, and the two districts that make up the northern region of the country feel quite different from Belize City or Cayo. Corozal and Orange Walk districts were flooded with refugees: German-speaking Mennonites fleeing the ravages of the Bolsheviks during the Russian Revolution via Canada, and Maya fleeing the Caste Wars, an indigenous Mexican revolt of the mid-19th century. The Mennonites still live in Orange Walk in large numbers and shun machinery, following a simple 19th-century Protestant lifestyle rooted in the Bible. The towns of northern Belize still retain a distinctly southern Mexican feel. People with broad Yucatec Maya faces speak English with the warm, resonant Caribbean tones of Belize City, but when talking amongst themselves, they switch smoothly into their own indigenous language or the lilting, staccato Spanish of Mexico.

Orange Walk District

The district's capital, Orange Walk Town, has little appeal for visitors, but is a useful jumping-off point for the attractions of Orange Walk's interior. The agricultural land that dominates the vicinity of the capital soon gives way to wild country. The Rio Bravo, which snakes across the district from the hills of Guatemala, is fringed with dense forest and marshland and broken by the roof combs of the ruined Maya cities of Lamanai and La Milpa. Wildlife is abundant, and the district is home to some of Belize's best rainforest lodges. ⟫ *For listings, see pages 185-188.*

Orange Walk Town → *For listings, see pages 185-188. Colour map A2. Population: 13,400.*

Important though Belize's second-largest town is to locals, Orange Walk attracts few visitors. Orange Walk took its name from a former orange orchard that once stood next to La Imaculada Church.

The 'Sugar Town', as it likes to call itself due to the region's prospering sugarcane industry, is Belize at its most multicultural, with a population drawn from the agricultural heartland of the country. Mennonites, Maya, Creole, Latin Belizeans and Chinese all congregate here

Orange Walk Town

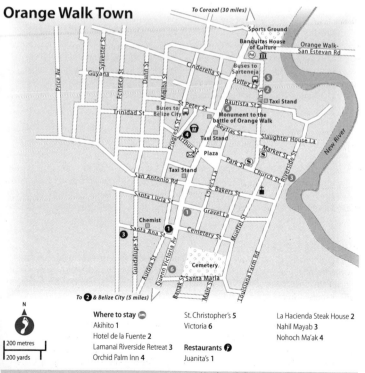

N
200 metres
200 yards

Where to stay 🛏
Akihito 1
Hotel de la Fuente 2
Lamanai Riverside Retreat 3
Orchid Palm Inn 4

St. Christopher's 5
Victoria 6

Restaurants 🍴
Juanita's 1

La Hacienda Steak House 2
Nahil Mayab 3
Nohoch Ma'ak 4

The Battle of Orange Walk

Orange Walk was the site of the most important battle fought in Belize during the Maya rebellion known as the Caste Wars. This revolt all but overthrew the Spanish in the entire Yucatán peninsula, claiming large swathes of modern-day Quintana Roo in Mexico for the Cruzob Maya (a northern group led by the charismatic leaders of a Mayan cult of the Talking Cross), which were not fully reconquered until after the First World War.

In the 1860s the Wars spilled across the border into Belize, when the chief of a Maya group loyal to the Mexicans was encouraged by the government in Mexico City to attack the north of British Honduras. Mexico hoped that by pretending to the Icaiche Maya that the territory would be theirs, they would finally wrest British Honduras from the control of perfidious Albion. The Icaiche, led by their irascible chief Marcus Canul, attacked villages and towns throughout the north of the colony and claimed many for the Maya. When the British in Orange Walk refused to pay taxes levied by Canul, he turned his attention to the district capital itself, attacking the town on 1 September 1872. The tiny outpost of just 1200 inhabitants was taken completely unawares. Chief military officer, Lieutenant Graham Smith was having a bath in the Officer's Mess when he heard gunshots. In a typical act of bungling British bravery, he grabbed his trousers, realised he'd left the keys to the arms store at home and rushed there to get them, in the face of hostile fire. His troubles were compounded by the fact that the door to the locker stood full in the face of the enemy rifles. Smith and Staff Sergeant Edward Belizario somehow avoided getting killed, dragging the heavy magazine out of the barracks to the soldiers, and, after prolonged fighting, they and a handful of civilian colonists managed to ward off the attack. Canul was fatally wounded in the process and died shortly after crossing the Rio Hondo on fleeing to Mexico. There is a small forgotten monument to the battle in Orange Walk Town.

to proffer their wares, and you are as likely to hear Spanish, Plautdietsch, Yucatec Maya or Mandarin spoken in shops and at bus stops in Orange Walk, as you are English.

The town huddles in two- and three-storey buildings along a bend in the pretty New River, which even here is deliciously wild. It was tiny until the late 18th century, but its population grew in the late 19th and early 20th centuries due to the influx of Manitoba Mennonites and refugees from the Yucatán caste wars. At this time, Orange Walk became the scene of the only battle yet officially to have been fought on Belizean soil (see box, above).

Arriving in Orange Walk Town

Getting there Buses from Belize City, Corozal and Guatemala arrive at the bus stop next to the market on Progresso Street (one block west of Queen Victoria Avenue) between Arthur and St Peter Streets. Progresso and Sarteneja buses use a stop on Main Street, opposite the St Christopher Hotel. ▶▶ *See Transport, page 188, for further details.*

Orientation The New River lies on the eastern outskirts, just two blocks from the town centre, where you'll find the market, Queen Victoria Avenue and the distinctly Mexican town square, which in Orange Walk Town is even referred to as La Plaza. Queen Victoria Avenue is essentially part of the New Northern Highway. Drive north along the Avenue

Don't miss ...

and you'll reach Corozal after some 30 miles; drive south and you'll get to Belize City after about 55 miles. There is no tourist office.

Places in Orange Walk Town

Unless you're buying sweetcorn or groceries, you'll not find much to do in Orange Walk. There's a **monument** ① *Queen Victoria Av*, to the battle that saved the town (see box, page 180) next to the sports ground (and diagonally opposite the plaza). And there's a pocket-sized cultural centre, **Banquitas House of Culture** ① *Main St at New River, T322-0517, Tue-Fri 1000-1800, Sat 0800-1200, free,* watching over a bend in the New River. Come here for a whistlestop tour of the district's history and see Maya ceramics from Lamanai, tools used by the logwood and mahogany cutters and the *chiclero* chewing gum collectors, lots of pictures of sugar cane, and views of Morelet's crocodiles basking on the adjacent river bank. **La Imaculada Church** ① *next to the river on the eastern edge of town,* has a lovely little grotto.

Lamanai → *For listings, see pages 185-188. Colour map A2.*

Set in a sea of misty, protected forest that runs green into Guatemala and watching over the warm, wild waters and wetlands of the New River lagoon, the archaeological reserve of Lamanai has the prettiest seat of any Mayan ruin in Belize. It also has one of the longest histories. We know from ceramics unearthed here that the site was first occupied in at least the Middle Pre-Classic period. It was finally abandoned by the Maya in the 18th century. Jaguars live in the area, there is a rich birdlife, and howler monkeys can often be seen in the trees. For more on jaguars and conservation of them through work at the Lamanai Field Research Center, see box, page 222.

Visiting Lamanai

Lamanai is on the banks of the New River Lagoon, 26 miles south of Orange Walk Town along the New River. The best way to reach Lamanai is by boat, easily arranged through hotels or tour operators in Orange Walk Town (see pages 185 and 188) or through general tour operators, such as **Black Orchid** (page 49) or **Belize Travel Services** (see page 39). The reserve can also easily be visited from neighbouring **Lamanai Outpost** jungle lodge, see page 186, and like Chan Chich and the Rio Bravo Conservation and Management Area, it's an excellent place to try to see jaguars. The mosquitoes can be voracious in the wet season, however, so wear trousers and bring repellent. The entry fee is BZ$10.

The site

Lamanai lies on one of the most crocodile-filled rivers in Central America and the river was clearly home to many of the reptiles when the site was named; Lamanai is a Spanish rendition of the Maya *lama'an ayin*, meaning 'submerged crocodile'. There are crocodile motifs all over the site. Most spectacular are the 5-m-high fibreglass renditions of the sixth- or seventh-century stucco carvings that were uncovered (and reburied) on the west side of the magnificent pyramid that lies in the extreme north of the site (named by unpoetic archaeologists as **Structure N9-56**). One shows a mask wearing a crocodile headdress. There are other carvings at Lamanai, notably the stone jaguar masks on Structure N10-9, colloquially known as the **Jaguar Temple**. A rather crude fibreglass reconstruction of a stela found at the site shows one of the city's aristocracy, Lord Smoking Shell, taking part in a ceremony. Few originals remain.

None of Lamanai's earliest buildings remain standing today. The oldest intact pyramid on the site is N10-43, known as **El Castillo**. It was constructed around 100 BC and is one of

Lamanai

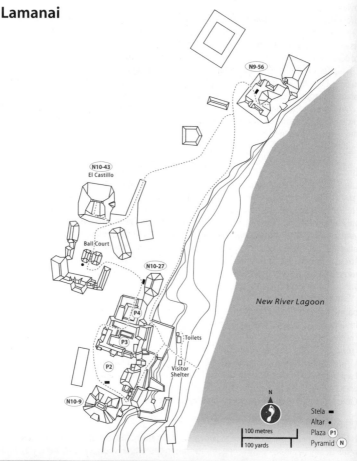

Border crossing

La Unión–Blue Creek

This remote, little-used porous border crossing lies near the Mennonite village of Blue Creek in northwestern Orange Walk District some 40 miles from Orange Walk Town. There are buses between Blue Creek and Orange Walk. There is no road across the border. The only means of crossing is by canoe ride (BZ$5). Then track down Mexican/Belizean immigration which is officially open daily 0700-1800, but in practice opens only sporadically. There are buses from La Unión to Chetumal or Xpujil in Campeche state.

the tallest pre-Classic Maya structures so far unearthed at 33 m. The views from the top, over the rainforest and the gently undulating New River, are superb. Looking down at the grassy plaza can be vertiginous.

Just to the south of El Castillo there is a **ball court**, dating from AD 900-950 and still with its stone centre marker. An offering discovered here in the 1970s included small amount of mercury, the first discovered in a Mayan ruin and thought to have come from Honduras.

The Lamanai **museum**, located at the main entrance, is one of the best site museums in Belize, with a large selection of artefacts, including crocodile figurines, worked obsidian blades and some stelae.

A short walk from the site at the village of **Indian Church** are ruins of a sugar mill built by the British. It dates from 1860-1875 when the British administered a 200 acre plantation. Also here are the 'Indian churches' themselves, the ruined buildings of a Spanish mission, built on one of Lamanai's pyramids in the 1570s.

Birdwatching

Lamanai lies at the centre of a two-sq-mile forest reserve that is contiguous with both the largest stretch of protected tropical forest north of the Amazon and the wetlands of the New River Lagoon. Birding here is excellent, and the pyramids offer the perfect canopy vantage point. As well as more common species, you can expect to see red lored and yellow-headed parrots, lineated and golden-fronted woodpeckers, keel-billed toucans, black-headed, violaceous and slaty-headed trogons and occasional ornate hawk eagles. The journey to Lamanai from Orange Walk, along the northern reaches of the New River, runs through gallery forest and is a habitat for numerous water birds, including limpkins, various rails, tri-coloured, agami and chestnut-bellied herons and various kingfishers.

Dedicated birders should consider staying at the adjacent **Lamanai Outpost** (see page 186), or **Hill Bank** (see page 186) further upstream. Both have superb birding and first-class guiding.

Mennonite villages → *For listings, see pages 185-188. Colour map A1.*

Lamanai lies close to **Blue Creek**, the largest of a number of Mennonite settlements in the area. Many inhabitants of these close-knit villages arrived in 1959 and were members of a Canadian colony that had migrated to Chihuahua, Mexico, to escape encroaching modernity.

Visiting Mennonite villages

It is possible to visit the Mennonites through **Lamanai Outpost**, see page 186, who offer a range of tours, including a fascinating day excursion to **Indian Creek** village. Guests

Mennonites

The Mennonites are a group of radical Protestants who follow the teachings and lifestyle espoused by the 15th-century Frisian Anabaptist theologian Menno Simons. Like the Lutherans, the Anabaptists were a group who railed against the baroque doctrine and cumbersome institution of the contemporaneous Catholic Church. Like most early Protestants, they returned to a simple interpretation of the scriptures, rejecting many of the sacraments and practising non-violence. Followers, who became known as the Mennonites, were persecuted throughout Europe both by the Catholic Church and by the nascent Protestant churches. This led them to form isolated communities, preserving a traditional way of life and shunning what they saw as the concupiscence of the outside world.

Over the centuries, the Mennonites themselves fragmented into groups including the Amish (named after Jacob Amman who led an attempt to reform the Mennonite Church in Switzerland and Bavaria). One group founded a large number of communities in Russia, after having been granted a great deal of land north of the Black Sea in present-day Ukraine by Catherine the Great. After the Russian Revolution, the farms were appropriated and thousands of Mennonites were murdered both and by Russian anarchists. Some fled to Germany, others to North America and eventually to Belize. There are now an estimated 10,000 Russian Mennonites in Belize, from the more liberal to the ultra-conservative Barton Creek Amish who do not use motors, paint or electrical machinery. All Mennonites still speak Plautdietsch, an old German dialect influenced by Dutch. It is possible to visit a Mennonite community, a fascinating and eye-opening experience (see page 183).

travel by horse and traps to the village, spend time with a family and have a traditional Mennonite lunch with prayers; a fascinating and, as far as we're aware, unique experience. Only in Belize can you take a tour to visit and spend time with the Mennonites.

The villages

Villages preserve their conservative traditions to varying degrees. All speak Plautdietsch (Low German) dialect, are exempt from military service and work community farms that supply Belize with most of its poultry, eggs, vegetables and furniture. **Blue Creek** is one of the least traditional, using machinery and motor tractors. Others, including **Indian Creek**, **Shipyard** and **Little Belize**, use only mules and distinctive horse traps. They shun modernity but are open to outsiders. The most conservative are the Amish, the group who featured in Peter Weir's *Witness* and who have a closed community at Barton Creek in Cayo. Some settlements, such as Neustadt in the west, have been abandoned because of threats by drug smugglers in the early 1990s.

Belize and Mexico have signed an agreement to build an international bridge from Blue Creek across the river to La Unión, together with a river port close to the bridge. It is not known when work will start; at present there is a canoe-service for foot passengers across the Blue Creek (see box, page 183).

Rio Bravo Conservation and Management Area (RBCMA) → *For listings, see pages 185-188. Colour map A1.*

This huge tropical forest reserve constitutes the second largest protected area in Belize after Chiquibul, covering 4% of national territory, or 260,000 acres. It is a crucial reserve of flora and fauna, with some 390 species of birds, 70 mammal species (including pumas, jaguars, ocelots and Baird's tapirs) and 200 species of trees. Since 2005 it has been the release site for the restoration of the near-threatened harpy eagle, the largest and most powerful eagle in the world. RBCMA has the highest density of jaguars in Belize and, possibly, Central America; for more on jaguars, see box, page 222.

RBCMA connects with the Guatemala Maya Biosphere Reserve (and through this, to Chiquibul) and with the Calakmul Biosphere Reserve (in Campeche, Mexico) to form the largest stretch of tropical forest north of the Amazon, covering 4.4 million acres. The reserve is managed by **Programme for Belize**, see page 25.

La Milpa
The Mayan site of La Milpa lies within the reserve. The ruins are said to be the second largest in Belize. They are very little excavated and are a short boat ride from Lamanai on a bluff overlooking the New River Lagoon at Hill Bank. For the species lists, see www. pfbelize.org. There is accommodation right next to La Milpa, see page 187.

Gallon Jug and beyond
The Rio Bravo Conservation and Management Area (RBCMA) is contiguous with the large private protected area (and ranch) of Gallon Jug immediately to the south on the frontier with Guatemala, where there is a superb upmarket rainforest lodge, **Chan Chich**, set within a Mayan ruin (see page 187). Gallon Jug is only accessible by staying at the lodge. The journey here passes through the Rio Bravo Conservation Area and offers some of the best chances of seeing wildlife, especially when arriving or departing at dusk or dawn. Like the RBCMA, Chan Chich is one of the best places to see jaguars in Central America. Birding is superb with very similar species to La Milpa (see the checklist on www.pfbelize. org). Another road has recently been cut south from Gallon Jug through Tambos to the main road between Belmopan and San Ignacio, but travel in this region is strictly a dry weather affair.

◉ Orange Walk District listings

For hotel and restaurant price codes and other relevant information, see pages 11-12.

● Where to stay

Orange Walk Town *p179, map p179*
\$\$ Hotel de la Fuente, 14 Main St, T322-2290, www.hoteldelafuente.com. Opt for the newest rooms in this hotel (next to the car park), refurbished in 2010 in mottled pink and decorated with paintings by a local (one-handed) artist. All have simple

wooden desks, flatscreen TVs, coffee-making facilities and generous en suites decorated in blue tiles.
\$\$ Lamanai Riverside Retreat, Lamanai Alley, T302-3955. Rooms here are simple – with lino floors, tiny en suites and modest furniture – but there is no better location. It's right on the river bank on the edge of town, with great views from the hammock-strung verandas. The adjacent *palapa* bar can get lively at weekends. Free Wi-Fi, bar and restaurant.

$$ Orchid Palm Inn, 27 Queen Victoria Av, T322-0719, www.orchidpalminn.com. This homely and centrally located townhouse hotel offers plain but well-kept white-paint and tile a/c or fan-cooled rooms, with firm mattresses, all with cable TV, Wi-Fi access and en suites. The hotel accepts credit cards and, like most in town, can organize boat tours to Lamanai.

$$ St Christopher's, 10 Main St, T302-1064, www.stchristophershotelbze.com. The garden rooms overlook a pretty bougainvillea garden next to the river. All are big and bright with lemon-yellow walls, desks, tables and chairs. Cheaper options are fan-cooled. The hotel runs good-value tours to Lamanai in conjunction with **Jungle River Tours**, see page 188.

$$-$ Akihito, 222 Belize–Corozal Rd, T302-0185, akihitolee@hotmail.com. The illustrious proprietor of this very simple hotel, Mr Lee, is a former professor at the Ocean University of China in Tsingtao. Fan-cooled rooms are very basic and in need of attention, but they are the cheapest in town. Most come with double beds and cable TV. The cheapest have shared bathrooms. Avoid those overlooking the street as they are a little noisy. Free Wi-Fi in most areas. Chinese food and breakfast available.

$$-$ Victoria Hotel, 40 Belize–Corozal Rd, T322-2518, www.victoriabelize.com. This big pink building on the edge of town may be well past its best, but rooms are clean, and this is the only hotel in town with a pool (when it's in use).

Lamanai *p181, map p182*

$$$$ Lamanai Outpost, New River Lagoon, T22-9444, www.lamanai.com. Nestled in flower-filled gardens surrounded by rainforest right next to the Lamanai ruins, and with gorgeous views across the spring-fed New River lagoon, this luxurious rainforest lodge is one of the most romantically situated in Belize. Unlike so many rooms in Belize, the a/c cabins here achieve levels of urban comfort without compromising their wilderness lodge identity. They are open to magnificent river views yet hidden behind layers of lush palms and tropical bushes, retaining a sense of privacy. Roofs are palm thatch, interiors rich with polished hardwood and furnished with rustic chic tables and chairs. Front decks are hung with hammocks. It has the best range of activities on offer in any rainforest lodge in Belize, with a perfect blend of community and nature-tourism. There are 8 activities a day to choose from, including participating in genuinely scientific monitoring programmes for Morelet's crocodile and jaguar (see box, page 222), visiting Mennonite communities (see page 183) or Lamanai, or kayaking and wildlife-watching in the New River wilderness. Best value when booked through the website as part of a package. There's an excellent restaurant and bar and Wi-Fi throughout. Credit cards accepted.

Rio Bravo Conservation and Management Area (RBCMA) *p185*

RBCMA's 2 lodges offer very different wilderness experiences and both are worth visiting. **La Milpa** is in the heart of the tropical forest, whilst **Hill Bank** is in the midst of the wetlands. Both are wonderful for seeing wildlife and are bookable through the **Programme for Belize**, see page 25. Price codes are per person, per night, including 3 meals and 2 guided tours on the property.

There is no effective public transport to **La Milpa** and **Hill Bank**. **Programme for Belize** charges BZ$180 each way per car (up to 3 people) from Orange Walk Town. To get to La Milpa by public transport, take one of the hourly buses running between Orange Walk Town and San Felipe village, which is 20 miles from La Milpa. La Milpa will pick up from San Felipe for BZ$110 per car (up to 3 people) or it's possible to hitch (see Transport, page 188). There is no public transport to Hill Bank.

$$$ Hill Bank. Accommodation here is similar to **La Milpa**, with fan-cooled dorms and doubles in large wooden huts with shared or en suite bathrooms. There are wonderful views over the shimmering waters of the New River Lagoon to the tropical forest beyond, and boat trips and forest walks offer a chance to see similar wildlife to La Milpa, whilst being in quite different habitats. Full species lists can be downloaded from www.pfbelize.org. Electricity and hot water are solar-generated, and the lodge practises sustainable tourism. Simple but generously served food is extra: breakfast is BZ$25, lunch BZ$36 and dinner BZ$50, as is guiding (see page 188).

$$$ La Milpa. This is a field station, and the basic, sex-segregated, fan-cooled wooden dorms and doubles with their shared bathrooms or en suites reflect this. All come with mosquito netting over the windows and double beds or bunks. Although the showers have hot water, there are no frills. The location, however, is superb. The field station sits in a lawned area surrounded by forest, a stroll away from the La Milpa ruins. The bird- and wildlife-watching is superb. White-tailed deer graze on the lawns, there are ocellated turkeys everywhere, and the forest is replete with rare species. Like **Hill Bank**, full species lists can be downloaded from www.pfbelize. org. There is solar-powered electricity and hot water, and the lodge practises sustainable tourism. The food and guiding on offer is the same as **Hill Bank**, above.

Gallon Jug

$$$$ Chan Chich, T223-4419, www.chan chich.com. Belize's most luxurious jungle lodge has 12 thatch-roofed *cabañas* set in the lawned plaza of a semi-excavated Mayan ruin amid pristine rainforest, which abuts both the Rio Bravo Conservation and Management Area (RBMCA) and the Mayan Biosphere Reserve in Guatemala. Each of the *cabañas* is beautifully appointed, flooded with light from high windows and comes with boutique hotel touches: Egyptian cotton sheets on the beds, designer-crafted en suite bathrooms with his and hers showers and huge make-up mirrors. Much of the meat and produce in the restaurant

(including decent coffee) comes from the Gallon Jug estate, which owns **Chan Chich**. The wildlife is superb, with great birding and a real chance to see big cats, which live in greater density in the area than anywhere else in Central America. **Chan Chich** offers a wide variety of guided tours, including guided wildlife and birdwatching, horse riding, kayaking, medicinal plant trails and night safaris. The best rates are available as packages through the website. The lodge has a mosquito-screened pool, internet facilities and practises some sustainable tourism (with solar-generated electricity, locally sourced produce and recycling).

🍴 Restaurants

Orange Walk Town *p179, map p179*
$$ La Hacienda Steak House, Belize–Corozal Rd, T302-1520. The big flatscreen TVs in this sports bar and steakhouse show English Premier League and Latin American football, as well as US sports. Portions from the restaurant are huge, from giant Porterhouse steaks to big rib-eye, grilled shrimp, buffalo wings and Mexican (not Tex-Mex) fajitas and tacos.
$$ Nahil Mayab, Sta Ana St at Guadalupe, T322-0831, www.nahilmayab.com. This small corner restaurant decorated with Maya stucco carvings and a children's playground is the best place in Belize for authentic Mexican cooking, with a huge menu of Yucatec Maya dishes like Pirix Pa'k (mashed boiled tomatoes sautéed with chopped onions and cilantro) and grilled snapper wrapped in plantain leaf (served with mushrooms, spaghetti and salad).
$ Juanita's, Sta Ana St at Aurora, T302-2677. Very cheap set meals, mostly consisting of various combinations of meat/fish/chicken, rice, beans and salad, but also Mexican food, including *huevos rancheros*, *huevos à la Mexicana*, tacos and Yucatán dishes.
$ Nohoch Ma'ak, Progresso at Arthur St. A menu of tasty but simple Mayan food and Belizean rice and beans standard dishes.

⚙ What to do

Orange Walk Town *p179, map p179*
Birdwatching
Ruben Arevalo, rudiablo@hotmail.com,
or through **Beyond Touring** (see page 26).
This Belize master naturalist and birding
guide from Indian Church village has been
guiding birders for well over a decade,
through work with **Lamanai Outpost** and
Beyond Touring.

Tour operators
Jungle River Tours, 20 Lover's Ln, T670-
3035. Wildlife-watching tours along the New
River, trips to the Mayan temples at Lamanai,
the New River Lagoon and to RBCMA, all at
some of the best prices in town.

**Rio Bravo Conservation and
Management Area (RBCMA)** *p185*
Birdwatching
La Milpa and Hill Bank lodges (see
page 186) both offer excellent

birdwatching and good guiding. Guiding
costs extra, from BZ$100 for 3-hr birding
trips, archaeological tours, night safaris and
jungle walks for up to 6 people.

⊖ Transport

Orange Walk Town *p179, map p179*
Bus
To **Belize City** (all stop at **Burrell Boom**
on request), more than 15 daily with
Gilharry and BBDC, 1st at 0500, last at
1845. To **Corozal** and **Santa Elena** on
the Mexican border, more than 15 daily
with Gilharry and BBDC, 1st at 0700, last
at 2100. To **Sarteneja** from in front of St
Christopher Hotel and the police station,
just before the bridge at 1200, 1340, 1700
and 1800, 2 hrs, BZ$6. To **San Felipe** (for
hitching to **La Milpa**), hourly buses from
0700, last at 1500.
     To **Mexico**: for ADO information on
the Belize City to Cancún bus and other
international routes, see box, page 40.

Corozal District

It's fun to arrive in Corozal from Mexico's Riviera Maya; the contrast couldn't be greater. Whizzing south past condo-lined beaches and crammed tourist towns you reach the border city of Chetumal, a hubbub of people hurrying through the hurly-burly of immigration. And then, Belize: quiet, calm and empty. Corozal town, which barely lies a street deep behind Corozal Bay, feels tiny enough, but get beyond its hinterland into the depths of the state and you'll leave tarmac for dirt. If you see another car at all, it'll be visible far off in the heat haze. There are no bridges across the creeks, just hand-winched wooden rafts, and no theme parks or resorts next to the winding, serpentine rivers and sky-blue lagoons. In places like tiny Sarteneja village, lost on the edge of the vast forests of the Shipstern Nature Reserve, it seems that there are more manatees than men. ►► For listings, see pages 191-194.

Corozal Town → *For listings, see pages 191-194. Colour map A2.*

Many tourists come to the district capital but only to catch a cross-border bus or boat to Ambergris Caye. But there is reason to stay: to take an afternoon trip to two of Belize's least-visited Mayan sites at Santa Rita and Cerros.

Arriving in Corozal Town
The airstrip is three miles south of town, taxi BZ$5. The bus terminal lies on Seventh Avenue four blocks northeast of the seafront. The best hotels lie two miles out of the town centre on

the road skirting Corozal Bay. A cab from the bus station to these hotels costs around BZ$7. The **Thunderbolt** dock which serves the cayes lies on the waterfront at the end of Second Street North. Corozal has no tourist office. ▸▸ *See Transport, page 194, for further details.*

Places in Corozal

There's only one structure to see at the Mayan ruins of **Santa Rita** ① *800 yds outside Corozal's city limits northwest along the Santa Rita Rd, next to the basketball court, no set opening hours, free,* a low bunker-looking building known as Structure 7-3rd, so it's hard to believe that Santa Rita was in all probability once the powerful Classic Mayan city of Chactemal, which lent its name to Chetumal across the border in Mexico. Much of the site was looted, not just for artefacts but also for building materials. The stones and foundations of Corozal were built out of the ruins of Santa Rita.

Around Corozal → *For listings, see pages 191-194. Colour map A2.*

From Corozal, a road leads seven miles northeast to **Consejo**, a quiet, seaside fishing village on Chetumal Bay. There is no public transport to Consejo; taxis cost from BZ$20. Six miles northwest of Corozal, to the right of the road to Chetumal, is **Four Mile Lagoon**, about a quarter of a mile off the road (buses will drop you there). There is great swimming

Corozal

To Santa Rita (800 yds, Mexican border & Chetumal (9 miles)

To Consejo

7th St North
6th St North
5th St North
4th St North
3rd St North
2nd St North

College Rd

11th AV
10th AV

Bus Station

Chemist

Thunderbolt Boats to San Pedro & Sartenja

Taxi Stand

2nd St South
3rd St South
4th St South
5th St South
7th St South
8th St South

9th AV
8th AV
7th AV

6th St

G St South

F St South
E St South
D St South
C St South
B St South
A St South

10th St South

4th AV
1st AV

To Orange Walk & Belize City

Corozal Bay

N

To Airstrip

200 metres
200 yards

Where to stay
Almond Tree **1**
Hok'ol Kin **2**
Maya World **3**

Mirador **4**
Sea Breeze **5**

Restaurants
Al's Café **1**
Chon Kong **2**
Jo Mel Inn **3**

and snorkelling in crystal-clear, wonderfully clean water, which is much better than a Corozal Bay. Stalls sell food and drinks available and it is only every busy at weekends.

The **Cerros** ① *daily 0800-1700, BZ$10*, are Mayan ruins sitting on a peninsula to th south overlooking Corozal Bay. There are three large buildings, a ball court and a pyrami fronted by stucco masks, whose most remarkable attribute is the glorious view from th summit over the brilliant-blue Caribbean Sea and the shimmering bay. Cerros is one of jus a handful of Mayan ruins with a sea view, but whilst the most famous one, Tulum, is overrun nowadays, you are unlikely to be disturbed by anything other than the balmy breeze an the flocks of birds and butterflies at Cerros. To reach Cerros, take a boat from Corozal, wal around the bay (a boat is needed to cross the mouth of the New River) or do the dry-seaso vehicular trail from Progresso and Chunox. For tours to Cerros, see What to do, page 192.

Northeast Corozal → *For listings, see pages 191-194.*

Towards Sarteneja
To reach wild northeastern Corozal from the district capital, you have to drive south t San Estevan (only 10 miles from Orange Walk) and then head northeast to Chunox and beyond. The road is spectacular: bone white and running through pristine Yucatán forest broken by sky-blue cenote lakes and lagoons. Progresso Lagoon lies in rushing Freshwate Creek, Cudjoe Lagoon is surrounded by dense bush and Barracouta Lagoon is one o dozens pocking the marshy forests and meadows around the Lowry's Bight estuary. There are no bridges, just hand-winched wooden ferries crossing clear-water rivers that look as clean and wild as they were in the days of the buccaneers and Baymen.

The road ends at tiny **Sarteneja**, a village as laid-back and gentle as a snooze in a hammock. It sits on the shallow seas of the enormous Chetumal Bay, one of the most important breeding grounds in the Neotropics for West Indian manatees; see box, page 224 The village only wakes up to go fishing or to party on Easter Sunday, see page 192. It was founded by refugees from the Caste Wars, see page 180, and there are still many Maya communities nearby where it is possible to organize a homestay (see page 169).

Shipstern Nature Reserve
① *Shipstern Nature Reserve visitor centre 3 miles west of Sarteneja, daily 0800-1800, www.shipstern.org, BZ$10.*
Immediately south of Sarteneja is the huge, sky-blue, brackish **Shipstern Lagoon**, brimming with American crocodiles, manatees, water birds and general wildlife. It forms the centrepiece of Corozal's most important protected area, the Shipstern Nature Reserve, protecting more than 27,000 acres of Yucatán forests, saline wetlands and lagoons. One of the habitats, the Yucatán dry forest, is completely unique to Shipstern and the Yucatán Peninsula and, after environmental degradation, is found in just four locations. Many of its plants and animals are unique; it's home to five cat species, including healthy numbers of jaguar, the endangered Baird's tapir and the Central American coatimundi. There are more than 70 species of reptiles and amphibians and over 270 of butterflies.

There are mounds covering buried Mayan buildings everywhere in Shipstern and a remote Mayan site, **Kakantunich**, deep in the forest. A botanical trail leading into the forest around the visitor centre has trees labelled with Latin and local Yucatec Maya names; a booklet is available. Be sure to visit the **Butterfly Breeding Centre** ① *daily 0800-1700, BZ$10 including excellent guided tour.* Visit on a sunny day if possible; on dull days the butterflies hide themselves in the foliage. Bring plentiful mosquito repellent.

irding The reserve is home to some 300 species of birds. A species list is available on www.shipstern.org. Joel Dias (see page 193) is a decent guide. Belize's only canopy tower es next to the visitor centre in Shipstern, with wonderful birdwatching in the trees. Since he establishment of the park many bird species depleted in the area are returning or ecovering. Some species, like the American woodstork and the roseate spoonbill, thrive in abundant numbers on Shipstern Lagoon, which is home to many other shore and wetland birds, including boat-billed herons, reddish egrets, white ibis, the rare black catbird and dozens of others. Forest species include abundant keel-billed toucans and endemic Yucatán species like Yucatán (aka yellow-lored) parrots, Yucatán woodpeckers, Yucatán poorwills, Yucatán nightjars, Yucatán jays, orange orioles and Yucatán vireos. Shipstern is also of prime importance for over-wintering migratory species from North America.

◉ Corozal District listings

For hotel and restaurant price codes and other relevant information, see pages 11-12.

● Where to stay

Corozal *p188, map p189*
The best hotels are strung along Bayshore Dr, a dirt road immediately to the south of the town.
$$$$ Almond Tree, 425 Bayshore Dr, T628-9224, www.almondtreeresort.com. The best hotel in town is an intimate, family-run affair overlooking the manatee-filled waters of Corozal Bay. A/c rooms are big, bright and spacious, with large French windows, sturdy and very comfortable hardwood beds, and en suites with faux-Seville ceramic wash basins and powerful hot-water showers. The warm and welcoming owners can organize trips around Corozal, from fishing, diving and snorkelling to visits to Maya ruins or Shipstern. There's a lovely pool, bar and restaurant, as well as Wi-Fi throughout and cable TV. They accept credit cards. Kayaks, bikes and complimentary coffee and juices.
$$$-$$ Mirador, 4th Av at 1st South St, T422-0189, www.mirador.bz. A big neoclassical 4-storey hotel right on the bay, offering homely a/c rooms with tiled floors, pretty wooden dressers, 2 queen-sized beds draped with Shanghai blankets, cable TV and functional en suites in grey tiles. There are larger rooms and suites for families, and the best have good bay views. Wi-Fi

throughout and internet access in the lobby. Credit cards accepted.
$$ Hok'ol Kin, 4th Av s/n, T422-3329, www.corozal.net. A/c rooms are plain and simple in this centrally located hotel, but breezy and well kept. The best are on the upper floors and have balconies slung with hammocks and sea views. All have small en suites. The hotel has Wi-Fi, cable TV and can arrange tours and transfers.
$$ Maya World, 16 2nd St North, T666-3577, byronchuster@gmail.com. If you arrive late and need to leave on an early bus, this simple hotel in a ramshackle old wooden house with bags of character is ideally placed right next to the bus terminal. Fan-cooled rooms are small but cosy and bright, all have en suites, and there's a living area with a communal TV.
$ Sea Breeze, 1st Av s/n, T422-3051, www.theseabreezehotel.com. Book Room 6 – the only one with a sea view – in this bright blue hotel overlooking the bay. Like the others it comes in whitewash and green tiles and has a queen-sized and a single bed – and not much else. The whole hotel, especially the en suites, could do with a little more care and attention, and a lick of paint, but it's good value and there's free Wi-Fi throughout.

Around Corozal *p189*
$$$ Cerros Beach Resort, www.cerros beachresort.com. Simple wooden and palm-thatch *cabañas* in a very small resort offering

food and tours. It's a short walk from the Cerros Mayan site.

Sarteneja p190
There are no street names or house number in Sarteneja.
\$\$ Fernando's Guest House, on seafront near centre of Sartaneja, T423-2085, sarteneja belize@hotmail.com. Simple rooms and cabins in whitewash and polished concrete with palm-thatch roofs. All have fans and are sparsely furnished. The hotel has a small restaurant and can organize tours.
\$\$-\$ Maya and Community Homestays, Sarteneja Homestay, SACD Office, T402-2677, or Ivett Nadia Cobb, T403-2677, www. travelbelize.org/accomodations/sarteneja-homestay, or book through **Sarteneja Tours**. The most interesting accommodation option is a homestay with a Mayan family in and around the village. Families can organize activities, teach Yucatec Maya and take you out on the lagoon or the ocean. Food costs BZ\$7 per meal.
\$ Backpacker's Paradise, T423-2016, T636-5677, http://backpackers.bluegreen belize.com. Simple en suite cabins 15 mins' walk north of the village, with communal areas that have mosquito screens and hammocks. There is also camping, a very simple restaurant and a kitchen. Activities arranged, friendly owners and an excellent website with directions and tips.
\$ Oasis Guest House, next to the BTL Tower, T660-9621. Simple fan-cooled rooms in a concrete and hardwood 2-storey building in the heart of the village, about 100 yds from the waterfront. All rooms have a shared balcony terrace and en suites with hot water. The owner can arrange boat trips and excursions.

Shipstern Nature Reserve p190
There is rather poor dorm accommodation (**\$**) at the visitor centre, BZ\$25 per person. Bring a mosquito net. You can also camp at the centre or just sling a hammock.

🍴 Restaurants

Corozal p188, map p189
\$\$ Chon Kong, 42 5th Av, T422-0169. Corozal's plushest restaurant has a big menu of Chinese standards: chow meins, chop sueys and crispy fried duck, as well as Belizean curries and Western dishes like steak and chips.
\$ Al's Café, 16 5th Av, T422-3654. Belizean standards like rice and beans are complemented by fried chicken, stewed pork, great juices (including tamarind and horchata, a milky rice drink) and sumptuous cakes; try the lemon pie.
\$ Jo Mel Inn, 2nd St at 5th Av, T402-2526. Locals come here for the regional speciality, cow foot soup. If that's not your thing then there's plenty more to choose from, including decent Mexican food: tamales, huevos à la Mexicana, fish steak and Belizean beans and rice favourites. The biggest portions are enough for 2 people.

✸ Festivals

Sarteneja p190
Easter Sun Popular regatta, with boat racing, dancing and music.

⏱ What to do

Corozal p188, map p189
Tour operators
Trips to **Cerros** can be arranged with **Almond Tree** and Hok'Ol K'in Guest House, see page 191, from BZ\$180 for a water taxi carrying up to 6.

Sarteneja p190
Tour operators
Sarteneja Adventure Tours, www.sartenejatours.com. Snorkelling, diving, boat trips, treks and visits to the Bacalar Chico Marine Reserve on northern Ambergris Caye, Shipstern and the Cerros Maya site. All guides are from the **Sarteneja**

Border crossing

Chetumal–Santa Elena

A popular crossing and often busy. Procedures can be slow, particularly at peak holiday times. No fresh fruit may be imported to Belize.

Currency exchange Plenty of money-changers. If entering Belize, it's not strictly necessary to change dollars as these are accepted everywhere at a fixed rate of 1:2. It's easier to change pesos here than inside Belize.

Mexican immigration Open 24 hours. Formalities are relaxed. Passengers exit the bus (without luggage) and show their passports with the FMM and DNI receipt (see below). They then get back in their vehicle, drive across the bridge and enter Belize immigration and customs, this time with their luggage. They are issued with a stamp permitting stays of up to 30 days. Extensions are available at any immigration office in Belize.

Belizean immigration Open 24 hours. When you leave Belize by bus, the first stop will be at Belize Immigration. Passengers exit the bus (without luggage) and show their passports. Those who have been in Belize for more than 24 hours must pay a departure tax of BZ$39.25, payable in local currency or US dollars. Passengers then get back in their vehicles and proceed to Mexican immigration and customs with their luggage, passports are stamped and visitors are given an FMM and a DNI form (see below).

Onwards to Belize Corozal is 12 km south. Ongoing connections to Belize City, three or four hours.

Onwards to Mexico Chetumal, 11 km from the border, offers connections to the Yucatán Peninsula and the beaches of Quintana Roo.

Border taxes Many visitors to Belize arriving from Mexico have reported problems with border tax payments. To clarify, all foreign nationals entering Mexico by air, road or sea must pay a *Derecho de No Inmigrante* (DNI) tax of MX$294 (roughly US$25). When arriving in Mexico by air the DNI is invariably included in the airline ticket price. When arriving in Mexico by land, the DNI must be paid before leaving the country. On arrival in Mexico you will be issued with a *Forma Migratoria Múltiple* (FMM) allowing a stay of 180 days in Mexico. The immigration officials will attach a piece of paper showing the amount to be paid for the DNI. Pay at any bank in Mexico. You will then be given a receipt which should be kept with the FMM. The fee is mandatory in almost all cases (even if the visitor is transiting through Mexico between two other countries regardless of the duration of the stay in Mexico). The fee is not mandatory if the visit is for seven days or less and the visitor returns to the country of original entry. Visitors coming into Mexico from Belize and catching a flight from Cancún can pay the DNI at Cancún airport. Aside from the DNI, there is no exit fee for leaving Mexico. There are reports that Mexican border officials in Chetumal demand a further US$20 'exit fee' on top of the DNI. Politely point out that you have already paid the DNI and decline to pay again.

Tour Guide Association, making this a decent community tourism company.

Shipstern Nature Reserve *p190*
Tour operators
Joel Dias, T627-3366, joel_shipstern@yahoo. com. Tours in the reserve from BZ$10 for trail

walking around the visitor centre to BZ$300 for trail walking and overnight camping deep in the forest, with a visit to the remote Kakantunich Maya ruins and to a wooden shelter on the edge of the pristine Shipstern Lagoon. Groups of up to 4 people.

● Transport

Corozal *p188, map p189*
Air
Maya Island Air flies daily to **Belize City** via **Caye Caulker** and **San Pedro** (for Ambergris Caye). Tropic Air flies daily to **San Pedro**. Private charters to **Sarteneja** cost about BZ$200 for the 30-min journey (compared with 3 hrs by road).

Boat
Thunderbolt (T610-4475, ambergriscaye. com/thunderbolt) to **Ambergris Caye** (via **Sarteneja** on request; ring ahead), leaves 0700 daily, BZ$50 one way, returning daily at 1500.

Bus
There are regular services daily to **Belize City**, 90 miles to the south, at least every hour, via **Orange Walk Town**, with Gilharry and BBDC, 1st at 0345, last at 1630. There are also over 15 buses daily to **Santa Elena** and the **Mexican border**, 9 miles to the north, BZ$3. See also box, page 193. To **Sarteneja** take the **Chunox** bus leaving at 1100 from Corozal post office, BZ$2. Change at Chunox for the bus to Sarteneja at 1300, BZ$3. Or go via Orange Walk Town.

To **Cancún**: For ADO information on the Belize City to Cancún bus and other international buses, see box, page 40.

Taxi
Belize VIP, T422-2725, belizetransfers.com. Transfers to **Chetumal**, **Tulum**, **Playa del Carmen**, **Mérida**, **Cancún**, **Flores** and **Tikal**. Also operates within **Belize**. Cheapest for a group.

Sarteneja *p190*
Bus
There are 4 daily to **Belize City**, 3-4 hrs, BZ$12. From Belize City take the Sarteneja Bus from the water taxi terminal, at 1030, 1200, 1600 and 1700. To **Corozal**, 1 daily via Chunox. From Corozal, take the Chunox bus leaving at 1100 from Corozal post office, BZ$2. Change at Chunox for the bus to Sarteneja at 1300, BZ$3. Or go via Orange Walk Town. To **Orange Walk Town**, 4 daily, 2 hrs, BZ$6. Buses from Orange Walk leave from in front of the San Christopher Hotel and the police station, just before the bridge, at 1200, 1340, 1700 and 1800. To **Chetumal** 1 a day, BZ$12. Buses from Chetumal for Sarteneja leave from the Mercado Nuevo at 1200.

Contents

Footprint features

Background

History of Belize

Earliest origins

Up until the 1990s most archaeologists believed that the first Americans had arrived around 11,400 Before Present (BP). They were known from a series of distinctively shaped bi-facially worked flint spear and arrow heads first discovered in Clovis, New Mexico, radio carbon dated in the 1950s to no older than 11, 400 BP. Artefacts from the **Clovis** people, as they came to be called, were later found all over North America, and the Archaeological Academy pieced together a neat and complete picture of the lives of these first Americans. They were primitive hunter-gatherers who had crossed the ice bridges from Asia when Russia and Canada were connected by a huge ice sheet. They hunted big woolly elephants called mastodons as they grazed on the vast American plains. Gradually, as time progressed, they spread south into what is now Belize and beyond, into South America.

We now know that whilst the Clovis most certainly existed, the story of the first Americans is far more complicated and much older. It was a series of discoveries in South America that first troubled the archaeological status quo. American archaeologist Thomas D Dillehay, working at a site in Chile called Monte Verde, found evidence of early Americans sleeping in hide-covered tents, consuming seafood and wild potatoes around 14,600 BP, more than 3000 years before the Clovis people were said to have crossed the ice bridge into North America. Other discoveries swiftly followed. In 1992, a Brazilian team led by Anna Roosevelt, granddaughter of Teddy, unearthed evidence for a sedentary Amazon civilization, based in caves at Monte Alegre, near Santarem in Brazil. These 'Pedra Pintada' Indians had been living off the rainforest about 11,000 years ago, making them roughly contemporary with the North American Clovis.

A British team, led by Dr Silvia Gonzalez of Liverpool's John Moores University, found footprints fossilized into volcanic ash which she and her team radiocarbon dated to 40,000 BP, declaring in a report to the BBC that 'It's going to be an archaeological bomb and we're up for a fight.' The most astonishing finds of all came from Brazil. In the late 1990s, scientists discovered the oldest known human fossil from the Americas. They called her Luzia, in homage to the famed, 3.2 million-year-old Ethiopian 'Lucy'. Analysis dated Luiza to well over 11,500 BP. But, most interestingly, Luiza did not look like American Indians. Her facial features were far closer to the native Aboriginal people of Australia, a people descended from the first Africans, whose origins reach back more than 60,000 years. Brazilian anthropologist Walter Neves had long claimed that the genetic diversity of the Native American peoples was far too great for them to have been descended from a handful of Bering Straits migrations. And then, more challenges came from Brazil. Sorbonne-educated Brazilian archaeologist Niéde Guidon discovered a series of hearths in the Brazilian outback, the earliest of which she dated to more than 45,000 BP, by far the most ancient date for human occupation in the Americas. Critics, mainly from the North American Clovis establishment, dismissed the hearths as a natural phenomenon resulting from seasonal brushwood fires. But subsequent dating obtained from calcite formations covering rock art from the same location revealed an equally revolutionary date of 36,000 BP, using thermoluminescence (TL dating).

The verdict on the First Americans is still out, with the dusty world of palaeoarchaeolgy split into two fevered camps, the Clovis die-hards and the Clovis denouncers, the most vocal accusing the principally North American establishment of not taking their research seriously. But the evidence against Clovis continues to mount, and go largely unnoticed by the rest of the world. The story of the true discovery of the Americas is still being written.

What's in a name?

There is a legend, perpetuated mostly by 19th-century historians, that Belize was first settled by a Scottish buccaneer, Peter Wallace or Willis. After leading a band on Tortuga Island, he was driven out by the French and found his way to Haulover Creek. Wallace and his men built a logwood camp, known as the Wallace Camp. By the time the Spanish came to know of it, the 'W' was softened, gradually turning into a 'V' and then a 'B': from Wallace to Valis to Balis to Beliss ... There is, however, little hard evidence for the Wallace settlement. The colony's earliest almanacs have not survived and there is no firm record of Peter Wallace, who definitely did exist, ever setting foot in Belize. Contemporary Belizean historians prefer another explanation. *Beliz* means 'muddy water' in Maya, something which can certainly be applied to the Belize River in rainy season.

Early Pre-Classic Maya

The same could be said of the story of the peoples we now know as the Maya. Only a fraction of the numerous Mayan sites that mound and ripple the earth from Mexico to Honduras have been excavated. Of the estimated 36,000 buildings at Belize's Mayan metropolis, Caracol, just 3000 have been carefully recorded and around 30 archaeologically explored. Tombs, obsidian artefacts, sweat baths and burial caches have been discovered at Caracol within the last five years (see www.caracol.org), a fact true of dozens of other Mayan sites across Central America and Mexico.

What we now believe is that the Maya as a civilization distinct from the other early peoples of Central and Southern Mexico and Central America first emerged in the Pre-Classic era (c 1800 BC to AD 250). It was during the Early Pre-Classic that the peoples of Mexico and Mesoamerica first took a species of wild grass called *teosinte* (*Zea Mexicana*) and cultivated it. Over hundreds of generations this plant would radically transform through selective breeding, its pods swelling to 10 times their original size and small hard seeds becoming big and succulent, until eventually it would become the only plant (prior to the invention of the terminator gene) able to reproduce only with the assistance of humans. It is from its seeds that man is created in the great Mayan creation myth recounted in the *Popul Vuh*; see box, page 200. We know the plant today as maize.

Maize enabled the hunter-gatherers who were living on the grassland plains (which then covered the Yucatán and Petén) to become sedentary. Some of the earliest settlements were around **Cuello** and **Corozal Bay** in present-day Belize. Stone digging tools were used to clear forest to cultivate maize and cotton from 3500 BC to 1200 BC in areas that would later become Maya towns and cities. By the Early Pre-Classic period, the settlers were shaping fired coil pottery which they used for storing liquids and cultivated produce, and making chocolate from roasted cacao beans.

But these people were proto-Maya. They had no pyramid temples, no elaborate mathematical system and no complex calendar. They were not yet obsessed with the stars. It was another civilization, the **Olmecs** who made them so. The Olmecs were the first pyramid builders in the New World. And they constructed their pyramid temples in emulation of the great volcanoes surrounding their homes at San Lorenzo and La Venta, in what is now Mexico, close to where they first lived. The temples were artificial sacred mountains and their flat summits were vantage points from which the Olmecs could watch the stars. When the proto-Maya were living in small villages in Belize, Guatemala and Chiapas, Mexico, the Olmecs already had a great civilization, spread across the Gulf Coast of Mexico in the modern-day states of Tabasco and Veracruz. The proto-Maya knew the Olmecs through trade and, from them, they learnt how to turn villages into cities, how to watch the stars and carve jade and stone. It was almost certainly the Olmecs who developed the Long Count and the base 20 mathematics used to calculate it, both of which were integral to what would become the Mayan Calendar (see page 201).

The rise and fall of the Maya

The Olmecs disappeared suddenly in around 500 BC, their cities abandoned or sacked. Their civilization collapsed, and as it did so, a handful of other civilizations, who had borrowed much of their culture, rose in their stead. In Central Mesoamerica, they were the Maya. By 900 BC Maya people in Ceibal in Guatemala were building low temples and carving jade, in emulation of the Olmecs, and the first Maya cities were being built in the Petén at **Tikal** (see page 107) in Guatemala and at **Cahal Pech** in Belize (see page 99).

By the Middle Pre-Classic (1000 BC-300 BC), the Maya – or as they are now known to archaeologists, the early Maya or Mamom civilization – had developed their own language and their population had increased markedly, with settlements all over what were then the grassy plains of the Petén and into Belize. They were producing distinctive monochrome pottery and mountain temples, in cities like **Nakbe** in Guatemala, and boiling chocolate drink in spouted teapots in **Colha** in Belize.

By the Late Pre-Classic period (300 BC-AD 250) the Maya had consolidated many of the traits which mark them out as a distinct civilization. They were building vaulted pyramids and palaces of limestone masonry with vaulted rooms and the distinctive V-shaped corbelled Mayan arch, at cities like Tikal in Guatemala and Lamanai, Cerros and Nohmul in Belize. These buildings were arranged around plazas with rows of elaborately carved standing stone tablets or stelae. Their art was highly sophisticated and brightly coloured. In Belize, as well as those cities listed above, the Maya had settled the entire Belize River valley and were spreading their influence through cities at Xunantunich, Cahal Pech, El Pilar and Pacbitún.

By the beginning of the Classic Maya era, the golden epoch of their civilization, the stelae adorning Maya cities and the lintels within temples from Tikal to Caracol were covered in writing recounting the great achievements of the cities' rulers and the rituals they performed to ensure their success. Priests and kings were planning the planting of crops, key events and the everyday life of the city according to the motions of the stars and auspicious days calculated from their elaborate Mayan calendar (see page 201). Temples and palaces became ever more monumental and richly decorated. The largest, such as **El Castillo** in Xunantunich and **Caana** in Caracol, were Cyclopean temple palaces which remain the tallest buildings in Belize. The cities, most notably Caracol, and the super-cities of Calakmul in Mexico and Tikal had long causeways or *sacbeob* leading from them to satellite towns and beyond. Classic-era Tikal was trading with the great Central Mexican civilization of Teotihuacan, some 700 miles to the west, which held a strong cultural and military influence over the Maya world until its collapse in the seventh century AD.

The Maya never had an empire as the Aztecs or the Romans, with the conquest of other nations organized from a central city state. They had a civilization, which was much more like the Hellenistic or Harappan World, where city states shared a common language and culture but existed not only independently of one another, but often in mutual conflict. There was no single great ruler. Belize, Guatemala and Petén Mexico were, in the words of the late great Mayan scholar Linda Schele, 'A Forest of Kings'. A handful of cities vied for supremacy, often allied to the two most dominant city-states: Calakmul and Tikal.

Stelae and lintels tell the story of constant conquest and rivalry. Tikal rose to supremacy through defeating and subsuming the city state of Uaxactun in the fourth century AD, and Calakmul and Caracol formed an alliance and conquered Tikal in the sixth century AD. At the height of their power, after the collapse of Teotihuacan, Maya cities dwarfed those of contemporaneous Europe, with populations in excess of 150,000, and had more advanced mathematics, and calendars. They also developed perspective in art 600 years prior to the Renaissance.

Around AD 800, the Maya civilization went into rapid decline, probably due to a widespread drought. Cities shrunk or were abandoned throughout Belize, where no new temples were built after AD 830. And war spread throughout the Maya world. Only a handful of Maya sites withstood the decline, most notably in Belize at **Lamanai**. From the ruins of the Maya world, a new, more modest Post-Classic civilization emerged in the Yucatán peninsula to the north, a hybrid of Mexican Toltec and Mayan which produced the pyramids of Chichén Itzá. When the Europeans arrived in Belize, the Maya world was divided between small rival factions: the **Dzuluinicob** of the Macal Valley and the **Chactemal** around Corozal Bay and Altún Ha.

Breaking the Maya Code

The painstakingly excavated ruined cities and their recovered artefacts tell us the story of what the Maya left. But they tell us very little about what the Maya believed. Until the late 1970s, we couldn't even read their writing, and eminent archaeologists, like J Eric S Thompson, were convinced that the glyphs unearthed at temples from Altun Ha to Palenque were rudimentary. It took a Russian linguist, Yuriy Valentinovich Knorozov, who had never been to the Americas, to crack the code, showing that like other ancient scripts such as Cuneiform, Maya glyphs had a phonetic component. Knorozov even went on to translate a handful of hieroglyphs. His ideas were dismissed by the archaeological establishment for 20 years, and he was even accused of using his papers to promote Marxist-Leninist ideology. A major breakthrough came at an archaeological conference at the Maya site of Palenque in 1973, when champions of Knorozov's approach translated a list of former rulers using his syllabic approach. Since then Mayan research has developed rapidly and, through the work of archaeologists and epigraphers such as Michael Coe, David Kelley and Linda Schele, we have a far clearer idea of who the Maya were and what they believed.

Maya cosmology

Much of our knowledge of Maya beliefs comes from the epigraphical and contemporary anthropological research carried out by academics like Linda Schele, Dennis Tedlock and David Freidel: a combination of what is written on the Maya buildings and surviving traditions preserved by contemporary Mayan indigenous groups. Further fragments have been gleaned from the various Spanish accounts, the handful of surviving Maya books and codices and the *Popul Vuh* (see box, page 200), a corpus of Mayan myths based on books burnt by the Spanish, but which were preserved orally and first written in European script in the late 16th century.

Like other pre-Columbian Americans, the Maya had an utterly different ontological approach to our own, rooted in **shamanism**, an apprehension of reality underlying all belief systems, which is found all over the world. Shamanism is a way of life: a journey of spiritual evolution in which the teacher and guide is the shaman. Although the ultimate goal is spiritual realization, few opt for the long, almost monastic path that takes them there. Shamanism is more often concerned with the correct ordering of everyday life

The Book of the Dawn of Life

The *Popol Vuh*, the Quiché Maya book of creation is one of the most important sacred books written in a native American language and one of the world's great myths. It is a corpus of sacred scriptures which tell the cosmic story of creation, as apprehended by the transcendental Maya imagination – from the shaping by the primordial, elemental Gods of material from nothingness, light from darkness and man from maize, to the rise of civilization and the Quiché Maya kings. The Quiche (who are one of the Maya peoples of Guatemala and Belize) who wrote the *Popol Vuh* did not regard it as a story at all, but as an *ilb'al* – 'a seeing instrument.' Through the *Popol Vuh* they saw their past, their future and, more importantly, their connection with the underlying forces that shape the material world. These forces are represented by Gods and heroes – most notably the hero twins who enable the final creation of humans by defeating death through cunning play of the Maya Ball Game.

The original *Popol Vuh* manuscript was conserved by a Dominican priest, Francisco Ximénez (28 November 1666–c 1729), written in Latinized Quiche Maya or possibly directly transliterated from original Maya glyphs. It was probably transliterated in an attempt to preserve the scriptures from the Spanish fires. The Maya wrote thousands of books or codices – folding bark manuscripts in the Maya's distinctive writing. Only three have survived.

events and the marking out of ritual and symbolic space. Everything from a hunt to the positioning of a building has to mimic the higher, divine world. For shamanic peoples, as for Catholic or Orthodox Christians, symbols are more than mere representations; they are the means by which the material world is tuned to the spiritual. Shamans, who educate initiates and oversee all the tribe's spiritual activities, are therefore priests and spiritual professors. Some have attained spiritual realization, either through intense deprivation or suffering, or the long process of shamanisitic education, others are merely the holders of tradition that has been passed on to them.

For the shaman, spiritual realization involves complete existential awareness of the fundamental absence of dualism. The shamanistic universe comprises two worlds, which coexist. Most obvious is the visible 'material' world, which is the realm of the senses and is governed by the quest for food. But underlying this is a spiritual 'invisible' world that we share with all objects and beings in the universe. This is the realm of pure being, archetype and spirit, and is the place in which we apprehend and even meet the cosmic and divine powers. Actions in the visible world must therefore be evaluated in terms of the invisible world, for this is ultimately where they derive their form and meaning: what we do belongs to the material world; what we are, belongs to the spiritual.

The Olmecs were the first great Shamanic civilization in Mesoamerica, developing the template which would be used and adapted not only by the Maya but by the great civilizations of central Mexico. The first Olmec pyramids were built in emulation of the symbolic location of material creation: the volcano of San Martín. They even had fluted sides. Into the base of their volcano pyramids, the Olmecs inserted huge stone stelae, showing their shaman rulers entering a trance-like state, communicating with archetypal spirits and divining and evaluating actions in the material world accordingly. One stela at the Olmec city of La Venta depicts a World Tree, a symbol of the axis mundi which lies at the heart of the Mesoamerican universe, with roots under the earth and branches in the heavens, linking the underworld kingdom of the dead, which would be called Xibalba by the Maya, with the middle kingdom of the Earth and the star-filled sky. World trees or *wacah chan* have been found all over the Maya world, depicted on the lid of a ruler's sarcophagus in Palenque or planted as Ceiba trees at the centre of Mayan cities. They would later come to be associated with the Milky Way. Opposite the first Mesoamerican pyramid, the Olmecs built a gateway to the shamanic spirit world in the form of a sunken court-shaped plaza, decorated with carvings of aquatic plants, symbols of the divide between the material and the spirit world. The Olmecs also propitiated gods through ritual bloodletting and human sacrifice.

The Olmec template for Mesoamerican civilization was adopted and elaborated by the Maya and changed little until the arrival of Cortés. Maya societies were theocracies, governed by a political and regal elite who ruled from temple-mountains, communicated with the spirit world in trance states, and recompensed its elemental and archetypal powers through blood-letting and sacrifice. An increased pre-occupation with divining and balancing the material and spiritual worlds led to the development of elaborate sacrificial ball games, taking place in sunken plazas decorated with aquatic symbols like those first built by the Olmecs. And, as the Maya believed that the relationship between the spiritual and the material was recorded in the stars, they developed an elaborate 260-day calendar to predict their movement. Every number and day had its own significance, each of the 20 day names had a specific deity and cardinal point and the calendar rotated in an anti-clockwise direction like a cog until a cycle of time had been completed. The cog fitted into another even more elaborate 365-day calendar, divided into 18 groups of 20 days plus an additional five days, all with a patron deity. When the two calendars were running concurrently it took 52 years for a cycle to complete.

These two calendars worked alongside a cyclical **Long Count**, broken-up into 52-year cycle divisions from the time of one creation to another. A stela at the Classic era city of Copán in Honduras calculates the Long Count to a 29-figure number using base 20 mathematics, the most sophisticated calculation ever accomplished anywhere to that date. The current Maya Long Count is set to end on the 23 December 2012.

The first Europeans

When Europeans came to Belize, Maya society was fragmented but there were still almost as many Maya in the country as there are people in Belize today. It was an ignominious arrival: a tiny sailing boat was shipwrecked near Corozal in 1511; of the handful of sailors who survived, five were sacrificed by the Maya and the remaining two, Geronimo de Aguilar and Gonzalo Guerrero, were enslaved. On landing on Cozumel in 1519 Hernán Cortés, the conquistador who would eventually overthrow the Aztecs, heard of their capture and sent gifts petitioning the Maya for their release. Aguilar returned, but Guerrero, who had by this time risen within Maya society and married Zazil Ha, daughter of King Nachan Kan, become the first European to settle in Belize. Guerrero would live up to his name, which means soldier in Spanish. He reportedly became a military adviser to the Maya and died fighting the Spanish invasion.

After Guerrero the Spanish left what is now Belize to its own devices and went on a campaign of pillage and plunder through the former Aztec Empire, aided by a Mayan princess from Cozumel and an army of Tlaxcalan warriors. In 1528 the conquistadores returned to Mexico's Yucatán peninsula, to the north of Belize, in the person of Francisco de Montejo, who based himself on Cozumel and waged an unsuccessful campaign to conquer the Yucatec Maya. His son continued the campaign, establishing a colonial capital at Mérida, a fort at Bacalar just north of Chetumal and a mission at Lamanai in Belize. He declared all the land to the south towards Belize and the west towards Tabasco state as Spanish. Belize was a province of Guatemala. This was despite the Maya not having been quelled, and despite the establishment of only tiny and scattered Spanish settlements in these areas.

Meanwhile the cruelties of the Spanish in the Americas were reaching the ears of the rest of Europe. On the one hand, the Spanish Crown had high ideals of justice and social order and a strong belief in the welfare of the indigenous Americans, commanding restraints and compassion and endeavouring to found schools and monasteries which would bring the conquered people into the fold of the Spanish nation. On the other, the colonies were burdened with the cynical reality of exploitative conquest carried out by idle and cruel aristocratic Spanish soldiers and their bands of cut-throat mercenaries fresh from expelling the Moors and the Jews from Spain. They massacred and enslaved the local people. The Dominican friar and campaigner against Spanish cruelty, **Bartolomé de las Casas** (after whom Mexico's San Cristóbal de las Casas takes its name), writes in *A Brief Report on the Destruction of the Indians* of typical treatment meted out by the Spanish in the 16th century:

'The Spaniards with their Horses, the Speares and Lances, began to commit murders, and strange cruelties: they entered into Townes, Borowes, and Villages, sparing neither children nor old men, neither women with childe, neither then that lay in, but that ripped their bellies, and cut them in peeces…. They laid wagers with such as with one thrust of a sword would paunch or bowell a man in the middest, or with one blow of a sword would most readily and most deliverly cut off his head, or that would best pierce his entrals at one stroake. They took the little Soules by their heeles, ramping them form the mothers dugges, and crushed their heads against the clifts… They murdered commonly the Lords and Nobility on this fashion: They made certaine grates of pearches laid on pickforkes, and made a little fire underneath, to the intent, that by little and little yelling and despairing in these torments, they might give up the Ghost. One time I saw foure or five of the principall Lords roasted and broiled upon these gredirons…'

The Buccaneers

Whilst the Spanish were massacring and pillaging the Mexicans and the few Maya of the northern Yucatán, Chiapas and Guatemala, the English chose to pillage the Spanish. This was under the full patronage of Queen Elizabeth I, who was incensed by Spanish territorial claims, granted by the Pope under the Treaty of Tordesillas. 'The Queen of England understands not why her or any prince's subjects should be debarred from the Trade of the Indies, which she could not persuade herself the Spaniards had any just title to by the Donation of the Bishop of Rome, to whom she acknowledges no prerogative much less authority in these cases,' she wrote in an edict of 1587, adding 'and this imaginary propriety cannot hinder princes from trading in those countries, or from transporting colonies into those parts thereof where the Spaniards do not inhabit.'

Her declaration was signed, sealed and delivered by British victory over the Armada the following year. It would provide justification for attacking Spanish towns and gold ships throughout the Americas, and for founding colonies throughout the Caribbean, including the capture of Jamaica and settlements on the Spanish Main in and around modern Belize and the Mosquito Coast of Nicaragua.

The edict and general abhorrence of the Spanish and their cruelty also inspired plucky and morally questionable Brits to sell up their wares and join crew making sail for the New World. They became known as buccaneers, a name derived from the Caribbean Arawak word *buccan*, a wooden frame for smoking meat, preferably manatee. The Dutchman Esquelim, an early journalist who lived among them, remarked that they scarce ate anything but flesh. The buccaneers were 'Boy's Own' characters who included pious teetotallers like Captain Bartholomew Roberts (who banned gambling on his ship and strictly observed the Sabbath) and sailors under patronage like Admiral Sir Francis Drake and later Welshman Henry Morgan (see below), who sacked Maracaibo, Portobello and Panama City, stealing a huge amount from the Spanish and leaving an island of red-haired illegitimate children who live to this day in Utila, a caye off the Honduran coast. Some had tiny, weather-beaten boats, bought in Europe from their life savings and barely able to make it across the Atlantic. Some wonder at how they managed to overpower and overthrow the much larger and better-armed Spanish galleons. In *Buccaneers of America* (1684), Esquemelin describes their method thus:

'Their first approach was made with great judgement, their tiny craft being so steered as to avoid the direct fire of the heavy artillery, while their picked marksmen attempted to shoot down the helmsmen and the sailors at the rigging. Then they got under the stern, proceeded to wedge up the rudder, and boarded the ship from several boats at once. The deck once reached, their personal dexterity, activity and courage were so marked that they rarely failed to overpower their opponents.'

The buccaneers found safe harbour in the region, when they were invited by Jamaica's Governor, Thomas Modyford, to base ships at Port Royal. And they plagued and panicked the Spanish for a century, together with their Miskito indigenous allies from the Nicaraguan and Honduran coast. The Miskito were divided into two groups, ethnic Native Americans and Miskito Sambu. Like the Garifuna people who would later settle in Belize, they were a mix of fugitive African slaves and local indigenous Americans. Both hated the Spanish with venom and pledged alliance to the British Crown. The last straw for Spain came at the end of the 1660s. In 1665, Henry Morgan and a crew of 107 men sacked Campeche, Trujillo and then, joining forces with a band of Miskito warriors, ascended the San Juan river into Lake Nicaragua and assaulted and captured the great city of Granada. The following year, Morgan and another Dutch buccaneer Edward Mansfield (nee Mansvelt) and their Miskito allies took Providence Island (now a territory of Colombia in the San Andrés archipelago) from the Spanish and founded a buccaneering base under the loose governorship of Thomas Modyford's brother James.

The Spanish were furious and fearful that the taking of Providence was just the first step in the conquest of the mainland. They attacked the settlement in great force, capturing James Modyford and subjecting him and a number of his associates to prolonged and brutal torture in Porto Bello. CH Haring, author of *Buccaneers in the West Indies in the XVII century*, describes their treatment as follows: 'Thirty-three were chained to the ground in a dungeon 12 feet by 10. They were forced to work in the water from five in the morning until seven at night… when weak for want of victuals and sleep, they were knocked down and beaten with cudgels so that four or five died. Having no clothes, their backs were blistered with the sun, their heads scorched, their necks, shoulders and hands raw with carrying stones and mortar, their feet chopped and their legs bruised and battered with the irons, and their corpses were noisome to one another.'

Meanwhile, in Europe, the English Crown had been negotiating peace with Spain since 1664, which was finally agreed upon under the Sandwich Treaty of Madrid of 23 May 1667. This effectively outlawed buccaneering. But it didn't stop the attacks.

Pirates of the Caribbean

Europe was a long way from Jamaica in the late 17th century, and Sir Thomas Modyford was determined to have his revenge on the Spanish after the sacking of Providence Island

and the deposing of his brother. After repeated intelligence reports, he was also fearful that the Spanish would next attack Jamaica. In 1666 Modyford had received an edict from George Monck, First Duke of Albemarle and Lord of the Admiralty, saying that the West Indies were exempt from the then ongoing negotiations with Spain and that the governor of Jamaica might still employ buccaneers if it would be beneficial to English interests in the Indies. Modyford chose to listen to Albemarle and ignore the Treaty of Madrid. He wrote to London: 'The Spaniards look upon us as intruders and trespassers, wheresoever they find us in the Indies, and use us accordingly: and were it in their power, as it is fixed in their wills, would soon turn us out of all our plantations; and is it reasonable that we should quietly let them grow upon us until they are able to do it? It must be force alone that can cut in sunder that un-neighbourly maxim of their government to deny all access to strangers.' And with that he despatched Henry Morgan and a privateer army with a fleet of 10 ships to Porto Bello, then one of the most important ports on the Spanish Main, in modern-day Panama.

Morgan captured Spanish clerics and forced them to climb ladders set against the fortified city's walls and pin them to the parapets. The Spanish killed many of their own priests, but Morgan's tactics prevailed and the pirates then climbed the ladders and hurled gunpowder grenades over the walls. The Spanish surrendered and the pirates ransacked Porto Bello and held it to ransom. After occupying the city for 15 days, they left it in smouldering ruins.

After their return, the wily Modyford sent Morgan to attack Caracas and another pirate, Captain Dempster, to harass Havana and Campeche. Knowing that he had all but declared war on Spain, he then petitioned London for several frigates to command the obedience of the privateers and to protect Jamaica from inevitable retaliatory attacks by the Spanish. Charles II sent the *Oxford*, a frigate of 34 guns. The governor's clever political manoeuvres had succeeded. Charles also instructed Modyford to continue to harry the Spanish and to employ privateers to do so. The *Oxford* was sent as private ship of war to join Morgan's fleet. Morgan then sacked Maracaibo and, in 1671, Morgan attacked and took Panama City, one of the wealthiest of all the Spanish possessions in the New World.

Baymen of the coast

Whilst Morgan and the privateers sponsored by the Jamaican governor continued their campaign, the smaller-scale adventurers who had hijacked Spanish ships before the Treaty of Madrid found themselves with increasingly less support from the English authorities. One of the cargoes they had plundered was logwood or, as it is now known, campeachy (*Haematoxylon campechianum*), named after Campeche on the western Yucatán peninsula whose environs was one of the locations of its first exploitation. When chopped into chips, moistened with water, fermented and treated with gaseous ammonia, campeachy yields copious brilliant green metallic crystals which were the base of a number of different dyes, used for calico cloth and woollen goods throughout Renaissance Europe. When mixed with various mordants, campeachy produces shades of blue and, when added to dilute acid, it turns a brilliant blood red. This versatility made chipped campeachy wood an extremely valuable commodity, selling at £100 a ton, the equivalent of nearly £200,000 in today's money.

Even before buccaneering was outlawed, the British were setting up extraction camps on the Spanish Main. But they had to be careful not to attract too much attention and share the same fate as Providence Island. Time and again, British set up camps near Campeche, along the Belize River and on the Mosquito Coast among their Miskito indigenous allies. Time and again, the Spanish would send a scout boat around the region, discover them and dispatch soldiers and gunboats from the Yucatán to dispel them. It wasn't an easy life, and it didn't attract savoury characters, as William Dampier (who would later become the first European to map Australia) observed in his book *Two Voyages to Campeachy*:

'Many of the cutters being good marksmen thought it a dry business to toil at cutting wood and so took more delight in hunting. But neither of these employments affected them so much as privateering. Therefore they often made sallies out in small parties among the nearest Indian towns, where they plundered and brought away the Indian women to serves them at their huts, and sent their husbands to be sold in Jamaica. Besides they had not their old drinking bouts forgot, and would still spend £30 or £40 a night at a sitting aboard the ships that came hither from Jamaica, carousing and firing off guns three or four days together. And though afterwards many sober men came into the Bay to cut wood, yet by degrees the old standers so debauched them, that they could never settle themselves under any civil government.'

It is probable that Dampier's picture of life in a Campeche settlement in the late 17th century held true for most of the logwood camps founded along the northern Central American coast. By the 18th century the largest logwood camps at Campeche had finally been completely expelled by the Spanish and the cutters were forced to concentrate on the far wilder shores of Belize and the Mosquito Coast. The former was remote, little visited by the Spanish and of little interest to them. The latter was almost unassailable to them, as the Spanish had never succeeded in subjugating the Miskito. As the settlements in Belize and the Mosquito Coast became ever more established, the logwood cutters began to call themselves Baymen, after the Bay of Honduras which faces both the Belizean and the Mosquito coasts, and which they now considered their homes. By the mid-18th century, there were permanent Baymen towns on the Belize River (at modern-day Belize City) and on St George's Caye. And the logwood trade had grown so much that the settlers had found the wealth to buy and transport several thousand African slaves from Sierra Leone.

Britain's attitude to the Baymen was identical to her attitude to Modyford's privateers. Diplomatically, they could not and did not defend them as colonists. Pragmatically they did much to support them and welcomed the revenue that logwood brought. Under the Convention of London of 1786, Spain agreed to allow logwood and mahogany harvesting, a settlement on St George's Caye and fishing rights. In return, the British would have to abandon their settlements on the Mosquito Coast. They would promise not to make any permanent land settlements on the mainland, install a system of government nor engage in agricultural activity. Britain agreed the quid pro quo, as much to protect Belize as to avoid having to handover Gibraltar at a later date. Nor did she abandon her alliance with the Miskito, meaning that the Mosquito Coast would be a British Protectorate in all but name.

By the end of the 18th century, the settlements had become both entrenched and prosperous enough for the Spanish to argue that they were in contravention of the Convention of London. Spain harried the Baymen. In 1798 Dublin-born *conquistador* and governor of the Yucatán, Arturo O'Neill de Tyrone y O'Kelly, decided to be done with them altogether. So in September of that year, he dispatched a mini-Armada to quell the logwood colonies in Belize and to retake them for the Empire.

Battle of St George's Caye

The Baymen were hopelessly outnumbered. Spain had 32 warships manned by 500 marines and reinforced by a land army of 2000 foot soldiers. There were some 700 Baymen, three sloops, two schooners and seven floating gun emplacements built from logwood rafts. The vessels boasted Hobbit names like *Tickler*, *Teaser* and *Towser*. Hearing of the impending attack, the British Governor in Jamaica dispatched the frigate *HMS Merlin*, under the command of Captain Moss. The Baymen and African slaves fought side by side against the Spanish and they were aided by Belize herself. On 3 September, the Armada tried to force its way through a narrow passage between the shoals and Montego Caye, but they were repelled under fierce gunfire. The following day the Spanish laid down stakes and beacons to guide them through the narrow passage, but the Baymen, who had far lighter and faster craft, removed them. A week later, the largest ships in the Armada attempted to engage the *Merlin* and the Baymen's fleet but were routed in a gun battle lasting just 2½ hours. By the time the Spanish had fled, they had suffered heavy losses, whilst not one of the Baymen had been killed.

The battle was a seminal moment for Baymen settlements in Belize. The Spanish did not trouble them again, and the confidence that resulted from the battle, and the peace of mind of knowing that they were finally free of harrying from Spain, would turn Belize Town from a settlement into a colony, and then the capital of a nation. And it would make a new people, the Belizeans, who have, to this day, not overcome their profound distrust of Spanish America.

Hypocrisy and the Honduras Settlement

After the Battle of St George's Caye, however, the hypocrisy continued, even as privateering was dying out in the Caribbean and the power of Spain was on the wane. The British absorbed 'the Honduras Settlement' into the Empire, as a colony by proxy through the few hundred Baymen. And they appointed a superintendent, a governor in all but name of what was a colony in all but name. In 1822 Spain lost Mexico and, shortly after it, much of Central America. As the short-lived Central American Federation came and went, life in the Honduras Settlement changed little. Despite fighting alongside the Baymen at the battle, there was no brotherhood in the colony until it was forced by the Abolition Act of 1833. Even the outlawing of the slave trade itself in 1807 had brought a duplicitous response from the Baymen. They argued that the anomalous status of the Honduras Settlement led the white minority to declare that it did not apply to them at all and they continued to buy people in the Caribbean and sell them into a hard and cruel life in the colony.

In Belize, slaves were used for cutting and hauling logwood and, increasingly, mahogany, working in scattered gangs in the forests, forcibly separated from their families in Belize Town. They referred to themselves by their original African nations such as Congos, Ashantis and Ebos, with the latter being so dominant ethnically that a quarter of early 19th-century Belize Town was known as 'Eboe Town'. In other parts of the Caribbean, the slaves were often treated abominably. Rape was commonplace, food was cruelly rationed and floggings widespread. Slaves in Belize rose up against the Baymen on four occasions, one of them requiring the British to send a gunship and soldiers to quell the rebellion. The last revolt was in 1820, necessitating the superintendent of the Honduras Settlement to declare martial law. He sent soldiers in to subdue the rebels, to discover that 'the Negroes who had first deserted and had excited others to join them, had been treated with very unnecessary harshness by their owner, and had certainly good grounds for complaint.'

It was a sign perhaps of change, which came in 1838 when slaves who had formally been freed by the Abolition Act of 1833 but forced to work as unpaid 'apprentices' were truly freed. Sixteen years later the Honduras Settlement was granted the first fruits of democracy when it gained a Legislative Assembly. Under the approval of Lord Palmerston, the Honduras Settlement finally became the Colony of British Honduras, a governor was appointed, and the Legislative Assembly was reduced to a Legislative Council, effectively diminishing the power of the local people and placing their fate in the hands of London's representative.

British Honduras

The new colony was basically a logging town with a few very isolated and tiny settlements devoted to timber extraction. Generations of persecution by the Spanish and their prohibition of agriculture meant that fledgling British Honduras imported all its food and produce. During the late 19th century, bananas, sugar and coffee were introduced to the colony. But the plantations where they were grown were owned by a just a few powerful landowners, or companies, one of which – later called the Belize Estate and Produce Company – came to own a fifth of national territory. As the population increased dramatically with an influx of refugees from the Yucatán Caste Wars, the disparity of wealth and power and the lack of national infrastructure became problematic. At the turn of the 19th century, much of the country was not only unchartered, it was completely unknown. British Honduras had been explored and exploited by boat. There were no railways and no real roads, just dirt tracks. Most Belizeans, including the governor himself, travelled from Belize City into the interior on flat-bottomed Mayan canoes called *pit-pans*; most were powered by hand.

Discontent and disharmony

By the early 20th century, the predominantly **Kriol** (Creole) British Honduran majority had seen very little improvement in their lot. And, whilst street lighting had been introduced to Belize City, there was still very little infrastructure. The disparity of wealth and power between the colonial authorities and the white-owned companies and landowners and the poor and predominanty Kriol majority was also beginning to foment anti-British sentiment. This came to a head after the First World War. Kriol British Hondurans leaving for the war had expected to fight alongside the white troops, but they found themselves treated like second-class subjects of the British Empire, assigned lackey jobs and often subject to racism.

When they returned to their flag-waving, patriotic black British Honduran wives and families, their bitterness was made even more acute. With the end of war and a collapse in demand for mahogany, the colony's prosperity slumped and ex-servicemen couldn't find work. They could no longer ignore the stark reality of colonial rule, where all the power was held by a few whites and where, even in their own homeland, Kriols were second-class citizens. In 1919 they rose up, rioting in Belize City, looting and attacking symbols of British rule. The anger and resentment that arose from this historical moment of revelation cannot be overstated. It echoes through contemporary Belizean fiction (in the writing of authors like Zee Edgell) and remains a potent symbol for many Kriol Belizeans to this day. And, whilst the rebellion was crushed, a strong black consciousness movement rose in its wake, inspired by the ideas and political action of **Marcus Garvey**. Garvey founded the Universal Negro Improvement Association (UNIA) in Jamaica in 1914 with the motto, 'One God, One Aim, One Destiny', to improve the conditions of those of African ancestry. In 1918 the UNIA began publication of the widely distributed *Negro World* newspaper and Garvey stated that 'There shall be no solution to this race problem until you, yourselves, strike the blow for liberty'. In 1920, a year after the Belize City riots, the UNIA opened a branch in Belize City and, in 1922, Marcus Garvey visited Belize. In the years that followed, British Hondurans asserted increasing pressure for equal rights and democracy.

When the British were taking the first tentative steps towards granting these, double disaster struck. First was the Great Depression which caused demand for mahogany and the colony's agricultural produce to plummet. Then came the devastating 1931 hurricane (see page 30), which flattened Belize City and laid waste to many of the plantations. Both gave Britain the excuse to clamp down governmentally, with London suppressing an

The Guatemala dispute

When Central American countries gained their independence from Spain, they determined that their national boundaries should be the same as those provincial boundaries as described by Spain under colonial administration. As Belize had never formally been lost to the Spanish Empire, but had been appropriated through stealth by Britain, Guatemala determined that Belize was in reality a province of Guatemala.

In 1945, a particularly bellicose Guatemalan government, sensing that Belize was about to become independent of a war-weakened and war-weary Britain, made plans to invade. The British responded vigorously. It had to do so on several other occasions throughout the 1960s and 1970s, delaying Belizean independence.

Britain's military presence in Belize and the routine flights made by Buccaneer and Harrier fighter-bombers over Belizean territory have much to do with the Guatemalan claims. In 1975 Guatemala and Britain came close to going to war over Belize. When Belize gained independence in 1979 they requested that British troops remain deployed in the country.

In December 2011, the UK government announced that the British military presence in Belize would be scaled down radically. Belizean Prime Minister Dean Barrow has made resolving the dispute his biggest goal and, meanwhile, both Belize and Guatemala have agreed to establish an 'adjacency zone' extending 1 km on either side of border and to continue negotiations to resolve the dispute.

incipient union movement led by Antonio Soberanis using unnecessary force. The British Treasury assumed control of the colony's finances and, in effect, its political fate, and British Honduras found itself in an intractable position. It could not pay its debts because it was under British control and it stayed under British control because it could not pay its debts.

Independence or bust

The Great Depression, the hurricane and then the Second World War could only postpone change. It began to become inevitable when Britain found itself bankrupt and in terminal decline after winning the war and with India's Independence in 1948, losing an Empire. The country could no longer afford its colonies. When **George Price**, a young Belizean university student and subsequent local politician, founded a new political party called the People's United Party he found support not only from his fellow countrymen but from the colonial authorities. They agreed to a general election in 1954, in which Price won with an overwhelming majority. Price became the leader of a government with limited powers of self-determination and, 10 years later, British Honduras gained self-government. In 1973, the country changed its name to Belize. Independence was now inevitable and desired by the British as much as the Belizeans. It was postponed only because the Belizeans did not want full independence during border disputes with Guatemala (see box, above), fearing they would be conquered. But it came eventually on 21 September 1981, with George Price as the first prime minister, a role he retained until 1984.

Post-Independence

The 1984 government of Manuel Esquivel, leader of the United Democratic Party (UDP), turned its eyes away from the Atlantic and looked resolutely north to the US, encouraging

North American investment, and fully adopting Reaganomics and privatization of the public sector. The US, who were very happy to have another foothold in Central America, strengthened the ties and granted Belizeans the most lenient immigration rights of any Central American nation. From the 1980s, thousands of Belizeans left to find their fortunes in the US, including famous names such as the athlete Marion Jones. Many returned to Belize or constructed lives between the two, and ties between the US and Belize are now arguably stronger than they ever were between Belize and Britain. The Belizean dollar is tied to the US dollar and the country has joined the Free Trade Area of the Americas (FTAA).

Belize remains a strong democracy and has a parliamentary system similar to Britain's. The National Assembly has two chambers: the Senate has 12 members appointed for a five-year term, whilst the House of Representatives has 31 members elected for a five-year term in single-seat constituencies. Like Britain, two parties dominate political campaigns: the loosely left-wing PUP and the right-wing UDP, whose leader Dean Barrow is the current prime minister. The next general elections are due in late 2012. The country's biggest source of revenue is tourism, which accounts for roughly a sixth of GDP and employs just under a third of all Belizeans.

Belize culture and customs

Music

The soundtrack for most hotel and resort stays in Belize is anodyne US rock, dominating Belize City's Love FM, or wafting out of bars in San Pedro. Local DJs in Belize City clubs often play reggaeton and other Caribbean beats. But many travellers leave Belize without realising that the country has a distinct and rich musical heritage. Whilst music in Belize reflects the country's diverse ethnic make-up, truly Belizean music comes from three basic roots: Europe, Africa and pre-Columbian America.

Marching bands and brukdown

The British brought military marching bands to the country. In the early days of the colony both the music and the presentation were European, but this quickly changed. Creole drummers took British drums, elements of percussive technique and fused these with West African rhythms. Carlinhos Brown, the great Brazilian percussionist, has said that exiled Africans in Latin America preserved cultural memory through rhythm and ritual, and the pounding, syncopated percussion of a Belizean marching band sounds far closer to maracatu or samba than anything you'd hear in Aldershot or Sandhurst. In the late 20th century, after a generation of Belizeans had spent many years in the US, the format of the drum parades changed too, becoming much closer to those in the US, with baton-twirling girl majorettes in spangly costumes. The best place to hear a Belizean marching band is at the annual **Bandfest**, which usually takes place in April; dates are available at tourist offices or on the Love FM website (www.lovefm.com).

Concurrent with the development of marching band music was the Creole working man's music called **brukdown**. This was originally sung by African loggers in the camps, who beat out rhythms on whatever they had to hand, from empty bottles to animal bones. In the 20th century, campfire brukdown was fused with Caribbean rhythms and melodic styles and accompanied by guitars, banjos, drums and, leftover from the campfire days, a donkey jaw-bone, whose teeth were rasped and rapped to produce a skiffle-like percussion sound. Brukdown bands include **Mr Peter's Boom and Chime** and **Brudda David Obi and his Cungo Beat**, who are more contemporary and politically sharp.

Garifuna music

Africa is most obviously preserved in the enchanting music of the Garifuna people. During colonial times, the Garifuna lived apart from British rule and culture, and were largely left alone. Memories of Africa were preserved strongly through ritual community drumming in the sacred *dugu* temples. The great heart drums which hang in these temples to this day are the symbolic backbones of the Garifuna communities. Traditional Garifuna drumming is undergoing a revival in Belize and can be heard at the *dugu* in **Punta Gorda** (which can be visited through Fubu, T669-0535, aba_iseni1@yahoo.com, and see below) and through the work of the **Lebeha Drumming Centre** in Hopkins (see page 140), and Creole drummer **Emmeth Young** in Gales Point (see page 52).

In the 19th and 20th centuries Garifuna rhythms and traditional African singing became fused with European instrumentation, notably guitars that were probably brought in from Spanish-speaking Garifuna communities in modern-day Guatemala or Honduras. A new style of Garifuna music was born from a particular rhythm called **paranda**, which then gave its name to this musical style: a gorgeous, lilting music that sways like the sea and which is instilled with a sweet underlying melancholy. Perhaps the greatest paranda musician still alive today is **Paul Nabor**, the keeper of the *dugu* in Punta Gorda (see box, page 211), whose music is profiled, alongside that of other musicians, on the wonderful *Paranda: Africa in Central America* CD.

Paranda is played on acoustic instruments. Another Garifuna rhythm, **punta**, was rendered contemporary when **Pen Cayetano** and his Turtle Shell Band (see box, page 212) electrified the style and all Belize with the creation of Punta Rock in the 1980s. Cayetano brought Garifuna music to the fore in Belize. He was followed by a succession of other Garifuna artists, such as Titiman Flores, Jeff Zuniga, Black Coral, Sounds Incorporated and **Andy Palacio** (see box, page 172).

Andy was born in Barranco in the far south of Toledo District on the border with Guatemala, closer to the Garifuna town of Livingston in that country than to his district capital of Punta Gorda. Andy had been gigging extensively in Garifuna Belize, Guatemala and Honduras when, in 1987, he was invited to come to London on a cultural partnership with Hackney, where he honed his musical and production techniques and recorded a number of songs, including 'Bikini Panti', a punta rock satire of Belize's tourist industry that became an airways and dance-floor classic in Belize. Andy then founded Sunrise Records, which released a compilation, *Punta Rockers*, firmly establishing punta rock as the national style. A string of releases by other punta rock bands – such as Waribagabaga and Children of the Most High – followed, together with Andy's first album *Come Mek We Dance*. By the 1990s, Punta was going from strength to strength, with the regular appearance of new bands, including the popular Punta Rebels, led by Lloyd Augustine.

Andy's music reached its highest mark when he met and collaborated with Cayo-based producer Ivan Duran. Duran brought state-of-the-art production techniques to Belizean records, which enabled them to compete on an international stage with releases from labels like Peter Gabriel's Real World. In 1995 Duran founded **Stonetree Records** (www. stonetreerecords.com). Andy released three albums with Stonetree: *Keimoun* (*Beat On*) in 1995 and *Til Da Mawnin* in 1997, which were punta rock releases. In 1999, the album *Paranda* was more reflective and melancholy. In 2000 he succeeded in lobbying UNESCO

Meeting Paul Nabor

Giant heart drums sit on a plinth at the entrance to Dangriga, one of Belize's biggest Garifuna towns, in the south of the country. They hang from the wooden walls inside Paul Nabor's Punta Gorda *dugu*, the most important Garifuna temple in the country. "The drums," he explains, as we sip sweet Belizean stout beer on wooden stools outside, "are used in sacred ceremonies by the Garinagu people. When people make ceremony to the ancestors we'll play all day and all night." Music and the spirit are one for the Garifuna, and music connects them with the ever-present past which imbued their everyday lives in Africa.

As if to emphasize the point, Paul beckons to one of his assistants, who brings a drum over whilst handing Paul his guitar. The 80-year-old winds his stiff fingers round the neck, crouches over the instrument and begins to sing paranda in a deep, sad baritone voice. The drums weave a hypnotic pattern and I feel like I'm slipping into a trance. The tropical sun looks richer, the leaves on the medicinal plants around the temple more brilliantly green and, for a moment, I leave seconds, minutes and hours for mythical time. It's as if I am invited for privileged communication with the Garifuna ancestors, whose stories and memories are preserved in rhythm and song.

I mention this to Paul when he finished playing. And he tells me the extraordinary story of how he was called to keep the *dugu*. Although he has been playing music all his life, Paul first worked as a fisherman. One night while on the high seas he had a sudden onset of paralysis which left him almost unable to move. Together with the paralysis came a blinding vision, a certainty that the only way he would be set free would be to return to the Garifuna community and visit the *dugu*. "I belonged there," he told me. "I was being called to work there." Barely able to use his body, somehow Paul managed to reach the shore many miles away. Friends wanted to take him to the hospital, but he refused, and begged to be brought immediately to the *dugu*. "My paralysis immediately left me," he said. "Today whenever somebody is feeling bad they come around here and I am working with them. We have a ceremony and we use the drums."

formally to make Garifuna language, music and dance part of the cultural World Heritage. And over the following years he assembled a core of accomplished Garifuna musicians who he would call the Garifuna Collective.

In 2007 Andy and the Collective had an astonishing breakthrough with *Wátina* (see box, page 172), which fused paranda, punta and ritual rhythms in a totally new, but rooted sound. The following year, just as he was becoming a world music superstar to rival the likes of Youssou N'Dour and Cesaria Evora, Andy died suddenly of respiratory failure after a massive stroke and heart attack. He was just 47 years old. "I decided to use music as a medium for cultural preservation," he said in an interview with US broadcaster NPR the year before he died, "At least we'd be able to use the language in the songs and keep them alive."

Andy's dream is being kept alive by a succession of other Garifuna artists from Belize and other Central American countries. Foremost is **Aurelio Martinez** from Honduras whose albums *Garifuna Soul* and *Laru Beya* have found widespread acclaim. Aurelio is a wonderful performer and plays regularly at Garifuna Settlement Day (see page 152) in both Dangriga and Hopkins.

"The big crowds here are a new phenomenon," he told Footprint when we interviewed him at Garifuna Settlement Day in Dangriga, "Andy Palacio's fight, and the fight of all

Pen Cayetano and Punta Rock

The Garifuna towns and villages of southern Belize have produced a legion of talented musicians and artists, none more so than Delivin 'Pen' Cayetano. Few musicians in the world can legitimately claim responsibility for single-handedly inventing a musical genre, but Pen can. He created Punta Rock in 1980, giving the country a national sound, just as it gained independence from Britain. In Pen's own words: "the Garifuna youth of Belize was losing their cultural foundations … they needed something to step with the time."

So Pen got some friends together and they experimented with rock instruments and Garifuna rhythms at his wooden weatherboard house at 5 Moho Road in Dangriga. As they played Pen, got the idea of speeding up the traditional punta rhythm, adding the electric guitar and the turtle-shell percussion, emblematic of the beach-based life of the Garifuna people. He called the new music 'Punta Rock' and named the group 'The Turtle Shell Band'.

The band started to perform by doing so-called roadblocks in Dangriga: gigging in the street. Then they moved to Belize City, playing in clubs like the Bunfire and Purple Cup. By the mid-1980s Punta Rock had blown through the tired ersatz Caribbean music scene like a hurricane. The Turtle Shell Band were ready for bigger things. They took Punta Rock into Mexico and the US, playing at the New Orleans Jazz Festival in 1983.

Pen's Punta Rock is written mostly in the Garifuna language. Songs talk about his people's history, calling for pride in Garifuna culture. Pen now lives in Germany, where he divides his time between his musical projects (notably with his family band the Cayetanos) and his burgeoning career as one of Belize's most successful artists. You can find out more about him and his music and art on his website www.cayetano.de.

Garifuna musicians, has been to bring Garifuna culture to our own countries. Small countries like Belize and Honduras have a problem appreciating what's their own, focusing so much more on what's from outside. There isn't a single radio station playing Garifuna music, nor can you hear our CDs played in bars, restaurants or hotels in Belize or Honduras. It's all US R'n'B, reggaeton or salsa. We simply have no outlet, no support. And yet Andy has helped to make us famous all around the world."

Travellers visiting Belize who request hotels and restaurants to play a Gaifuna CD will not only find a captivating new genre of music, they will help that music and the Garifuna language, to survive.

Mayan marimbas

Received wisdom tells us that the marimba – a wooden xylophone with a delicious soft sound, also known as the Mayan *tocomates* – was invented by Africans and brought to the Americas in the 16th century. But the Maya in Guatemala and Belize claim it for their own and insist that Maya people have been playing marimbas for over 1000 years. You will find a marimba tucked away in the community hall or church of most Belizean Mayan villages. Mayan marimbas are huge, multi-keyed wooden instruments which often require two musicians to play them. They have a deep sonorous sound. In villages they are usually the accompaniment to singing, but Maya-mestizo marimba fusion bands play everything from ballads to jazz, accompanied by drums, double bass and even guitar. You can hear them playing at festivals and special events throughout the country, especially in Cayo and the Mayan heartland of Toledo.

Ten essential Garifuna CDs and DVDs

Andy Palacio – *Wátina* His classic and multi-award-winning release.
Aurelio Martinez – *Garifuna Soul* Similar to *Wátina* with wonderful playing and breadth of mood.
Aurelio Martinez – *Laru Beya* Garifuna music meets West Africa in a masterful fusion.
Lugua & the Larubeya Drummers – *Bumari* Pure Garifuna percussion.
Mr Peters & His Boom & Chime – *Berry Wine Days* Rum-soaked Creole music with infectious percussion and accordion.
Pen Cayetano & the Turtleshell Band – *Punta Rock* The CD that established

a new musical style.
Three Kings of Belize – A musical documentary DVD, profiling paranda singer Paul Nabor, Mayan marimba player Florencio Mess and Creole accordionist Wilfred Peters of the Boom & Chime band.
Various – *Paranda* The best introduction to this gentle, melancholy music.
Various – *This is Belize* Belizean party music from Punta Rock to Brukdown and national reggae.
Various – *Umalali* The melancholy and memory of Africa in the singing of Garifuna village women.

People

Belize is a melting pot of peoples. The **white Belizean** elite, who dominated the country when it was British Honduras still exist as a tiny but powerful minority. Its most infamous representative is the previous owner of Belize Telecom, Belize Bank and large swathes of properties and land, Michael Ashcroft. He was nominated for his knighthood by the Belizean government and his website states, 'If home is where the heart is, then Belize is my home.' It certainly seems to have been for tax purposes. Despite being a UK Conservative Party chairman and one of their biggest donors, Ashcroft admitted in 2010 to non-domicile UK tax status, a year after he was recorded as 37th on the annual *Sunday Times* Rich List. Belizean attitudes to him are mixed. In 2011, the *Guardian* in the UK reported that Belize Bank, 'a bank with close links to Lord Ashcroft will be accused in a British courtroom of keeping $10m destined for social housing' in Belize. Ashcroft was subsequently investigated over other business dealings by the BBC's investigative journalism programme *Panorama* in 2012.

The largest ethnic group along the Belizean coast and, politically and culturally, the most powerful are the **Kriol** (Creole) people. These are the descendants of the Baymen and former slaves and speak their own Kriol form of English, which sounds similar to the Kriol spoken in countries like Guyana and Jamaica. There are many well-known Kriol Belizeans, including the sprinter Marion Jones and all three recipients of the country's highest medal of honour, the Order of the National Hero: the cyclist and historian Monrad Metzgen, and Philip Goldson and George Price, who were instrumental in the movement for Belizean Independence. Kriol writers include the poet and statesman Colville Young and novelist Zee Edgell.

The Kriols make up around a quarter of Belize's population and are the second largest ethnic group in Belize after **Mestizo Belizeans**. Mestizos are mixed race descendants of indigenous American and non-American mostly Spanish-speaking peoples, who make up around 48% of the population. They are the largest group in the Belizean interior and are predominantly made up of economic migrants and Central American refugees who fled Guatemala, Nicaragua and El Salvador during the 1980s civil wars. Those who do not speak

Kriol or English are sometimes referred to as Spanish, a term not loved by Mestizo Belizeans and indicative to them of the tension that exists between the Mestizo and Kriol communities.

The third largest ethnic group in Belize are the **Maya**, who comprise about 10% of the population. Very few of the Belizean Maya are direct descendants of those who built the temples you see in Belize. Those people migrated elsewhere many centuries ago. But all are the descendants of the people who built the great pre-Columbian cities of Mesoamerica. They fall into three distinct cultural-linguistic groups: the Yucatec Maya, made up largely of refugees from the Caste Wars and concentrated in the north of the country and in Cayo; the Mopan Maya (often incorrectly called simply 'the Maya' by Belizeans) who arrived mostly in the late 19th century and settled in Cayo; and the largest group, the Qe'chi (Kekchi) Maya, who are comprised mainly of economic migrants from the Cobán region of Guatemala and are concentrated in Toledo District.

The **Garifuna** (or, more correctly, the Garinagu) people make up around 6% of the Belizean population. They have a fascinating story similar to that of the Surinamese *Saramaccans*, the Nicaraguan *Mestizo Sambus* and the peoples of the *Quilombos* of Brazil. It is a story as full of joy, tragedy and perennial lament as their wonderful music. It begins in West Africa in the 1660s with two British ships chartered to transport slaves to the sugar plantations of the southern Caribbean. After their Atlantic crossing, the ships foundered off the coast of San Vicente and the Africans escaped to a new freedom. Over decades, their community in exile intermingled with the native Arawak and Caribs of San Vicente and, by the mid-1700s, their union had given birth to a new society and language created from a fusion of their combined roots. This new people came to be known as the Garinagu, the Black Caribs, and are nowadays called the Garifuna, the singular form of Garinagu.

The 18th-century Garifuna society on San Vicente had become prosperous and self-sufficient; so much so that it attracted the attention of the British and French who were determined to appropriate the Garifuna's fertile fields and seas. When the Garifuna refused to sell or be cajoled off their lands, the British provoked them to open war and the French funded their army. The Garifuna were doomed. After finally losing to the British, the decimated and dying remnants of their society were forced from San Vicente and transported by the British to the tiny island of Roatan. From here they spread to the coast of nearby Central America, setting up villages from Belize to southern Honduras where they flourished once more. Garifuna towns in Belize include Dangriga, Hopkins and Punta Gorda, and famous Garinagu people include Pen Cayetano, Andy Palacio, Paul Nabor and the Honduran Garifuna singer Aurelio Martinez (see Garifuna music, page 210).

Belize also has a large population of **Russian Mennonites** (see box, page 184) divided into isolationist Amish, conservative and liberal groups. Mennonites live principally in Cayo and Orange Walk districts. There are also two small Asian ethnic groups: Indians (or East Indians as they are called in Belize) and Chinese. Fewer than 500 Indians were brought in as indentured labourers on the sugar plantations of the mid- to late-19th century. Their descendants live throughout Belize today but, unlike Indians in Guayana and Trinidad, they have retained very little of their root culture and do not speak Hindi or follow Asian religions, although the tiny handful of immigrant modern Indian business and retail owners do. The Chinese are the hidden economic power of Belize. Almost all shops and retail businesses are run by Belizean Chinese and Taiwanese. The first Chinese arrived in 1865 as farm workers in Toledo and have mostly been fully assimilated into Belizean society. Many more Chinese, mostly from Kwangtung Province, and Chinese Taiwanese arrived in the latter half of the 20th century to establish businesses through the Belize government's Economic Citizenship Programme.

Belize land and environment

Geography

Belize is the second smallest country in Central America after El Salvador, covering an area of 8866 sq miles, making it a little larger than Wales, slightly smaller than Belgium and around the same size as the US state of New Hampshire. It's also the least densely populated country in Central America. By far the greatest percentage of the population lives in Belize City. Beyond the district capitals, Belize is pretty much empty.

Geology and landscape

Like Mexico's Yucatán Peninsula immediately to the north, Belize is a big block of limestone submerged under swampy top soil and dense forest in the centre and south and covered in low shrubby Yucatán dry and moist forest in the north and northeast. The limestone is pocked with numerous caves, most of which have never been explored and the most extensive of which extend for tens of miles. There are many underground rivers and cenotes, or sinkholes, lakes and lagoons. The limestone reaches its highest point in the Cockscomb Range and the foothills of the Maya Mountains, where the largest cave systems are found.

The **Maya Mountains** themselves are a geological anomaly in Belize and are made up of a large block of ancient granite, worn down to crags and cracked into deep canyons with plunging waterfalls, which reach their most impressive at Mountain Pine Ridge. For many years Belize's highest mountain was thought to be Victoria Peak, a rocky bluff which juts out of the Maya Mountains like a worn tooth in the southern Cockscomb Range. A fresh survey has revealed it to be Doyle's Delight at 1124 m, just 4 m higher, which was only climbed for the first time in 2008.

The Maya Mountains run roughly parallel to the coast and are separated from the Atlantic by a low flat plain lying at roughly 10 feet above sea level and averaging 15 miles wide. This is mostly covered in swamp land and dense forest, broken by agricultural land and cut by half a dozen rivers, many of which were used by the Baymen to extract timber. The largest are the New and Hondo rivers in the north, the Monkey and Sarstoon in the south and the Belize River (and its tributaries the Macal and Mopan) in the centre of the country, which divides as it reaches the sea, one branch forming Haulover Creek where Belize City lies.

The limestone block that underlies lowland Belize extends offshore for about 20 miles to the edge of the **Belize Barrier Reef**. This reef forms one of the wildest and most pristine sections of the 560-mile-long Mesoamerican Barrier Reef System which extends south to the Bay Islands of Honduras and north to Cancún. It is the longest barrier reef system in the Atlantic and probably the third longest in the world after the Great Barrier Reef in Australia and the New Caledonia Barrier Reef in the South Pacific. Between the reef and the shore are extensive sand flats, which, in places, are shallow enough to walk through for miles and which offer superb fly fishing. These deepen to small trenches and rise to tiny islets or cayes, some sandy and some made up principally of mangroves. The largest of these, lying in Belize's north, is **Ambergris Caye**, which is in reality not a caye at all, but a peninsula stretching south from Mexico's Riviera Maya and cut by a Mayan canal at the Belize–Mexico border just south of Xcalak.

Beyond the Barrier Reef are three atolls: the **Turneffe Atoll** and **Lighthouse Atoll** in the north and **Gover's Atoll** in the south. In addition, the southernmost section of the barrier reef forms a series of mini-atolls or faroes which include Laughing Bird Caye.

Flora and fauna

Belize is very rich in flora, with an estimated 4000 species of flowering plants including 730 tree species and 280 orchids. These are distributed over a variety of habitats affected by elevation, humidity and rainfall; the variety is far greater in Belize than would be expected in an equatorial region. For what may seem like mere forest to the untutored eye is radically divergent to the botanist, who sees an enormous range of tropical and sub-tropical forest types within this tiny country, supporting different communities of plants and animals. The country is a superb destination for wildlife enthusiasts.

Littoral forests line the coast of Belize from Corozal to Toledo, except where they have been felled to make way for human development. They fall into two types. Strand forests lie along beaches, dominated by common trees, such as coconut, cocoplum, sea grape, buttonwood and introduced species including casuarina (she-oak), Norfolk Island pine and cajeput. Mangrove forests are made up of different groups of woody salt-tolerant plants. You will see them along the coast, around lagoons and on many cayes, a number of which are formed entirely of mangrove. The dominant species are white mangrove, black and, the largest of all, red mangrove. Mangrove forests are also home to buttonwood, swamp caway and marsh fern, amongst others.

Behind the littoral forests are a variety of **coastal plain forests**. In the north the coastal plain forests are constituted of pines (such as Pine Ridge), dominated by Caribbean pine, calabash, palmetto palm; bajo swamp forest, which are very thick and spiny with low canopies and stands of cabbage palms, give-and-take palms, spiny bamboo and wild grape; logwood swamp (on the edge of lagoons like Crooked Tree), dominated by logwood, a small – 8-m-tall or less – woody tree with a fluted, crooked trunk; transitional broadleaf forest (Broken Ridge), with light-demanding species such as cecropia, wild cotton, bay cedar and yemeri; cohune palm forest (aka Cohune Ridge), dominated by the feathery cohune palm, and broadleaf hardwood forest (High Ridge), which has closed canopy tropical forest with large tropical ficus and inga and swamp dogwood, often found on the edges of the larger rivers in lowland Belize. There are also small pockets of tropical savannah grasslands and seasonally wet meadows in the coastal plains, particularly in southern Belize District.

These coastal plains are dotted with other types of forest: semi-deciduous broadleaf (or high ridge) in the hills of the Rio Bravo Conservation Area, with stands of mahogany and chicle; marshy forest around Gales Point; limestone karst hill forests with abundant chicle, ramon and wild mammee in the foothills of the Maya Mountains, and Yucatán dry and moist forests northeast of Corozal and in the Shipstern Nature Reserve.

The Belizean Highlands behind the coastal plain are dominated by the forests of the Maya Mountains. These are of a varied type. **Mountain Pine Ridge** is a unique Belizean habitat, with a unique species, the mountain pine (*Pinus oocarpa*) related to the more common Caribbean pine. This is broken with tropical oaks and other trees like matapal. The **Maya Mountains** and **western upland forests** lie at the base of the Pine Ridge and have similar species to the forests of the Rio Bravo Conservation Area, together with sapodilla, banak and ironwood. In the high uplands of the Cockscomb Range, especially Doyle's Delight and Victoria Peak, there are small pockets of **cloud forest**, rich with bromeliads and rare orchids.

The forests of Toledo in the south are the wettest in Belize and are the only true **tropical rainforests** in the country, with large buttress-root trees, hundreds of epiphytic orchids and characteristic tree species like rosewood, Santa Maria, banak and ceiba.

Belize's endangered or threatened birds and mammals

Birds
Black rail
Black catbird
Buff-breasted sandpiper
Brown pelican
Yellow-headed parrot
White-crowned pigeon
Painted bunting
Ocellated turkey
Least tern
Keel-billed motmot
Harpy eagle
Guianan crested eagle
Great curassow
Golden-winged warbler
Cerulean warbler
Golden-cheeked wood warbler

Mammals
Baird's tapir
Giant anteater
Guatemalan black howler monkey
West Indian manatee
Jaguar
Margay
Ocelot
Long-tailed otter
Van Gelder's bat
Spectral bat
Yucatán brown brocket deer
White-lipped peccary

Birds

Belize has some 600 species of birds, around the same number as the Congo and slightly fewer than Costa Rica, which has 838. However, birds are easy to see in Belize, facilities and guides are excellent and, unlike many Latin American countries, it is straightforward and quick to get around the country. Of these species, more than half do not reach the Temperate Zone and are therefore truly tropical. Of those that do reach the Temperate Zone, 80% are seasonal visitors to Belize passing through on migration or wintering in the country. Birding checklists are available on the internet (see www.birdinginbelize.com/bird_checklist.html) and a print-out is useful for any trip to the country.

Europeans, Asians and Australians will expect to find dozens of families not encountered back home. However, North Americans used to birding in Florida might be surprised to learn that there are 15 families they will see in Belize that are not found in the US or Canada: tinamous, sungrebes, ovenbirds, woodcreepers, jacana, antbirds, potoos, antthrushes, motmots, cotingas, puffbirds, manakins, jacamars, bananaquit and toucans.

Belize has no true endemics. But it does have some very rare and locally confined species and some really spectacular ones. The former include Yucatán Peninsula endemics: black catbirds, Yucatán jays and Yucatán vireos, all easily seen in Shipstern Nature Reserve (see page 225). The latter include scarlet macaws, orange-breasted falcons, agami herons, ornate hawk eagles, ocellated turkeys and, if you're very lucky, harpy eagles.

Antbirds, antthrushes and antpittas These are undistinguished small forest birds that live in the lower parts of the forest canopy and feed on insects. A number of the species have learnt to follow troops of marauding soldier ants as they sweep through the undergrowth, catching startled insects as they attempt to escape. There are nine species of antbirds in Belize and one species each of anthrush and antpitta.

Bananaquits, honeycreepers, American sparrows and yellow finches These small seed-eating birds mostly live high in the forest canopy and are associated with flowering trees, from which the bananaquit, which has a black head with a white eye stripe and a yellow breast, sucks nectar.

Cotingas These are generally beautifully coloured forest and forest-edge birds. Males have elaborate plumage, glamorous colours and often engage in an ostentatious courtship display. There are some 71 species in total, two of which live in Belize: the brilliant blue lovely cotinga and the dull, brown rufous piha, which has a characteristic screech-like call.

Cuckoos and anis Belizean cuckoos, of which there are six species, are not the chubby brood parasites of Europe, but are slim birds most often seen darting across open country to a bush or trees where they sit utterly motionless. Their relatives, the anis, are black, shiny birds who commonly hunt and nest in groups. In some groups all individuals contribute to one single community nest. Belize has two species.

Hummingbirds Belize has just over a twelfth of all the world's hummingbird species, 26 in all. Most are brilliantly iridescent and weigh just a few grams. A few, like the white-necked Jacobin, are far larger, even perching to suck nectar from flowers. All are capable of stunning, acrobatic flight. These are the only birds which can fly backwards, propelled by rapidly beating wings which flap in a figure-of-eight motion, with a rotor effect a little like helicopter blades. Male hummingbirds are usually more spectacular than females. Many of Belize's hummingbirds are threatened or vulnerable.

Jacamars, puffbirds and motmots Jacamars and motmots are among the most beautiful Belizean birds, with long, often rigid, tail feathers and bright colours. You'll often see motmots perched on low branches on the edge of the forest in areas like the Macal River. Jacamars feed on insects caught on the wing. Puffbirds are related to both but lack their cousins' spectacular plumage. There are six species in Belize.

Jays and ravens Belize's corvids or crows are mostly brilliantly coloured jays, such as the spectacular electric blue Steller's jay or the pretty green jay. They include locally confined species like the Yucatán jay. All are forest dwellers and there are four species, as well as the common raven. Most jays are gregarious, living in groups of five or 10, foraging within a restricted home range and calling raucously to each other from tree to tree. All are highly intelligent birds.

Manakins Belize has four species of these enchanting, brightly coloured wren-like birds, the prettiest of which is the red-capped manakin. All male manakins spend most of their lives performing in a *lek*, a tiny clearing in a grove of bamboos or thick vines. Here they dance, flit and flash colour from bright chests and throats for their dull-coloured females. They are most easily seen in Rio Bravo and Gallon Jug.

Mockingbirds and thrushes Thrushes are famous in Europe for their exquisite songs. Whilst most thrush species live in the Old World, there are a handful in the Neotropics, which also have beautiful songs. In Belize there are 12 species, including the bright blue red-breasted eastern bluebird and the clay-coloured robin. Mockingbirds resemble thrushes and, like them, have sylph-like calls, but they are more closely related to starlings.

They are some of the best mimics in the Neotropics and include the near-threatened black catbird. There are only three species in Belize.

Nightjars and potoos You'll most easily see nightjars at dusk on dirt roads in the forest, darting from the ground to catch insects caught in the car headlights. During the day they are impossibly well camouflaged, their brown plumage perfectly blending in with leaf mould and dry twigs. Belize's eight species include the whip-poor-will. The two potoo species are even more difficult to spot. They perch completely stationary on the end of a dead tree branch, their grey colour and head angle mimicking a severed wood stump. At night they let out a plaintive, mournful rising whistle.

Orioles and other icterids There are 19 species of these lively and versatile birds in Belize. They include the inquisitive jet-black, yellow-eyed grackles, the brightly coloured orioles and the caciques and oropendolas, which make pendulous scrotum-like nests hanging from trees in forest. Some like the giant cowbird, which places its young in the nests of oropendolas, are parasitic.

Ovenbirds There are more than seven species of small, brown ovenbirds in Belize, most of them almost identical. They are named not because they taste good roasted, but because some of them produce rock-hard oven-shaped clay nests.

Parakeets, parrots and macaws There are no birds more strongly associated with the Caribbean and the Buccaneer past than these engaging, brilliantly coloured social birds. Belize has 12 species, including a rare subspecies of scarlet macaw, the bird famous for sitting on Long John Silver's fictional shoulder.

Pigeons and doves There are 20 species in Belize, most of them small, shy forest birds.

Raptors Belize has some spectacular raptors, including the world's largest eagle, the harpy eagle, and the king vulture, with black and white plumage and a red and violet head. The commonest raptors are the red-headed turkey vultures and the wedge-beaked, crested caracara (Mexican eagle), which preys on nestlings. Others include ospreys and black-collared hawks (which have a buff back and a distinct black ring around their necks), both of which are commonly seen on lagoon sides in places such as Crooked Tree. There are 12 species of owl and 17 of hawk, which include the orange-breasted falcon, seen most easily on Mountain Pine Ridge.

Swifts, swallows and martins Although they closely resemble each other in appearance and in their speedy, swooping flight, swifts are more closely connected to hummingbirds than they are to swallows. There are seven swift species in Belize and 11 swallows and martins, including the cave and the mangrove swallow.

Tanagers This large, Neotropical family of finch-like birds includes some of the most colourful species in the region. There are some 27 species in Belize. These include the beautiful bright red summer tanager, and the crimson- and yellow-headed western tanager.

Tinamous, chachalacas, turkeys, guans and currasows These big forest floor and low canopy birds are some of the first to disappear when forests are cleared and hunted.

Tinamous are shy pheasant-like birds more heard than seen. Their mottled or dull brown colour makes them hard to see against the dark tropical forest floor where they live. Listen out for their plaintive whoop-like calls. There are four species in Belize. The turkeys and their cousins – the guans, currasswos and chachalacas – are large birds living in the trees or on the ground. Turkeys and guans have brightly coloured wattles. Chachalacas have a very loud staccato call. There is one species of each in Belize, including the spectacular ocellated turkey, which can easily be seen at La Milpa, and the near-threatened great curassow.

Toucans and barbets Belize's national bird, the keel-billed toucan, is one of the three species found in the country, the others being the collared aracari and the rarer emerald toucanet, which is most easily seen at Caracol. Toucans are often mobbed by smaller birds, for, while they are mainly fruit-eaters, they also raid nests and eat fledglings.

Trogons The brightly coloured, iridescent trogons include one of the most spectacular birds in Central America, the resplendent quetzal, whose turquoise plumage is offset by a crimson breast. Quetzals are rainforest birds that had a mythical status for Mesoamerican peoples. Belize's other four trogons are only a little less spectacular and include the brilliant yellow and black violaceous trogon and emerald and red slaty-tailed trogon.

Tyrant flycatchers This huge group of perching birds comprises 429 species worldwide and 60 species alone in Belize. Most are small plain-coloured birds more heavily built than their Old World cousins, with broad, flat beaks which they use to snatch insects from the air in a dizzying acrobatic flight.

Vireos and warblers There are 65 species of these agile, small bush birds. Warblers are generally busy and brightly coloured little birds, though wood warblers are generally reddish-brown. Vireos look similar with heavier bills and are typically greenish in colour. Both families are insectivorous. The rare Yucatán vireo is found in Shipstern Nature Reserve.

Water birds Belize's diverse wetland areas – from rivers, lakes and lagoons to mangrove forests and isolated offshore cayes – are a habitat for dozens of water bird families. These include 18 species of bitterns, herons and egrets (including the rare reddish egret), 13 species of rail (including the purple gallinule), two species of grebe, ocean goers such as white-tailed tropicbirds, frigatebirds, boobies and three species of shearwaters, flamingos, pelicans and the ubiquitous neotropical cormorant and the related anhinga, which is similar but with a long, thin neck. There are some 17 species of ducks and geese in Belize, many of them migratory.

Woodpeckers and woodcreepers Belize has 11 species of woodpeckers, many of them with bright head plumage, and 10 of woodcreepers, which are dull brown forest birds perfectly camouflaged against tree trunks. They too use their bills to dig out insects from under tree bark. Both bird families have a characteristic, fluttering flight.

Wrens These tiny birds with characteristically upright, spring tails catch mosquitoes and gnats on the wing. There are 10 species in Belize, including the tiny house wren, which has one of the greatest ranges of any perching bird in the world – nesting from Canada to southern Argentina, often in houses and garages – as its name would suggest.

Mammals

Most visitors who come to Belize and who are not birdwatchers want to see Belize's big mammals, most notably the jaguar and Belize's largest mammal, Baird's tapir (see box, page 133). Forest cats are notoriously hard to see, and jaguars even more so. Your best chance is at the Lamanai Outpost, Chan Chich or Rio Bravo. However, with 132 species, there are plenty of other mammals to see whilst you're searching. They include four other felines: pumas, which are even tougher to see than jaguars; labrador-sized ocelots; the slightly smaller margay, which spends much of its life in the trees, and jaguarondi, which looks like an elongated house cat and has a colour that varies from black to tan.

Belize's other carnivores include grey foxes, inquisitive white-nosed coatimundis, forest-dwelling relatives of the racoon, aggressive Neotropical badgers called grison, and one of the largest weasels in the world, the fox-sized tayra. There are also Neotropical river otters, whose numbers have been heavily depleted through hunting, nocturnal, arboreal racoons called cacomistles, and placid kinkajou or night walkers, whose big eyes shine brilliant orange in torchlight.

Belize's smaller mammals include forest rodents like the cat-sized paca (aka gibnut), armadillos, tree-dwelling tamandua anteaters, two skunks, six opossums and 14 bats, including vampires and the greater fishing bat, which flies by night and plucks fish from rivers and lakes with its feet.

There are two monkey species: the Mexican black howler (see box, page 45) and the scarcer and more timid Central American spider monkey, which moves in troops high in the canopy of pristine rainforest in search of fruits and seeds.

Marine mammals include the West Indian manatee (see box, page 224) and several species of dolphin.

Reptiles and amphibians

There are two crocodile species in Belize: the smaller freshwater Morelet's crocodile and the bigger and more powerful American crocodile, which lives off the cayes and in the larger lagoons, and which can grow up to 6 m long. Five species of marine turtle nest on Belize's beaches, including the world's biggest reptile, the leatherback, which can weigh up to half a ton and measure over 3 m long. The lazy, long-necked Central American river turtle (aka hickatee) was once very abundant in Belize's rivers. It is now on the critically endangered list after intense hunting for its meat, eggs and shell.

Belize has more than 50 snakes, which you will be very lucky to see. Most are very shy or nocturnal. A handful are dangerously venomous (see page 18), which makes it likely that every snake you see will be harmless. Species include some brilliantly coloured boas, vine snakes and reclusive, mottled and venomous forest vipers like the fer-de-lance.

Marine life

Belize is one of the Atlantic's premier dive and snorkel destinations, with one of the region's two barrier reefs (the other being off Providence Island), three of just 10 to 20 Caribbean atolls and numerous cayes, with fringing and shallow reefs. There is nowhere in the Caribbean region with more variety of marine environments and the marine fauna is abundant. You will see fish in far greater numbers and variety in Belize than anywhere else along the Mesoamerican Barrier Reef, including Cozumel, and there is a real chance of seeing spectacular wildlife like whale sharks.

Reef systems are constituted of the skeletal build-up of coral over thousands of years. Only a thin outside layer of coral is alive: the polyps set in a chalky shell. The polyps form

Jaguars: conserving biodiversity in Belize

Belize is home to five species of wild cats, including the three largest cats of the Neotropics: the jaguar (*Panthera onca*), the puma (*Puma concolor*) and the ocelot (*Leopardus pardalis*), as well as two smaller predatory felids: the jaguarundi (*Puma yagouaroundii*) and the margay (*Leopardus weidii*). The jaguar, known locally as 'tiger', is the largest predator and a keystone species in the Americas. It is a national icon in Belize with a prominent role in the country's culture dating back to the early Mayan civilizations, who revered the jaguar god Balaam.

The jaguar's present range extends from Mexico, through Central America and into northern Argentina, with occasional sightings in southern USA. The jaguar has a sturdy, muscular build with a broad head and a yellow-tan coat patterned with black rosettes that are individually distinct. Black jaguars also exist but are uncommon in Belize. Their average body weight is 73 kg and an average body length of 1.3 m plus 60 cm for its tail. The jaguar requires densely forested areas to hunt and is often

described as a nocturnal species, but it is most active at dawn and dusk. Jaguars are opportunistic hunters that prefer large prey such as deer, tapir and peccary, but whose diet also includes small mammals, reptiles and birds.

The jaguar is a near-threatened species on the IUCN list and, in Belize, population strongholds are thought to be within the country's protected areas of the Cockscomb Basin Wildlife Sanctuary, the Chiquibul Forest Reserve and the Rio Bravo Conservation Area. Jaguar populations, however, are still declining. All wild cats are under threat of fragmentation where connected landscapes are diminishing rapidly. In 2010, the Labouring Creek Jaguar Corridor Wildlife Sanctuary was established as part of a central jaguar corridor to provide a protected landscape between Belmopan and Belize City that connects protected areas in northern and southern Belize. Even with these efforts, population numbers are increasingly fragmented and there is a steady rise in human-wildlife conflicts as people and wild

communities or colonies which fight each other for reef space, digesting their neighbours in saprophytic nocturnal attacks.

Caribbean reefs differ from those in the Indo-Pacific in several ways. First, they have no algal ridge. These are prevalent in the Indo-Pacific where waves are much stronger and are composed primarily of encrusting calcareous red algae that forms a cement-like barrier to the initial impact of incoming ocean waves. Secondly, because Caribbean reefs are not pounded by such strong waves, there is an abundance of soft corals, sponges and gorgonians, which proliferate both in the depths and on the coral ridge, where the reef meets the deep ocean, adding to the biodiversity and the visual impact of the reef. Thirdly, the Caribbean reefs developed in isolation from those in the Pacific after the isthmus of Panama closed, some three to four million years ago. Their species are distinct though similar to those in the Pacific. Whilst the Caribbean is far less biodiverse, Belize is the most biodiverse marine location in the region, with about 65 to 75 species of hard corals and some 500 to 700 reef-associated fish species. In the Bahamas, by contrast, there are some 40 to 50 coral species and some 480 fish species.

Belize's 75 hard corals species and 36 soft come in an array of sizes and colours. Among the largest are the greater star and boulder corals, which form huge caramel-coloured animals are forced to share a landscape. Major threats to wild cat populations are largely due to habitat loss and fragmentation, but also include the illegal trade in pets and body parts, retaliatory hunting due to livestock and poultry being attacked, and poaching of their wild prey base as game meat. Unfortunately, in communities that border natural areas, and a natural source of wildlife, conflicts emerge because of there is no economic benefit and no shared responsibility of wildlife conservation.

Research on wild cat conservation in Belize has been exceptionally good but is focused in protected areas. Local communities are often not targeted and may be the key to effective wildlife conservation as the Lamanai Field Research Center, in collaboration with the University of Florida, has discovered from its community-based camera-trapping programme in northern Belize. This ongoing project documents a substantial number of wild cats moving through and using a very human-dominated landscape, illustrating that a grassroots conservation programme is able to instill awareness, promote respect for threatened species and a widespread wildlife appreciation. The jaguar has become the poster child for wildlife conservation throughout the Americas and, as such, when an umbrella species is preserved, wildlife within the same terrestrial systems is simultaneously conserved. Biodiversity is a valuable commodity, biodiversity protection is an alternative land use and conservation is meaningless without thinking of the long-term. New measures should be geared towards conservation of natural forests and managed landscapes, designing strategies that reduce land-use changes and implement a partnership between people and wildlife.

By Venetia Briggs-Gonzalez, PhD, a biologist working on big cat conservation with the **Lamanai Field Research Center** (www.lamanai.org), which run conservation and ecotourism projects you can join through **Lamanai Outpost Lodge** (see page 186).

mounds across the reef. A colony can grow up to 3 m in diameter. Plate corals and sheet corals are found on the outer edges of the reef wall, lettuce coral on the surface, and large expanses of stag or elkhorn coral – like fields of abrasive tusks – lie in between. Soft corals, sea fans and gorgonians – like spindly ostrich feathers – are attached to the reef walls where the current is most variable, to trap particles of water-borne food. Big filter-feeding barrel sponges often lie nearby.

The entire reef community is populated by crustaceans, nudibranch molluscs and fish. Tiny blennies and gobies hide in crevices. Surgeon fish swim over the reef heads in loose congregations. Disc-shaped butterfly and angel fish swim between the reef blocks, together with shoals of barbelled goatfish and grunts, which emit a strange guttural sound as they chew. Parrot fish flap in between on overly large pectoral fins, and trigger fish chomp at the coral with powerful front-pointing jaws. Moray eels, with their characteristic bared fangs, undulate from holes, and larger fish like grouper hide under the reef blocks: the striped tiger grouper in shallower reef and the 2-m-long rare jewfish in deeper water.

On the sand flats between the coral heads you'll see bar jacks – often in mating pairs, one silvery and the other almost jet black – as well as big stingrays, gracefully gliding spotted eagle ray and, perhaps, a turtle.

Manatees

West Indian manatees are one of three species of sea cows or sirenians living in warm, shallow seas around the Americas and Australasia. They take their name from the sirens, the seductresses whose songs lured countless Greek mariners to their doom and who Odysseus escaped by having his crew rope him to the mast of his ship. Sirens came to be associated with mermaids, and scientists postulate that manatees might be the source of the mermaid myth.

But even after months at sea in an all-male population, you'd have to be desperate to kiss a manatee. Like other sirenians, manatees pluck vegetation from shallow seas with hard, bristly mouths. They spend almost all their lives grazing and farting. It's by the bubbles of gas produced from both ends that manatee-spotting guides find them. And they're no delicate, alluring, silver-voiced beauties. An adult female manatee can weigh as much as 600 kg and her song is a succession of whines, grunts and squeals.

All sirenians are endangered. The largest species, the whale-sized stellar's sea cow, is extinct, wiped out in a generation by hunting mariners. The Amazon manatee almost suffered the same fate. The dugong is vulnerable to hunting, too, and to habitat depletion, and there have been dramatic falls in their numbers. West Indian manatees are protected in most countries where they are found, but they are nonetheless rare or extinct over much of their former range. In the US, many are killed annually by boat prows or propellers and, throughout the Caribbean and Neotropics, manatees are suffering habitat loss. Belize is one of their last strongholds.

In the deeper water off the reef you will see torpedo-shaped toothsome barracuda – often at the edge of your vision, watching you with unnerving intensity – and big grey snapper. Apart from nurse sharks, sharks are uncommon in the western Caribbean. Bull sharks and grey reef sharks are occasionally seen off the atolls and, in snapper spawning season, whale sharks visit the South Water Caye Marine Reserve (see page 144).

National parks

Belize has one of the highest percentages of protected areas of any country in the world, with 92 reserves of varying levels of protection, covering 44% of national territory (a total of 2.6 million acres) and the percentage is going up. These areas are protected under different management structures. Around 1.9 million acres is set aside as terrestrial reserves, including archaeological sites, while 392,970 acres are marine reserves and 317,615 acres are protected by private conservation initiatives. Although much of Belize is protected, its ecosystems are under increased threat and pressure from high deforestation rates (especially the tropical forests of the west, where timber and wildlife are poached mostly by trespassers from Guatemala), rapid coastal development, improper solid waste management and oil exploration on the reefs and atolls. The country has strong legislation but weak institutional and legal frameworks and a lack of transparency. For more information, see box, page 69.

Some of Belize's protected areas are tiny, inaccessible or not open to visitors and we do not include all these areas in the main body of the book. Others are included in the text in some detail. Our personal favourites are listed below.

Northern Belize **Shipstern Nature Reserve** (which is not formally protected – with pristine Yucatán dry and moist forest, unique birds and vast, remote lagoons filled with American crocodiles and manatees); **Rio Bravo Conservation and Management Area** and **Gallon Jug** (comprising a huge area of tropical forest with one of the highest mammal and bird biodiversity levels in the country; probably the best place to see jaguar in Belize); **Lamanai** (beautifully located Mayan ruins nestled in forest next to a river lagoon fringed with wet meadows).

Belize District **Crooked Tree** (large lakes and some of the best birdwatching in the country); **Spanish Creek** (wildlife-filled forest, lakes and meadows); **Community Baboon Sanctuary** (the best place to see howler monkeys in Belize).

Cayo District Actun **Tunichil Muknal** (a cave in the heart of the forest filled with stunning speleological formations and Mayan artefacts); **Chiquibul Forest Reserve** (part of the largest stretch of tropical forest north of the Amazon, little-visited and packed with wildlife); **Caracol** (Belize's largest and most spectacular Mayan ruins); **Xunantunich** (towering pyramids in a stunning tropical forest setting); and **Mountain Pine Ridge** (a uniquely Belizean highland ecosystem with rare trees, birdlife and dozens of waterfalls).

Northern Cayes **The Blue Hole** (a perfectly circular, deep sink-hole in the reef leading to a system of underwater caves); **Half Moon Caye Natural Monument** (pristine white sands, mangrove forest and some of the best wall-diving in the country); **Hol Chan Marine Reserve** (superb, diverse diving, reefs and marine life); **Bacalar Chico Marine Reserve** (wonderful diving and snorkelling in a variety of reef and marine habitats, wet meadows, mangrove forests and eel grass beds); **Caye Caulker** (shallow reef with excellent snorkelling and diving and a large stretch of littoral forest); and **Turneffe Flats** (an isolated atoll with superb diving and fishing).

Southern Belize **Sapodilla Cayes** (remote sandy islands fringed with well-preserved reef and covered in littoral forest); **Gladden Spit** and **Silk Cayes** (with some of the best diving in Belize, including the chance to dive with whale sharks); **Cockscomb Basin Wildlife Sanctuary** (the only designated jaguar preserve in Central America); **Mayflower Bocawina National Park** (excellent birdwatching and walks to waterfalls and Mayan ruins lost in the forest); **South Water Caye Marine Reserve** (a string of islands set in pristine but threatened reef); and **Glover's Reef** (Belize's most biodiverse atoll, with some of the best diving in the Atlantic).

Books on Belize

Archaeology and art

Kelly, Joyce, *An Archaeological Guide to Northern Central America* (University of Oklahoma Press 1996). A detailed and scholarly site-by-site analysis of the Mayan sites of Belize, Guatemala and El Salvador with maps and potted histories. There is a companion guide to the sites of the Yucatán.

Miller, Mary Ellen, *The Art of Mesoamerica* (Thames and Hudson fourth revised edition 2012). This study is one of the best introductions to the art of the region, from the Olmecs to the Aztecs, with extensive material on the Maya, and information on the ritual context and evolution of the art.

Fiction and poetry

Edgell, Zee, *Time and the River* (Heinemann 2007). A portrait of Belizean society during the time of slavery from the viewpoint of the daughter of a slave and a slave-owner.

Fairweather-Belgrave, Carrie, *Parchment Pages: Speak to Me in Poetry* (Identity 2010). Powerful verses, each a vignette of Belizean life, from one of the country's most gifted poets. Published just before her death in 2011.

Fisk, Pauline, *In the Trees* (Faber 2010). Belize's charms, curses and contradictions seen through the eyes of a young Londoner on a quest that takes him through the country's cities and jungles searching for his father and himself.

Hyde, Evan X, *Feelings* (Angelus Press 1975). Short stories from an Amandala journalist, the country's leading black activist and founder of the United Black Association for Development (UBAD).

Various, *Memories, Dreams and Nightmares* (Cubola Books 2005). A short story anthology from many of Belize's leading women writers including Zee Edgell, Zoila Ellis, Felicia Hernadez and Kathy Esquivel, laying bare the country's colonial bitterness and racial tensions.

Watler, John Alexander, *Cry Among Rainclouds* (Daafy Publishing 2001). Belize's most popular novel from one of the most beloved and respected Kriol writers in Belize

Young, Colville, *From One Caribbean Corner* (Angelus Press 1983). Creole and English poems written by the current governor general of Belize, founding member of the Liberal Party and pedagogical specialist.

History

Bradley, Leo, *Glimpses of Our History*. Moments from Belize's history up until Independence from one of the country's most respected historical writers.

Caiger, Stephen L, *British Honduras Past and Present* (George Allen and Unwin, 1951). The least dry of the various histories of what was British Honduras when the book was written, with entertaining chapters on the first years of the colony and a narrative panache which brings the incidental protagonists to life.

Dobson, Narda, *A History of Belize* (Longman Caribbean 1973). A well-researched history of the country until the years just before Independence. It is strong on human geography and economics, but out of date on the pre-Columbian Maya.

Haring, CH, *The Buccaneers in the West Indies in the XVII Century* (Methuen 1910). A methodically documented account of the exploits of Henry Morgan and the early buccaneers with quoted eye-witness accounts from contemporaneous sources.

King, Emory, *The Great Story of Belize 1 & 2*. A rip-roaring history of Belize by one of the country's best known writers. King was born in Florida and arrived in Belize in 1953 when the yacht he was on ran aground on the Belize Barrier Reef at English Caye. He fell in love with the country and adopted it as his own. King also wrote many novels, the best known of which is *The Little World of Danny Vasquez*.

Reed, Nelson, *The Caste War of the Yucatán* (Stanford University Press, revised edition 2001). The classic account of the conflict which swept across the Yucatán from the mid-18th century to the early 20th and which resulted in Belize's only official land battle: the Battle of Orange Walk (see box, page 180).

The Maya

Coe, Michael, *The Maya* (Thames and Hudson eighth revised edition 2011). The best all-round summary of the history, thought and achievements of the pre-Columbian Maya.

Schele, Linda, Freidel, David and Parker, Joy, *Maya Cosmos* (Perennial 1995). An astonishing analysis of Mayan ontological, epistemological and metaphysical thought gleaned from pre-Columbian Maya writings and the preservation of traditional thought of the modern Maya.

Tedlock, D (trans), *The Popol Vuh* (Touchstone 1996). The classic translation of the corpus of Maya myths and scriptures with an illuminating introduction by Dennis Tedlock, one of the world's leading authorities on the Maya.

Natural history

Arvigo, Rosita, et al, *Rainforest Remedies* (Lotus Press revised edition 1998). An illustrated guide to 100 pharmacologically active Belizean plants with descriptions of their morphology, habitat, traditional medicinal usage and a summary of the results of pharmacological research on each species, genus or family. The book includes a fascinating introduction on Mayan medicine which the author learnt from Don Elijio Panti (see page 101), amongst others.

D'Abrera, Bernard, *Butterflies of the Neotropical Region* (Hill House 1987). A lush multi-volume, hardback magnum opus devoted to the butterflies of the region.

Deloach, N and Humann, P, *Reef Fish Identification: Caribbean, Bahamas, South Florida* (New World Publications 2011). A comprehensive scholarly guide to 281 of the more common fish found on the region's reefs, illustrated with excellent photographs.

Emmons, Louise, et al, *Neotropical Rainforest Mammals* (University of Chicago Press 1990). An illustrated scholarly field guide, which is not exhaustive and which includes only forest-dwelling species. However, the descriptions of the animals, their behaviour, conservation status and distribution are first class.

Kricher, J, *A Neotropical Companion* (Princeton University Press, revised edition 1999). The classic introduction to the ecology, biology, flora and fauna of the region.

Lee Jones, H and Gardener, D, *Birds of Belize* (Christopher Helm 2004). An excellent accurate and scholarly illustrated field guide to almost all the species so far recorded in the country.

Reid, Fiona, *Mammals of Central America and Southeast Mexico* (Oxford University Press 2009). The only field guide to offer comprehensive coverage of all Central American mammals.

Suarez, A and Gorter, U, *Belize Marine Guide* (Rainforest Publications 2009). The only illustrated field guide solely devoted to the reef fish, marine mammals, sport fish and sea turtles of the Belize Barrier Reef.

Travelogues

Huxley, Aldous, *Beyond the Mexique Bay* (Chatto and Windus 1934). The author made a brief visit to Belize on his way between the Caribbean and Guatemala. His descriptions are colourful but in general he's churlish about Belize and offers few illuminating insights on the country.

Paxman, Jeremy, *Through the Volcanoes* (Michael Joseph 1985), 'Belize City,' writes Paxman, 'had the air of an African ground-nut port after 20 years of ground nut blight'. His acerbic wit fails to veil the very thin nature of both his travels in Belize and his observations.

Contents

Footnotes

Basic Spanish for travellers

Learning Spanish is a useful part of the preparation for a trip to Latin America and no volumes of dictionaries, phrase books or word lists will provide the same enjoyment as being able to communicate directly with the people of the country you are visiting. It is a good idea to make an effort to grasp the basics before you go. As you travel you will pick up more of the language and the more you know, the more you will benefit from your stay.

General pronunciation

Whether you have been taught the 'Castilian' pronunciation (z and c followed by i or e are pronounced as the *th* in think) or the 'American' pronounciation (they are pronounced as s), you will encounter little difficulty in understanding either. Regional accents and usages vary, but the basic language is essentially the same everywhere.

Vowels

a	as in English *cat*
e	as in English *best*
i	as the *ee* in English *feet*
o	as in English *shop*
u	as the *oo* in English *food*
ai	as the *i* in English *ride*
ei	as *ey* in English *they*
oi	as *oy* in English *toy*

Consonants

Most consonants can be pronounced more or less as they are in English. The exceptions are:

g	before *e* or *i* is the same as *j*
h	is always silent (except in *ch* as in *chair*)
j	as the *ch* in Scottish *loch*
ll	as the *y* in *yellow*
ñ	as the *ni* in English *onion*
rr	trilled much more than in English
x	depending on its location, pronounced *x*, *s*, *sh* or *j*

Spanish words and phrases

Greetings, courtesies

hello	*hola*	I speak Spanish	*hablo español*
good morning	*buenos días*	I don't speak Spanish	*no hablo español*
good afternoon/ evening/night	*buenas tardes/ noches*	do you speak English?	*¿habla inglés?*
goodbye	*adiós/chao*	I don't understand	*no entiendo/ no comprendo*
pleased to meet you	*mucho gusto*	please speak slowly	*hable despacio por favor*
see you later	*hasta luego*		
how are you?	*¿cómo está? ¿cómo estás?*	I am very sorry	*lo siento mucho/ disculpe*
I'm fine, thanks	*estoy muy bien, gracias*	what do you want?	*¿qué quiere? ¿qué quieres?*
I'm called...	*me llamo...*		
what is your name?	*¿cómo se llama? ¿cómo te llamas?*	I want	*quiero*
		I don't want it	*no lo quiero*
yes/no	*sí/no*	leave me alone	*déjeme en paz/ no me moleste*
please	*por favor*		
thank you (very much)	*(muchas) gracias*	good/bad	*bueno/malo*

Questions and requests

Have you got a room for two people?	When does the bus leave (arrive)?
¿Tiene una habitación para dos personas?	*¿A qué hora sale (llega) el autobús?*
I'd like to make a long-distance phone call	Where is the nearest petrol station?
Quisiera hacer una llamada de larga distancia	*¿Dónde está la gasolinera más cercana?*

How do I get to_?	*¿Cómo llego a_?*	When?	*¿cuándo?*
How much does it cost?	*¿Cuánto cuesta?*	Where is_?	*¿dónde está_?*
	¿cuánto es?	Where can I buy tickets?	*¿Dónde puedo comprar boletos?*
Is service included?	*¿Está incluido el servicio?*	Why?	*¿por qué?*
Is tax included?	*¿Están incluidos los impuestos?*		

Basics

bank	*el banco*	market	*el mercado*
bathroom/toilet	*el baño*	note/coin	*el billete/la moneda*
bill	*la factura/la cuenta*	police (policeman)	*la policía (el policía)*
cash	*el efectivo*	post office	*el correo*
cheap	*barato/a*	public telephone	*el teléfono público*
credit card	*la tarjeta de crédito*	supermarket	*el supermercado*
exchange house	*la casa de cambio*	ticket office	*la taquilla*
exchange rate	*el tipo de cambio*	traveller's cheques	*los cheques de viajero/los travelers*
expensive	*caro/a*		

Getting around

aeroplane	*el avión*	to insure yourself against	*asegurarse contra*
airport	*el aeropuerto*		
arrival/departure	*la llegada/salida*	luggage	*el equipaje*
avenue	*la avenida*	motorway, freeway	*el autopista/ la carretera*
block	*la cuadra*		
border	*la frontera*	north	*norte*
bus station	*la terminal de autobuses/camiones*	south	*sur*
		west	*oeste (occidente)*
bus	*el bus/el autobús/ el camión*	east	*este (oriente)*
		oil	*el aceite*
collective/fixed- route taxi	*el colectivo*	to park	*estacionarse*
		passport	*el pasaporte*
corner	*la esquina*	petrol/gasoline	*la gasolina*
customs	*la aduana*	puncture	*el pinchazo/ la ponchadura*
first/second class	*primera/segunda clase*		
		street	*la calle*
left/right	*izquierda/derecha*	that way	*por allí/por allá*
ticket	*el boleto*	this way	*por aquí/por acá*
empty/full	*vacío/lleno*	tourist card/visa	*la tarjeta de turista*
highway, main road	*la carretera*	tyre	*la llanta*
immigration	*la inmigración*	unleaded	*sin plomo*
insurance	*el seguro*	to walk	*caminar/andar*
insured person	*el/la asegurado/a*		

Accommodation

air conditioning	*el aire acondicionado*	power cut	*el apagón/corte*
all-inclusive	*todo incluido*	restaurant	*el restaurante*
bathroom, private	*el baño privado*	room/bedroom	*el cuarto/*
bed, double/single	*la cama matrimonial/*		*la habitación*
	sencilla	sheets	*las sábanas*
blankets	*las cobijas/mantas*	shower	*la ducha/regadera*
to clean	*limpiar*	soap	*el jabón*
dining room	*el comedor*	toilet	*el sanitario/excusado*
guesthouse	*la casa de huéspedes*	toilet paper	*el papel higiénico*
hotel	*el hotel*	towels, clean/dirty	*las toallas limpias/*
noisy	*ruidoso*		*sucias*
pillows	*las almohadas*	water, hot/cold	*el agua caliente/fría*

Health

aspirin	*la aspirina*	diarrhoea	*la diarrea*
blood	*la sangre*	doctor	*el médico*
chemist	*la farmacia*	fever/sweat	*la fiebre/el sudor*
condoms	*los preservativos,*	pain	*el dolor*
	los condones	head	*la cabeza*
contact lenses	*los lentes de contacto*	period/sanitary towels	*la regla/las toallas*
contraceptives	*los anticonceptivos*		*femeninas*
contraceptive pill	*la píldora anti-*	stomach	*el estómago*
	conceptiva	altitude sickness	*el soroche*

Family

family	*la familia*	husband/wife	*el esposo (marido)/*
brother/sister	*el hermano/*		*la esposa*
	la hermana	boyfriend/girlfriend	*el novio/la novia*
daughter/son	*la hija/el hijo*	friend	*el amigo/la amiga*
father/mother	*el padre/la madre*	married	*casado/a*
		single/unmarried	*soltero/a*

Months, days and time

January	*enero*	Monday	*lunes*
February	*febrero*	Tuesday	*martes*
March	*marzo*	Wednesday	*miércoles*
April	*abril*	Thursday	*jueves*
May	*mayo*	Friday	*viernes*
June	*junio*	Saturday	*sábado*
July	*julio*	Sunday	*domingo*
August	*agosto*		
September	*septiembre*	at one o'clock	*a la una*
October	*octubre*	at half past two	*a las dos y media*
November	*noviembre*	at a quarter to three	*a cuarto para las tres/*
December	*diciembre*		*a las tres menos*
			quince

it's one o'clock	*es la una*	in ten minutes	*en diez minutos*
it's seven o'clock	*son las siete*	five hours	*cinco horas*
it's six twenty	*son las seis y veinte*	does it take long?	*¿tarda mucho?*
it's five to nine	*son las nueve menos cinco*		

Numbers

one	*uno/una*	sixteen	*dieciséis*
two	*dos*	seventeen	*diecisiete*
three	*tres*	eighteen	*dieciocho*
four	*cuatro*	nineteen	*diecinueve*
five	*cinco*	twenty	*veinte*
six	*seis*	twenty-one	*veintiuno*
seven	*siete*	thirty	*treinta*
eight	*ocho*	forty	*cuarenta*
nine	*nueve*	fifty	*cincuenta*
ten	*diez*	sixty	*sesenta*
eleven	*once*	seventy	*setenta*
twelve	*doce*	eighty	*ochenta*
thirteen	*trece*	ninety	*noventa*
fourteen	*catorce*	hundred	*cien/ciento*
fifteen	*quince*	thousand	*mil*

Food

avocado	*el aguacate*	goat	*el chivo*
baked	*al horno*	grapefruit	*la toronja/el pomelo*
bakery	*la panadería*	grill	*la parrilla*
banana	*el plátano*	grilled/griddled	*a la plancha*
beans	*los frijoles/ las habichuelas*	guava	*la guayaba*
beef	*la carne de res*	ham	*el jamón*
beef steak or pork fillet	*el bistec*	hamburger	*la hamburguesa*
boiled rice	*el arroz blanco*	hot, spicy	*picante*
bread	*el pan*	ice cream	*el helado*
breakfast	*el desayuno*	jam	*la mermelada*
butter	*la mantequilla*	knife	*el cuchillo*
cake	*el pastel*	lime	*el limón*
chewing gum	*el chicle*	lobster	*la langosta*
chicken	*el pollo*	lunch	*el almuerzo/ la comida*
chilli or green pepper	*el ají/pimiento*	meal	*la comida*
clear soup, stock	*el caldo*	meat	*la carne*
cooked	*cocido*	minced meat	*el picadillo*
dining room	*el comedor*	onion	*la cebolla*
egg	*el huevo*	orange	*la naranja*
fish	*el pescado*	pepper	*el pimiento*
fork	*el tenedor*	pasty, turnover	*la empanada/ el pastelito*
fried	*frito*	pork	*el cerdo*
garlic	*el ajo*		

potato	*la papa*	spoon	*la cuchara*
prawns	*los camarones*	squash	la calabaza
raw	*crudo*	squid	*los calamares*
restaurant	*el restaurante*	supper	*la cena*
salad	*la ensalada*	sweet	*dulce*
salt	*la sal*	to eat	*comer*
sandwich	*el bocadillo*	toasted	*tostado*
sauce	*la salsa*	turkey	*el pavo*
sausage	*la longaniza/ el chorizo*	vegetables	*los legumbres/ vegetales*
scrambled eggs	*los huevos revueltos*	without meat	*sin carne*
seafood	*los mariscos*	yam	*el camote*
soup	*la sopa*		

Drink

beer	*la cerveza*	juice	*el jugo*
boiled	*hervido/a*	lemonade	*la limonada*
bottled	*en botella*	milk	*la leche*
camomile tea	*la manzanilla*	mint	*la menta*
canned	*en lata*	rum	*el ron*
coffee	*el café*	soft drink	*el refresco*
coffee, white	*el café con leche*	sugar	*el azúcar*
cold	*frío*	tea	*el té*
cup	*la taza*	to drink	*beber/tomar*
drink	*la bebida*	water	*el agua*
drunk	*borracho/a*	water, carbonated	*el agua mineral con gas*
firewater	*el aguardiente*		
fruit milkshake	*el batido/licuado*	water, still mineral	*el agua mineral sin gas*
glass	*el vaso*		
hot	*caliente*	wine, red	*el vino tinto*
ice/without ice	*el hielo/sin hielo*	wine, white	el vino blanco

Key verbs

to go	**ir**	there is/are	*hay*	
I go	*voy*	there isn't/aren't	*no hay*	
you go (familiar)	*vas*			
he, she, it goes, you (formal) go	*va*	**to be**	**ser**	**estar**
we go	*vamos*	I am	soy	estoy
they, you (plural) go	*van*	you are	eres	estás
		he, she, it is, you (formal) are	es	está
to have (possess)	**tener**	we are	somos	estamos
I have	*tengo*	they, you (plural) are	son	están
you (familiar) have	*tienes*			
he, she, it, you (formal) have	*tiene*	This section has been assembled on the basis of glossaries compiled by André de Mendonça and David Gilmour of South American Experience, London, and the Latin American Travel Advisor, No 9, March 1996		
we have	*tenemos*			
they, you (plural) have	*tienen*			

Index → Entries in **bold** refer to maps

Advertisers' index

About the author

Alex Robinson is a photographer and writer who has been published by *Wanderlust*, *Sunday Times Travel*, the *Independent*, *Vanity Fair* and *Departures* magazine, amongst others. He was part of a team who won a national magazine award in the USA, an Editora Abril journalism award in Brazil and was runner-up in the Friends of the Earth International photography competition. He is a fellow of the Royal Geographical Society, where he has lectured on Belize.

Acknowledgements

With great thanks to the following people: Gardenia and Raphael, Elizabeth Robinson, Jo Williams for fastidious editorial work and Alan Murphy for commissioning the book. In Belize thanks to Nick Davies – for tireless and selfless enthusiasm about Belize and professionalism above and beyond excellent, Luky Bol for her efficiency and helping out hugely, Doug Thompson and family for the welcome and for being the epitome of Belizean hospitality, warmth and wisdom, Emerald Wong and her family for a wonderful time in Belize City, for her warmth and kindness and for introducing me to her namesake and grandmother, the unforgettable Carrie Fairweather-Belgrave, Venetia Briggs for the jaguars and Ivan Duran for bringing Belizean music to the world and sparing his time to talk to me. Thanks to Doug and Veronique, Ian and Kate at Hickatee, Mariam at the San Ignacio hotel, Eduardo and family at Huun Chik for superb guiding, inspiration and help, Chef Rob and his family for great food and conversation, Mark and Ruben at Lamanai for true inspiration and running a great operation, Cahal Pech, Nadege at Mystic River for her style and warmth, Chan Chich, Almond Tree, Mike at Midas for the bright lights of San Ignacio, Fiona at San Ignacio, Caye Casa, Victoria House for unforgettable food, Laura Rendell-Dunn at JLA, Hamanasi, Hidden Valley, La Milpa and Hill Bank Field Stations, Hugh Parkey's, Aurelio Martinez for the interview, Paul Nabor for the honour of allowing me into the *dugu*, Fubu Ainsworth, everyone at Royal Palm, Portofino for being indeed a 'Porto muy fino', and for great food, Joanna on Caye Caulker for her hospitality and for sharing her photography enthusiasm, Island Magic, Jackson and Ruth out on the Lighthouse Reef for a wonderful (but too short) time, may there be many more and may I be able to congratulate you in person, Louis in Aguacate village, Chabil Mar, Hopkins Bay, Hamanasi, Kaana, Macaroni Hill, Semhar and Amanprit for sharing a shark filled snorkel trip and interviews to the wonderful warm people of Belize….. and to Peter Eltringham who first shared knowledge and enthusiasm about Belize with me and who is very greatly missed.

Credits

Footprint credits
Project Editor: Jo Williams
Layout and production: Emma Bryers
Proofreader: Sophie Jones
Cover and colour section: Pepi Bluck
Maps: Kevin Feeney

Managing Director: Andy Riddle
Content Director: Patrick Dawson
Publisher: Alan Murphy
Publishing Managers: Felicity Laughton,
Jo Williams, Nicola Gibbs
Marketing and Partnerships Director:
Liz Harper
Marketing Executive: Liz Eyles
Trade Product Manager: Diane McEntee
Account Managers: Paul Bew, Tania Ross
Advertising: Renu Sibal, Elizabeth Taylor

Photography credits
Front cover: Mark Lewis / Getty Images
Back cover: Frans Lanting/FLPA

Colour section
All images by Alex Robinson

Printed in India by Replika Press Pvt Ltd

Publishing information
Footprint Belize
1st edition
© Footprint Handbooks Ltd
July 2012

ISBN: 978 1 907263 61 3
CIP DATA: A catalogue record for this book
is available from the British Library

® Footprint Handbooks and the Footprint
mark are a registered trademark of
Footprint Handbooks Ltd

Published by Footprint
6 Riverside Court
Lower Bristol Road
Bath BA2 3DZ, UK
T +44 (0)1225 469141
F +44 (0)1225 469461
footprinttravelguides.com

Distributed in the USA by Globe Pequot
Press, Guilford, Connecticut

Every effort has been made to ensure that
the facts in this guidebook are accurate.
However, travellers should still obtain advice
from consulates, airlines, etc about travel
and visa requirements before travelling.
The authors and publishers cannot
accept responsibility for any loss, injury
or inconvenience however caused.

THE BEST OF BELIZE chosen by millions of travellers

Hamanasi Adventure

Cave Tubing R "us"

Maya Beach Hotel Bistro

Top-rated places to stay

Hamanasi Adventure and Dive Resort, Hopkins
⊙⊙⊙⊙⊙
"The treehouses are awesome!!"

The Phoenix Resort
San Pedro
⊙⊙⊙⊙⊙
"Fabulous, small, intimate resort"

Coco Plum Island Resort
Dangriga
⊙⊙⊙⊙⊙
"The best honeymoon spot"

Amazing attractions

Cave Tubing R "us"
Belize District
⊙⊙⊙⊙⊙
"The caves were gorgeous"

Actun Tunichil Muknal
Cayo
⊙⊙⊙⊙⊙
"Fun for the fit and brave traveler"

Hol Chan Marine Reserve
San Pedro
⊙⊙⊙⊙⊙
"Prepare to be thrilled"

Popular restaurants

Maya Beach Hotel Bistro
Placencia
⊙⊙⊙⊙⊙
"The chocolate soufflé is exquisite"

Tutti Frutti
Placencia
⊙⊙⊙⊙⊙
"Great and unexpected gelato shop"

The Secret Garden Restaurant, Placencia
⊙⊙⊙⊙⊙
"Super spot in paradise"

◎◎ tripadvisor®

Plan your perfect trip with millions of candid traveller reviews.

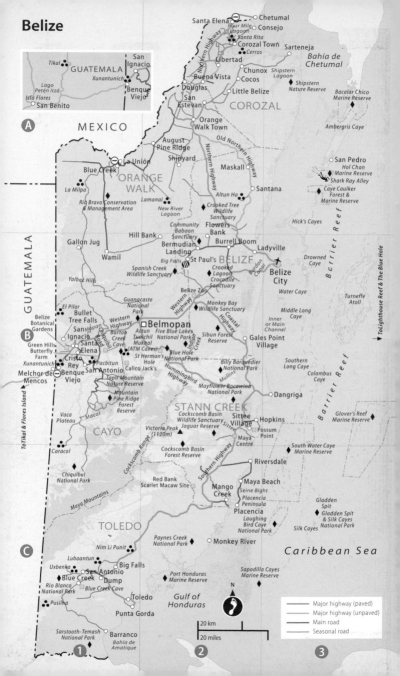